NIETZSCHE AND THE CLASSICAL TRADITION

UNIVERSITY OF NORTH CAROLINA
STUDIES IN THE GERMANIC LANGUAGES
AND LITERATURES

Initiated by RICHARD JENTE (1949–1952), *established by* F. E. COENEN (1952–1968)

Publication Committee

SIEGFRIED MEWS, EDITOR   JOHN G. KUNSTMANN   GEORGE S. LANE

HERBERT W. REICHERT   CHRISTOPH E. SCHWEITZER   SIDNEY R. SMITH

For other volumes in the "Studies" see pages 276 ff.

Send orders to: (U.S. and Canada)
The University of North Carolina Press, P.O. Box 2288
Chapel Hill, N.C. 27514
(All other countries) Feffer and Simons, Inc., 31 Union Square, New York, N.Y. 10003

NUMBER EIGHTY-FIVE

UNIVERSITY
OF NORTH CAROLINA
STUDIES IN
THE GERMANIC LANGUAGES
AND LITERATURES

Studies in
Nietzsche and the Classical Tradition

Edited by

James C. O'Flaherty, Timothy F. Sellner,
and Robert M. Helm

CHAPEL HILL
THE UNIVERSITY OF NORTH CAROLINA PRESS
1976

© University of North Carolina
Studies in the Germanic Languages
and Literatures 1976

Library of Congress Cataloging in Publication Data

Main entry under title:

Studies in Nietzsche and the classical tradition.

(University of North Carolina studies in the Germanic languages
and literature; no. 85)
Includes bibliographical references.
1. Nietzsche, Friedrich Wilhelm, 1844–1900—Addresses, essays,
lectures. I. O'Flaherty, James C. II. Sellner, Timothy F., 1938–
III. Helm, Robert Meredith. IV. Series: North Carolina. University. Studies in the Germanic languages and literatures; no. 85.

B3317.S78   193   75-22444
ISBN 0-8078-8085-X

Manufactured in the U.S.A.

Contents

Acknowledgments

The editors wish to express their great appreciation for the initial encouragement and continuing interest of Professor Herbert W. Reichert of the University of North Carolina at Chapel Hill in the present project. They wish further to express their gratitude to Wake Forest University for the generous grant which has made possible the publication of the volume. Not least are they grateful to Mrs. Mary C. Reid, secretary of the German Department, Wake Forest University, for her efficiency and unfailing patience in the typing of the manuscript. Permission to reprint articles appearing in the volume as individual chapters granted by the following publishers is gratefully acknowledged: Yale French Studies (Ch. VI, in part); Walter de Gruyter & Co. (Ch. VII, in translation); Athenäum Verlag, GmbH (Ch. VIII); Doubleday & Co., Inc. (Ch. XV).

Introduction

Reminiscing years later about his scathing attack on *The Birth of Tragedy*, an unrepentant Wilamowitz asserted that Nietzsche had become "the prophet of a non-religious religion and an unphilosophical philosophy."[1] Whether this statement is found wanting or not, it is certainly true that Nietzsche regarded his prophetic, Zarathustran role as paramount. If it is the essential role of the prophet to turn his glance to the past in order to project his vision with more confidence into the future, surely no one has fulfilled more faithfully the dual requirements of that office than Friedrich Nietzsche. For while his most cherished (and provocative) thoughts concern the future—the vision of the *Übermensch* and the idea of eternal return—Nietzsche's critical reckoning with the two great streams of cultural influence in the Western world, the Judaeo-Christian and the Graeco-Roman, may yet prove to be his most important contribution to Western thought. In the present volume all the essays revolve to some degree around the central problem of Nietzsche's relation to the classical tradition. The term "classical tradition" here signifies not the actual culture of the Greeks and Romans, but that culture as it has been interpreted (or misinterpreted) by various representative thinkers in the course of European history. The essays are, for the most part, comparative studies, i.e., it is the aim of the authors to contrast Nietzsche's interpretation of the classical tradition, or some aspect of it, with that of representative thinkers and creative writers drawn from significant periods of European history. Thus, the question whether or not Nietzsche's interpretation is closer than that of others to the historical facts about the Greeks and Romans is left open.

The advantage of such an approach as that adopted here is obvious. By setting Nietzsche's version side by side with that of another, in many cases equally genial, interpretation of the classical tradition we gain a deeper insight into his mind, and at the same time an insight into the minds of those with whom his thought is brought into juxtaposition. Since Nietzsche's critical interests cover an astonishingly wide range of subjects within the classical tradition, he affords an unusual number of opportunities for comparative studies of the kind to be found in the following pages. It is readily conceded that a certain arbitrariness and subjectivity necessarily inheres in a compilation of this kind. Some readers will miss a treat-

[1] Ulrich von Wilamowitz-Möllendorff, *My Recollections 1848–1914*, trans. G. C. Richards (London: Chatto & Windus, 1930), p. 152.

ment of this or that thinker in relation to Nietzsche, and in some cases with complete justification, but the editors have had to work within certain practical limits. The collection of studies is offered with no claim to completeness of coverage—whatever "completeness" would mean in such a context—of so large and manifold a subject.

The volume includes essays from each of the following areas: age of the Church Fathers; Scholasticism; the Renaissance; the Enlightenment; Weimar Classicism; Romanticism; nineteenth-century Decadence. Of the fifteen essays included in the volume, five have previously appeared in some form: one has been published in German as part of a larger study (Ch. VII); one has been considerably expanded (Ch. VI); one has appeared in English as part of a larger study (Ch. XV); one has been reprinted essentially without change (Ch. VIII); although written for the present collection, one essay (Ch. I) appeared earlier, with permission of the editors, in somewhat altered form. Thus, eleven of the essays were written expressly for the present volume.

There is no question but that Nietzsche's influence is today both widespread and steadily increasing. Yet he remains, and is certain to remain, a highly problematic figure for Western civilization. For European man is inescapably heir to the Judaeo-Christian tradition and to the Platonism which Nietzsche reprobated. These components of our Western culture may have undergone considerable transformation in the course of two millenia, often quite secularized in the case of the former and distorted in various ways in the case of the latter, but they remain as essential ingredients of our civilization. Nietzsche, who coveted the title of "Antichrist" and who would replace the worship of Christ with that of Dionysus, invoked the culture of the ancient Greeks to effect his purpose. Since this is so, one is justified in raising the question as to whether he correctly understood the Greeks.

Despite the fact that the studies offered here are not concerned with the answer to that question they may serve as a sort of prolegomenon to the search for an answer as well as a stimulus to the individual's own coming to terms with Nietzsche's conclusions. Not only will the reader find in the following essays numerous divergences from Nietzsche's understanding of the Greeks, but he will often encounter agreement with or anticipation of Nietzsche's views in the most unlikely quarters. The truth is that there is probably not a single important idea in Nietzsche's works which has not at one time or another been advanced by a predecessor. Yet the recognition of such a fact by no means diminishes his originality, for in the case of his works the whole is indeed greater than the parts. While one cannot speak of a "system" in connection with his philosophy, it is characterized by a unity provided not merely by a pervading ethos but also by what Bertrand Russell, one of his most penetrating and hostile critics, concedes to be "the consistency and coherence of his doctrine."[2]

[2] Bertrand Russell, *A History of Western Philosophy* (New York: Simon and Schuster, 1945), p. 760.

It is highly significant that a classical philologist like Hugh Lloyd-Jones, heir to the rigorous scholarly tradition of a Wilamowitz, should, exactly a century after the publication of *The Birth of Tragedy*, espouse a view of Nietzsche in many ways diametrically opposed to that of his great German predecessor. Professor Lloyd-Jones' essay, "Nietzsche and the Study of the Ancient World" (Ch. I), may well serve as an introduction to our subject in general as well as to the specialized discussions of the succeeding chapters.

For the most part, the chapters which follow deal with the theme of the volume in chronological order, beginning with Nietzsche's relationship to one of the most important of the Church Fathers. Thus in his essay, "Plato in the Thought of Nietzsche and Augustine" (Ch. II), Robert M. Helm demonstrates that, while Augustine and Nietzsche generally agree in their understanding of the Platonic philosophy, they radically disagree in their evaluation of it. (Augustine's and Nietzsche's essential agreement regarding the historical Plato, we may observe in passing, provides a striking contrast to Hamann's and Nietzsche's radical divergence regarding the historical Socrates, as we shall see later in Ch. VIII.) In her thoroughly documented study, "Aristotle in the Thought of Nietzsche and Thomas Aquinas" (Ch. III), Hedwig Wingler shows how both thinkers concur in rejecting the rationalistic content of Aristotle's philosophy, but disagree fundamentally as to what should take its place and as to the usefulness of the Aristotelian logic.

Nietzsche ordinarily holds creativity and the active life to be superior to knowledge and the contemplation of truth. Yet his own visionary experience "6000 feet beyond man and time" in the woods of Lake Silvaplana would seem to belie that judgment. In his comparative psychological study of Dante, the Aristotelian Christian, and Nietzsche, the neo-pagan antagonist of Christianity, entitled "Between *Inferno* and *Purgatorio*: Thoughts on a Structural Comparison of Nietzsche with Dante" (Ch. IV), Eugen Biser calls attention, among other things, to the striking parallel between Dante's vision of the Circle of Heaven—"the Celestial White Rose"—and Nietzsche's sudden illumination regarding the idea of "eternal recurrence." Not only the parallel concerning the content of the visions, but also the similar circumstances under which the two men experienced their mystical visions are underscored.

Although the essays of Kurt Weinberg and Peter Heller both deal with Nietzsche's relationship to French culture, they approach their subject from different angles, and thus supplement each other. Professor Weinberg, who is chiefly concerned with aesthetics, makes it clear in his study, "The Impact of Ancient Greece and of French Classicism on Nietzsche's Concept of Tragedy" (Ch. VI), why the German philosopher's theory of tragedy thoroughly justifies his dictum that "the nature of the French is much closer to the Greeks than the nature of the Germans," at least in so far as that nature is reflected in the French neoclassical drama. Professor Heller, on the other hand, approaching his subject from the standpoint of social philosophy in the chapter entitled "Nietzsche in His Relation to Voltaire and Rousseau" (Ch. VII), illuminates the paradox that Nietzsche felt an affinity both for Voltaire, the advocate of high culture and sophisticated civilization, and for Rousseau, the advocate of a return to nature. This central problem of nature and civilization in Nietzsche's thought will emerge again in connection with his relationship to nineteenth-century Decadence (cf. Ch. XIV).

Nowhere perhaps are the manifold possibilities for diverse, yet viable interpretations of the classical tradition more evident than in the case of the diametrically opposed views of Socrates which we encounter in the case of Hamann and Nietzsche. In the chapter, "Socrates in Hamann's *Socratic Memorabilia* and Nietzsche's *The Birth of Tragedy*" (Ch. VIII), James C. O'Flaherty calls attention to the fact that the conception of each of these seminal German thinkers springs from his basic epistemological position. Karl Schlechta, in his essay, "The German 'Classicist' Goethe as Reflected in Nietzsche's Works" (Ch. IX), explicates the reasons for Nietzsche's final rejection of Goethe's (and Winckelmann's) conception of classical antiquity. Professor Schlechta emphasizes the central role which metaphysics and a concern for "style" played in the development of Goethe's classicism. In dealing with the other great exponent of Weimar Classicism, Friedrich Schiller, Helmut Rehder notes in his study, "The Reluctant Disciple: Nietzsche and Schiller" (Ch. X), the close parallel between that poet and Nietzsche. Thus he writes: "Nietzsche . . . in spite of his repeated declarations of faith in Goethe, manifested a fundamental sentiment and structure of mind which linked him to the beliefs and precepts of Schiller."

In the past far more scholarly ink has been expended on Nietzsche's influence on others than on the influences which shaped his own thinking, especially on those arising from within the German tradition to which he was immediate heir. In a richly documented study, "Nietzsche and the Tradition of the Dionysian" (Ch. XI), Max L. Baeumer traces the genesis and development of this important concept in the more than a century preceding *The Birth of Tragedy*. In so doing, Professor Baeumer examines the concept in the writings of such diverse thinkers, scholars, and poets as Winckelmann, Hamann, Herder, Novalis, Hölderlin, Heine, Creuzer, Bachofen, Schelling, and others. As a result, a rare and revealing perspective on Nietzsche's philosophy is gained. Ralph S. Fraser's study, "Nietzsche, Byron, and the Classical Tradition" (Ch. XII), traces the complex relationship of these two ardent, but dissimilar Graecophiles through the various stages of Nietzsche's attitude toward the English poet, ranging from uncritical youthful admiration to a final, more realistic appraisal. It is interesting to note that, although Nietzsche admires the French tragedians of the seventeenth century for adhering to the dramatic unities, and therefore for their ability "to dance in chains" (cf. Chs. VI, VII), he is nevertheless critical of Byron for doing so in dramas such as *Manfred*.

Heinrich Heine, with his distinction between "Hellene" and "Nazarene" and with his emphasis on Dionysus as the "savior of the senses" and the "divine liberator," is clearly a forerunner of Nietzsche's philosophy. It is Sander L. Gilman's thesis in the chapter "Parody and Parallel: Heine, Nietzsche, and the Classical World" (Ch. XIII) that, despite Nietzsche's initial quarrel with Heine over the nature of Greek myth and over Heine's style, Nietzsche's later "awareness of the parallels between his fate and that of Heine led to . . . total identification with the poet."

According to Mark Boulby, "it can be demonstrated that, especially in Nietzsche's later years, his manipulation of Roman and Greek material is something of a touchstone of his relationship to the so-called Decadent Movement." In discussing this relationship as well as his relationship to Stefan George, Boulby stresses the antithetical nature of Nietzsche's notion of the "classical"—namely, the paradox of the will, which is seen both as the source of order and of chaos. It is precisely Nietzsche's conception of the paradoxical will, Professor Boulby contends, that separates him from the Decadents (see Ch. XIV: "Nietzsche and the *Finis Latinorum*"). In the course of these studies the problematic character of Nietzsche's idea of nature has already come to light in another context (cf. Ch. VII).

Two of the contributions to the present volume relate Nietzsche's ideas concerning Greek culture to different areas of contemporary aesthetics. In *The Birth of Tragedy* Nietzsche states that "the highest goal of tragedy and art in general is reached" when "Dionysus speaks the language of Apollo, and Apollo finally the language of Dionysus." Marcus Hester, in his study "The Structure of Tragedy and the Art of Painting" (Ch. V), throws light on the complex relationship which results when this *communicatio idiomatum* of the Dionysian and the Apollonian takes place. Analyzing the relationship in terms of contemporary aesthetic theory, Professor Hester shows how Nietzsche's ideas may be fruitfully extended to art criticism. In the concluding chapter, "Nietzsche and the Death of Tragedy" (Ch. XV), Walter Kaufmann argues that Nietzsche was in error with regard to the reasons for the demise of Attic tragedy, and, further, that his followers are wrong in their conception of tragedy in our own time. "Neither in Athens nor in our time has tragedy perished of optimism; its sickness unto death was and is despair." Avoiding the clichés of traditional criticism, and taking a fresh look at the representative dramas of Aeschylus, Sophocles, and Euripides, Professor Kaufmann sees adequate reason to invert Nietzsche's scheme and to consider Aeschylus rather than Euripides as the genuine optimist among the Greek tragedians.

Although five of the present essays were originally written in German (none has appeared previously in English) it was deemed best to render them into English, as well as the quotations from Nietzsche and others, in order to reach the widest possible readership in this and other English-speaking countries. Peter

Heller translated his own essay into English; the remaining four were read and approved by the author in each case. The book addresses itself not only to specialists in literature and philosophy but also to the general reader who seeks a better understanding of Nietzsche's place in the history of Western thought.

31 July 1974   James C. O'Flaherty

Key to Abbreviations

Individual works by Nietzsche:

GT   *Die Geburt der Tragödie (The Birth of Tragedy)*
U   *Unzeitgemäße Betrachtungen (Untimely Meditations or Thoughts out of Season)*
MA   *Menschliches, Allzumenschliches (Human, All-Too-Human)*
S   *Der Wanderer und sein Schatten (The Wanderer and His Shadow)*
M   *Morgenröte (The Dawn or The Dawn of Day)*
FW   *Die fröhliche Wissenschaft (The Gay Science or The Joyful Wisdom)*
Z   *Also sprach Zarathustra (Thus Spoke Zarathustra)*
J   *Jenseits von Gut und Böse (Beyond Good and Evil)*
GM   *Zur Genealogie der Moral (On the Genealogy of Morals)*
G   *Die Götzen-Dämmerung (The Twilight of the Idols)*
A   *Der Antichrist (The Antichrist)*
WM   *Der Wille zur Macht (The Will to Power)*

Editions of Nietzsche's works:

GOE   *Werke: Großoktavausgabe,* ed. Elisabeth Förster-Nietzsche et al. (Leipzig: Naumann, 1894–1904), 15 vols.; 2nd ed. (1901–13), 19 vols., indicated by: GOA(2). Vol. XX, published as a partial index to 2nd ed. (Leipzig, 1926).

MusA   *Gesammelte Werke: Musarionausgabe,* ed. Richard Oehler, Max Oehler, and F. C. Würzbach (Munich: Musarion Verlag, 1920–29).

HKG   *Werke und Briefe: Historisch-Kritische Gesamtausgabe,* ed. under supervision of the "Stiftung Nietzsche-Archiv" (Munich: Beck, 1933–42), 9 vols.

K   *Sämtliche Werke in zwölf Bänden,* ed. Alfred Bäumler (Stuttgart: Kröner, 1964–65). The twelve vols. are reprints of Nos. 70–78, 82–83, and 170 in *Kröners Taschenausgabe* series, and are identified by the series number in italics, followed by the page number, e.g.: *70,* 48; *71,* 49, etc. The last vol. (*170*) is Richard Oehler's index to the previous vols.

W   *Werke in drei Bänden,* ed. Karl Schlechta (Munich: Carl Hanser, 1954–56; 1966). *Nietzsche Index* to foregoing (Munich, 1965).

WKG   *Werke: Kritische Gesamtausgabe,* ed. Giorgio Colli and Mazzino Montinari (Berlin: de Gruyter, 1967 ff.), about 30 vols. planned.

GB   *Gesammelte Briefe,* 5 vols. in 6 (Leipzig:.Insel, 1902–9). Volume V consists of two separately bound parts, designated V/1 and V/2.

I

Nietzsche and the Study of the Ancient World[*]

HUGH LLOYD-JONES

The late Eduard Fraenkel (1888–1970) once remarked to me that the most powerful factor in the difference of outlook between Wilamowitz and his own generation was the influence of Nietzsche. I remembered his remark when, looking back at the end of a study of early Greek religion and thought undertaken in terms of the concept of *dike*, that term which can mean "justice," but can also mean "the order of the universe which the gods maintain,"[1] I found the turning-point in the modern understanding of early Greek thought to be the publication just a hundred years ago of Nietzsche's *The Birth of Tragedy*.

In Germany, the importance of Nietzsche's influence upon classical studies has been recognized a good deal more clearly than it has been in English-speaking countries. Notably, Karl Reinhardt, who had perhaps the finest feeling for poetry and the most sensitive understanding of the Greek intellectual world among Wilamowitz' pupils, grew up under this influence;[2] Nietzsche's friend Paul Deussen was a habitué of his father's house. Many German and Italian scholars have been more or less aware of it. In English-speaking countries scholars have been less willing to recognize it, at least until lately.

This is largely due to the unfortunate prejudice which for most of this century has prevented most American and English people from recognizing the immense importance of this writer; a comparable case is that of Wagner. That prejudice is due largely to the evil work of Nietzsche's sister, a Nazi before the Nazis, who took over all his papers and did her best to credit him with her own detestable opinions; it was also fostered by the excessively strong language in which Nietz-

[*] This is the text of a lecture given at Wake Forest University in November 1972 and later repeated at various other centers. I am painfully aware that some parts of it will seem elementary to students of Nietzsche and other parts to classical scholars; but I have decided to print it in the form in which it was delivered. It was published in a slightly modified form in *The Times Literary Supplement* (21 February 1975), pp. 199–201. I would like to thank Professors James O'Flaherty and Heinz Wenzel for their encouragement, and Professor Rudolf Kassel for useful criticisms.

[1] *The Justice of Zeus* (Berkeley: University of California Press, 1971).

[2] See Uvo Hölscher, *Die Chance des Unbehagens: 3 Essais zur Situation der klassischen Studien* (Göttingen: Vandenhoeck & Ruprecht, 1965), pp. 31 f.

sche's fatal vanity and his natural resentment at the neglect he suffered led him to express himself.

In our time there is no excuse for such a misconception of Nietzsche; Karl Schlechta's edition of 1954–56 began the necessary task of a proper publication of the vast mass of material in the Nietzsche-Archive at Weimar, and now the splendid complete edition of Colli and Montinari[3] has come half way to a satisfactory completion of the work. In America Walter Kaufmann's pioneer study has made it easier for the reader to do justice to Nietzsche;[4] from different points of view, R. J. Hollingdale and Arthur Danto[5] have supplemented his work. There is ground for hope that even in English-speaking countries the general reader may come to realize how impossible it is to understand the origins of existentialism, and other movements now prominent, without taking account of this formerly proscribed writer; how great a part of the advance in understanding the workings of the human mind popularly ascribed *en bloc* to Freud properly belongs to Nietzsche; and how Nietzsche's reservations about language point forward to the linguistic philosophy of Wittgenstein.

It is generally known that Nietzsche in his mature philosophy took the motive force of all human activities to be the will to power and saw the only hope of improvement in the future in the procreation of more specimens of a superior type of human being, the *Übermensch*. On the surface that sounds akin to Nazi doctrines, and Elisabeth Nietzsche told Hitler that he was what her brother meant by an *Übermensch*. She lied. First, Nietzsche made it abundantly clear that he regarded racial purity as a delusion, and thought the highest human types resulted from a racial mixture; we can now know that he often spoke with special admiration of the Jews. Secondly, when Nietzsche spoke of power, he meant much more than the strength that can achieve physical or political domination. In its highest manifestations, he thought, the will to power produced great saints or great artists; his favorite example of the *Übermensch* was not Napoleon, but Goethe. The educated reader is nowadays aware that Freud's view that the erotic instinct is the mainspring of human behavior made it fatally simple for people to make fun of Freud by taking as literal the meta-language which he had to use in order to expound his theory. Thus when Freud says that an infant is in love with his mother he is using not ordinary language but a meta-language. In the language of ordinary life his statement is absurd, so that people who neglect the distinction can make fun of him. But nowadays educated readers will not do this in the case of Freud; and there is no reason why they should do it in the case of Nietzsche.

[3] WKG. For key to abbreviations see p. xvii above.

[4] Walter Kaufmann, *Nietzsche: Philosopher, Psychologist, Antichrist* (Princeton: Princeton University Press, 1950).

[5] R. J. Hollingdale, *Nietzsche: The Man and His Philosophy* (Baton Rouge: The Louisiana State University Press, 1965); Arthur C. Danto, *Nietzsche as Philosopher* (New York: Macmillan, 1965).

Nietzsche is commonly regarded, even by people who know how much people like his sister have misrepresented his real views, as a dangerous subverter of established ethics. He himself is partly to blame, for he often uses language that gives color to this notion; it recalls to Dodds,[6] for instance, the arguments of the immoralist Callicles in Plato's *Gorgias*. Yet as Kaufmann has pointed out, Nietzsche is not an immoralist, except in the sense that he criticizes modern notions about morals. From the moment when, as a schoolboy, he came in contact with the views of Darwin, Nietzsche rejected the belief in God. He thus denied the existence of a divine sanction for morality; and being strongly opposed to a distinction between spirit and matter, he rejects abstract notions of the good like that of Plato. He is concerned to base a relativist ethics upon a realistic psychology. But that does not make him an immoralist. His superman is no more overbearing than Aristotle's megalopsych. The passions, he holds, should be subordinated to the will to power; but they must not be weakened or repressed, but sublimated by the controlling action of the will. Courage is the supreme virtue, and pity is looked on with suspicion; but generosity is commended, and the power to be pursued is not power in the sense of arbitrary dominion over others. Instinctual reactions are favored, but instinct must be controlled by reason.

Unlike Kant and Hegel, but like most great philosophers, this man of genius was not a professional philosopher. But he was for ten years a professor in an important university; and he was by training and profession a classical philologist, and from an early age he showed a very marked aptitude for that subject, one which in Germany in his time and for long before and long after was of central importance to the whole culture of the nation. In the formation of his philosophy he was influenced by many modern thinkers, including, for example, Spinoza and Hume, Kant and Hegel, Darwin and Lamarck, Schopenhauer and Wagner. But his impetus towards philosophy derived initially from his study of the ancient world, and not only of its philosophy but still more of the religious and intellectual climate in which those philosophies developed.

Like many original thinkers, Nietzsche found himself at odds with the members of his own profession. His first book was savagely attacked by some of them and condemned in conversation by others;[7] and after ten years he resigned his chair to concentrate upon philosophy. These facts, and also the nature of their own training, have caused some of his interpreters to write as if Nietzsche had only drifted into classical philology by mistake, and to ignore the part played by the influence of Greek antiquity in the formation of his opinions. That, I think, is a mistake.

I am no philosopher, but a classical scholar, and much of what I have to say is concerned with *The Birth of Tragedy;* but I think it unfortunate that so many

[6] E. R. Dodds, *Plato, Gorgias* (Oxford: Clarendon Press, 1959), p. 387 f.
[7] See below, pp. 7 ff.

people begin the study of Nietzsche by reading this, or by reading *Thus Spoke Zarathustra*. The overheated tone of the former work and the biblical and prophetic manner of the latter are not calculated to reassure the skeptically or empirically minded reader. But Nietzsche is in many ways a skeptic and an empiricist. He detested Hegel, he finally rejected Wagner, and he purified himself from the influence of the latter's music by listening repeatedly to *Carmen*. Correspondingly, he often writes in very different style, sharp, elegant and crisp. "Only a genius," he said, "can write clearly in German." Nietzsche certainly survives the test. What makes his philosophy difficult to understand is his habit of stringing together separate aphorisms or disconnected paragraphs; that is why it is hard to get a general view of his philosophy till you have read all of him. Still, it is a delight to read him; he is one of the greatest writers of German prose, and might be considered a greater writer than any philosopher since Plato.

To understand Nietzsche's criticisms of the classical philology of his time, and also the importance of the subject in his own formation, one must take account of the history of classical studies in Germany, and indeed in Europe. In modern times there have been two revivals of interest in the ancient world. The first arose in Italy during the late middle ages and reached its climax there during the fifteenth and in France during the sixteenth century; its impetus was finally exhausted by the wars and superstitions of the early seventeenth century. The second originated late in that same century, reached a high point in Germany late in the next, and maintained great vigor until 1914; since then, its impetus has been declining under the pressure of the wars and superstitions of our own time. Despite the progress in Greek studies made by individuals like Politian and the great French scholars of the sixteenth century, the first renascence was largely concerned with Greek civilization in its Latin dress. The second concentrated far more upon Greek; and with its beginning, Greek literature for the first time reentered the bloodstream of European civilization in an undiluted form.

Before the second renascence, classical philology had seldom been anything but a secondary pursuit. Men used it to perfect some other skill; they were first divines, lawyers or doctors, and only in second place classical scholars. Nietzsche rightly noted[8] that a new era dawned on 8 April 1777, when Friedrich August Wolf, entering the university of Göttingen, insisted on being set down as "studiosus philologiae."

Yet at its beginning the second renascence was, like the first, a movement of men eager to make use of the ancient world to illuminate the modern. German classicism had its links with the universities; yet it was not an academic but a literary movement. Winckelmann was in a sense a great scholar, but he was less concerned with art history than with art itself; Lessing and Goethe made serious and sustained efforts to become familiar with the ancient world, but did so not for

[8] WKG, IV-1, 90.

the sake of scholarship but for that of literature and art. During the early stage of this second renascence, even professional scholars had something of this attitude. Johann Gottfried Hermann was a close student of Kant, and interpreted Aristotle's *Poetics* in the light of Kantian aesthetics; he and Wolf[9] were both in touch with Goethe, and helped him in his Greek studies. Karl Otfried Müller's history of Greek literature is a learned book which the general reader as well as the scholar can enjoy and admire. The link between the two worlds is seen most clearly in the person of Wilhelm von Humboldt, eminent both as scholar and as statesman and prominent among the founders of that University of Berlin which was to provide Europe with the pattern of a modern education.

But philology could not remain unaffected by the vast development of historical studies that marked the nineteenth century. In the early decades the older type of literary scholarship, personified by Hermann, came into conflict with the newer type, making use of the findings of archaeology, epigraphy, and the new science of comparative linguistics, personified by Karl Otfried Müller, August Böckh, and Friedrich Gottlieb Welcker. On the whole the victory rested with the latter; what was now called the science of the ancient world, *Altertumswissenschaft*, was dominated by the historical outlook. Not all the scholars of this period lost touch with literature. We can remark, for instance, the link between romanticism and the new growth of a historical sense; the new historical writing, rich in cultural and social detail, owed a debt to the romantic novels of Scott, as Ranke, for example, was well aware.[10] But it was now that scholarship became separated from literature, and indeed from other departments of life. Seduced by the example of the natural sciences, whose results seemed so easily to be expressed in concrete terms, scholars showed an increasing appetite for facts collected for their own sake and an increasing pride in "production"; specialization was carried to an extreme degree, and the new historicism came to despise, as sentimental and superficial, the classicism of the age of Goethe. Of course by no means all scholars of the new type were dull or dry; but in the new climate dullness and dryness throve. By 1869, when Nietzsche began his professorial career, the second renascence was showing distinct signs of a decline.

Born in 1844, Nietzsche was educated at Schulpforta, by far the most famous classical school of Germany, which had educated Ranke and—four years after Nietzsche—Wilamowitz, as well as countless classical philologists of note. In this strict establishment, in the face of the keenest competition, Nietzsche won high honors; and he maintained his progress after entering the University of Bonn in 1864. At the end of his first year, the famous quarrel between Otto Jahn and

[9] See the references to the two men in the index of Ernst Grumach's *Goethe und die Antike: Eine Sammlung* (Potsdam: E. Stichnote, 1949).

[10] See H. R. Trevor-Roper, *The Romantic Movement and the Study of History: John Coffin Memorial Lecture delivered before the University of London on 17 February 1969* (London: Athlone Press, 1969), pp. 13 ff.

Ritschl[11] ended in the departure of the latter to Leipzig, and Nietzsche was among those who followed him. Nietzsche might have been expected to side with Jahn, whose strong aesthetic sense came out in his famous life of Mozart and in his pioneer studies in Greek art, rather than with Ritschl, whose claim to fame lies in his immense services to the study of early Latin, particularly Plautus. But in fact Nietzsche attached himself to Ritschl, for whom, as he noted, philology meant the attempt to understand an entire civilization. Ritschl was so much impressed by Nietzsche's work that in 1869 he secured his appointment, at the age of 24, as Professor Extraordinarius at Basel; he became full professor a year afterwards.

Karl Reinhardt, who cannot be accused of prejudice against Nietzsche, has written that "the history of philology has no place for Nietzsche; his lack of positive achievement is too great."[12] It is true that his contribution to detailed scholarship is comparatively small; but when we remember that he gave up his chair at thirty-five, he must be acknowledged to have made himself a place in the history of the subject, even if we think only in terms of concrete achievement. His early work on Theognis (1864)[13] is interesting chiefly on account of the resemblance of this poet's uncompromisingly aristocratic outlook with Nietzsche's own. His doctoral thesis[14] advanced the investigation of the problem of the sources of the second-rate compiler Diogenes Laertius, on whom part of our knowledge of the history of Greek philosophy unfortunately depends. More interesting, from the point of view of Nietzsche's own development, is his work on Democritus;[15] but we should hardly read it now if it were by another author. On the other hand, the three articles on Greek rhythmic[16] contain a statement of the case against believing in a stress accent in Greece that is referred to with approval in Paul Maas' standard manual on Greek metre.[17] A distinct contribution to learning is made by Nietzsche's work on the fictitious contest between Homer and Hesiod preserved in an ancient life of Homer;[18] his guess that the work depended on the *Mouseion* of the late fifth-century sophist Alcidamas, ridiculed

[11] For an excellent brief account of the quarrel, see Alfred Körte, *Die Antike*, 11 (1935), 212 f. Nietzsche's letter to Rohde of 8 October 1868 shows that the attack on Jahn in *Die Geburt der Tragödie* that so angered Wilamowitz (cf. *Erinnerungen, 1848–1914* [Leipzig: K. F. Koehler, 1928], p. 129) had been provoked by Jahn's unfavorable criticism of Wagner. Körte, p. 216 f., shows how strongly Wilamowitz sided with Jahn in the quarrel with Ritschl's supporters.

[12] In a lecture on "Die klassische Philologie und das Klassische," given in 1941; see *Vermächtnis der Antike: Gesammelte Essays zur Philosophie und Geschichtsschreibung*, ed. Karl Becker, 2nd ed. (Göttingen: Vandenhoeck & Ruprecht, 1966), p. 345.

[13] MusA, I, 209 f.

[14] MusA, II, 33 f.; cf. I, 299 f.

[15] MusA, II, 85 f.

[16] MusA, II, 279 f.

[17] Paul Maas, *Greek Metre*, trans. Hugh Lloyd-Jones (Oxford: Clarendon Press, 1962), sec. 4, p. 4.

[18] MusA, II, 369 f.

by Wilamowitz in 1916, was confirmed when J. G. Winter published a Michigan papyrus in 1925.[19] It is more interesting to note that in this study we see the origins of Nietzsche's important observation of the significance in Greek life of contests and competitions. This is emphasized in the history of Greek culture of Jacob Burckhardt,[20] a senior colleague of Nietzsche in the University of Basel; and though Burckhardt always kept his distance from Nietzsche, and later came to mistrust him, it seems certain that this feature of his work was due to Nietzsche's influence. The lecture notes published in the Musarion edition of Nietzsche's works in 1920[21] are highly interesting to students of the origins of his philosophy, or of the general contribution to the understanding of Greek thought which I shall come to presently; but they contain little positive establishment of concrete facts. In that respect, Nietzsche has rather more to his credit than Reinhardt's judgment would imply; Reinhardt, who himself was denied by some colleagues the title of philologist, may have been afraid to claim too much for him. But Nietzsche's own achievement in professional scholarship is trivial in comparison with his general contribution to the understanding of Greek life and thought.

The main elements of this are present in *The Birth of Tragedy*, published in 1872. This work was greeted with derision by most of his professional colleagues. Soon after publication it was bitterly attacked in a pamphlet entitled *Philology of the Future*, with allusion to Wagner's "Music of the Future," by a doctor of philology four years Nietzsche's junior and like him an alumnus of Schulpforta. This was Ulrich von Wilamowitz-Möllendorff, destined to become the most celebrated Greek scholar of his time. Nietzsche was defended in an open letter to a Swiss newspaper by no less a person than Richard Wagner, and in a pamphlet no less bitter than that of Wilamowitz and bearing the unfortunately chosen title of *Afterphilologie* by his friend and contemporary Erwin Rohde, destined in the 1890s to bring out a study of Greek beliefs about the soul that is one of the landmarks in modern classical scholarship; then Wilamowitz returned to battle in a second pamphlet. The firm of Olms has lately reprinted all this literature inside one cover.[22] It makes distressing reading; the over-excited tone and utter lack of humor of all parties to the dispute—it is significant that the most moderate of them was Richard Wagner—is the kind of thing that makes foreigners despair of the

[19] *Transactions of the American Philological Association*, 56 (1925), 121 f.; M. L. West, *Classical Quarterly*, 17 (1967), 433 f. believes that the papyrus comes from a manuscript of Alcidamas; G. S. Kirk, ibid., 44 (1950), 149 f., E. R. Dodds, ibid., 46 (1952), 187 f., and G. L. Koniaris, *Harvard Studies in Classical Philology*, 75 (1971), 107 f., think lines 15–23 come from Alcidamas; R. Renehan, ibid., 85 f., thinks that "we must either accept the entire papyrus as a fragment of Alcidamas or pronounce it an obscure piece of Greek of unknown authorship" (ibid., p. 104).

[20] See especially *Griechische Kulturgeschichte* iv, 84 f., rpt. in *Gesammelte Werke*, VIII (Darmstadt: Wissenschaftliche Buchgesellschaft, 1962), 84 f.

[21] MusA, II, 337 f.

[22] *Der Streit um Nietzsches "Geburt der Tragödie,"* ed. K. Gründer (Hildesheim: Georg Olms Verlagsbuchhandlung, 1969).

whole German nation. The condemnation of his book by older, more established scholars may have distressed Nietzsche more. Usener, the great authority on Greek religion, pronounced its author "dead from the point of view of scholarship"; and Nietzsche's own teacher, Ritschl, was more polite but hardly less severe.[23] On the other hand, Rohde in a letter of 12 January 1873 claims that Jacob Bernays recognized in the book ideas that had long been in his mind.[24] This, if true, is highly significant, for Bernays had a more penetrating intelligence than either Usener or Ritschl.[25]

Considered as a work of scholarship, *The Birth of Tragedy* has many failings. As Wilamowitz saw, it contains some annoying mistakes in scholarship; and the author even leaves out several facts which might have been used to support his thesis.[26] That thesis, that tragedy originated through a synthesis of Apollonian and Dionysian elements, is as a statement of fact to say the least unprovable; and the defectiveness of the arguments confidently asserted to prove it is rendered doubly infuriating by the over-confident and hectic tone in which it is written. Nietzsche failed entirely to control the two intellectual passions which at that period of his life had taken possession of him, the passion for Schopenhauer and the passion for Wagner. The later passion was not simply for Wagner's music, but for his critical writings, so that Nietzsche took over from his hero the notion that Wagnerian opera was in a real sense a revival of Greek tragedy. In consequence, the importance assigned to music in the emergence of tragedy is quite out of proportion. Wilamowitz rightly pointed out that the very different music of ancient Greece was always kept in strict subordination to the words. Later Nietzsche came to regret that he had ever added to the original fifteen sections of the book the ten sections about Wagner with which it concludes.

Nietzsche's Apollo and Dionysus bear an obvious resemblance to the notions of idea and will in the philosophy of Schopenhauer. Later, when Nietzsche had abandoned his Schopenhauerian dualism in favor of a monistic position, he would have operated with Dionysus only. The manner in which the two elements became interfused, and the whole functioning of the Dionysian, are described in over-heated tones not calculated to appeal to the judicious reader; and the

[23] See Charles Andler, *Nietzsche: Sa vie et sa pensée* (Paris: Éditions Bossard, 1920–31), II, 59.

[24] See ibid.; cf. *Nietzsches Briefwechsel mit Erwin Rohde*, ed. Elisabeth Förster-Nietzsche and Fritz Schöll (Leipzig: Insel Verlag, 1923), p. 273.

[25] On Bernays, see A. Momigliano, "Jacob Bernays," *Mededelingen der Koninklijke Nederlandse Akademie van Wetenschappen*, afd. Letterkunde, Nieuwe Reeks, Deel 32, No. 5 (1969), 17.

[26] It is astonishing that Nietzsche does not mention Aeschylus' trilogy about Lycurgus, in which the devotees of Dionysus seem to have clashed with those of Apollo, led by Orpheus; see Karl Deichgräber, *Göttingische Gelehrte Nachrichten*, 8 (1938–39), 231 f. for critical discussion; the fragments are on pp. 25 f. of Hans Joachim Mette, *Die Fragmente der Tragödien des Aischylos* (Berlin: Akademie Verlag, 1959). See in particular fragment 83 (the texts with evidence for the clash between the two cults) and fragment 71, the wonderful fragment describing Dionysiac revelry which is preserved by Strabo X, 3, 16.

assertion that tragedy was killed by an alliance between Euripides and Socrates, grounded as it is on a belief in a community of opinion between these two persons, which is wholly unacceptable, leaves the book wide open to attack. Its author himself later became dissatisfied with it; in 1886 he wrote that he should have done what he had to do "as an imaginative writer."[27] Yet with all its appalling blemishes it is a work of genius, and began a new era in the understanding of Greek thought.

Through Nietzsche's writings runs a vein of criticism of the view of the Greek world taken by the old classicism, much as he preferred its attitude to antiquity to that of the new historicism. Behind the calm and dignity praised by Winckelmann, Nietzsche saw the struggle that had been needed to achieve the balance; he saw that the Greeks had not repressed, but had used for their own purposes, terrible and irrational forces. Nietzsche, and not Freud, was to invent the concept of sublimation, so important in his mature philosophy. Nietzsche saw the ancient gods as standing for the fearful realities of a universe in which mankind had no special privileges. For him what gave the tragic hero the chance to display his heroism was the certainty of annihilation; and tragedy gave its audiences comfort not by purging their emotions but by bringing them face to face with the most awful truths of human existence and by showing how those truths are what make heroism true and life worth living. In comparison with such an insight, resting on a deeper vision of the real nature of ancient religion and the great gulf that separates it from religions of other kinds, the faults of Nietzsche's book, glaring as they are, sink into insignificance.

Reinhardt[28] says that Nietzsche did not discover the Dionysian element in Greek thought, for archaeologists, whose work he had neglected, knew about it before. He might have added that the investigation of the whole problem of the irrational did not begin with Nietzsche. Its origins may be seen in the now forgotten but perhaps still instructive controversy stirred up by the symbolistic theories of the Heidelberg professor Creuzer; his book on Dionysus appeared in 1809 and his *Symbolik und Mythologie der alten Völker, besonders der Griechen* in 1810–12. Reinhardt might have inquired whether in Basel Nietzsche had become acquainted with Bachofen, whose work might well have influenced him. According to Reinhardt, Rohde would have written his great book *Psyche* without the influence of his early friend. Perhaps that is true; perhaps the spirit of the time made it inevitable that the anthropologically minded scholars of the Cambridge school should approach Greek antiquity in the light of Durkheim's teaching; and that the course of classical studies should be transformed by the great movement that culminates, or seems to us to culminate, in *The Greeks and the Irrational* of E. R. Dodds.[29] But the man who first set this in motion was

---

[27] In his introduction to the reprint of that year.

[28] See n. 12 above.

[29] E. R. Dodds, *The Greeks and the Irrational* (Berkeley: University of California Press, 1951).

Nietzsche; and by that alone he acquired an importance in the history of philology far greater than that which his positive discoveries of fact could have won him. More significantly still, Nietzsche's writings show an unprecedented insight into the nature of divinity as the Greeks conceived it. The scholars of modern times who have best apprehended this are Reinhardt himself and Walter F. Otto.

Anyone who shares the view of Nietzsche's importance in the history of scholarship which I have put forward must accord some interest to the criticism of scholarship and scholars which are scattered through his writings, particularly those of the early period. We see these criticisms beginning to take shape in the notes for a course entitled "Introduction to Philology," which Nietzsche delivered in the summer of 1871. This remarkable document may be read in the Musarion edition;[30] the criticisms of contemporary practice which it implies arise naturally out of the subject-matter, and lack the almost waspish sting they carry in Nietzsche's later writings. Above all, Nietzsche insists that the philologist must love his subject; in listing the three requirements of philology: a bent for teaching, "delight in antiquity" ("Freude am Altertume"), and pure desire for knowledge, he clearly gives special consideration to the second. Modern classical education, he ruefully remarks, is designed to produce *scholars;* how different that is from the purpose of the Greeks themselves! There is something comic, he says, about the relation of scholars to the great poets.[31] The most important thing, and the hardest, is to enter into the life of antiquity and to feel the difference. He warns against overspecialization, and insists that the acquisition of knowledge is a means and not an end; in defiance of the spirit of his time, he pleads for concentration on the real classics, which have a permanent value. In a magnificent passage he insists upon the essential simplicity of the Greeks; they are "naiv," he says, and this word connotes both simplicity and depth.

In the essay on the future of German cultural institutions of 1872,[32] Nietzsche attacks philologists as being unable to teach their pupils art and culture. In the essay of 1874 on the uses and disadvantages of history, very similar arguments are directed against historians. The four *Untimely Meditations,* published between 1873 and 1876, were originally to have numbered eight. The fifth was to have been entitled "We Philologists"; a number of the notes collected for it have appeared in the Colli-Montinari edition.[33]

[30] MusA, II, 337 f.

[31] Nietzsche would have enjoyed the poem of Yeats that begins, "Bald heads, forgetful of their sins."

[32] WKG, III-2, 133 f.

[33] WKG, IV-1, 87 f. The merit of having translated a selection from these notes and of having drawn attention to their importance belongs to William Arrowsmith, "Nietzsche on Classics and Classicists," *Arion,* 2 No. 1 (Spring, 1963), 5–18 and 2, No. 2 (Summer, 1963), 5–27. His brief introductions to them are admirably vigorous, but devote too much of their limited space to the negative side of Nietzsche's attitude. Nietzsche's views on this topic have to be considered in their historical context and in some detail. Otherwise there is danger of their being invoked to give a charter to

From this early date in his career, Nietzsche, more than any German writer of his time, condemned the vulgarization and brutalization of many elements of German life and culture which acquired such frightening momentum from the foundation of the Empire in 1871. He was now beginning to emancipate himself from Wagner's influence; and the more he did so, the more scathingly he attacked the crude and stupid nationalism which saw in the triumph over France convincing evidence of the superiority of German culture. He saw that this affected science and scholarship, just as much as it affected trade, commerce, and technology. Dominated by the prevailing materialism, scholars had become fatally ambitious to emulate the positive and concrete achievements of natural science. The passionate devotion to antiquity that still marked German scholarship had become mechanized; and most members of the vast learned profession that had been created were devoted to the accumulation of facts for their own sake. So far as it concerns German classical scholarship, Nietzsche's criticism finds a striking parallel in Housman's inaugural lecture given at Cambridge in 1911.[34] Yet what Nietzsche says about his own profession is only a part of his criticism of German culture in general.

The preference accorded to classical studies, he says in "We Philologists," is due to ignorance of the rest of antiquity; to false idealization of the humanity of the Greeks, who were really less humane than Indians or Chinese; to the arrogance of schoolmasters; to the tradition of admiration of the Greeks inherited from Rome; to prejudice for, or against, Christianity; to the belief that where men have so long dug there must be gold; to aptitude and knowledge derived from philological studies. In sum, it derives from ignorance, false prejudice, wrong inferences, and professional interest; he speaks also of escapism, "Flucht aus der Wirklichkeit." The grounds for this preference have one by one been removed, and one day people will notice this. Many philologists, he thought, had drifted into the profession without being really suited to it. Such people were unfit to teach others, because they had no real conception of the object of their study; if they could grasp the real nature of antiquity, they would turn from it in horror. He accused scholars of lack of respect for antiquity, excess of respect for one another, having ideas above their station, sentimentality, and loose rhetoric. Classical culture, he said, was for the few; there ought to be special police to stop people from being bad scholars, as there ought to be a special police to stop people from playing Beethoven badly. He thought people would get more out of the subject if they began the study late in life. He quotes with approval Wolf's remark that people who are not scholars may understand the ancients better, if they have a real affinity with them, than people who are. The most notable

people who wish to write about the classics, but who lack the ability or the industry to equip themselves to do so competently.

[34] Published under the absurd title "The Confines of Criticism" by the Cambridge University Press, 1969.

products of our study of the ancient world, he said, are not scholars, but Goethe, Wagner and Schopenhauer; later in his life, he might have said Goethe, Leopardi and himself.

What comment can be made on these criticisms? It is easy to see that Nietzsche became dissatisfied with philology partly because it gave no scope for his philosophic and prophetic mission. *The Birth of Tragedy* turned out to be not a work of scholarship, but an imaginative construction; and Nietzsche was right when he finally took the advice of Wilamowitz and gave up his profession. But to say that hardly disposes of Nietzsche's criticisms. It must be recognized that many other persons, by no means prejudiced against the subject, have held that, at the time when Nietzsche began his professorial career, philology was passing through a difficult period, when one wave of inspiration had become exhausted and the next had not yet gathered strength.

In the event, philology made a remarkable recovery, thanks to the great generation of Nietzsche's contemporaries. With the example of Mommsen to guide them, and by an immense *tour-de-force* of comprehensive learning, men like Eduard Meyer, Hermann Diels, Eduard Schwartz, Friedrich Leo, and above all Wilamowitz broke down the barriers between specialized compartments of the subject. Wilamowitz in a lecture at Oxford[35] once said that as Odysseus in the underworld had to give the ghosts blood before they could speak to him, so the philologist had to give the spirits blood—his own—before they would reveal their secrets. By the astonishing vitality of his teaching and writing, and with the aid of his colleagues, Wilamowitz was able for a time to put off the crisis of philology. But throughout his lifetime the dangers indicated by Nietzsche were drawing nearer.

During the 1920s Werner Jaeger tried to institutionalize the now evident reaction against historicism by proclaiming the need for a "third humanism" in the wake of the two revivals of interest in ancient culture of the past. Philology was not to renounce the burden of comprehensive learning imposed on it by the nineteenth century; how could it, without degenerating into mere *belles-lettres?* But it was to publish its official divorce from history; and while it went about its business, it was to keep reminding itself that it was all the time reflecting on its purpose. So Jaeger rewrote the intellectual history of the Greeks from the standpoint of culture conceived as education, and produced one of the most respected, and one of the dullest, learned books of our century.

Bruno Snell in a famous review of Jaeger[36] truly said that the business of philology is not to proclaim new humanisms, but to investigate and present

---

[35] Ulrich von Wilamowitz-Möllendorff, *Greek Historical Writing, and Apollo: Two Lectures Delivered before the University of Oxford, June 3 and 4, 1908*, trans. Gilbert Murray (Oxford: Clarendon Press, 1908), p. 25.

[36] *Göttingische Gelehrte Anzeigen*, 197 (1935), 329 f., rpt. in *Gesammelte Schriften* (Göttingen: Vandenhoeck & Ruprecht, 1966) pp. 32 f.

antiquity with honesty and truth. The self-conscious attitude recommended by Jaeger has fortunately not caught on. But to do in our time what Snell demands is not easy. Unless the noble conception of the unified study of the ancient world as a whole is to be abandoned, a large labor force is needed; and in the nature of things most of these laborers must be mere technicians. Can we do without them?

Nietzsche was prepared to sacrifice the concept of antiquity as a whole, and to concentrate attention on the really creative period of Greek thought. Wilamowitz asked, "What can we do for philology?"; Nietzsche preferred to ask, "What can philology do for us?" To the classicists, with whom Nietzsche's standpoint has so much in common, the ancients had supplied a pattern, an ideal standard of excellence; for the historicists with their relativistic outlook no such thing could exist. Even those who do not accept the notion of an ideal pattern may feel that we must get from antiquity what we can; and in modern conditions, which have notably reduced our labor force, that is what we are being forced to do. Even in modern conditions, and in our new awareness of the dangers of historicism, we cannot renounce the idea of *Altertumswissenschaft* as a unity; if only as an ideal notion, it must still be kept in mind. But scholarship involves a subject as well as an object; and if our studies are to enhance the value of life, we must ask the questions which will yield the most interesting results. Often the people who ask those questions are those who, like Nietzsche, are not restricted by narrowly professional limits. Such people have to guard against reading back into the ancient world the things they want to find in it. All generations have to some extent done that, as, when we look into the past of scholarship, hindsight easily reveals. At least we can be quick to suppress movements which are still looking for what our predecessors wanted to discover, and instead look for those things in the past—real things to the best of our ability—which our own position in history makes it possible and desirable for us to find. That can be done, if it can be done at all, by him who is willing to enter in imagination completely into the life of the past, while carrying back with him as little as possible of the mental furniture of the present. In the past, we can find working models of culture and civilization that may be of value to us when we make our own experiments. The main value of historical scholarship is that it can furnish such models to those who can make profitable use of them. Nietzsche himself was such a one. Ernst Howald[37] rightly says that Nietzsche owed nothing to philology, but much to antiquity; and in a few pages of *The Twilight of the Idols*, written in 1888, the last year of his activity,[38] Nietzsche speaks of his debt to the ancients in a tone of open-minded detachment. He acknowledges a debt to Sallust, who he says awoke his feeling for

---

[37] Ernst Howald, *Nietzsche und die klassische Philologie* (Gotha: F. A. Perthes, 1920), p. 1. Brief as it is, Howald's lecture is necessary reading for anyone seriously interested in the subject. It well deserves to be reprinted. See also the literature quoted by Marcello Gigante in the course of his excellent remarks about Nietzsche in *La parola del passato*, 156 (1974), 15 ff.

[38] WKG, VI-3, 148 f.

style and for the epigram as a stylistic medium, and to Horace; the sketch for this chapter in the notebooks adds Petronius.[39] To the Greeks, he says, he owes no such definite impressions; he repeats what he has written earlier, that the Greeks are more remote from us than the scholars of his day believed. We may well wonder whether he was altogether true to his earlier self at this point; but one can understand his wish to avoid the all too easy self-identification with the Greeks of so many of his contemporaries. His skepticism about Plato extends to style as well as matter; Plato, like a true decadent, wrote in too many different styles, a judgment in which he fortifies himself by quoting "the most refined judges of taste of antiquity"—an odd way of referring to Dionysius of Halicarnassus. His relief from Plato has always been Thucydides; Thucydides, and also Machiavelli's *Prince*, have always been close to him because of their unconditioned will to take nothing for granted and to see reason in reality. Thucydides, who for Nietzsche incarnates all those Sophists whom he much preferred to Socrates and Plato, is the great summation, the last revelation of that strong, strict, hard factuality which lay in the instinct of the early Greeks. Plato, he says, is a coward in the face of reality.[40]

Next, with the German classicists in mind, Nietzsche rejects all attempts to see in the Greeks beautiful souls, golden means or other types of perfection. Their strongest impulse was the will to power, and all their institutions arose from safety regulations, to protect themselves from the potentially explosive matter lying all around them. The inner tension in a Greek state burst out in ruthless external enmities; strength was a necessity, and so was realism.

He himself, Nietzsche claims with pride, has been the first to see the significance of Dionysus; Burckhardt saw at once the importance of his discovery. He pours contempt on the matter-of-fact, rationalistic explanation of Dionysiac mysteries given by Creuzer's learned antagonist, Christian August Lobeck. Goethe would not have understood the mysteries; therefore Goethe did not understand the Greeks. They signified eternal life, the eternal return of life, a triumphant Yes to life beyond death and change; true life as the continuance through generation, through the mysteries of sexuality. The key to the concept of tragic feeling, misunderstood by Aristotle, was given him, he claims, by the psychology of orgiasm. Tragedy—and here he is correcting his own early treatment—is far removed from the pessimism of a Schopenhauer; it is above all an affirmation of life. Its purpose is not to free us from terror and pity nor to purge us by allowing us to discharge these feelings, but by means of them to allow us to participate in the eternal delight of being, that delight which incorporates also the delight of annihilation.

---

[39] WKG, VIII-3, 436.

[40] It must have been in unconscious memory of this remark that I wrote: "The first important failure of nerve was that of Plato." *The Justice of Zeus*, p. 136.

It is not hard to see that in the formation of philosophy designed to meet the needs of his own time Nietzsche made use of the work of many modern thinkers. The influence upon him of classical antiquity receives less attention in most current manuals; even the exhaustive study of Charles Andler,[41] who painstakingly lists every conceivable influence upon Nietzsche's thought, hardly does it full justice. It would, I think, have been better apprehended if it had been easily resolvable into the influences of individual philosophers. Thus the love-hate relationship with Socrates which Nietzsche often mentions has received much attention; yet this is not positive but negative. The truth is that in building his philosophy Nietzsche used not so much the doctrines of any individual ancient thinkers, not even that of Heraclitus, whose thought seems to provide several striking parallels, as the religious and ethical attitude held generally in Greece down to the fifth century, and expressed, with variations, by many Greek poets, historians and thinkers. The influence of Greek ethics upon Nietzsche's ethics is, or should be, obvious. Equally undoubted, in my view, is the influence of the early Greek world outlook upon his philosophy. The Greek universe was god-controlled, but not anthropocentric; the gods granted men occasional favors, but ruthlessly held them down in their position of inferiority; it was in the face of this that heroes showed their heroism. Nietzsche's theory of tragedy contains the essence of his whole metaphysic; so that the Greek influence on this can hardly be disputed. An important difference is that the Greeks, unlike Nietzsche, believed tha gods controlled the universe. But, as modern experience has shown, a metaphysic like that of Nietzsche is not necessarily atheistic.[42]

[41] See n. 23 above.

[42] Dr. Peter Walker, Bishop of Dorchester, draws my attention to the influence of Nietzsche upon Dietrich Bonhoeffer, who even finds in Nietzsche's *Übermensch* "many of the traits of the Christian made free, as Paul and Luther described him." André Dumas, *Dietrich Bonhoeffer, Theologian of Reality*, trans. Robert McAfee Brown (New York: Macmillan, 1971), p. 285.

II

Plato in the Thought of Nietzsche and Augustine

ROBERT M. HELM

On an August day in the year 386, Aurelius Augustinus, his last defenses against Christianity crumbling under the onslaught of a child's voice and a passage of Scripture, felt the weight of sin lifted from him and found the love for God which was to become the dominant passion of his life.

In August of 1886, with the publication of *Jenseits von Gut und Böse*, Friedrich Nietzsche pronounced his judgment on that earlier day in Milan: "The passion for God . . . . There is sometimes an Oriental ecstasy worthy of a slave who, without deserving it, has been pardoned and elevated—for example, in Augustine, who lacks in a truly offensive manner all nobility of gestures and desires."[1]

In the fifteen centuries separating Augustine's conversion from Nietzsche's contemptuous evaluation of it, the Platonic Christianity espoused by the Saint of Hippo had exercised an enormous influence on the institutions which shaped the values of the Western world. Nietzsche, from the earliest years of his young manhood, had dedicated himself to a radical reordering of those values.

He brought to the task a critical mind and a formidable arsenal of learning. Despite the savage and often unfair attacks on him by his fellow philologists, he had confidence in his own scholarship and did not hesitate to assail traditional Christian writings on the ground of philological inadequacies not unlike those of which he had been accused by his opponents:

> *The philology of Christianity.* How little Christianity educates the sense of honesty and justice can be seen pretty well from the writings of its scholars: they advance their conjectures as blandly as dogmas and are hardly ever honestly perplexed by the exegesis of a Biblical verse. Again and again they say, "I am right, for it is written," and the interpretation that follows is of such impudent arbitrariness that a philologist is stopped in his tracks, torn between anger and laughter, and keeps asking himself: Is it possible? Is this honest? Is it even decent? . . .

---

[1] J, pt. 3, sec. 50. (For key to abbreviations see p. xvii above.) Unless otherwise noted, all translations from Nietzsche are those of Walter Kaufmann in *Basic Writings of Nietzsche*, The Modern Library (New York: Random House, 1968), *The Portable Nietzsche* (New York: Viking, 1954), or (with R. J. Hollingdale) *The Will to Power* (New York: Vintage Books, 1968).

In the end, however, what are we to expect of the after-effects of a religion that enacted during the centuries of its foundation that unheard-of philological farce about the Old Testament? I refer to the attempt to pull the Old Testament from under the feet of the Jews—with the claim that it contains nothing but Christian doctrines and *belongs* to the Christians as the *true* Israel, while the Jews had merely usurped it. And now the Christians yielded to a rage of interpretation and interpolation which could not possibly have been accompanied by a good conscience? [2]

In view of Augustine's importance as a prime architect of Christian thought and his vulnerability to charges of arbitrary interpretation of classical philosophy and the Scriptures, it is curious that Nietzsche's writings contain so little in the way of direct attack on him. Certainly Nietzsche had a full measure of the love of intellectual combat which he attributed to the Greek poets and philosophers, and he was seldom really at his best polemically until he could identify the ideas with which he was in conflict with a flesh-and-blood adversary.

Two reasons may be suggested for his reluctance to challenge Augustine directly. In the first place, although it is clear that he had strong objections to the sort of Hellenic-Jewish synthesis which reaches full development in Augustine's writings, Nietzsche must have regarded the Augustinian fusion simply as the inevitable result of a revolution in thought that had its origins centuries earlier in post-Periclean Athens.

In the second place, Nietzsche's failure to cross swords with Augustine in any serious way may have been due in part to the low opinion he had of him as a man. It is clear from his statements about himself and the ambivalence of his attitude toward Socrates that Nietzsche enjoyed jousting with adversaries sufficiently worthy of his steel to be honored with an enmity not unmixed with reverence. He thought Augustine merely a "Christian agitator," one of a clever but "unclean lot,"[3] an incomplete man:

> In an age of disintegration that mixes races indiscriminately, human beings have in their bodies the heritage of multiple origins, that is, opposite, and often not merely opposite, drives and value standards that fight each other and rarely permit each other any rest. Such human beings of late cultures and refracted lights will on the average be weaker human beings: their most profound desire is that the war they *are* should come to an end. Happiness appears to them, in agreement with a tranquilizing (for example, Epicurean or Christian) medicine and way of thought, preeminently as the happiness of resting, of not being disturbed, of satiety, of finally attained unity, as a "sabbath of sabbaths," to speak with the holy rhetorician Augustine who was himself such a human being.[4]

A more suitable antagonist, from Nietzsche's point of view, was Plato, heir to Socrates, assimilator into Greek thought of foreign ideas, and forerunner of

[2] M, sec. 84.
[3] A, sec. 59.
[4] J, sec. 200.

Augustinian Christianity. Acknowledging in Plato the nobility that he could not find in Augustine, Nietzsche includes him in a select list of "royal and magnificent hermits of the spirit"[5] whom he recognizes as his honored teachers:

> I, too, have been in the underworld, like Odysseus, and shall be there often yet; and not only rams have I sacrificed to be able to speak with a few of the dead, but I have not spared my own blood. Four pairs it was that did not deny themselves to my sacrifice: Epicurus and Montaigne, Goethe and Spinoza, Plato and Rousseau, Pascal and Schopenhauer. With these I must come to terms when I have long wandered alone; they may call me right and wrong; to them will I listen when in the process they call each other right and wrong. Whatsoever I say, resolve, or think up for myself and others—on these eight I fix my eyes and see their eyes fixed on me.
>
> May the living forgive me that occasionally *they* appear to me as shades, so pale and somber, so restless and, alas, so lusting for life—while those men then seem so alive to me as if now, *after* death, they could never again grow weary of life. But *eternal aliveness* is what counts: What matters "eternal life" or any life![6]

He finds in Plato a full measure of the Greek love of combat, "an overwhelming craving to assume the place of the overthrown poet and to inherit his fame."[7] Plato's artistic achievements are attributed to his desire to show that he is a greater myth-maker, playwright, and orator than any of his predecessors, and his triumph is crowned by his final repudiation of the arts in which he has sought and achieved success through sheer love of a good fight.

If Plato's pleasure in conflict and contempt for pity earn him Nietzsche's respect, they do not acquit him of complicity in the corruption of the West. It is Plato, after all, who provided the literary vehicle for Socratic rationalism and who, under Socrates' influence, advocated a proscription of the tragic art which, for Nietzsche, represents the fullest flowering of the Greek spirit. In Nietzsche's eyes, a great piece of philosophic mischief took place in the prison cell where Socrates drank the fatal draught. "*The dying Socrates,*" he observes, "became the new ideal, never seen before, of noble Greek youths: above all, the typical Hellenic youth Plato, prostrated himself before this image with all the ardent devotion of his enthusiastic soul."[8] With the conversion of Plato to Socratism, the natural development of philosophy was summarily arrested. "It is no idle question," Nietzsche says, "whether Plato, if he had remained free from Socratic enchantment, would not have found a yet higher type of the philosophic man, which type is forever lost to us."[9]

If youth was responsible for Plato's initial commitment to Socratism, the

[5] Ibid., sec. 204.

[6] *Mixed Opinions and Maxims*, sec. 408.

[7] *Homer's Contest* (see Kaufmann, *The Portable Nietzsche*, p. 36).

[8] GT, sec. 13.

[9] MA, Book I, sec. 261. *Werke: Dünndruckausgabe*, ed. Alfred Bäumler (Leipzig: Kröner, 1930), II, 213 (author's translation).

specific shape of his own thought was, in Nietzsche's view, formed at a somewhat later period:

> *Every philosophy is the philosophy of some stage of life.* The stage of life at which a philosopher found his doctrine reverberates through it; he cannot prevent this, however far above time and hour he may feel. Thus Schopenhauer's philosophy remains the reflection of ardent and melancholy *youth*—it is no way of thinking for older people. And Plato's philosophy recalls the middle thirties, when a cold and a hot torrent often roar toward each other, so that a mist and tender little clouds form and under favorable circumstances and the rays of the sun, an enchanting rainbow.[10]

Nietzsche had a classical scholar's familiarity with Plato's writings. Augustine, clearly better acquainted with the thought of the Neo-Platonists than with that of Plato himself, seems, nevertheless, to have read some of the dialogues. The two men are substantially in agreement concerning the effects of his philosophy on the classical mind in rendering it susceptible to Christianity. Their attitudes toward its influence, however, are markedly different.

Augustine holds that if Plato were alive and could be asked whether a man who could persuade the world of the high truths of Platonic philosophy would not be worthy of divine honors, he would reply that "being the bearer and instrument of God on behalf of the true salvation of the human race, such a man would have earned a place all his own, a place above all humanity."[11] Jesus the Christ is, according to Augustine, the man in whom the Platonic promise is fulfilled.

For Nietzsche, on the other hand, the age that Plato brought to an end was greater than the one which he brought into being. Socratic dialectic and Euripidean drama, in which cold, calculating reason replaces Dionysian instinct and frenzy, find their fulfillment in a new art form created by Plato. Deprecating tragedy, along with all the other arts as imitation of imitation, Plato tried to create a mode of artistic expression which would rise above what is commonly taken for reality and represent directly the realm of Ideas: The result was the dialogue, a mixture of all the literary and dramatic styles and forms which had gone before it and, in fact, the model of the novel, "which may be described as an infinitely enhanced Aesopian fable, in which poetry holds the same rank in relation to dialectical philosophy as this same philosophy held for many centuries in relation to theology: namely, the rank of *ancilla*."[12] A result in literature and philosophy has been, in Nietzsche's view, the substitution of a spirit of optimism for a true sense of tragedy.

He regards the presence of Socratism in Plato's philosophy—the optimistic

---

[10] *Mixed Opinions and Maxims*, sec. 271.

[11] Augustine, *Of True Religion*, 3.3 *Augustine: Earlier Writings*, ed. and trans. John Burleigh (Philadelphia: Westminster Press, 1953), p. 227.

[12] GT, sec. 14.

and utilitarian identification of badness with ignorance—as an alien intrusion for which Plato himself was really too high-minded: "Plato did everything he could in order to read something refined and noble into the proposition of his teacher—above all, himself. He was the most audacious of all interpreters and took the whole Socrates only the way one picks a popular tune and folk song from the streets in order to vary it into the infinite and impossible—namely, into all of his own masks and multiplicities in a jest, Homeric at that: what is the Platonic Socrates after all if not *prosthe Platōn opithen te Platōn messē te Chimaira*."[13]

Noble intent was not enough. Under Plato's influence, classical thought strayed farther and farther from the original forms it had taken in the works of the great Greek tragedians and the pre-Socratic philosophers. In the last analysis, indeed, Nietzsche regards Plato rather than Socrates as the real turning point in the history of Western thought:

> With Plato something quite new begins, or, as can be said with equal justice, since Plato, philosophers lack something essential in comparison with that republic of geniuses from Thales to Socrates. Whoever wishes to express himself spitefully about those older masters may call them one-sided and their *epigones*, with Plato at the head, many-sided. It would be more accurate and unprejudiced to conceive the latter as philosophic mongrel characters, the former as pure types. Plato himself is the first grand mongrel character and distinctly stamped as such, both in his personality and in his philosophy. Socratic, Pythagorean, and Heraclitean elements are joined together in his ideology; it is, therefore, no typically pure phenomenon. As a man too, Plato intermingles the traits of the royally reclusive, all-sufficient Heraclitus, of the gloomily compassionate and legislatorial Pythagoras, and of the psychologically proficient dialectician Socrates.[14]

Nietzsche judges all post-Platonic philosophers to be such hybrid characters. They are founders of sects which oppose the older Hellenic culture. The pre-Platonic thinkers, in whose ranks Nietzsche, in this context at least, includes Socrates, were true Greeks, types of the philosopher who "guards and defends his native country."[15] After Plato, on the other hand, the philosopher "is in exile and conspires against his fatherland."[16]

One reason for the alienation is, in Nietzsche's view, to be found in the assimilation by Plato and his successors of elements from a variety of cultures. A principal difference between Augustine and Nietzsche lies in their evaluation of this process.

Augustine, concerned to find the hand of God moving in the Greek world, welcomes every evidence that Platonic philosophy may have been influenced by

13 J, sec. 190.
14 Nietzsche, *Die Philosophie im tragischen Zeitalter der Griechen*, sec. 2, *Friedrich Nietzsches Werke*, I, 268 (author's translation).
15 Ibid., p. 269.
16 Ibid.

the revealed truth given through the Jews. In *De Doctrina Christiana*, he rejects the theory that Jesus may have learned from Plato. Appealing to the authority of Ambrose, he asks whether the great Bishop did not, "when he had considered the history of the pagans and found that Plato had traveled in Egypt during the time of Jeremias, show that Plato had probably been introduced to our literature by Jeremias so that he was able to teach or to write doctrines that are justly commended."[17] Discovering that Plato was born too late to have met the prophet and too early to have read the Septuagint translation, Augustine still maintains in *De Civitate Dei* that Plato could have become familiar with the contents of the Jewish Scriptures through conversation or by delving into literature.[18]

The description of the creation of the heavens and the earth in the first book of Genesis is compared, as one instance of this apparent influence, with Plato's account of the uniting by God of earth and fire, the latter element being located in the heavens. Augustine speculates, with equally questionable plausibility, that the inclusion of two other elements, air and water, may have been based on the verse: "the spirit of God was stirring above the waters." Air is identified with spirit in popular Greek thought, his reasoning goes, and so Genesis could have been the source of Plato's elements.[19]

Augustine finds in the Scriptures an idea consonant with Plato's definition of a philosopher as one who loves God, and he sees in Plato's writings a recognition of the God of the Old Testament:

> . . . the most palpable proof to my mind that he was conversant with the sacred books is this, that when Moses, informed by an angel that God wished him to deliver the Hebrews from Egypt, questioned the angel concerning the name of the one who had sent him, the answer received was this: "I AM WHO AM. Thus shalt thou say to the children of Israel: He who is, hath sent me to you," as though, in comparison with Him, who, being immutable, truly is, all mutable things are as if they were not. Now, Plato had a passionate perception of this truth and was never tired of teaching it. Yet, I doubt whether this idea can be found in any of the works of Plato's predecessors except in the text: "I AM WHO AM, and you shall say to them: He who is hath sent me to you."[20]

In spite of his low opinion of Christian philology, Nietzsche shows little inclination to challenge Augustine's interpretation of Plato's thought on philological grounds. Like Augustine, he sees abundant evidence of foreign influence in Platonic philosophy, and he is critical of the Semitic flavor which Augustine

[17] Augustine, *On Christian Doctrine*, 2.28, trans. D. W. Robertson, Jr. (New York: Liberal Arts Press, 1958), p. 64.

[18] Augustine, *De Civitate Dei*, 8.11.

[19] Ibid.

[20] Augustine, *The City of God*, 8.11, trans. Gerald G. Walsh, et al. (New York: Image Books, 1958), pp. 160–61. (All references to *The City of God* hereinafter cited are to this edition.)

values. Maintaining that Christianity inherited a megalomania from its Jewish
background, he nevertheless continues: ". . . on the other hand, Greek moral
philosophy had already done everything to prepare the way for and to make
palatable moral fanaticism even among the Greeks and Romans—Plato, the
great viaduct of corruption, who first refused to see nature in morality, who had
already debased the Greek gods with his concept 'good,' who was already marked
by Jewish bigotry (—in Egypt?)"[21]

No overall prejudice against Jews need be read into such observations as
this, and indeed, Nietzsche characterizes himself as a foe of anti-Semitism. In his
writings, he praises the early Hebrew ethos and frequently expresses his admiration for the Jews as a people. Moreover, even his criticisms of the Jewish elements
in Platonism and Christianity, though scathing enough, usually show more
restraint than his attacks on his fellow Germans. Nevertheless, he does see non-
Hellenic influences, in particular those with Jewish origins, as destructive of the
vigor and purity of the older Greek culture. After Socrates, these innovations
become, in his opinion, an ineradicable source of corruption. Plato is an "instinctive Semite and anti-Hellene,"[22] and a Stoic "is an Arabian sheik wrapped
in Greek togas and concepts."[23] Late in his career, defecting from his earlier
identification of Socrates as the last of the truly Greek philosophers, he accords
this distinction to the Sophists. "When Socrates and Plato took up the cause of
virtue and justice," he says, "they were *Jews* or I know not what."[24] Christianity
is only a continuation of "the fight that had already begun against the *classical*
ideal and the *noble* religion."[25] It is "Platonism for 'the people.' "[26]

Both Augustine and Nietzsche find the principal significance of Socrates
and Plato in the emergence of morality as the dominant element in philosophy.
"To Socrates," Augustine says, "goes the credit of being the first one to channel
the whole of philosophy into an ethical system for the reformation and regulation
of morals."[27]

Nietzsche, although recognizing the presence of a moral element even in
pre-Socratic metaphysics, maintains that with Socrates and Plato, morality
ceases to be a matter of instinct and becomes a self-conscious rational discipline,
conveniently provided with an ideal, if fictional, metaphysical foundation:

> *In praxi*, this means that moral judgments are torn from their conditionality,
> in which they have grown and alone possess any meaning, from their Greek and
> Greek-political ground and soil, to be denaturalized under the pretense of sublima-

---

[21] WM, sec. 202.
[22] Ibid., sec. 195.
[23] Ibid.
[24] Ibid., sec. 429.
[25] Ibid., sec. 196.
[26] J, "Preface."
[27] Augustine, *The City of God*, 8.3, pp. 146–47.

tion. The great concepts "good" and "just" are severed from the presuppositions to which they belong and, as liberated "ideas" become objects of dialectic. One looks for truth in them, one takes them for entities: one *invents* a world where they are at home, where they originate.

In summa: the mischief has already reached its climax in Plato—and then one had need to invent the abstractly perfect man as well:—good, just, wise, a dialectician—in short, the scarecrow of an ancient philosopher: a plant removed from all soil: a humanity without any particular regulating instincts; a virtue that "proves" itself with reasons. The perfectly absurd "individuum" in itself! Unnaturalness of the first water.—

In short, the consequence of the denaturalization of moral values was the creation of a degenerate type of man—"the good man," "the happy man," "the wise man."—Socrates represents a moment of the profoundest perversity in the history of values.[28]

In so corrupting morality, Plato is seen as having had necessary recourse to the holy lie, originally a priestly prerogative, and, Nietzsche is careful to point out, an Aryan rather than a Semitic one. The holy lie, in promoting a concept of good and evil divorced from such natural predicates as "useful," "harmful," "life promoting," "life retarding," and the like, necessitates a claim to authority here and hereafter as a source of powerful sanctions for the enforcement of an unnatural rule of conduct. To provide that authority and those sanctions, the holy lie posits God, an afterlife, conscience, morality, and revealed truth.

It may be noted that Plato, in the *Republic*, justifies a lie for pious ends in defense of a social stratification not too much at variance in form, at least, with that favored by Nietzsche himself. It is presumably with this in mind that Nietzsche cites Plato as an authority for the value of "a real lie, a genuine, resolute, 'honest' lie."[29] He does not hesitate, however, to brand the *Republic* as an instance of the sort of cold-blooded, reflective Aryan influence[30] responsible for the *pia fraus*, which is, in such a context, "more offensive to the free spirit, who has 'the piety of the search for knowledge' "[31] than the *impia fraus* because it results in "the worst mutilation of man that can be imagined presented as the 'good man.' "[32]

The holy lie, in support of an unnatural moral system, must be distinguished form the legitimate lie of the artist, which Nietzsche defends, for:

. . . art, in which precisely the *lie* is sanctified and the *will to deception* has a good conscience, is much more fundamentally opposed to the ascetic ideal than is science: this was instinctively sensed by Plato, the greatest enemy of art Europe has yet

---

[28] *The Will to Power*, sec. 430.
[29] GM, "Third Essay," sec. 19.
[30] WM, sec. 142.
[31] J, sec. 105.
[32] WM, sec. 141.

produced. Plato versus Homer: that is the complete, the genuine antagonism—there the sincerest advocate of the "beyond," the great slanderer of life; here the instinctive deifier, the *golden* nature. To place himself in the service of the ascetic ideal is therefore the most distinctive *corruption* of an artist that is at all possible; unhappily, also, one of the most common forms of corruption, for nothing is more easily corrupted than an artist.[33]

Whether it does or does not really rest on a lie, a universal ethical system goes hand-in-hand with the claim that there is an absolute truth. Here again, Augustine and Nietzsche agree substantially in their interpretation of Plato's thoughts but differ sharply in their evaluation of it.

According to Augustine, the philosopher, as seen by Plato, is engaged in "a hunt for happiness which ends only when a lover of God reaches fruition in God,"[34] and he praises the Platonists, "who acknowledged the true God as the author of being, the light of truth and the giver of blessedness."[35]

Similarly, Nietzsche speaks of "the Christian faith, which was also Plato's, that God is truth, that truth is *divine*."[36] Plato is asserted to have "wanted to employ all his strength—the greatest strength any philosopher so far has had at his disposal—to prove to himself that reason and instinct of themselves tend toward one goal, the good, 'God.' "[37] As contrasted with Augustine's wholehearted approval of the spirituality and theocentricity he saw in Platonic philosophy, however, Nietzsche's attitude toward Plato's "invention of pure spirit and the good" is one of incredulity. "How could the most beautiful growth of antiquity, Plato, contract such a disease?" he asks. "Did the wicked Socrates corrupt him after all? Could Socrates have been the corrupter of youth after all? And did he deserve his hemlock?"[38]

Certainly, Augustine's theory of knowledge is Platonic in character. While acknowledging the claims of sense experience and an instrumental use of reason in the conduct of practical affairs, he stresses the final goal of liberation from the senses and the attainment of the wisdom and happiness which result from contemplation directed toward a supernatural end. Plato's mathematical entities are reflected in Augustine's treatment of the ideal geometrical figures by which mutable and imperfect circles and lines are judged, while principles not unlike Plato's ἀρχαί provide the standards by which specific aesthetic and ethical judgments are made. Moreover, Plato's comparison of the sun with the Idea of the Good in the *Republic* finds its counterpart in Augustine's treatment of God as the light by which the nature of intelligible things is made evident to the

[33] GM, "Third Essay," sec. 25.
[34] Augustine, *The City of God*, 8.8, p. 156.
[35] Ibid., 8.5, p. 151.
[36] GM, "Third Essay," sec. 24.
[37] J, sec. 191.
[38] J. "Preface."

intellect, "just as the eye of the flesh sees the things that lie about it in this corporeal light."[39] In his earlier writings, he seems to have entertained sympathetically the Platonic doctrine of Reminiscence, but it is apparently repudiated in *De Trinitate*.[40]

Nietzsche, while rejecting the Platonic doctrine of Ideas, is not impervious to its attractiveness as contrasted with the attempt to derive explanatory principles from naive reliance on sense data:

> Conversely, the charm of the Platonic way of thinking, which was a *noble* way of thinking, consisted precisely in *resistance* to obvious sense-evidence—perhaps among men who enjoyed even stronger and more demanding senses than our contemporaries, but who knew how to find a higher triumph in remaining masters of their senses—and this by means of pale, cold, gray concept nets which they threw over the motley whirl of the senses—the mob of the senses, as Plato said. In this overcoming of the world, and interpreting of the world in the manner of Plato, there was an *enjoyment* different from that which the physicists of today offer us—and also the Darwinists and anti-teleologists among the workers in physiology, with their principle of the "smallest possible force" and the greatest possible stupidity.[41]

Plato's real difficulty, as Nietzsche sees it, lies in the fact that a philosophy based on morality makes Truth an absolute good and the search for it an unconditional duty. However, a search for that Truth sufficiently honest and diligent to satisfy the moral imperative must at last lead to the denial that any such goal can be attained and thus to intellectual nihilism.

According to Nietzsche, we must examine the whole question of truth from a different standpoint. It is not, as Plato supposed, something absolute and unchanging and neither are the men who seek it:

> What separates us most thoroughly from all Platonic and Leibnizian ways of thinking is: we believe in no eternal concepts, eternal values, eternal forms, eternal souls: and philosophy, so far as it is science and not legislation, to us means only the broadest extension of the concept "history." From etymology and the history of language we take the view that all concepts have evolved [*sind geworden*], many are still evolving: and moreover in such fashion, that the most general concepts, being the *falsest*, must also be the oldest. "Being," "substance," "absolute [*Unbedingtes*]," "sameness," "thing"—: at the first and earliest period, thought devised for itself these schemata, which in fact contradict the world of becoming most thoroughly, but which *seemed* to correspond to it as a matter of course, given the obtuseness and all-the-sameness [*Einerleiheit*] of consciousness as it began in the lower animals. . . .[42]

[39] Augustine, *The Trinity*, 12.15.24, trans. Stephen McKenna (Washington, D.C.: Catholic University of America Press, 1963), p. 366.

[40] Ibid.

[41] J, sec. 14.

[42] *Nachgelassene Werke*, 1882–88, sec. 21. Trans. George A. Morgan in *What Nietzsche Means* (Cambridge, Mass.: Harvard University Press, 1941), p. 243.

The changing and partial character of knowledge does not, in Nietzsche's view, entitle us to think in fragmentary fashion. A system of thought with some sort of wholeness is as appealing to him as to any other philosopher, but the wholeness must be a product of organic growth and not of deliberate rational construction. "Such dogmatic men as Dante and Plato," he says, "are *farthest* from me and perhaps thereby most fascinating: men who dwell in a trimly built and firmly believed house of knowledge."[43]

Nietzsche's preference for a dynamic as opposed to a static conception of knowledge is reflected in his wholehearted approval of empirical method and his distrust of scientific concepts, which seem to him to imply a Platonic view of knowledge:

> Every concept originates through our equating what is unequal. No leaf ever wholly equals another, and the concept "leaf" is formed through an arbitrary abstraction from these individual differences, through forgetting the distinctions; and now it gives rise to the idea that in nature there might be something besides the leaves which would be "leaf"—some kind of original form after which all leaves have been woven, marked, copied, colored, curled, and painted, but by unskilled hands, so that no copy turned out to be a correct, reliable, and faithful image of the original form.[44]

Nietzsche's regard for mathematics and logic as sources of knowledge is considerably lower than Plato's. They are, to be sure, useful disciplines for a variety of practical enterprises, but, far from revealing the nature of reality, they actually obscure it. Perfect circularity, a purely fictitious product of thought, could never, in Nietzsche's view, be legitimately thought of as having greater reality than an approximately circular object of experience. Knowledge in the Platonic sense is impossible, for there is no intelligible absolute Being to be known.

Augustine's acceptance and Nietzsche's rejection of a Platonic transempirical reality have their inevitable corollary in their differing evaluations of Plato's conception of nature and man. Augustine regards Plato as committed in the *Timaeus* to a doctrine of creation not too much at variance with his own theory of *creatio ex nihilo*:

> Surely, in matters which the mind of man cannot penetrate it is better simply to believe what God tells us, namely, that the soul is not co-eternal with God but was created out of nothing. To justify their refusal to believe this, the Platonists have been content with the argument that nothing can be everlasting unless it has existed eternally. What, however, Plato himself expressly stated is that the world and those gods whom God put in the world began to be and had a beginning, although they

[43] *Nachgelassene Werke*, sec. 55. Cited by Morgan.

[44] Nietzsche, "On Truth and Lie in an Extra-Moral Sense" (see Kaufmann, *The Portable Nietzsche*, p. 46).

will have no end, since the will of the all-powerful Creator will keep them in existence forever.[45]

Augustine draws attention to a statement by Plato that God was filled with delight at the completion of His creation, like an artist pleased with his work. This does not, Augustine holds, necessitate the attribution to the Creator of any sense of discovery or recognition of novelty, and he denies that Plato places God in time. "For, not in our way does God look forward to the future, see the present, and look back upon the past, but in a manner remotely and profoundly unlike our way of thinking."[46]

In his discussion of Plato's doctrine of creation, Augustine points to a further instance of the subordination of metaphysics to morality: "Even Plato says that the best reason for creating the world is that good things should be made by a good God. It may be that he read this scriptural passage or learned it from those who had, or, by his own keen insight, he clearly saw that 'the invisible things' of God are 'understood by the things that are made,' or, perhaps, he learned from others who had clearly seen this."[47]

Augustine again has recourse to Plato in his treatment of questions about human souls. For both thinkers, the soul is immaterial and substantial. With some revision, Augustine appropriates Plato's arguments for its immortality. Rather than holding, with Plato, that the soul is in its own right the principle of life and thus cannot die, he maintains that it derives its being and essence from God and that, being grounded in the Divine Life, the individual soul has life as its own essence and so is not subject to death. In Platonic fashion, the soul is also declared to be indestructible because it is capable of apprehending indestructible truth.

Augustine suggests that his own view of souls as direct creations of God is not incompatible with Plato's position: "Of course, when Plato taught that the lesser gods, made by the Supreme God, were the makers of the mortal part of all other animals, he knew that the immortal part came from God; therefore, he maintained that the lesser gods were responsible not for our souls but only for our bodies."[48]

Augustine uses Plato's declaration in the *Timaeus* that animal life is essential to a perfect and beautiful universe[49] as an argument against the Platonists' contention that souls are placed in bodies as punishment for sins occurring in some state of pre-existence. He nowhere commits himself to any theory as to when souls come into existence, and most of his speculation on the origin of individual souls is concerned with the question of whether God creates each soul individually

---

[45] Augustine, *The City of God*, 10.31, p. 197.
[46] Ibid., 11.21, p. 227.
[47] Ibid., p. 228.
[48] Ibid., 12.27, p. 266.
[49] Plato, *Timaeus*, 41c.

or whether all souls were originally created in Adam's. His interest in the subject is, perhaps, more theological than philosophical, though he would certainly draw no sharp distinction between the two disciplines.

In contrast to Augustine, Nietzsche holds distinctly anti-Platonic views of nature and man. The world is in no way dependent upon a god or gods:

> And do you know what "the world" is to me? Shall I show it to you in my mirror? This world: a monster of energy without beginning, without end; a firm, iron magnitude of force that does not grow bigger or smaller, that does not expend itself but only transforms itself; . . . a sea of forces flowing and rushing together, eternally changing, eternally flooding back, with tremendous years of recurrence, with an ebb and a flow of its forms; . . . this, my *Dionysian* world of the eternally self-creating, the eternally self-destroying, . . . do you want a *name* for this world? A *solution* for all its riddles? A *light* for you, too, you best-concealed, strongest, most intrepid, most midnightly men?— *This world is the will to power—and nothing besides!* And you yourselves are also this will to power—and nothing besides![50]

In Nietzsche's world-view, there is no immutable unconditioned, rational reality lying behind the world of change. Reality is itself the becoming which Plato mistakenly tries to transcend, and "the world has no goal, no final state, and is incapable of being."[51] "This beautiful world history is, in Heraclitean terms, 'a chaotic pile of rubbish.' "[52]

His rejection of a Platonic universe does not commit Nietzsche to atomistic materialism, which he dismisses as "one of the best refuted theories there are."[53] His own view of the nature of things is, indeed, far removed from the usual mechanistic formulations of classical materialism. As for the world constructed by the speculative imagination of the scientist, it too is suspect, as resting on essentially Platonic foundations:

> The truthful man, in the audacious and ultimate sense presupposed by the faith in science, *thereby affirms another world* than that of life, nature, and history; and insofar as he affirms this "other world," does this not mean that he has to deny its antithesis, this world, our world? . . . It is still a *metaphysical faith* that underlies our faith in science—and we men of knowledge of today, we godless men and anti-metaphysicians, we, too, still derive *our* flame from the fire ignited by a faith millenia old, the Christian faith, which was also Plato's, that God is truth, that truth is *divine*.—But what if this belief is becoming more and more unbelievable, if nothing turns out to be divine any longer unless it be error, blindness, lies—if God himself turns out to be our *longest lie?*[54]

[50] WM, sec. 1067.
[51] WM, sec. 1062, p. 546.
[52] *Notes* (*1873*), 6.334 f.
[53] J, sec. 12.
[54] GM, "Third Essay," sec. 24 (quoted from *Die Fröhliche Wissenschaft*, sec. 344).

Nietzsche summarily rejects the theory of the creation of the world which Augustine attributes to Plato. "We need not worry for a moment about the hypothesis of a *created* world," he says. "The concept 'create' is today completely indefinable, unrealizable; merely a word, a rudimentary survival from the ages of superstition; one can explain nothing with a mere word."[55]

As for the conception of the soul "as something indestructible, eternal, indivisible, as a monad, as an *atomon:* this belief ought to be expelled from science!" Nietzsche says, but he goes on to add: "Between ourselves, it is not at all necessary to get rid of 'the soul' at the same time, and thus to renounce one of the most ancient and venerable hypotheses—as happens frequently to clumsy naturalists who can hardly touch on 'the soul' without immediately losing it. But the way is open for new versions and refinements of the soul-hypothesis; and such conceptions as 'mortal soul,' and 'soul as subjective multiplicity,' and 'soul as social structure of the drives and affects,' want henceforth to have citizens' rights in science."[56]

To the Platonic view of immortality, Nietzsche opposes his own doctrine of eternal return, one of the most significant and, at the same time, most puzzling features of his philosophy. Seen from one standpoint, the theory seems to suggest little more than an unending recurrence based on the questionable notion that, given a world limited in extent but unlimited in duration, any event must be repeated an infinite number of times:

> If the world may be thought of as a certain definite quantity of force and as a certain definite number of centers of force—and every other representation remains indefinite and therefore useless—it follows that, in the great dice game of existence, it must pass through a calculable number of combinations. In infinite time, every possible combination would at some time or another be realized; more: it would be realized an infinite number of times. And since between every combination and its next occurrence all other possible combinations would have to take place, and each of these combinations conditions the entire sequence of combinations in the same series, a circular movement of absolutely identical series is thus demonstrated: the world as a circular movement that has already repeated itself infinitely often and plays its game *in infinitum*.[57]

Nietzsche insists that this concept is not merely mechanistic. It may not be immediately obvious, however, why he describes it as "this highest formula of affirmation that is at all attainable"[58] or why his outlook underwent a change not unlike that associated with experiences of religious conversion when, walking in the woods by the lake of Silvaplana in 1881, he stopped by a pyramidal rock

---

[55] WM, sec. 1066. The word translated as "indefinable," reportedly illegible in the manuscript, is rendered as "*undefinierbar*" in German editions.

[56] J, sec. 12.

[57] WM, sec. 1066.

[58] "Thus Spoke Zarathustra," *Ecce Homo*, sec. 1.

and found himself overcome by a conviction that all things must return. The exhilaration this revelation produced in him would seem an inappropriate response to a vision of a senseless universe repeating a meaningless history throughout a time without beginning and without end.

From the popular point of view, Nietzsche acknowledges, such a prospect would be all but unendurable. No ordinary man could cheerfully will his own return and the recurrence of everything that happens to him during his lifetime. If this "hardest idea"[59] is to be borne, one must be prepared to revalue all his values, assert the will to power, accept uncertainty and strive for the creation of the Superman. If, like Zarathustra, a man can see himself as a maker of his own destiny rather than as a pawn of fate, he can affirm the values of his life and joyfully will to live again and again throughout eternity.

The precise nature of the theory of recurrence has been the subject of considerable speculation. Nietzsche's aversion to discussing such matters in traditional metaphysical terms frustrates any attempt to arrive at a clear concept of time and eternity which could safely be attributed to him, and it is possible that his view may be more complex than would seem to be indicated by the quasi-mechanistic formulation of a finite world in infinite one-directional time. In any event, the real significance of the concept lies not so much in the recurrence itself as in the realization of it by one who has the sort of experience which overwhelmed Nietzsche as he stood by his pyramidal rock "6000 feet beyond man and time."[60] In being able to will his own return, one brings eternity into the present moment. "That *everything recurs*" Nietzsche says, "is the closest approximation of a world *of becoming* to a world of being."[61] The doctrine thus reconciles as ideals "the two most extreme modes of thought—the mechanistic and the Platonic."[62]

Platonic influence is clearly evident in Augustine's treatment of virtue, derived from classical sources, but interpreted in Christian terms:

> As to virtue leading us to a happy life, I hold virtue to be nothing else than perfect love of God. For the fourfold division of virtue I regard as taken from four forms of love. For these four virtues (would that all felt their influence in their minds as they have their names in their mouths!) I should have no hesitation in defining them: that temperance is love giving itself entirely to that which is loved; fortitude is love readily bearing all things for the sake of the loved object; justice is love serving only the loved object, and therefore ruling rightly; prudence is love distinguishing with sagacity between what hinders it and what helps it. The object of this love is not anything but God, the chief good, the highest wisdom, the perfect harmony.[63]

---

[59] WM, sec. 1059.

[60] "Thus Spoke Zarathustra," *Ecce Homo*, sec. 1.

[61] WM, sec. 617.

[62] WM, sec. 1061.

[63] Augustine, *On the Morals of the Catholic Church*, 15, trans. R. Stothert in *Basic Writings of Saint Augustine*, Whitney J. Oates, ed., (New York: Random House, 1948), p. 331.

Nietzsche too, though his ethical outlook is quite different from Augustine's, occasionally discusses virtue in terms of four qualities. In *Morgenröte*, they are given as "Die guten Vier / *Redlich* gegen uns und was *sonst* uns Freund ist; *tapfer* gegen den Feind; *großmütig* gegen den Besiegten; *höflich*—immer: so wollen uns die vier Kardinaltugenden."[64] In *Jenseits von Gut und Böse*, a somewhat different set of virtues is proposed: "Und Herr seiner vier Tugenden bleiben, des Mutes, der Einsicht, des Mitgefühls, der Einsamkeit."[65]

Nietzsche's view of Plato became more acerbic with the passage of time. In *Götzen-Dämmerung*, or *Wie man mit dem Hammer philosophiert*, written near the end of his active life, he expresses a strong preference for Roman literature over Greek and sums up his earlier objections to Plato in a surprisingly bitter passage:

> For heaven's sake, do not throw Plato at me. I am a complete skeptic about Plato, and I have never been able to join in the admiration for the *artist* Plato which is customary among scholars. In the end, the subtlest judges of taste among the ancients themselves are here on my side. Plato, it seems to me, throws all stylistic forms together and is thus a first-rate decadent in style: . . . To be attracted by the Platonic dialogue, this horribly self-satisfied and childish kind of dialectic, one must never have read good French writers—Fontenelle, for example. Plato is boring. In the end, my mistrust of Plato goes deep: he represents such an aberration from all the basic instincts of the Hellene, is so moralistic, so pre-existently Christian—he already takes the concept "good" for the highest concept—that for the whole phenomenon Plato I would sooner use the harsh phrase "higher swindle" or, if it sounds better, "idealism," than any other. We have paid dearly for the fact that this Athenian got his schooling from the Egyptians (or from the Jews in Egypt?). In that great calamity, Christianity, Plato represents that ambiguity and fascination, called an "ideal," which made it possible for the nobler spirits of antiquity to misunderstand themselves and to set foot on the bridge leading to the cross. And how much Plato there still is in the concept "church," in the construction, system, and practice of the church.[66]

Augustine and Nietzsche are alike in having a polemic rather than an expository purpose in their references to Plato. Both see in him a challenger of earlier pagan values and a foreshadower of Christianity. Both suppose him to have been strongly influenced by Semitic views, probably acquired in Egypt. Both characterize his philosophy as having an essentially moral orientation. Both offer interpretations of Plato's epistemological and metaphysical positions which, though strikingly similar, point up with clarity the difference between the two men in their attitudes toward the fabric of Western thought. All in all, Nietzsche accepts so much of the Augustinian portrait of Plato that he can hardly accuse

64 M, sec. 556, *Nietzsches Werke in Zwei Bänden*, ed. Gerhard Stenzel (Salzburg: Verlag "Das Bergland Buch," 1950), II, 542.

65 J, sec. 284. Stenzel, p. 817.

66 "What I Owe to the Ancients," G, sec. 2.

Augustine of any great philological impropriety in his treatment of Platonic thought without laying himself open to the same charge.

In all fairness, it should be recognized that Nietzsche acknowledges the sort of distortion inherent in his representation of Plato:

> Every society has the tendency to reduce its opponents to caricatures—at least in imagination—and, as it were, to starve them. Such a caricature is, e.g., our "criminal." Within the aristocratic order of values, the Jew was reduced to a caricature. Among artists, the "philistine and bourgeois" became caricatures; among the pious, the godless; among aristocrats, the man of the people. Among immoralists it is the moralist: Plato, for example, becomes a caricature in my hands.[67]

Perhaps it was inevitable that, in the course of Nietzsche's career, the Plato whom he originally honored with his respect would be seen more and more as a scapegoat to be loaded with the sins of Christendom. In the last analysis, though they had quite different purposes, his portrait of Plato is little different from that painted by Augustine. But the elements of caricature present in both cannot diminish the value of the tribute implicit in the fact that two thinkers of the stature of Augustine and Nietzsche, separated by fifteen hundred years and looking at the world from almost diametrically opposed points of view, could nevertheless agree in acknowledging Platonic thought to be the key to any true understanding of the Western mind.

[67] WM, sec. 374.

III

Aristotle in the Thought of Nietzsche and Thomas Aquinas

HEDWIG WINGLER

TRANSLATED BY TIMOTHY F. SELLNER

> Among other things Nietzsche's dictum, "God is dead," would say to us: There is no "ultimate meaning," and "behind" the world there is no "authentic being" of the kind of "Unmoved and Self-Subsisting Being" which Aristotle sought in his *Metaphysics*. There is no Purposive Will to which everything is teleologically related.
>
> —Hermann Wein, *Positives Antichristentum* (1962)

> Clearly it is any being as being whose principles we are trying to explain.
>
> —Aristotle, *Metaphysics*, E 1 (trans. *Richard Hope*)

From the end of the eighteenth century on, interest in Aristotle had been growing steadily due to the fact that great value had been placed on his writings as documents illustrating the development of philosophy. Important editions of his works were being published, and it was the historical consciousness of the flourishing field of classical philology in particular which manifested a preference for Aristotle, who, in addition to his concern for the principles of systematization and analysis, had also to a certain extent made use of the historical method in his writings.

Thus it is not at all unusual that Friedrich Nietzsche, at a time when he was still studying classical philology at the University of Leipzig, should prepare a seminar lecture (1867) on the lists of the writings of Aristotle stemming from the period of classical antiquity, and that he should express the intention in 1868—never carried out—of writing a dissertation entitled "de Aristotelis librorum indice Laertiano," which would thus have been an elaboration of the seminar lecture. On the other hand, he writes in another letter from the same year: "My field of criticism now encompasses, among other things, almost all of Greek philosophy, with the exception of Aristotle. . . ."[1]

[1] HKG (*Briefe*), II, 264. (For key to abbreviations see p. xvii above.)

In Nietzsche's lectures in Basel from the years 1869 to 1879 Aristotle is treated within the framework of the usual topics in the field of classical philology;[2] the only thing which could be considered unusual is Nietzsche's special treatment of the Pre-Socratics during his academic years. Also within the realm of the expected is his demand for a "precise interpretation of Aristotle and Plato" within the academic profession, at a time (1871) when Nietzsche, the classical philologist, was competing—unsuccessfully, as it turned out—for the professorship in *philosophy* at his University in Basel. This professorship was then given to Rudolf Eucken, whose appointment prompted Nietzsche to write in a letter the following ironic remark: ". . . our new philosopher is going to deliver his inaugural address on the 'obvious' theme: 'The Significance of *Aristotle* for the Present Age.' "[3]

But in spite of this conventional ranking of Aristotle with Plato, Nietzsche did not possess an edition of Aristotle in the original Greek, whereas it can be shown that he most certainly read a number of the dialogues of Plato in the original. Aristotle, it would appear, was an author whose works he scarcely got around to reading thoroughly in the original, even though he resolved to do so on a number of occasions.

On the other hand, two works from the secondary literature are especially important. The first is the *History of Materialism* (*Geschichte des Materialismus*) by Friedrich Albert Lange, with which Nietzsche had been acquainted from the year 1866 on. Lange influenced Nietzsche to reject the purely historical approach to the Greek philosophers and, instead, to study them for their "contemporary" value.[4] The second work is *The Philosophy of the Greeks* (*Die Philosophie der Griechen*) by Eduard Zeller, which Nietzsche, however, used mainly as a source. In addition, the collection of fragments published in 1863 by Valentin Rose under the title *Aristoteles Pseudepigraphus*, which was known by Nietzsche from 1866 on, must also be mentioned as one of the primary sources of Nietzsche's knowledge of Aristotle.

The numerous references to Aristotle—partly in Greek, partly in German—which are to be found in the lecture manuscripts can be traced directly to the secondary literature, which was generously utilized by Nietzsche, above all during the period when he was in Basel. In other respects, the list of sources

[2] See Johann Stroux, *Nietzsches Professur in Basel* (Jena: Frommann, 1925) and esp. GOA, XVII-XIX.

[3] HKG (*Briefe*), III, 104, 167.

[4] See esp. Hermann Josef Schmidt, *Nietzsche und Sokrates* (Meisenheim am Glan: Hain, 1969), p. 306; Fr. A. Lange, *Geschichte des Materialismus und Kritik seiner Bedeutung in der Gegenwart* (Iserlohn: Baedeker, 1866, rpt. 1873, 1876); Eduard Zeller, *Die Philosophie der Griechen* (Tübingen: Fues, 1844–52), vols. I–III. There are no visible traces of Nietzsche's use of Diogenes Laërtius, *Lives and Opinions of Famous Philosophers*, in connection with Aristotle, though this is a book which is important for Nietzsche's reckoning with tradition in other cases.

compiled by the editors of the Large Octavo Edition is quite inadequate, above all for the three *Philologica* volumes, which comprise Nietzsche's manuscripts on classical philology and the philosophy of the ancients, and especially the manuscripts of the lectures in Basel. Here the critical edition of Colli and Montinari will, for the first time, provide greater clarity and precision, since the practice followed and the criteria used by the editors in the selection of references for the Large Octavo Edition are dubious.

I am indebted to Curt Paul Janz in Basel, who is certainly the best authority on Nietzsche's life, for a valuable personal communication concerning Nietzsche's work on Aristotle's *Rhetoric*. Janz has recently published an article containing a list of the university lectures and of the reading material used by Nietzsche at the "Paedagogium," the *Gymnasium* in Basel, where it was his obligation to teach classical languages concurrently with his duties as a professor at the University. Thus it is logical to assume that he read "selections from the *Gorgias* of Plato and the *Rhetoric* of Aristotle" with his pupils in the Summer Semester of 1874 at the *Gymnasium*.[5] During the Winter Semester following this Nietzsche lectured on the "*Rhetoric* of Aristotle" at the University. Consequently, it can be shown that he worked with the Greek text of the *Rhetoric*, even if he did continue to rely on secondary material—here, for example, on Friedrich Blass' *History of Rhetoric* (*Geschichte der Beredsamkeit*)—for his treatment of the theme. In any case, however, the lectures and fragments of his literary remains reveal everywhere that Aristotle was on his mind or that he encountered him in his work, and even in his published papers he deals at length with him.

Nietzsche frequently passed judgment on Aristotle's literary style—for example, by saying that "the bare bones" were at times all too visible.[6] In the same vein he writes: "In the case of Thucydides the pleasant sensation with which one moves a lock with a key: a laborious yielding by degrees, but well-ordered and continually coming closer to its goal. With Aristotle one sees the bare bones." In his lecture on the "History of Greek Literature" (in the winter of 1874 and summer of 1875) we find a rather long passage on Aristotle as a writer, containing the following evaluation of the extant works, in which Nietzsche shows himself to be thoroughly aware of the difference between the extant systematic works and the lost dialogues: ". . . never again has there been such abstinence from all *charités*. No flesh, no life; no concern with effect—one hears the rattle of bones."[7]

Nietzsche became acquainted with Aristotle by way of classical philology,

---

[5] The quotation is from Hans Gutzwiller, "Friedrich Nietzsches Lehrtätigkeit am Basler Paedagogium 1869–76," *Basler Zeitschrift*, 50 (1951), 180. The essay by Janz, who directed my attention to the article above, has just appeared. See "Friedrich Nietzsches akademische Lehrtätigkeit in Basel 1869–1879," *Nietzsche Studien*, III (Berlin: de Gruyter, 1974), 192–203. The reference to Gutzwiller appears on p. 192.

[6] WKG, IV-4, 367; the quotation following is from WKG, IV-1, 118 f.

[7] GOA, XVIII, 77; the passage following, GOA, IX, 81 (spring, 1870).

and in his lectures during the period of his professorship at Basel he refrained from almost all criticism and personal opinion in philosophical matters. Nevertheless, it was not long before he began to ridicule what he called philological "hod-carrying," including his own work in the field: "Most of the 'burning issues' of classical philology are rather *insignificant* in the face of the central issues, which, to be sure, are perceived only by a few. How unimportant is the question of the sequence of the Platonic dialogues! How fruitless is the question of the genuine-ness of Aristotle's works!"

Nietzsche's relationship to Aristotle belongs to the larger theme of the former's preoccupation with classical antiquity. It has been shown that even in his philological lectures (and this is even more true for the writings which were not limited by his academic responsibilities) Nietzsche *creates* a Hellenism pre-cisely by refusing to view the heritage of antiquity purely as a theoretical problem. In the study of antiquity Nietzsche does not seek history but rather the essence of classicism. A good example of this is to be found in his lecture on the study of classical philology (summer, 1871). Ernst Howald writes: "Above all it is a question of his teleological inclination, which exerts an ahistorical effect, and his personification of a people, an approach which is fully and properly discredited today. . . ."[8] Related to this is the fact that Nietzsche's argument does not base itself on evidence, but merely uses the latter for purposes of ornamentation—an embarrassment traceable to Nietzsche's breach with classical philology.

It is evident that the person of Aristotle was not a main figure in Nietzsche's reckoning with tradition; indeed, it is obvious that Aristotle as a figure in philo-sophical tradition was far less provocative for Nietzsche than, for example, Socrates and Plato. It is my thesis that the reasons for this lie less in the philosophi-cal themes and problems *per se* (Nietzsche was very much interested in certain Aristotelian methods of inquiry and solutions), but rather in the fact that the figure of Aristotle and also his "style," in the broadest sense of the word, capti-vated and held his imagination to a far lesser degree than those of Socrates and Plato.

Nietzsche's reckoning with the content of Aristotle's works takes place chiefly in his writings on aesthetics (the critique of culture) and in his critiques of morality and scholarship. It is in the realm of aesthetics that Nietzsche's reckoning with Aristotle from the standpoint of theme and purpose emerges most clearly. In *The Birth of Tragedy, or Hellenism and Pessimism* (1872) there is to be found—very near the conclusion of the treatise, in order that he once again may make a sharp differentiation between an aesthetic and a moral phenomenon—the most important observation on Aristotle and "our own aestheticians," by which he means the entire tradition with the exception of Richard Wagner:

[8] Ernst Howald, *Friedrich Nietzsche und die klassische Philologie* (Gotha: F. A. Perthes, 1920), pp. 13 f., also p. 9. Likewise Karl Schlechta, *Der junge Nietzsche und das klassische Altertum* (Mainz: F. Kupferberg, 1948).

Not since Aristotle has anyone provided an explanation of the tragic effect from which one can infer aesthetic states or aesthetic activity on the part of the audience. Now pity and fear are to be urged toward a mitigating discharge through the solemn events, now we are to feel ourselves . . . elevated and inspired in the sense of a moral contemplation of the world; and as sure as I am that precisely this, and only this, constitutes the effect of tragedy for countless individuals, just as clearly does it follow that none of these, including their aestheticians who give interpretations, have ever experienced tragedy as an *art* of the highest form. Aristotle's catharsis, that pathological discharge which the philologists are not sure whether to classify as a medical or moral phenomenon, reminds us of a remarkable idea of Goethe's: "Were the ancients also superior to us in that the highest degree of pathos would have been for them only aesthetic play-acting, whereas for us the truth of nature must also play a role in bringing forth such a work?" This profound ultimate question of Goethe's may at present be answered in the affirmative, now that we have experienced with amazement in the case of the musical tragedy just how the highest pathos can indeed be only an aesthetic performance.[9]

The famous passage in Aristotle reads: "Tragedy is the imitation of an . . . action . . . in such a manner that . . . through pity and fear a catharsis of precisely these emotions is brought about."[10] In direct contrast to this Aristotelian interpretation stands Nietzsche's interpretation, in which the aesthetic spectator is elevated above the pathological-moral process. Nietzsche uses the tragic myth to "sweep over" into the metaphysics of art, "without transgressing into the realm of pity, fear, or of the moral and sublime."[11] Except for this, there is little mention of Aristotle in this treatise; on the other hand, Nietzsche's continuous polemic against Socrates and Plato is of much greater importance, since they rejected tragedy because it depicted only that which was pleasant, and not that which was useful. In his struggle against the optimistic dialectic and anti-Dionysian tendencies of Euripides, Socrates, and Plato, Nietzsche's resistance to Aristotle never comes to the point of a direct attack, even though the line of demarcation between his own position and that of Aristotle is drawn clearly enough.

This is also the way Nietzsche came to interpret it later; in the preface to his *Birth of Tragedy* entitled "An Attempt at Self-Criticism" (1886) he states as his goal: "to view science through the eyes of the artist, but art through the eyes of life. . . ." To this also belongs another self-interpretation of Nietzsche's, this time from the *Twilight of the Idols* (1888), which, because it seemed so important to him, he cites in *Ecce Homo* (1888) as well. He had, he says, drawn his concept of tragedy from Greek drama in order now to understand himself as a tragic philosopher: "*Not* to be set free from terror and pity, not to purify oneself from a dangerous affect by means of a violent discharge—the way Aristotle misunder-

[9] W, I, 122.
[10] Aristotle, *Poetics*, VI, 1449b, 24 ff.
[11] GT (W, I, 131); the passage following, ibid., pp. 11, 79.

stood it—rather to go beyond the concepts of terror and pity and *to be oneself* the eternal joy of becoming—that joy which also includes the joy in destroying."[12]

Nietzsche also expresses disagreement with Aristotle regarding the problem of imitation. Greek tragedy and Italian opera are frankly interpreted as deviations from nature: "This is where nature *should be* contradicted! . . . The Greeks go far in this direction . . . as a matter of fact they have done everything they could to counteract the elemental effects of images inspiring fear and terror—but with all due deference to Aristotle, *they simply did not want fear and pity.* Not only did he fail to hit the nail on the head but he most assuredly missed it entirely when he spoke of the ultimate purpose of Greek tragedy! . . . The Athenian went to the theater *to hear beautiful speeches! . . .*"[13] In the final analysis it was Nietzsche's own era that he had in mind, and even here he is interpreting according to his desire for an artists' metaphysics. At that time he admired above all the musical works and aesthetic writings of Richard Wagner. "They are definitely the most important aesthetic writings we have . . . In them everything—problem and solution—is experienced, endured, and victoriously achieved; no foolish canonizing or swearing by Aristotle, such as we find even in Lessing, intervenes."[14] Nevertheless, Aristotle often serves Nietzsche at a later time, after his enthusiasm for Wagner had already ended, by providing a contrast to his own ideas and goals.

Subsequent to this period of enthusiasm for Wagner, Nietzsche's criticism of Aristotle, going beyond that contained in *The Birth of Tragedy*, concentrates on three specific areas. The first criticism is directed at Aristotle the historian. Aristotle, Nietzsche says, has incorrectly interpreted Greek tragedy—that is, tragedy in its highest form, represented by the figure of Aeschylus—by taking into consideration only the drama as practiced by Euripides, and thus sanctioning the drama which is designed chiefly to be read. In the case of Aeschylus, he states, the chorus and music stood at the very center of the play. Aristotle in his Philistinism considered the work of art a product of artistic insight rather than a result of the artistic nature.[15] It is the "learned," scientific approach for which Nietzsche reproaches Aristotle, in addition to his criticism of Aristotle the historian, and it is this approach, he maintains, which continues to foster historical error. We ought finally to free ourselves, he says, from "that screech-owl of Minerva, Aristotle, who was himself already alienated from that great artistic instinct which his teacher Plato still possessed even in his mature period . . . ," and we ought to study works of art for ourselves.[16]

---

[12] G (W, II, 1032).

[13] FW, Aphorism 80, "Art and Nature" (W, II, 89 f.), with reference to Aristotle's *Poetics*, VI.

[14] HKG, IV-1, 298 (literary remains from the summer of 1875, with reference to *Richard Wagner in Bayreuth*).

[15] GOA, IX, 45, 67, 80, 212, esp. from preliminary studies to the lectures "Das griechische Musikdrama" and "Sokrates und die Tragödie" (1869, 1970).

[16] GOA, IX, 267 (literary remains, 1870–71).

The second criticism, already expressed somewhat less harshly in *The Birth of Tragedy*, has to do with the catharsis theory. In an important passage we find a polemic against Schopenhauer, whom Nietzsche takes to task even more harshly at the same time he is refuting Aristotle: "What is tragic?—I have repeatedly put my finger on Aristotle's great misunderstanding in believing that he sees the tragic affects to lie in two *depressing* emotions, in terror and in pity. . . ." It is incorrect, he continues, to view art as a symptom of decay or as serving to bring about a decline, "for it is simply not true that through the excitation of these two emotions [namely terror and pity] one is 'purged' of them, as Aristotle seems to believe. . . . This theory can be refuted in the most cold-blooded way, namely, by measuring by means of a dynamometer the effect of a tragic emotion. The result will be such that only the absolute mendacity of an utter dogmatist can misconstrue it: that tragedy is a *tonicum*. . . ."[17]

Nietzsche "put his finger on the great misunderstanding" most definitely when he criticized the misinterpretation of fear and pity "from the standpoint of the soul of the artist and the writer."

> Are pity and fear really supposed to be discharged through tragedy, as Aristotle would have it, so that the spectator returns home more serene and with less passion? It is the case with several physical processes, for example with sexual pleasure, that a lessening and temporary depression of the drive sets in after the need has once been satisfied. But fear and pity are not in this sense needs of certain organs which demand satisfaction. And in the long run every drive is in fact *strengthened* through practice in the attainment of its satisfaction, in spite of such periodic lessenings. It would be possible for pity and fear in each individual case to be alleviated and discharged through tragedy; nevertheless as a whole they could be made greater by means of the effect of tragedy, and Plato was entirely right when he stated that man becomes through tragedy, on the whole more fearful and lachrymose. . . .[18]

With that formulation we have arrived at the third point in Nietzsche's treatment of Aristotle's aesthetics. Nietzsche, along with Plato, sees tragedy and art as a "*tonicum*," not as a "purgative," as Aristotle does. But while Plato—very Socratically, in Nietzsche's view—demands as a consequence his negation of tragedy, Nietzsche himself derives precisely from this interpretation his affirmation, not only of art, but also of life. Just how closely connected the themes of art, life, and the critique of metaphysics are for Nietzsche, even at a much later period, and to what extent they resemble his earlier works in their mode of expression, can be seen from a section from the *Antichrist*, in which Christianity and Schopenhauer are condemned in his discussion of pity.

---

[17] W, III, 828, Aphorism 851 of the so-called *Will to Power;* cf. also Aphorism 852.
[18] MA, Vol. I, part 4 (W, I, 571, sec. 212). Cf. also HKG, IV-2, 450 (literary remains, 1876).

On the whole, pity clashes with the law of evolution, which is the law of *selection*. It preserves what is ripe for extinction. . . . Pity is nihilism *put into practice . . . hostility to life*. Schopenhauer was hostile to life; that is why pity became a virtue for him. . . . Aristotle, as we know, considered pity to be a pathological and dangerous condition which one would do well to attack from time to time by means of a purgative—and he understood tragedy as a purgative. As far as the instincts of life are concerned, we ought in fact to be searching for a means of giving such a pathological and dangerous accumulation of pity as is represented by the case of Schopenhauer (and unfortunately also by our entire literary and artistic *décadence* from St. Petersburg to Paris, from Tolstoi to Wagner) a prick, so that it would *burst*. . . ."[19]

To be sure, it is doubtful whether Nietzsche's "pity" and the "*eleos*" of Aristotle or Christian pity come close to each other at all in this particular sense. I assume that they do not. And even Aristotle's use of the term does not amount to much more than the placing of scenery on a stage. It nevertheless is clear that Aristotle was present in Nietzsche's thinking up to the end, even if his concern was a contemporary one, namely to take aim at Schopenhauer utilizing Darwinian ammunition. This is not the place to pursue further the extent to which Nietzsche, by rejecting the category of utility in art, sets himself apart not only from Aristotle, but also from the theoreticians of the nineteenth century, insofar as this century attempted to unite the concept of utility in art with the principle of realism. One must not, however, overlook also the other aspect of his "liberation of art" from nature—is not in Nietzsche's case the liberation of art also a liberation from society, the hypostatizing of art as a "culture-creating" force?

The goal of the coming culture does not lie in this world. . . . Does not every true work of art wrest a confession from us which belies Aristotle's claim [i.e., tragedy as imitative representation]? Is it not nature which imitates art? Does she not, in the restlessness of her becoming, imitate with stammering and inadequate speech that which the artist expresses in pure form? Does she not long for the artist to deliver her from her incompleteness?[20]

True, this "proposition of Aristotle's" concerning imitative representation is cast into doubt by Nietzsche, but instead of discussing it thoroughly he chooses rather to use it merely for emphasis and the personification of an opposing view. Nietzsche himself idealized the position of art and did not recognize the dialectical tension between projection and reflection in which art also finds itself. In a purely formalistic manner he rendered Greek tragedy absolute in the form of a willful reconstruction of his own making, completely ignoring the evolution of art and of artistic values.[21] He disassociated them both from their social contexts, and yet wished to assign a social task to them, namely the creation of culture. In this

---

[19] A, sec. 7 (W, II, 1168–69).

[20] GOA, X, 320 (ca. 1874).

[21] Concerning the reaction at that time among classical philologists, see Howald, pp. 15–27.

idealistic misunderstanding he is altogether wrong with respect to Aristotle, who, in his analyses in the *Poetics* (Ch. VII, 1450b) as well as in the *Metaphysics* (1078a, 31–36), adheres essentially to an inherited concept of artistic creation instead of creating his own norms. Aristotle adheres to the concept of artistic practice, which at the same time implies for him a social practice. This also becomes clear from his catharsis-theory.

In this way tragedy was thought by Aristotle to make use of fear, depression, and pity in order to bring the emotions of the audience rapidly to a high pitch by means of the dramatic action; afterwards the soul was freed of these emotions. This is what Nietzsche told his students in Basel without further commentary—at least we find none in the final written form of these lectures.[22] But perhaps in taking this position Aristotle was merely reflecting the state of affairs as it existed in his own time. Perhaps this *was* the task of tragic art. Paul Gohlke has rendered plausible a political interpretation of the catharsis-theory by maintaining that "cathartic" music and poetry do justice to the demand that something be offered to the masses, and thus Aristotle's interpretation of catharsis is congenial to notions of democracy.[23] But precisely this interpretation is contrary to the standpoint of Nietzsche. Without being in a position to pursue this problem further at the present time, however, perhaps I may summarize here: "Aristotle" is for Nietzsche one of the collective concepts which he uses in order to place into relief and give contour to his own viewpoint in aesthetics and art theory—a viewpoint which was in no case always a fixed and constant one.

In the field of aesthetics Aristotle was for Nietzsche a classical author who was so important for tradition that he could not be disregarded. "The desire to have some certainty in aesthetics seduced us into worshiping Aristotle; I think it will gradually be proved that he knows nothing of art, and that what we admire so much in him is only the echo in his writings of the wise discourse of the Athenians."[24] In the realm of ethics Aristotle likewise represents a traditionally central figure who cannot be ignored. The "Aristotelianism of morality" belongs to "all these moralities"; along with the Stoics' indifference toward the emotions and Spinoza's destruction of the emotions, it is "that lowering of the emotions to a harmless level at which they are permitted to gain satisfaction—the Aristotelianism of morality. . . ." To this critique, which is, so to speak, a comparative history of existing moralities there is also to be added his mention of the "Aristotelian presuppositions" which, along with the ecclesiastical and courtly moral sanctions, was a part of that tyranny against "reason" and "nature" which prevailed during the history of "the long subjugation of the spirit." Nevertheless, Aristotle does receive praise in his treatment of certain questions dealing with ethical matters,

---

[22] GOA, XVIII, the lecture entitled "Geschichte der griechische Literatur," Part 3, 1875–76.

[23] Paul Gohlke in the Introduction (p. 17) to his translation of the *Poetics* of Aristotle (Paderborn: F. Schöningh, 1959).

[24] HKG, IV-1, 119 (1875). The quotations following are from J, secs. 198 and 188.

especially when it is a case of bearing witness to the "whole of Greek antiquity" as an ideal especially in contrast to Nietzsche's own era and to Christianity. In this case Nietzsche uses Aristotle to emphasize his point.

But Nietzsche is not concerned with the question of which of the existing moralities is to be preferred, but rather with abolishing morality as such. Here, as we know, he also invokes the name of the Greeks, that is, the Pre-Socratics."[25] In his posthumous work "Philosophy in the Tragic Age of the Greeks," he would have Anaxagoras utter the following words when reflecting upon the cosmos and also when viewing the Parthenon: "Becoming is not a moral phenomenon, but merely an artistic one."[26] Apparently Nietzsche had been stimulated in this by a statement of Aristotle's, for he continues: "Aristotle relates that Anaxagoras answered in the following way the question as to why existence was precious to him at all: 'In order to view the heavens and the whole order of the cosmos.' He treated physical objects so devoutly and with the same mysterious awe with which we stand before an ancient temple. . . ."

Whether Nietzsche captures with that the sense which either Aristotle or Anaxagoras had in mind is open to question. Ernst Howald has stated with regard to Nietzsche's posthumous fragments on Greek philosophy that no matter how clever these fragments may be, the completed sections are just as tedious in their historic formulation, and that one must observe carefully "how much the view of the author toward the diversity of history has been weakened—every one of them, Anaximander, Empedocles, and Heraclitus, are all half-Nietzsches. This pseudo-history no longer has anything to do with those things which science sees in them."[27] Nevertheless, we should regard as important here only the fact that Nietzsche also hearkens back to the Pre-Socratics for the purposes of overcoming morality. The Greeks, Nietzsche says, first began to lose their ingenuousness through Socrates, and "their myths and tragedies are a great deal wiser than the ethics of Plato and Aristotle. . . ."[28]

Nevertheless, in general it is true for the discussion of morality (and to a lesser extent for the discussion of aesthetics and science, although not so exclusively) that Aristotle, as a great philosopher of tradition, simply cannot be ignored. He is perceived as a "venerable classicist" who has been "rigorously and soberly" interpreted through the centuries, and it was Nietzsche's ambition to influence the future of his age as greatly as Aristotle had that of his own. The relationship between Plato and Aristotle can be compared here to that between

[25]For a thorough description of this development in Nietzsche's philosophy, see Karl Schlechta and Anni Anders, *Friedrich Nietzsche: Von den verborgenen Anfängen seines Philosophierens* (Stuttgart-Bad Cannstatt: F. Fromann, 1962), and my review in English of this book in *Philosophy and History*, German Studies Section I, I (Tübingen: German Studies, 1968), 42–45.

[26] W, III, 410; the Aristotle quotation is from the *Eudemian Ethics*, I, 1216a, 11 ff.

[27] Howald, p. 33.

[28] "Wissenschaft und Weisheit im Kampfe," W, III, 339 (WKG, IV-1, 183 f.).

Nietzsche and Schopenhauer, namely, that of the pupil who refutes his former teacher.[29] In this regard Nietzsche was, so to speak, personally interested in Aristotle.

Nietzsche's criticism of the concept of teleology in previous moralities leads to his rejection of morality. Aristotle becomes for him the embodiment of the opposite position: "Happiness as the final goal of the individual life. Aristotle and everyone! Thus it is the dominance of the concept of purpose which has been the ruination of all previous moralists. 'There must be a Why? to life!' (To this Schopenhauer even added the concept of the unconscious purpose!) That even the rational, conscious life is involved in the development of life without purpose —*ego*. The essence of all activity is purposeless or indifferent in the face of a multiplicity of purposes."[30]

Nietzsche then proceeds to discuss the theme of science versus philosophy. At an earlier time he had already investigated purpose and cause, behavior and cognition in terms of their mutual dependence—as a critique of ideology, so to speak. An example of this is his criticism of Socrates, the prototype of theoretical man, and of his metaphysical illusion "that thought, by means of the clue of causality, can fathom the deepest abysses of being, and that thought is capable not only of understanding being but even of *correcting* it."[31] This theme—the negation of rationality and the rejection of a logical basis for knowledge and behavior— leads directly to Nietzsche's confrontation with Aristotle's concept of science, or to put it more clearly, to his image of Aristotle as an embodiment of theoretical man in general.

Also regarding the problem of morality and science Aristotle is, like Plato, a key—and this by virtue of Nietzsche's singular method, already mentioned several times before, of illustrating his analyses and diagnoses by means of historical personages, and even of personifying the results. For both Aristotle and Plato, knowledge constitutes the greatest happiness. Nietzsche's own interpretation is to be found in his literary remains: "The greatest happiness, as Plato and Aristotle understood it, does *not* lie in intuitive understanding (genius of Schopenhauer!), rather the source of this happiness lies in the active intellect operating according to dialectical principles. This interpretation of the greatest happiness is, of course, based on subjective judgments, but for such subjects I am grateful."[32]

For to consider knowledge as a means to happiness is, Nietzsche says, a "great naiveté."[33] From this same period we also find similar conclusions—for example, that philosophy since Socrates had become moral philosophy, because

---

[29] GOA, XII, 216 (from 1881–83) and WKG, V-1, 417 (Literary remains from the spring of 1880).

[30] GOA. XIII. 161 f. (ca. 1883–84).

[31] GT, W, I, 84.

[32] WKG, V-1, 440 (fragments from the literary remains dating from the period of the *Morgenröte*, 1880); cf. M, Aphorism 550 (W, I, 1270).

[33] W, III, 551 (So-called *Will to Power*. Aphorism 449).

philosophers were searching for *happiness*. "Aristotle conceived of his God as one concerned only with pure knowledge, without any feeling of love whatsoever; and he himself probably had his best moments when he coldly and clearly (and happily) enjoyed the rapturous giddiness provided by the broadest generalities. To perceive the world as a system and such a system as the culmination of human happiness—how the schematic mind here betrays itself!"[34] Also in this context falls Nietzsche's criticism of the idea of purpose as a category of ethics as well as of science. Once more we encounter a formulation which refers to Aristotle: "We have not yet freed ourselves from the logical mania of the ancients: they valued nothing more highly than dialectic, and therefore 'intentions,' 'purposes.' "

The summation of this theme—the transition from the critique of morality to that of science—can be gleaned from a passage in which Socrates is viewed as a turning-point: "The unbiased view of man is missing in all the Socratics, who focus on those detestable abstractions 'the Good' and 'the Just'. . . . They [the Greeks] lose, through Socrates, their ingenuousness. Their myths and tragedies are a great deal wiser than the ethics of Plato and Aristotle, and their Stoics and Epicureans are poor in contrast to their earlier poets and statesmen."[35] Thus on the one hand, Aristotle belongs to those who complete, along with Socrates, the transition from philosophy to morality.

On the other hand, however, Nietzsche does not consider Aristotle to be "typically Greek," precisely because he sets himself apart from the "culture and art of the Hellenes," and indeed, from the practice of Socrates as well, in that for him [Aristotle] "the practical drive of philosophy comes to a standstill," and "understanding in itself becomes the goal. . . . Only the Peripatetics (and not the other post-Socratics) apply their energies to science. . . . It is one of the great attributes of the Hellenes," he says, "that they were not able to transform the best of what they had into reflection," while Aristotle is "the greatest man of the intellect," and it is for just this reason that he is lacking in depth and simplicity. Aristotle, "the first logician," is simply not a genuine Hellene for Nietzsche (a notion which is probably intended to exculpate the Greeks), but "half-Macedonian." To this he attributes Aristotle's strength in the field of science, for as a "Macedonian" he did not share the "antipathy of classical Hellenism to the rigors of science (as well as to the rigors of life)." Aristotle symbolizes for Nietzsche the ultimate stage of consciousness (reflection) of life.[36]

Such ideas are similar to those in *The Birth of Tragedy*, where "Socratic man" figures as the embodiment of the "theoretical optimist" who "attributes to knowledge and understanding the power of a panacea, and perceives error as evil in and of itself." Here, too, we find reference to the "powerful illusion" of

---

[34] GOA, XIII, 103; the quotation following, ibid., p. 162 (literary remains from 1882–88).
[35] "Wissenschaft und Weisheit im Kampfe," W. III, 339.
[36] GOA, XVII, 351 f. (summer semester, 1871) and GOA, XVIII, 139, 144, and 165 (1875–76).

science. Later, when, as a professor in Basel, he was occupied with the history of Greek literature and philosophy, he elaborated even further this antithesis between the Pre-Socratics as lovers of wisdom and Aristotle as descending to the level of pure scholarship. First intimations of this notion are already present around 1870–71. "Aristotle, absolute knowledge," is the pithy formulation in his literary remains.[37]

To be sure, there is one time when Nietzsche "forgets" his criticism of of Aristotle, namely when he violently attacks the ontology of Parmenides. He accuses Parmenides of committing an error in logic by confusing existence and essence, "Dasein" and "Wesen." Aristotle and Kant are invoked as logicians who forbade the drawing of inferences from the concept to being, from essence to existence, which Nietzsche immediately uses as a confirmation of the fact that knowledge and being are "the most contradictory of all realms."[38] In this passage Aristotelian logic becomes a useful instrument for determining formal errors in the process of reasoning.

Nevertheless, this agreement with Aristotle must not be overrated, for it is quickly restricted by Nietzsche when he states: "There is no touchstone to discover error which has to do with content and not with form." And as far as Parmenides himself is concerned, Nietzsche is of the opinion that "the later Greek systems (Aristotle) had conceived of the Eleatic problems too superficially,"[39] that is to say, the "being" of Parmenides cannot be adequately criticized by Aristotle's "thought."

When Nietzsche speaks of Aristotle himself and not of his relationship to other authors, his criticism of the Aristotelian concept of knowledge is quite central and consistent. As an example we might mention the highly ironical section "For Whom Truth Exists."[40] It exists namely for those, Nietzsche maintains, who, like Aristotle, do not seek consolation and healing in truth. For the others, however, who do seek such consolation, there will be disappointment: for them there is only the reproach of "cold indifference, barrenness, and inhumanity" in the face of science. Here Nietzsche sees very clearly the weaknesses of the historicism of historical studies and of the positivism of the natural sciences, which latter disciplines were pressing forward to a success that was purchased with the loss of the question as to the Why? of life. It is my thesis that Nietzsche had the conditions of his own time in mind when he spoke of the contrast between philosophy and science embodied in the "pre-Platonic" philosophers, on the one hand, and the "scientist" Aristotle, on the other, whom he identifies with "absolute" science. Nietzsche himself stands on the side of philosophy; his

---

[37] GT, W, I, 86; literary remains: GOA, IX, 263 (1870–71).

[38] "Die Philosophie im tragischen Zeitalter der Griechen," W, III, 389 f.; the quotation following, ibid.

[39] GOA, XIX, 129 (Lecture from summer, 1872).

[40] M, Book V, Aphorism 424 (W, I, 1220).

experience with classical philology as a science, which was held in such high regard by the conservative bourgeoisie of the time, was a great disappointment. But as I have indicated above, Nietzsche's condemnation of science in general was much more a condemnation of the methods of science.

"In the blind desire to know everything at any price," he maintains, "science is pressing on without any selectivity or sense of distinction whatsoever with regard to all that is knowable; philosophical thought, on the other hand, is always on the trail of things which are most worth knowing, of the greatest and most important knowledge,"[41] whereby philosophy itself sets the norm for greatness. The various "basic epistemological positions" [materialism, sensualism, idealism] are accordingly exposed by Nietzsche on the basis of an ideology-critique as consequences of value judgments.

It is not possible here to enter into a discussion of Nietzsche's problematic position involving a circle of relativism, nihilism, and axiology. Nevertheless it is a central question for Nietzsche's total philosophy, for in the final analysis the consequences of Nietzsche's political thought are bound up with his negation of the basis for truth *and* untruth, namely with his negation of the postulate of reason, with the result that the "ideologists of inhumanity" profited from his glorification of irrationality.[42] On the other side stands Aristotle, whose first premise of the *Metaphysics* states: "All men strive toward knowledge by nature. . . ." These two ideas represent anthropological opposites, the analysis of which is itself in need of an ideology-critique. In any case, philosophy as a basic science is only to be postulated on a rational basis.[43]

For Nietzsche, however, Aristotle can quickly and unceremoniously become "Aristotle," a sort of code-name for the prototype of the scholarly and scientific man whom he disdained. In a posthumously published preliminary sketch to "Richard Wagner in Bayreuth" we read that Wagner "holds sway over the religions and the historical disciplines, and yet he is the very antithesis of a polyhistor, of a compiling, surveying and ordering talent (such as Aristotle was for nature)."[44] The editors add here in a note that "Humboldt" was changed to "Aristotle" by means of a correction. In the text Wagner had immediately previous to this been given the title "Anti-Alexander," which was most certainly

---

[41] "Die Philosophie im tragischen Zeitalter der Griechen," W, III, 364; the quotation in the line following, W, III, 547; the so-called *Will to Power*, Aphorism 580.

[42] Cf. especially Georg Lukács, *Die Zerstörung der Vernunft* (Neuwied am Rhein: Luchterhand, 1955); further H. H. Holz in the Introduction to Volume III of the *Studienausgabe von Nietzsches Werken* (Frankfurt am Main: Fischer Bücherei, 1968); Hermann Wein, *Positives Antichristentum* (Den Haag: Nijhoff, 1962); Jan Broekman, *Strukturalismus* (Freiburg: Karl Alber, 1971); pp. 29 f. of the latter work deal with Nietzsche's relativism.

[43] Cf. Erhard Albrecht, "Vom Nutzen des Studiums der griechischen Philosophie," *Sitzungsberichte der deutschen Akademie der Wissenschaften zu Berlin, Klasse für Philosophie, Geschichte, Staats-, Rechts- und Wirtschaftswissenschaften*, 1966, No. 5, especially pp. 27 ff. concerning Aristotle.

[44] WKG, IV-1, 285 (summer, 1875); the editor's note is from WKG, IV-4, 395.

the reason for crossing out "Humboldt" and arriving at the age in which both Aristotle and Alexander flourished, whereby Wagner gained further in stature by vanquishing Alexander as the creator of culture and Aristotle as the "ruler over the intellectual disciplines."

There exists yet another special problem for Nietzsche with regard to the question of knowledge, namely the problem of logic. In the unmasking of the principle of contradiction (or of the excluded middle) in Aristotle's thought, Nietzsche offers the opinion that this principle—quite in contrast to the way in which Aristotle conceived of it—is not at all the most certain of the principles on which all demonstrations are based, but in fact the opposite is true: it is an "*imperative* for that which should be taken for true." The same reproach is reserved for logic as for the ontology of Parmenides, namely, the reproach of setting up linguistic hypostatizations as realities, "of conceptualizing a metaphysical world, that is to say, a 'real world' (which is, however, a duplication of the world of appearances)."[45]

Aristotelian logic is criticized because, in overestimating conceptual knowledge, it takes linguistic-logical (grammatical) categories to be categories of being: "The conceptual injunction against contradiction arises from the belief that we are able to form concepts, the belief that a concept not only designates the essence of a thing, but comprehends it as well. . . . Logic (just like geometry and arithmetic) is valid in fact only in terms of fictitious truths which we ourselves have created. Logic is the attempt to understand the real world in terms of an ontological scheme which we ourselves have established; or, more correctly, the attempt to make the world 'susceptible of formulation' and calculable for us. . . ." Nietzsche saw that knowledge directed toward disposability (prognosis) not only brings happiness through understanding, but also power—namely, the power to dispose by means of calculation in all empirical and analytic sciences, whether those of "nature" or society. His prejudice is the pessimism of power— he does not see the possibility of control by social power, even of the conclusions reached by science.

One thinker above all was superior in Nietzsche's mind to Aristotle and his dual-valued logic, which was only able to speak in terms of an undialectical either-or, namely, Heraclitus. The essence of reality as becoming and passing away had revealed itself to this thinker. Heraclitus, according to Nietzsche, rejects the logic of reason, "and this he does so unhesitatingly in such statements as 'everything always bears its antithesis within itself,' that Aristotle accuses him before the tribunal of reason of the most terrible crime of having sinned against the law of contradiction."[46] Nietzsche senses that his own standpoint is not

[45] W, III, 537 (WM, Aphorism 516); the quotation following, ibid., 538. On the problem of Aristotelian cognitive logic, see E. Albrecht, p. 28. Aristotle approaches all basic questions of epistemology from a naturalistic, anti-Platonic standpoint, rather than from an idealistic one.

[46] "Die Philosophie im tragischen Zeitalter der Griechen," W, III, 370 f. The Aristotle quotation is from the *Metaphysics*, 1005b, 20 ff.

congenial with Aristotelian logic, but with the dialectical logic of Heraclitus, even though his pessimism distinguishes him with regard to the knowability of the world from dialecticians of the idealistic as well as the materialistic sort. By rejecting the logic of Aristotle he places himself on the side of Heraclitus, whose statement of antitheses quite clearly contradicts the principle of the excluded middle. But Heraclitus' dialectic does not lead to such an epistemological nihilism as that from which Nietzsche's hostility to science arises.[47]

Hostility to science was also characteristic of long centuries between Aristotle and Thomas Aquinas. It was expressly directed against erudition or "polymathy," as Aristotle would call it. In Hellenism and above all in early Christianity it drew its arguments from the Socratic rejection of natural science in which ethics would be ignored. Olof Gigon notes in this regard: "The much-discussed hostility to learning of early Christian literature [is inseparable] from the old Socratic rejection of natural philosophy."[48] Socrates considered only "the affairs of men" to be a suitable theme for critical reflection; on the other hand, one must not, in the case of the Pre-Socratics, speak of such a separation of "ethics" and "natural philosophy"—and this is true for Heraclitus as well—which is probably one reason for Nietzsche's high regard for the Pre-Socratics. Nietzsche first encountered cognition as a final goal in the writings of Aristotle, and his rejection of it here is vehement enough. If he had read Aristotle in context and not, as he doubtless did, collected quotation upon quotation for the purpose of achieving, by taking statements out of context, an even stronger emphasis of his own, he would then have had a much less clear conscience about branding Aristotle as the "absolutizer" of science. For the ethical writings of Aristotle alone, to cite an example, would have sufficed to reveal other goals in life than knowledge, and to bring about the realization that particularly in the case of Aristotle knowledge is *not* taken to be hostile to life.[49] Only when we get to Nietzsche do we first encounter this notion.

The early Christianity of which Gigon speaks, as well as the Middle Ages, were acquainted chiefly with Aristotle's writings on logic. Not until about 1200 did the remaining works of Aristotle gradually become known in Latin translations from the Arabic and Greek. "Thus by the time that Aquinas began his teaching career at Paris the Aristotelian philosophy had become known to the medieval Christian world."[50] Aristotle was accepted enthusiastically in part, and in part his writings were forbidden by the Church—for example, the *Metaphysics* and the *Physics* in 1210 and 1215 in Paris. However, the suppression had little effect.

[47] Concerning Nietzsche's epistemology, see also Jürgen Habermas in his concluding remarks to *Friedrich Nietzsche: Erkenntnistheoretische Schriften* (Frankfurt am Main: Suhrkamp, 1968).

[48] Olof Gigon, *Die antike Kultur und das Christentum* (Gütersloh: G. Mohn, 1966), pp. 54, 66.

[49] Cf. Aristotle, *Eudemian Ethics*, 1216 a-b.

[50] F. C. Copleston, *Aquinas* (Harmondsworth, Middlesex: Pelican Books, 1955), p. 61.

In such a way the advocates of Aristotelianism were resisted. Siger of Brabant, for example, a contemporary of St. Thomas, was silenced by means of imprisonment. He taught that material nature was eternal, not created by God, and that the individual soul was mortal. He is truly "Aristotelian" in that he sought to emancipate himself from Christian faith by appealing to philosophical truth, while Thomas Aquinas saw the problem precisely in terms of the question "whether the teachings of Scripture [of the Gospel] not only can become the object of an act of faith, but also of a deductive process analogous to that of Aristotelian science."[51] In sharp contrast to this stands this great opponent of Thomas Aquinas at the University of Paris, Siger of Brabant, the Averroist who advocated the doctrine of double truth, philosophical and theological, and consciously avoided the assimilation of Aristotelian doctrines to those of Christianity. Aristotle taught that the world was eternal and that God was not its creator—and thus the Aristotelian system seemed to have no place for Christianity.

Copleston points out that while Bonaventura, who was also a contemporary of St. Thomas, considered Aristotle to be a great scholar, he did not feel that the latter deserved to be called a "metaphysician."[52] St. Thomas' success, in contrast to Siger *and* Bonaventura, resulted from the fact that he was able to come to terms with Aristotle effectively. Aquinas took over from Aristotle whatever seemed valid to him, and intended to show that those statements of Aristotle which were incompatible with Christianity stemmed from false premises. He deals with Aristotle much the way Aristotle does with the Pre-Socratics—a builder of systems is not interested in his predecessors for historical reasons, rather it is "the terms and categories of his own thinking which he . . . applies."[53]

At this point I find it necessary to digress for a moment and to make an observation concerning methodology. My examination of Nietzsche's relationship to Aristotle has been conducted strictly along philological lines, taking as its basis the sum total of references to Aristotle in the texts of Nietzsche's works which have been published up to this time. In so far as they related to his philosophical reckoning with Aristotle, I have classified them according to theme: aesthetics, the critique of morality, science and its critique—and then presented and interpreted the main passages. (As a consequence of the particular character of Nietzsche's lectures in Basel it turns out that, while Aristotle often receives mention, he is nonetheless, aside from the exceptions presented and cited above, not treated in a very fruitful way with regard to the philosophical part of his works.)

[51] R. Guelluy, *Philosophie et théologie chez Guillaume d'Ockham* (Louvain: É. Nauwelaerts, 1947), p. 42.

[52] Copleston, *Aquinas*, p. 63.

[53] Werner Jaeger in his review of H. Cherniss, *Aristotle's Criticism of Pre-Socratic Philosophy* (Baltimore: The Johns Hopkins Press, 1935), appearing in the *American Journal of Philology*, 58 (1937), 350–56.

It is hardly possible, however, to utilize such a method in analyzing Aquinas' relationship to Aristotle, and it is certainly not possible within the framework of this investigation. Copleston, in appealing to Étienne Gilson in his great work, *A History of Philosophy*, states as a procedural method that the philosophy of Thomas Aquinas "must be regarded in the light of its relation to his theology, . . . and it is a mistake to collect the philosophical items from St. Thomas's works, including his theological works, and construct a system out of them according to one's own idea of what a philosophical system should be. . . ."[54] I also concur with Copleston in the question concerning the Commentaries on Aristotle when he adds that it "is true to say that the loss of a theological work like the *Summa Theologica* would be a major disaster in regard to our knowledge of St. Thomas's philosophy, whereas the loss of the Commentaries on Aristotle, though deplorable, would be of less importance. . . ." In a lengthy section Copleston deals with the difficulties which arose for St. Thomas out of his attempt to "reconcile" the autonomous, naturalistic system of Aristotle with theology. I shall choose two examples, specifically, the concept of authority in political theory and the concept of the soul, in order to illustrate some of the problems which are bound up with "St. Thomas's utilization of Aristotle," to use Copleston's phrase. Along with Aristotle, Thomas Aquinas sees the social nature of man as anchored in his physical needs; the individual is dependent upon society.

> Since every community of human beings is directed at a certain necessity of life, that community will be a perfect one which has for its goal the possession by the individual of that which is continually necessary for the preservation of life. The state is, however, such a community. For it is inherent in the nature of the state that everything is to be found in it which is necessary for the preservation of human life. . . . [Aristotle] describes the ends to which the state, according to its nature, has been organized: it arose first and foremost for the sake of human life, namely to insure that men were able to find enough to live on.[55]

This same argument, that of the spiritual needs of the individual, is also invoked by Thomas Aquinas as proof of a supernatural order, and with that he goes beyond Aristotle in an essential point. Franz Faller has demonstrated this in the relationship of the Commentaries on Aristotle to the other writings of Thomas Aquinas, and explained the transposition from a system of secular concepts to a spiritual one.[56] St. Thomas first takes up Aristotle's observation that

[54] F. C. Copleston, *A History of Philosophy* (Westminster, Md.: Newman Press, 1955), II, 306–7 for this and the quotation following; see also pp. 423–34.

[55] Thomas de Aquino, *In octo libros politicorum Aristotelis expositio*, Editio Alumnis univ. Lavellensis (Quebec: Reprod. Photo-Litho Tremblay and Dion, 1940), p. 13 (*Commentarius in Pol. I, 1*).

[56] Franz Faller, *Die rechtsphilosophische Begründung der gesellschaftlichen und staatlichen Autorität bei Thomas von Aquin* (Heidelberg: F. H. Kerle, 1954).

society is a totality and an organism. The whole exists before the part, and the organic body serves as an analogy to the societal "body." St. Thomas continues: "In view of its nature and perfection, the whole must unquestionably exist before the part. . . . If the whole man is destroyed, then it is not a hand or a foot which remains, but only these parts in a figurative sense, in the sense that the stone hand of a statue is also called a hand. Thus, with the dissolution of the whole, the part is destroyed as well."[57] Faller has described in detail how this conception of the state as an organism leads to the question regarding the principle of unity in such an organism, and regarding the way St. Thomas locates this principle of unity in the concept of authority.[58] Law and justice are grounded upon authority. Here St. Thomas follows the concept of law and authority which Aristotle developed from his concept of the organism: the individual human being must find a place within the whole, and this he does according to the law. According to Aristotle, the individual cannot exist outside of this law. He recognized in the state a community based on authority, that is, the state is defined by authority, and authority is the essential element in the community and the state—not only in the ethical sense, but in that sense pertaining to the philosophy of law, just as it is also understood by Thomas Aquinas. Faller states: "Consequently, in so far as one acknowledges society and thus also the state to be a legal community, one must necessarily arrive at law and authority as the form-giving principle of society and of the state." This principle accords with the thought of both Aristotle and Thomas Aquinas.

But while Aristotle defines political authority with only the citizens of the state in mind, and thus in human or temporal terms, for Thomas Aquinas, whose gaze is fixed on the church, the temporal legally established authority is superseded by divine authority. For St. Thomas human society as a community ordained by nature is unthinkable without divine authority, and according to him law is of divine origin, just as the state is ordained by God.[59] In terms of church history it is an important fact that in Thomas Aquinas' writings—quite in contrast to Augustine's *City of God*, for example—there exists no rigid antithesis between the sinful earthly city and the City of God, rather the attainment of a harmonious hierarchy was envisaged.

Aristotle also provides the starting point for Thomas Aquinas with regard to his doctrine of the soul. Aristotle maintains that the soul is the form of the body, while the body is "substratum and matter." "It is necessary, then," he states, "that the soul be a substance in the sense of the specifying principle of a physical body, potentially alive. Now substance [in this sense] is act; it will therefore be the act

---

[57] Thomas Aquinas, *Comm. in Pol.* I, 1 (Ed. univ. Lavall., p. 15), on Aristotle's *Politics*, I, 1, 1253a, 20.

[58] Faller, p. 70; also p. 28. The passages in the *Politics* are from Book I, 1, 1252a ff. and Book III, 14, 1285b, 29 ff.

[59] Especially in *De Regimine Principum*; in quite the opposite vein, Aristotle's *Politics*, I, 1, 1252 ff.

of a body of this sort. . . . Hence it is unnecessary to enquire whether the soul and body be *one*, any more than whether the wax and the impression made in it are one; or in general, the matter of anything whatever, and that of which it is the matter."[60]

St. Thomas takes the notion from Aristotle that the soul is the form of the body, but he calls it an immortal form created by God. In so doing he contradicts Aristotle, who specifically emphasizes that "the soul can neither exist without the body, nor can it be a body itself. For it is not a body, but something which is bound up with the body." Wilhelm Nestle points out that this particular passage was intended by Aristotle as a polemic against the dualistic concept of the Pythagoreans as well as of Plato.[61]

For Thomas Aquinas the soul is both the form of the body *and* immortal. By virtue of its immortality, it will actually be united again with the body after their separation: "It is therefore contrary to the nature of the soul to be without the body. But nothing which is contrary to nature can be perpetual. Hence the soul will not for ever be without the body. Therefore since the soul remains for ever, it should be united again with the body, and this is what is meant by rising [from the dead]. The immortality of souls seems then to demand the future resurrection of bodies."[62]

It has been stressed that Aristotle vehemently denied that the soul lived on after death. Copleston enlarges on this: "The human psyche is [for Aristotle] the principle of biological, sensitive and certain mental functions, and it is the form of the body; but precisely because it is the form of the body it cannot exist in separation from the body. . . ."[63] Here St. Thomas differs in a very basic way from Aristotle, "even though Aquinas does not himself make this point very clear. Hence it is not true to say that he slavishly reproduced Aristotle's theories, however much he may have been influenced by them." At another point Copleston had stressed "that the synthesis of Christianity and Aristotelianism in St. Thomas's thought was in some respects rather precarious . . . ,"[64] and that the Aristotelian philosophy of finality could not as such be taken over by orthodox Scholasticism. With regard to both the concept of political authority and the anthropological concept of the soul, "natural," Aristotelian truth is overcome by the supernatural belief of the Church.

Étienne Gilson, the great authority on medieval philosophy, has stated very

[60] *De anima*, II, 1, 412a, 1 ff.; the passage following, ibid., II, 2, 414a. The first quotation is cited from: Aristotle, *De anima*, in *The Version of William of Moerbeke and the Commentary of St. Thomas Aquinas*, trans. Kenelm Foster et al. (London: Routledge and Kegan Paul, 1951), pp. 163–64.

[61] *Aristoteles, Hauptwerke*, ed., trans., introd. Wilhelm Nestle, 3rd ed. (Stuttgart: Kröner, 1941), p. 155, n. 1.

[62] Thomas Aquinas, *Contra gentiles*, IV, 79.

[63] Copleston, *Aquinas*, pp. 163 and 164.

[64] Copleston, *History of Philosophy*, II, 424.

pointedly that 'whatever metaphysics is to be found in the writings of Thomas Aquinas or Duns Scotus is their own, in each case based on the formulations of Aristotle, which they take over at their own risk and which derive their significance from the concept of *esse* or of *ens infinitum*, which Aristotle *had not intended*, and which he would not have understood. . . ."[65] Gilson emphasizes the great difference between Scholastic theology and that of Aristotle: the latter has a God who did *not* create the world *ex nihilo* and who never interferes in its affairs in a providential way, but who abandons the world to the law of necessity, which can only be interrupted by chance, a world in which man is only an ephemeral individual. Aristotelian metaphysics was a direct extension of Aristotelian physics: "Those thinkers of the Middle Ages who proceeded from the *science of Aristotle*, precisely because they refused to speak as theologians, naturally arrived, like Averroës, at the same metaphysics as Aristotle." As E. Albrecht has shown, philosophy (in the original sense of science) is subordinate to theology.[66]

Thomas Aquinas makes out of Aristotelian philosophy "something rather different from historic Aristotelianism" (Copleston). Other scholars, too, in full acknowledgement of the impetus toward new approaches which have arisen from the rediscovery of Aristotle's writings after 1200—especially the *Politics*—have confirmed these findings. Especially instructive are the findings of Lorenzo Minio-Paluello, who has examined the Aristotelian tradition in philosophy and science and remarked almost with astonishment that the *doctor angelicus* had "written nearly word-for-word, sentence-for-sentence commentaries on the *Metaphysics*, *Physics*, *De anima*, *Nichomachean Ethics*, *Politics*, *De caelo*, as well as other treatises. But when we look for proof of Aristotle's influence on the remaining works of Aquinas, we are surprised to discover what important Aristotelian propositions had *no* influence on his thinking."[67] As a matter of fact, in much of what St. Thomas "translates" from Aristotle is to be found a "direct antithesis to Aristotelianism." An example of this is the discussion of the order of creation found in the *Summa Theologica* as contrasted with the Aristotelian "prime mover" of the *Physics*.

"The Greek philosopher," Copleston writes, "was concerned with the problem of motion, in the wide sense of becoming, whereas Aquinas made the problem of existence the primary metaphysical problem. The former asked what things are and how they come to be what they are, but he did not raise the question why they exist at all or why there is something rather than nothing."

---

[65] Étienne Gilson in the Appendix to A. Hayen, *Der heilige Thomas von Aquin gestern und heute,* trans. Robert Scherer (Frankfurt am Main: J. Knecht, 1954), pp. 114 f.

[66] Gilson, p. 107; Albrecht, p. 26.

[67] Lorenzo Minio-Paluello, "Die Aristotelische Tradition in der Geistesgeschichte," *Aristoteles in der neueren Forschung,* ed. Paul Moraux (Darmstadt: Wissenschaftliche Buchgesellschaft, 1968), p. 321. (Original title: "La tradition aristotélicienne dans l'histoire des idées," *Actes du Congres de l'Association Guillaume Budé* [Lyon: Les Belles Lettres, 1958 (1960), pp. 166–85].

Copleston underscores the great difference between the two questions and then continues:

> In his *Tractatus logico-philosophicus* (No. 644) Wittgenstein stated that "not *how* the world is, is the mystical, but *that* it is." If the word "metaphysical" is substituted for the word "mystical," this statement, though it would not be entirely acceptable to Aquinas, can serve as an illustration of the difference between the philosophy of the historic Aristotle and that of Thomas Aquinas. The change in emphasis doubtless owed a lot to the Judaeo-Christian tradition, . . . but that there was a change can hardly be denied.[68]

If one supplies to the *question* concerning the existence of the world the *answer* that it has no meaning, we have come full circle to Nietzsche. Thomas Aquinas answers this question by affirming transcendence, while Nietzsche's entire philosophy consists in the struggle to eliminate this transcendence.[69] "Saint" Thomas and the "Antichrist" Nietzsche certainly do have in common, however, the fact that they subordinate science and scientific philosophy to other modes of dealing with the question of existence. This separates both of them from Aristotle's theory and practice of rationality. In the case of St. Thomas, it is Christian faith which stands above science; in the case of Nietzsche it is scepticism and the denial of veridical knowledge. To this extent Nietzsche embodies the antithesis of the Thomistic world-view—not only, in terms of content, as the "Antichrist," but also methodologically, as an aphorist in opposition to all systematization. Thomas Aquinas strives to surmount reason with faith; Nietzsche strives to nullify it—"the destruction of reason."[70] And one can read from the political history of our century just how Nietzsche's theory of irrationality turned into the practice of inhumanity.[71]

[68] Copleston, *Aquinas*, p. 64 f.

[69] F. C. Copleston, *St. Thomas and Nietzsche*, The Aquinas Society of London Papers, No. 2 (London: Blackfriars, 1944) inquires into the difference between the two thinkers. Cf. also Friedrich Nietzsche, *Menschliches, Allzumenschliches*, 98 (W, I, 775): "If we had not remained to some extent *unscientific* beings, what could interest us in science at all! . . . *cognition would be a matter of indifference to a purely cognizant being.* We differ from the pious and the believer not in the quality, but in the quantity of belief and piety; we are satisfied with less . . ."

[70] Cf. the interpretation of Nietzsche in Lukács, *Die Zerstörung der Vernunft*.

[71] Concerning Nietzsche's relationship to fascism, see also H. H. Holz's introduction to the four-volume *Nietzsche-Studienausgabe* and Copleston, *St. Thomas and Nietzsche*, which describe how the political failure of the middle-class in the nineteenth century was perpetuated through the glorification of Friedrich Nietzsche, its most fascinating representative.

IV

Between *Inferno* and *Purgatorio:* Thoughts on a Structural Comparison of Nietzsche with Dante *

EUGEN BISER

TRANSLATED BY CHERYL L. TURNEY

Friedrich Nietzsche, more than almost any other figure of intellectual history, continues to provide a stimulus for structural comparisons. This is all the more striking, since he emphatically challenges his reader with the admonition: "Above all do not misunderstand me!"; and at the same time he is on the alert for the one who will "defend and define" him against the misunderstandings which nevertheless threaten him. The analogy between the lives of Nietzsche and Hölderlin—attested by a close relationship of ideas—attracted attention early.[1] In an ingenious sketch from his last productive period, the philosopher Franz Brentano, who died after a long Odyssey in Switzerland, even draws a comparison between Nietzsche and Jesus,[2] while Nietzsche's Russian contemporary, Vladimir Soloviev, believed he recognized in the figure of the mentally ill philosopher of Basel the contours of the Antichrist.[3] The astonishing correspondence of the lives of Nietzsche and Kierkegaard has repeatedly been emphasized, most penetratingly by Karl Jaspers.[4] My own Nietzsche book (1962) supple-

---

* Quotations from the *Divine Comedy* are from the translation of J. A. Carlyle, Thomas Okey, and Philip H. Wicksteed in The Modern Library Editions (New York: The Modern Library, 1950); the quotation from Dante's *Vita Nuova* is from the translation of Mark Musa (Bloomington: Indiana University Press, 1962); the passages from Augustine are from the translation of F. J. Sheed, *Confessions of St. Augustine* (New York: Sheed & Ward, 1942); translations from *Thus Spoke Zarathustra* are by Walter Kaufmann (New York: Viking Compass Press, 1966); the longer passages from Nietzsche's other works are cited from his *Basic Writings of Nietzsche* (New York: The Modern Library, 1968).

[1] In this connection see for example Ernst Bertram, *Nietzsche: Versuch einer Mythologie* (Berlin: Bondi, 1919), pp. 251, 282 f.

[2] "Nietzsche als Nachahmer Jesu" in Franz C. Brentano, *Die Lehre Jesu und ihre bleibende Bedeutung,* ed. Alfred Kastil (Leipzig: F. Meiner, 1922) pp. 129–32.

[3] The most important documents dealing with this comparison, of which only the essay "Die Idee des Übermenschen" (1899), the Lermontow-review of 1899 and "Die Kurze Erzählung vom Antichrist" (1900) may be expressly mentioned, were published by Ludolf Müller in the collection of essays, *Wladimir Solowjew, Übermensch und Antichrist: Über das Ende der Weltgeschichte* (Freiburg i. Br.: Herder, 1958).

[4] In this connection see Karl Jasper's exhaustive structural and motif comparison in the first of the

mented these studies with a parallel treatment of Nietzsche and his Russian critic, Soloviev;[5] this was after Leo Schestow had compared Nietzsche and Dostoevski in his 1924 study of the same name,[6] as "twin-brothers," molded by similar experiences. Nietzsche's own references to figures of cultural history whom he approached with remote sympathy, occasionally with pronounced love-hate, lead further along the track of a structural comparison. After Pascal, who first springs to mind in this connection, comes Dante. For along with the tasteless apostrophe to Dante in *The Twilight of the Idols* as the "hyena who composes poetry among the tombs,"[7] there are also such serious sentences as: "Such dogmatic men as Dante and Plato are the farthest from me and therefore the most attractive."[8] This statement attracts attention because it corresponds most exactly to the broken structure of relationships, which is always to be observed in Nietzsche's biography.[9]

Just as none of Nietzsche's friendships endured without a breach, so there was no intellectual relationship which did not suffer from a period of critical alienation. Even Schopenhauer, whom he initially greatly admired, was no exception:

> What he taught is laid aside,
> What he lived will long abide.[10]

In the case of Dante the alienation is incomparably greater. Yet that fact does not invalidate either the legitimacy nor the intensity of the relationship. Before pursuing this subject and seeking to identify specific parallels, one will do well to keep in mind first of all the decisive difference which Nietzsche sees between himself and Dante. It consists originally for Nietzsche, as his reference in *Human, All-Too-Human* shows, in an awareness of the historical distance which separates him from Dante and from the direction of art which he represented, since that species of art can never, for a sensibility such as Nietzsche's, come to flower again, a species "which like the *Divine Comedy*, the pictures of Raphael, the frescoes of Michelangelo, the Gothic cathedrals presuppose not only a cosmic, but also a metaphysical significance of the art object."[11] Nevertheless, the epochal distance

---

lectures published under the title *Vernunft und Existenz* (Munich: Piper, 1960), pp. 7–41. Jaspers gave these lectures in the spring of 1935 at the University of Groningen, Holland.

[5] *"Gott ist tot"*: *Nietzsches Destruktion des christlichen Bewußtseins* (Munich: Kösel, 1962), pp. 267 f.

[6] Leo Schestow, *Dostojewski und Nietzsche: Philosophie der Tragödie* (Cologne: Marcan, 1924), p. 9.

[7] G, "Streifzüge eines Unzeitgemäßen," sec. 1. (For key to abbreviations see p. xvii.)

[8] *Die Unschuld des Werdens*, II, K, *83*, sec. 220.

[9] See Karl Jaspers' discussion of the limits of Nietzsche's capacity for friendship and his loneliness in *Nietzsche: Einführung in das Verständnis seines Philosophierens* (Berlin and Leipzig: W. de Gruyter & Co., 1936) pp. 69–76.

[10] First lines of the quatrain on Arthur Schopenhauer.

[11] MA, I, sec. 220.

between the two is only the symptom of an incomparably deeper one which has to do with differing modes of thought and which cannot be overcome by any return to an earlier mode. Nietzsche emphasizes the difference in the most pointed way possible when he reckons Dante along with Plato among the "dogmatic men," and in elaboration of this characterization calls him "one in whom the Catholic Church is perfectly epitomized."[12]

What Dante is reproached with here is elucidated by the critical comparison with Zarathustra in *Ecce homo*, in contrast to whom Dante was "merely a believer" and "not one who first creates truth."[13] Nietzsche's criticism of Dante reaches its climax accordingly in a reproach directed at all immanental systems. The note from his posthumous papers which characterizes the "dogmatic men like Dante and Plato" as those "who live in a properly built and solidly believed-in house of knowledge," already aims in this direction; this is true whether it is constructed out of one's own materials or out of the building materials of tradition. In contrast to this, what follows praises the incomparably greater strength which is necessary to maintain oneself in an "incomplete system, with free unsettled views." The greatness of the poet of the *Divine Comedy* is decisively relativized by the standard set here. It is greatness within a given system, but not greatness which, as Nietzsche demanded for himself and the future, holds good in the overcoming of systems or even in the gaining of the new intellectual vistas which are thereby made possible. Nietzsche's feeling of aversion for Dante increases to the point of passion in the passage: "I wish Dante went completely against our taste and stomach."[14] The presumption expressed in *The Dawn* is that Dante and those intellectually related to him had "penetrated into the lusts of power," and that consequently the secret of love remained closed to him.[15] This presumption reveals that more than merely a philosophically conditioned aversion is manifesting itself here. With the inscription over the gate of hell: "I too was created by eternal love," Dante, inspired by a "terrifying ingenuity," committed "a gross blunder" which betrays his own alienation. For "over the gate of the Christian Paradise and its eternal bliss would, with greater justice, stand the inscription: 'I too was created by eternal hate'—supposing that a truth might stand above the gateway to a lie!"[16] On a higher plane of reflection, which Nietzsche attains in a note found in his posthumous papers, he concedes: "I believe that whoever has divined anything of the most fundamental conditions for any growth in love will understand why Dante wrote above his Inferno: 'I too was created by eternal love.'"[17]

Indications of this kind of "meeting one half way" are especially important

---

12 *Die Unschuld des Werdens*, I, K, *82*, sec. 538.
13 *Ecce Homo*, "Also Sprach Zarathustra," sec. 6.
14 *Die Unschuld des Werdens*, I, K, *82*, sec. 473.
15 M, II, sec. 113.
16 GM, I, sec. 15.
17 W, III, 893.

in Nietzsche's case, for they allow us to recognize, more reliably than thematic correspondences, the abiding affinity present in verbal contradictions. The statement that for him "such dogmatic men as Dante and Plato" are the "most fascinating" precisely because they are, structurally speaking, at the farthest remove from him, also aims in this direction. But this remark reduces his affinity with Dante to the level of merely aesthetic interest. The actual relationship is incomparably more comprehensive and profound, even though, amid the considerable number of negative statements, positive statements worth mentioning are scarcely to be found. That fact should not, however, be misleading as far as a structural comparison is concerned. What is compared lies as a rule outside of the data with which critical self-awareness concerns itself. Therefore it is to be more easily determined "from the outside" than by reference to autobiographical data. At only one point do Nietzsche's autobiographical writings shed light on our problem—admittedly without express reference to Dante. It has to do with the initial visionary experience of his "Un-Divine Comedy," that of Zarathustra. At this point we must examine the positive evidence, before taking up thematic motif-comparisons.

In spite of all that separates them, Dante and Nietzsche are in agreement in so far as they created the most personal of their works in each case out of the "stuff" of an inspirational experience: Dante, the *Divine Comedy;* Nietzsche, his "son," *Zarathustra.* As far as the visionary nucleus of the *Divine Comedy* is concerned, it will suffice to call to mind Romano Guardini's observations on this matter. In his essay "Vision and Poetry" (1946) this perhaps most sensitive interpreter of the *Divine Comedy* in the modern period takes the position that a visionary experience lies at the basis of the work, even though this assumption is only confirmed—except for a hint at the end of the *Vita Nuova*—by the fact that the structure and diction of the work are to be explained more readily with its help than without it. Following the concluding sonnet of the artificial early work, Dante writes:

> After this sonnet there appeared to me a miraculous vision in which I saw things that made me resolve to say no more about this blessed one (Beatrice) until I should be capable of writing about her in a more worthy fashion. And to achieve this I am striving as hard as I can, and this she truly knows. So that, if it be the wish of Him in whom all things flourish that my life continue for a few years, I hope to write of her that which has never been written of any other lady.

On the basis of these autobiographical statements Guardini favors the hypothesis that Dante at the height of his mature years—"in the middle of the journey of our life"—fell into a crucial entanglement, an aporetic situation such as the opening lines of his cosmic poem describes (*Inferno* I, 1–3), a situation which was finally clarified by means of a visionary experience.[18] Since not only his

---

[18] The text is cited at the end of the chapter.

relationship to Beatrice but also the meaning of life was apparently affected by the crisis, the clarifying vision has a double perspective. It is first of all a fulfilling re-encounter with Beatrice; the reunion scene which is described in Canto XXIX of the *Purgatorio* is, to be sure, anything but an intimate event. Dante introduces Beatrice as queen of a solemn ceremonial procession, stylized as Divine Wisdom, surrounded in ranks by redemptive figures, beginning with Christ appearing in the image of a griffin, on down to the personified Holy Scriptures and to the virtues intertwined in an allegorical round-dance. Yet love enthralled him with the same vehemence and ardor he felt at the time when he, still at the threshold of youth, first saw the child Beatrice. All the more harsh is the effect created by the first words of the Transfigured One, whom a confirmation of the old bonds of love by no means concerns, but rather the ending of the alienation in which the beloved has so deeply entangled himself, an alienation so profound that he was to be helped only by means of a journey through the three kingdoms of the other-world, by "a trip around the world," to invoke the words of Heinrich von Kleist in his essay on the marionette theater. She reprimands him, reproaches him with his erotic aberrations and his entanglement in the folly of illusory images, and finally forces him to lift his eyes to her, so that, gazing into her countenance, he may comprehend the full magnitude of his misery. Everything in this scene has the character of an ecstatic concentration of time. The childish initial experience is repeated in the expiatory dialogue of the eyes which, for its part, redeems in a painfully rapturous way the promise which was made at that time and since then repeatedly broken.

As a clarifying vision, the sight of the celestial white rose in Canto XXX of the *Paradiso* corresponds to the eclipsing of the meaning of life. What is clarified here is not anything of the kind that is usually sought behind the word "meaning." But no doubt the whole being of the beholder falls under the spell of an over-powering experience of light which rescues him from his distraction and over-comes his deterioration, bringing about the concentration of an existence lovingly devoted, lovingly knowing, lovingly reconciled with itself. The following verses refer to this: "So there shone around me a living light, leaving me swathed in such a web of its glow that naught appeared to me" (XXX, 49–51). What Dante once even gives formal expression to when he speaks thus of the genesis of the vision of Paradise: "All its appearance is composed of rays reflected from the top of the First Moved, which draweth thence its life and potency" (XXX, 106–8), becomes understandable from the event itself: in its greatness the rose therefore remains "near," since present in it is nothing objective, but only the goal which lies beyond all objects and this side of all that is merely subjective. And it is the consummation of that which exists as a whole, experienced in mystical anticipa-tion, the perfect resolution of the many into the one. About this Dante writes: "Near and far addeth not nor subtracteth there, for where God governeth without medium the law of nature hath no relevance" (XXX, 121–23).

Guardini says of this image, which manifests none of the familiar dimensions: "It lies beyond space and time, in the pure present; so there is in it no distance but everything is visible everywhere. Of its final meaning we must perhaps say: everywhere in the rose its whole form and the complete fullness of its content is present."[19] Since every individual separateness dissolves in the unifying field of this symbol of perfection, it follows for him "that the rose bursts into blossom everywhere and each individual beholds it there where it concerns him, that is, at the place where he stands."[20] Applied to Dante, this means that only in so far as he is "prepared for the union" is he able "to behold the rose as the inclusion of creation and history within the simplicity of the Divine Light."[21] And conversely, lost in the visionary contemplation of perfection, he now "becomes sure of the meaning of his own life" and is free from the entanglements in which he found himself at the beginning."[22]

Nietzsche's inspirational experience which led to the writing of *Zarathustra* has no comparable relationship to a "muse" embodying the creative purpose, unless one sees it in a compensatory connection with the pitiably shattering relationship with Lou Salomé.[23] The only record of this relationship is to be found in the late, stylized account in *Ecce homo*. There Nietzsche writes, looking back to the genesis of his *Zarathustra*:

> The fundamental conception of this work, the idea of eternal recurrence, this highest formula of affirmation that is at all attainable, belongs in August 1881: it was penned on a sheet with the notation underneath, "6000 feet beyond man and time." That day I was walking through the woods along the lake of Silvaplana; at a powerful pyramidal rock not far from Surlei I stopped. It was then that this idea came to me.[24]

After a few statements characterizing and dating the various stages in the origin of the work, in which a reference to the *Hymn to Life* composed by Nietzsche for a text of Lou Salomé is inserted, he poses the question:

> Has anyone at the end of the nineteenth century a clear idea of what poets of strong ages have called *inspiration?* If not, I will describe it.—If one had the slightest residue of superstition left in one's system, one could hardly reject altogether the idea that one is merely incarnation, merely mouthpiece, merely a medium of over-powering forces. The concept of revelation—in the sense that suddenly, with

[19] Romano Guardini, *Vision und Dichtung: Der Charakter von Dantes Göttlicher Komödie* (Tübingen and Stuttgart: Wunderlich, 1946), p. 41.

[20] Ibid., p. 44.

[21] Ibid., p. 46.

[22] Ibid.

[23] *Friedrich Nietzsche, Paul Rée, Lou von Salomé: Die Dokumente ihrer Begegnung*, ed. Ernst Pfeiffer (Frankfurt a. M.: Insel Verlag, 1970); further, E. F. Podach, *Friedrich Nietzsche und Lou Salomé: Ihre Begegnung 1882* (Zurich: Niehans, 1938).

[24] *Ecce Homo*, "Also sprach Zarathustra," sec. 1.

indescribable certainty and subtlety, something becomes *visible*, audible, something that shakes one to the last depths and throws one down—that merely describes the facts. One hears, one does not seek; one accepts, one does not ask who gives; like lightning, a thought flashes up, with necessity, without hesitation regarding its form—I never had any choice.

A rapture whose tremendous tension occasionally discharges itself in a flood of tears—now the pace quickens involuntarily, now it becomes slow; one is altogether beside oneself, with the distinct consciousness of subtle shudders and of one's skin creeping down to one's toes; a depth of happiness in which even what is most painful and gloomy does not seem something opposite but rather conditioned, provoked, a *necessary* color in such a superabundance of light; an instinct for rhythmic relationships that arches over wide spaces of forms—length, the need for a rhythm with wide arches, is almost the measure of the force of inspiration, a kind of compensation for its pressure and tension . . .

This is *my* experience of inspiration; I do not doubt that one has to go back thousands of years in order to find anyone who could say to me, "it is mine as well."[25]

In view of the evident euphoria underlying these self-revelations there are those who see Nietzsche's inspirational experience in connection with his disease. The chief spokesman for this group is Karl Jaspers, who, especially on the basis of his background in psychiatry, and in view of Nietzsche's great initiatory experience, speaks of the latter's break-through to actual awareness of his life's-task, and remarks concerning this decisive turning-point in his thought:

Anyone who reads his letters and other writings in chronological order, keeping both past and future in mind and thus consciously observing the temporal relations of the utterances to each other, cannot escape an extraordinarily strong impression that Nietzsche underwent at this time the most profound change that he had ever experienced. It is revealed not only in the contents of his thinking and in new creations, but also in the forms which his experience assumes; Nietzsche submerges himself, as it were, in a new atmosphere; what he says takes on a different tone; and the mood that permeates everything is something for which there are no harbingers and indications prior to 1880.[26]

Then in an express reference to the course of Nietzsche's illness he writes:

. . . the contrast between the attacks and the periods free from them is henceforth overshadowed by the more incisive new contrast between the *intensified* states of a creative experience of being and the terrible melancholy of weeks and months of *depression*. In accordance with this is the fact that Nietzsche, while going through his mental "desert" between 1876 and 1880, remains spiritually sovereign and in no way feels that he has lost ground. . . . Not until after 1881 does he come to know the sudden changes from nothing to something and the relapse into nothingness;

[25] Ibid., sec. 3.
[26] Jaspers, *Nietzsche*, p. 78 f.

thereafter, he not only seizes upon the great affirmation with jubilation, but he experiences its necessity with despair during periods when it does not arise. A dependable, even state never occurs. The ups and downs are extraordinary. While looking back on these years he writes: "The vehemence of my mood-swings was frightful during the past years.[27]

To this Jaspers adds the following important observation:

> The various states of mystical light, dangerous shuddering at the boundary, and creative inspiration are limited to the years 1881–1884. From 1885 on there is no longer any mention of such feelings, experiences of being, and revelations. When Nietzsche on a later occasion writes that he is "without hold" and "can easily be blown away overnight through a storm" and that his situation is "one of being unable to climb up or down, very high, but constantly near danger, without any answer to the question, Whither?" (to Gast, '87), this is now said without reference to experienced states but rather out of concern for his task, while those earlier utterances proclaim the boundary experience he actually lived through.[28]

Jaspers deduces from this that a "biological factor" exerted an unusually strong effect on Nietzsche's thought precisely in this decisive phase, even though he leaves open as unanswerable the question as to the nature of this factor. With unerring diagnostic insight he aligns Nietzsche with those existential thinkers whose lives present themselves as control-tests of their thought, and whose thought in turn presents itself as an intellectual sublimation of their own existence; in so doing Jaspers relegates him, even more precisely, to that group of persons for whom disease exerts a decisive influence on the creative process. It is just in this regard, however, that Nietzsche again moves into the vicinity of Dante, whom the opening lines of the *Divine Comedy* present in a state of deepest confusion and perplexity: gone astray in a dark forest-canyon, troubled by demonic animals, incapable of escaping his critical situation by virtue of his own strength and intelligence. The aporetic situation in which Dante finds himself corresponds perfectly to the symptoms of a disease. On the other hand, one must view this in Nietzsche's case in connection with his personal and professional conflicts: the final break with Wagner is followed by a severe illness, which causes Nietzsche to resign from his teaching post early in 1879; in the summer of 1881, when Nietzsche conceives the idea of eternal recurrence, a suddenly developing crisis of a psycho-physical nature precedes the precipitously disintegrating relationship with Lou Salomé. In both cases inspiration follows crucial shocks so directly that one can say of them, to borrow an expression from Dante, that they could find succor only through a visionary escape from their accustomed horizons. In spite of the similarities, profound differences do of course persist, so much so that at times the impression could arise that in juxtaposing Dante and Nietzsche one is

[27] Ibid., p. 80.
[28] Ibid., p. 81.

comparing the fundamentally incomparable. Nevertheless, the differences concern less the points of departure—characterized by astonishing agreements—than the course and the destination of the journeys. Measured against the model of the *Divine Comedy*, Nietzsche knows no paradise, unless one sees in the idea of eternal recurrence a structural counterpart to the white rose of Paradise and its circles described by the round-dances of the blessed ones. Nietzsche's journey is consciously limited to the two lower regions. For, like Faust, he has pledged himself to the task, and envisions the fulfilled repose of peaceful oneness at best as a fleeting possibility. When Zarathustra, at the beginning of the Fourth Part of the work is sitting before his hut, looking out across the abysses to the sea, his animals ask him: " 'O Zarathustra, are you perhaps looking out for your happiness?' 'What matters happiness?' he replied; 'I have long ceased to be concerned with happiness; I am concerned with my work.' " [29] And likewise he cries out at the end of the entire work: " 'My suffering and my pity for suffering—what does it matter? Am I concerned with *happiness?* I am concerned with my *work*.' "[30] Seen in terms of the panorama sketched by Dante, Zarathustra-Nietzsche thus ranges himself with the penitents at the foot of the Mount of Purgatory, who, bent and groaning under oppressive burdens, mark the place where the poem, which is otherwise so completely given over to theory, approaches most closely the practical world, indeed even the world of physical labor:

> As to support ceiling or roof is sometimes seen for corbel a figure joining knees to breast,
> which of unreality begetteth real discomfort in him who beholds it; in such wise saw I these when I gave good heed.
> True it is that more and less were they contracted, according as they had more or less upon them, and he who had most patience in his bearing, weeping seemed to say: "I can no more."[31]

Finally, landscape-scenery in the background of both works also points to the *Inferno-Purgatorio* mood. The "pyramidal rock not far from Surlei," in the vicinity of which the idea of eternal recurrence dawned on Nietzsche, reminds one inevitably of the great mass of stone which the other-world travellers saw looming up before them at the foot of the Mount of Purgatory. Unexpectedly they hear a voice beside them:

> At sound of it each of us turned him round, and we saw on the left a great mass of stone, which neither I nor he perceived before.
> Thither drew we on; and there were persons, lounging in the shade behind the rock, even as a man settles him to rest for laziness.[32]

[29] Z, IV, "Das Honigopfer."
[30] Ibid., "Das Zeichen."
[31] *Purgatorio*, Canto X, 130–39.
[32] *Purgatorio*, Canto IV, 100–105.

The reverse line that leads from the landscape-experience of Dante to that of Nietzsche is traced by Kurt Leonhard in his biography of Dante:

> It is well known . . . that Dante received some concrete impressions for the sur-realistic landscapes of the *Inferno* directly in the valleys of the Alpine foot-hills between Verona and Trento just as he had earlier in the mountains of Casentino. On the other hand, the Lunidiana could have evoked some of the romanticism of the *Purgatorio*. Do these mountain-terraces, precipitous coasts, coves, stretches of sea not belong to the same figurative landscape which were likewise, five hundred years later, to serve Nietzsche as a model for the scenery of Zarathustra?[33]

Among the multiplying similarities, however, we should not lose sight of the decisive and incisive difference, namely, that of the unequal length of the journeys. While Dante rises to the heights of the empyrean, Nietzsche does not succeed, apart from a fleeting approach, in quitting the environs of the *Inferno* and *Purgatorio* landscapes. That fact, to mention the basic cause, stems from his loneliness. Even his ecstasies are autistic. Whenever he is elevated it is always simply by the bootstraps of his own emotions. The result is that Zarathustra, in spite of his dancing-songs, his hymnic betrothal to the world ("The Seven Seals"), and his discourse on children and marriage, lacks the dimension of love. Quite different Dante, who from the beginning is under the spell of the beautiful eyes of one who escorts him to the heights of the Paradiso, even though she must entrust the beloved on the first two journeys to the guidance of Vergil and, on his last ascent, to the guidance of the mystic Bernard. Through these figures likewise the love of Beatrice is carrying out its purpose, only now in an altered form. It overcomes the force of gravity which clings to him, and which is in-creased still further by his guilt in life. With its help he traverses the entire range of the dimensions of the other world and of the spheres of existence symbolized by them. It is no accident that the motif of freedom, which is central in the *Divine Comedy*, is lacking in *Zarathustra*. The latter work is simply a monologue re-volving about itself, when measured against this emancipatory statement, born of the impulse of love.

Against the background of these differences, the common elements become all the more striking. They involve first of all the point of departure and goal. As far as the latter is concerned, we should remember that in the case of Zarathustra we have to do with a mere bordering on that which in Dante's case is actually attained. As far as the similarity of the initial life-situations is concerned, they provide that agreement which Nietzsche himself recognized, and which is formally confirmed in a letter written in 1879. On 11 September of that year Nietzsche writes to Peter Gast from St. Moritz:

---

[33] Kurt Leonhard, *Dante Alighieri in Selbstzeugnissen und Bilddokumenten* (Reinbek b. Hamburg: Rowohlt, 1970), p. 65.

I am at the end of the thirty-fifth year of my life, the "middle of life" as it has been called for a millenium and a half. Dante had his vision at this age and speaks of it in the opening lines of his poem. Now I am in the middle of life, so "encompassed by death" that it can overtake me at any hour; the nature of my suffering compels me to think of a sudden death, from convulsions. . . . As far as that is true, I feel like the oldest of men, but also from the fact that I have accomplished my life's work. I have contributed a good drop of oil, that I know, and for that I shall not be forgotten.

Concerning this we should simply note that, barely two years later, the visionary experience also occurs, even though certainly not in such a way that it has the power to lure him out of the morbid landscape in which he sees himself settled. His way proceeds, with one exception, across the inner fields of punishment and purification. And that means, to speak plainly, that his thought remains fraught with conflict without mounting, like that of Dante's, above the realm of conflicts to the realm of resolved contradictions. An impressive document of the near-approach to the goal of perfection, which I have hinted at as the "exception," is the chapter "At Noon" incorporated in the "Fourth and Last Part" of *Zarathustra*, though structurally it is quite foreign to it.[34] At the point of falling asleep, his consciousness growing dim, Zarathustra experiences here, even though ever so fleetingly and darkened by sleep, the anticipation of a great happiness, which presents itself to him in a twofold way—as the perfection of the world and as his union with it:

> Falling asleep, however, Zarathustra spoke thus to his heart: Still! Still! Did not the world become perfect just now? What is happening to me? . . . What happened to me? Listen! Did time perhaps fly away? Do I not fall? Did I not fall—listen!—into the well of eternity? What is happening to me? Still! I have been stung, alas—in the heart? In the heart! Oh, break, break, heart, after such happiness, after such a sting. How? Did not the world become perfect just now? Round and ripe? Oh, the golden round ring—where may it fly?

The "golden round ring" has a twofold meaning. It is the symbol of eternal recurrence, sign of the boundless world, eternally revolving within itself, without why or wherefore, devouring itself and giving birth to itself over and over. And it is the ring of Zarathustra's betrothal to this perfection which has attained complete self-sufficiency. The proximity to the *Divine Comedy* is, in spite of all distance, considerable. Even Dante sees the goal of fulfillment in the symbol of the circle, which, to be sure, differentiates itself triadically in the sense of the Christian doctrine of the Trinity: "In the profound and shining being of the deep light appeared to me three circles, of three colors and one magnitude; one by the second as Iris by Iris seemed reflected, and the third seemed a fire breathed equally from one and from the other."[35]

[34] See Karl Schlechta, *Nietzsches großer Mittag* (Frankfurt a. M.: Klostermann, 1954), pp. 67–72.
[35] *Paradiso*, Canto XXXIII, 115–20.

The agreement extends even to the motif of the visionary sleep, except that for the *Divine Comedy* the fruitful moment is not as for Zarathustra that of falling asleep but that of awakening. In this sense Dante's guide for the last ascent, the mystic St. Bernard, declares:

> But since the time that doth entrance thee fleeth, here let us make a stop, like to the careful tailor who to the cloth he hath cutteth the garment;
>
> and let us turn our eyes to the Primal Love, so that gazing toward him thou mayst pierce as far as may be into his shining.[36]

The decisive difference appears in the distinction between falling asleep and awakening. What Nietzsche merely glimpses as a possibility, disappearing again in the very act of appearing, is vouchsafed to Dante in the form of a possession into which one comes at the moment of awakening to it. One can perhaps make the distinction clear in connection with Augustine's reflection on the vision appearing to him during a conversation with his mother in Ostia shortly before her death, in which he touches upon the region of *aeterna sapientia*, of eternal wisdom with the beating wings of his heart (*modice toto ictu cordis*), an approach which is just as fleeting as it is fervent. Looking back on this experience, Augustine asks himself: ". . . if this could continue, and all other visions so different be quite taken away, and this one should so ravish and absorb and wrap the beholder in inward joys that his life should eternally be such as that one moment of understanding for which we had been sighing—would not this be: 'Enter thou into the joy of Thy Lord?' "[37]

What Augustine hoped for only hypothetically, as a temporally unrealizeable continuation of the ecstatic experience of mystical union, is granted to Dante in the timeless moment when he perceives, as in a flash of lightning, the identity of the human countenance and the triadic figure of God:

> As the geometer who all sets himself to measure the circle and who findeth not, think as he may, the principle he lacketh;
>
> such was I at this new-seen spectacle; I would perceive how the image consorteth with the circle, and how it settleth there;
>
> but not for this were my proper wings, save that my mind was smitten by a flash wherein its will came to it.
>
> To the high fantasy here power failed; but already my desire and will were rolled—even as a wheel that moveth equally—by the Love that moves the sun and the other stars.[38]

[36] *Paradiso*, Canto XXXII, 139–44.

[37] Book 9; this and the following translation are from Sheed, pp. 201, 200, respectively. For an interpretation of the Ostia-vision, see the discussion in my book, *Theologische Sprachtheorie und Hermeneutik* (Munich: Kösel, 1970), pp. 59 ff., 381–85, which deals extensively with the various motifs of the *Divine Comedy* (pp. 70, 83–87, 386).

[38] *Paradiso*, Canto XXXIII, 133–45.

That is the vision which does not allow the beholder to fall back onto the levels already passed, just as its object, the Eternally One, can never retreat again behind the multiplicity of commonplace things. Quite different is Augustine, who, after a fleeting contact with the realm of wisdom, sinks wearily back into the commonplace realm from which he started: "Then sighing, and leaving the first fruits of our spirit bound to it, we returned to the sound of our own tongue, in which a word has both beginning and ending. For what is like to your Word, Our Lord, who abides in himself forever, yet grows not old and makes all things new!"

Upon closer inspection this is also the situation of Zarathustra. Certainly, time sinks for him above all, to borrow the expression from the chapter "At Noon," into the "well of eternity" (Löwith) so that it appears as if permanence is vouchsafed to the moment and the *nunc stans* of an anticipated eternity is attained.[39] Yet this impression is relativized by Zarathustra's concrete experience of time. He reaches the goal of the time-transcended moment only in the almost timeless moment when he sinks into a sleep, which, as we learn quite incidentally at the end, probably did not last very long. So the contact with a no doubt great but finally unassimilated potentiality remains: "Thus spoke Zarathustra and arose from his resting-place beside the tree as if from a strange intoxication."[40]

With this difference is causally connected one of the two individual motifs, which may finally be mentioned. It consists in the admonition not to look back, known as early as the myth of Orpheus, and also echoed in Jesus' instruction to his disciples. "No one who puts his hand to the plow and looks back is fit for the kingdom of God," is Jesus' answer to the request of a prospective disciple who wished to take leave of his family before the final enlistment as a disciple (Luke 9:62)—which admonition becomes manifest here, in its positive intention, as an absolute commitment, absolute devotion. In Dante's poem the motif emerges twice, first in the mouth of Beatrice, who "with the voice of an angel" exhorts Vergil, struck by her starry gaze, to come to the aid of the one lost in the forest ravine: "My friend, and not the friend of fortune, is so impeded in his way upon the desert shore, that he has turned his back for terror; and I fear he may already be so far astray, that I have risen too late for his relief, from what I heard of him in Heaven."[41]

The second and central occurrence of the motif is the word of the angel-guard at the entrance upon the path of purification, who, with the point of his sword, scratches the seven-fold sign of their guilt upon the foreheads of all who enter, and imparts the warning on no account to look back: "Then he pushed

[39] Karl Löwith, *Weltgeschichte und Heilsgeschehen: Die theologischen Voraussetzungen der Geschichtsphilosophie* (Stuttgart: Kohlhammer, 1953), pp. 198 ff., trans. by Hermann Kesting under the title *The Meaning of History*.

[40] Schlechta, *Nietzsches großer Mittag*, p. 71.

[41] *Inferno*, Canto II, 62–63.

the door of the sacred portal, saying: 'Enter, but I make you ware that he who looketh behind returns outside again.' "[42] Apart from a note in Nietzsche's unpublished papers, this motif seems to be lacking. There he writes almost with catch-words: "presupposition: bravery, patience, no 'turning back,' no fervor to go forward."[43] To this he adds in the form of a *nota bene:* "Zarathustra, confronting all earlier values parodistically, out of his abundance." However, if, as this appended note indicates, parody is the means to escape the force that would draw us backwards, its antithesis, pity, is from all indications the quintessence of a mode of thought and behavior turned backwards and living in retrospection. If one follows the line indicated by this conjecture, if one thus seeks the missing motif under the pseudonym "pity," one discovers it quickly and indeed at the place where the strains of thought intertwined in *Zarathustra* converge and at the same time open themselves to a possible new beginning, namely, in the final chapter, "The Sign." Once again there is mention of a stone, fraught with great meaning, which immediately calls to mind the "pyramidal rock not far from Surlei." Here Zarathustra gains insight into his "last sin," his bond through pity, with the higher men, the representatives of values which he has already transcended and dismissed, who because of this bond hang on him like leaden weights, crack his self-will, and thus curb his last upward flight:

> And once more Zarathustra became absorbed in himself, and he sat down again on the big stone and reflected. Suddenly he jumped up. "Pity! Pity for the higher man." he cried out, and his face changed to bronze. "Well then, *that* has had its time. My suffering and my pity for suffering—what does it matter? Am I concerned with *happiness?* I am concerned with my work . . . this is *my* morning, *my* day is breaking: *rise now, rise, thou great noon!*"[44]

In sober terms this means that Zarathustra denies himself pity in order to be wholly himself, because for Nietzsche pity is the essence of the romantically broken, second-hand existence, an existence characterized by unreconciled and therefore fatally intervening mediation.[45]

With the aim of achieving integral wholeness, this motif touches upon another in which there is admittedly only a partial agreement between Dante's and Nietzsche's thought. And even this agreement is evident only provided that one views the point of comparison as far as Nietzsche is concerned in the context of his remark about Lou Salomé contained in a letter in which he introduces her

---

[42] *Purgatorio,* Canto IX, 130–32. See my article "Bilder der Buße: Betrachtungen über Dantes Purgatorio," in *Wort und Antwort,* 14 (1973), 33–42.

[43] W, III, 896.

[44] In connection with this passage, see H. M. Wolff, *Friedrich Nietzsche: Der Weg zum Nichts* (Bern: Francke, 1956), pp. 209–23.

[45] Details in my study, *Theologie und Atheismus: Anstöße zu einer theologischen Aporetik* (Munich: Kösel, 1972), pp. 27 ff., 55–64.

to Peter Gast as follows: "she is as discerning as an eagle and brave as a lion, and yet after all a very girlish child who will probably not live very long."[46] With an inversion of the first terms the same sequence of metaphors reappears in the related passage, the speech of Zarathustra "On the Three Metamorphoses."[47] As the explanation of the sequence of motifs by Zarathustra indicates, it is based on a hierarchical scheme which leads upward and over the preliminary stages of heteronomy and autonomy represented by the metaphors "camel" and "lion" to the goal of an unquestionably independent self-consciousness, symbolized by the "child." This is a purely anthropological conception to which, in the case of Dante, a specifically Christological conception corresponds, a conception determining the fragmentary nature of the correspondence. In Canto XXXI of the *Purgatorio* the wanderer in the other-world sees, reflected in the unveiled eyes of Beatrice, the griffin harnessed to the carriage of the Church, which in its dual form, the lion-like body and the heavenward-reaching wings, symbolizes the Christ, the God-Man:

> As the sun in a mirror, not otherwise the twofold beast was beaming within them, now with the attributes of one, now of the other nature.
> Think, reader, if I marvelled within me when I saw the thing itself remain motionless, and in its image it was changing.[48]

Reflected in Beatrice's star-bright eyes, the chimerical griffin-figure separates itself for Dante, as Kurt Leonhard interprets the passage, into the two aspects intertwined within it so that at one time the one, at another, the other dominates: that of the eagle pointing to the divinity of Christ, and that of the lion symbolizing His unconditioned humanity.[49] If one adds the medium of the vision, the reflecting eyes of Beatrice, the original duality finally finds its completeness in a triad, albeit by no means composed of equals. What results from this process is certainly not like Nietzsche's model of ascent, but is rather the opposite, namely, a figurative representation of the condescension in which the incomprehensible mystery of the God-Man is translated into the alternating images which are reflected in Beatrice's eyes. Moreover, a linkage of motifs follows here in the fact that, analogous to the "mirror" of Beatrice's eyes, there also appears among the metaphors and images of Zarathustra "the child with the mirror." Zarathustra awakens one morning so troubled by the recollection of a dream that he asks himself: "Why was I so startled in my dream that I awoke? Did not a child step up to me, carrying a mirror?"[50]

---

[46] Letter of 13 July 1882.

[47] See Karl Löwith, *Nietzsches Philosophie der ewigen Wiederkehr des Gleichen* (Stuttgart: Kohlhammer, 1956), pp. 28 ff.; also, his *Weltgeschichte und Heilsgeschehen*, pp. 190 ff.; further the discussion in my study, "*Gott ist tot*," pp. 171. ff., 239 ff.

[48] *Purgatorio*, Canto XXXI, 121–26.

[49] Leonhard, *Dante Alighieri*, p. 130.

[50] Z. II, "Das Kind mit dem Spiegel."

Although the full extent of the agreement becomes clear only in the succession of the visions—as Zarathustra perceives in the child's mirror the danger threatening his doctrine, likewise Dante sees in the frightening images which follow the danger to which the Church, overwhelmed by the French monarchy, is exposed—nevertheless so much that is common stands out that one can speak of a genuine correspondence. As we hardly need to stress, this correspondence extends to all of the motif-groups. By virtue of the common element of the mirror the highest stage in Nietzsche's sequence of figures parallels so closely Dante's configuration that between the two a genuine, though not rationally demonstrable, correspondence seems to prevail. Or does the secret structural relationship between Nietzsche's atheism and the Christian faith manifest itself in a sudden flash of insight? Does even Dante's conception of salvation possibly appear here, mirrored in Beatrice's gaze, as the answer to the question which the highest of the Zarathustra-symbols, the child, poses, precisely in its unquestionable self-sufficiency?

However risky a comparison of Nietzsche with Dante may appear at first glance, nevertheless a series of clear analogies could be adduced pursuant to this brief investigation. A detailed comparison of motifs could without doubt expand it by a considerable number. But not too much would be gained. For the result would likewise be relativized by the circumstance which we should note in conclusion; and that is a recognition of the fact that the demonstrated affinity is merely of an episodic and transitory nature. It concerns the period of the incubation and genesis of *Zarathustra*, and yields thereafter to an increasing divergence. In the relationship between Dante and Nietzsche, the contradiction, at least the feeling of distance, as indicated by the notice from his unpublished papers cited earlier, is definitive.[51] The common element limits itself temporally—to borrow Nietzsche's expression in a letter to Peter Gast (11 September 1879)—to "the middle of life." Substantively it consists of endurance—and in the creative mastery—of the same aporetic situation which Nietzsche in the same context describes as a "being encompassed by death," and which impels Dante to utter the confessional opening verses of his poetic work:

> In the middle of the journey of our life I came to myself in a dark wood where the straight way was lost.
> Ah! how hard a thing it is to tell what a wild, and rough, and stubborn wood this was, which in my thought renews the fear!
> So bitter it is, that scarcely more is death.[52]

[51] See note 8 above.
[52] *Inferno*, 1–7.

V

The Structure of Tragedy and the Art of Painting

MARCUS HESTER

My purpose is to analyze the structure of tragedy in *The Birth of Tragedy* and show how Nietzsche could have used his insights to develop terms in which one could analyze specific paintings. My basic theses thus will come from *The Birth of Tragedy*, though I suggest continuities with later works. To start we must ask: What sort of things are the Dionysian and the Apollinian? Are they gods or are the gods only paradigmatic expressions of psychological drives? Nietzsche unfortunately freely changes the terms they qualify. However, "Trieb" in various forms occurs significantly. The Dionysian and the Apollinian are basically artistic drives, and the Greek gods are only symbols and paradigmatic manifestations of these basic drives or energies. The Apollinian is the drive to individuation, the drive to set boundaries important in the Greek ethical concepts of balance, proportionality, right limits and the negative concept of hubris. The drive to individuation shows itself in plastic delineation and in other visual delineations, as in dream images. The Dionysian is the drive to unity and oneness, and its analogy is intoxication. The nature of these drives is well developed by others.[1]

Another preliminary which must be emphasized is how freely Nietzsche shifts the category or kind of thing he is explaining in tragedy and other arts. Apparently he assumed that these dual drives can freely assume different forms within and even across categories.[2] As illustrations of such shifting one may cite the following: the characters Prometheus and Oedipus are different manifestations of the Dionysian (GT, sec. 10); Kaufmann suggests that Antigone is Apol-

---

[1] Rose Pfeffer, *Nietzsche: Disciple of Dionysus* (Lewisburg, Pa.: Bucknell University Press, 1972). For convenience, given the many editions of Nietzsche, I shall throughout refer to sections except where further specification is necessary. (For key to abbreviations see p. xvii above.) Unless otherwise noted, all translations are those of Walter Kaufmann in *Basic Writings of Nietzsche*, The Modern Library (New York: Random House, 1968), *The Portable Nietzsche* (New York: Viking, 1954), or (with R. J. Hollingdale) *The Will to Power* (New York: Vintage Books, 1968).

[2] Here he is influenced by the concept of the free transformation of the gods. (See GT, sec. 10.) Also there is a hint of his later idea that energy, drive or force is able to express itself in different forms. Sexual energy as sublimated may flow into apparently non-sexual channels such as artistic creation. And a final factor in the free shifting of the kind of thing Apollinian and Dionysian qualify is inherent in the use of polar concepts.

linian, Cassandra is Dionysian.[3] More radical than transformations within the category of character are cross-category analogies. There are whole arts which, vis-a-vis other arts, are Dionysian or Apollinian. Painting is Apollinian, music Dionysian (GT, sec. 1). Yet among examples of an art which is primarily Apollinian, for example, painting, there are examples which are Dionysian or Apollinian. Raphael is Dionysian. Mozart is probably Apollinian. The Dorian mode definitely is Apollinian (GT, sec. 2). An art which is primarily Dionysian with respect to other arts may contain examples which are Apollinian with respect to other examples. Further, within a medium considered as a whole, both Apollinian and Dionysian aspects may be evident. Tone and flow of melody is Dionysian. Even instruments are Apollinian (cithara) or Dionysian (flute) (GT, sec. 2). In sum, within a single work of art, Nietzsche often cites a Dionysian or Apollinian element or character. Within an art there are examples which are Dionysian or Apollinian with respect to each other. (Homer is Apollinian, Archilochus is Dionysian.) Finally, a whole art is sometimes said to be Dionysian or Apollinian with regard to other arts. There is free shifting in comparing aspects, particular works and whole genres. Nietzsche gives only the briefest hints about these transformations, and we shall simply have to say that he assumes artistic energies can find equivalences within and across categories. Nietzsche does not give any explanation of why these equivalences are equivalent, but we must add that no one yet can explain these important inter-category and inter-art resonances. In this paper I shall explore only a limited number of transformations. With these preliminaries aside, I now turn to my main subject.[4]

THE STRUCTURE OF TRAGEDY

In discussing the birth or origin of tragedy, Nietzsche deals with both the origin of the *elements* of tragedy (elements such as the chorus versus the scene) and with the *content* represented or shown by the elements. (The distinction here is not

---

[3] *Basic Writings of Nietzsche*, p. 47 n.

[4] Because of the free transformation into very different types of things by Dionysian and Apollinian drives, one cannot give a fixed answer to the question of how they are related. Specifically, if one is speaking of the Dionysian and Apollinian elements of tragedy, the relation is very different than that between Dionysian or Apollinian characters. Characters *interact*, and the action emerges from their interaction. The chorus as a Dionysian element, however, *discharges itself into* Apollinian imagery. What "Dionysian" or "Apollinian" as adjectives qualify is very important, and when "Dionysian" now qualifies one sort of thing and in another context a very different sort of thing (for example, Dionysian *chorus* versus a Dionysian *character* in Cassandra), the relation of Dionysian and Apollinian must be very different. Stated differently, when Dionysian drive transforms itself into a different kind of thing, the kind of thing or category of thing has its own inertia which cannot be changed completely by the drive. A drive is partially pulled into the orbit of the nature of that in which it is manifest. An adjective qualifies a substantive, but it does not destroy the substantive's nature. A Dionysian chorus is a very

the usual one of form and content but rather the distinction of structure and content). Not only is the Dionysian the source of the chorus as an element of tragedy, but the satyr chorus has a Dionysian nature. Likewise, the Apollinian is the source of the element of scene, but represented in the scene can be content that is Apollinian or Dionysian. Sometimes Nietzsche means a Dionysian or Apollinian element or part of tragedy, at other times he means that the content of the element is Dionysian or Apollinian in character. However, it will be seen that this dual level of meaning can be reconciled.

By "element of tragedy" I mean a functional part or role in the sense that the spectators, chorus and scene are functional parts. The elements of tragedy are parts of the whole which is tragedy. Nietzsche himself occasionally refers to Dionysian or Apollinian parts ("Teile") (GT, sec. 9). And typically, being the kind of dichotomistic thinker he is, Nietzsche sees all the rich elements which make up tragedy (spectator, chorus, music, poetry, dance and image) gravitating into two basic parts, parts labeled, of course, Dionysian and Apollinian. "Accordingly, we recognize in tragedy a sweeping opposition of styles: the language, color, mobility, and dynamics of speech fall apart into the Dionysian lyrics of the chorus and, on the other hand, the Apollinian dream world, and become two utterly different spheres of expression" (GT, sec. 6). Further, Nietzsche immediately begins to think of these two parts in terms of a very basic model which I call the self-object model.[5] The self is the center of experience, the moving center of its world, a point about which the phenomenal world spreads (GT, sec. 5). The objects of this center of the world are all sorts of objects of consciousness (varying from "empirische Realität," to "Vorstellung," "Schein," "Bild," "Traum," etc.). Here Nietzsche is influenced by the Kant-Schopenhauer line of thought. Later, specifically in Husserl, the way of expressing this point is to say that all mental acts are intentional, that every mental act has its appropriate sort of object,[6] that for every noesis there is a noema.

different sort of thing from a Dionysian character, and the relation of a Dionysian chorus to the Apollinian element of scene is very different from the relation of a Dionysian character to an Apollinian character. Many Nietzsche scholars assume, falsely I think, that one can specify one sort of relationship between Apollinian and Dionysian.

[5] Strictly speaking, there are several self-object models, two being shown below. Further, I realize that later Nietzsche rejects the entification of the self, and I use the term here only out of grammatical convenience. Later he shifts to what I would call an energy–object model, and that model shows the basic structure of the will to power. The energy–object model is anticipated in many ways in the self-object model, and I am deliberately paralleling the two. Nietzsche later rejects a certain romantic flavoring of *The Birth of Tragedy* and the weak pessimism it occasionally expresses. Also his break with Wagner caused modification of the concept of genius and the associated concept of inspiration examined below. (See J, sec. 188; MA, I, pt. IV, secs. 155, 156, 163–65.) But I think it is important to emphasize that the self-object model is an anticipation of the basic structure of the will to power.

[6] Edmund Husserl, *Ideas: General Introduction to Pure Phenomenology*, trans. W. R. Boyce Gibson (London: George Allen and Unwin, Ltd., 1958), pp. 116 f.

We might diagram the structure of the Apollinian self-object model as follows:

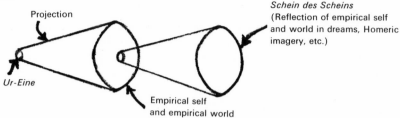

In my use of the term "projection" I mean that a basic but categorically imperceptible (primordial self) causes or projects a lesser, shadowy reality such as an appearance, dream image or hallucination. (See note 5.) The empirical self is a projection of the primoridal self ("Ur-Eine"), and the world of imagery is a reflection of the projected empirical world. It is this basic model, as simplified in the next diagram below, which pervades Nietzsche's understanding of the structure of the tragedy. Further, and very importantly, the basic concepts of Dionysian and Apollinian often refer respectively to the self and projected image parts of this model and *not* to represented content. I think this particular sense of Dionysian and Apollinian, that is, as respectively the primordial self versus the projected world (self-object model), has not been sufficiently emphasized in the Nietzsche literature.

In a state of ecstasy, as in tragedy when the spectators are excited by the chorus, the first reflection (empirical self and world) is bypassed or short-circuited, so to speak. The spectator forgets his ordinary roles and appearances and also those of other spectators. A mystical and unified self emerges which directly discharges itself into Apollinian imagery (GT, secs. 7, 8). The new and more literal self-object model is thus:

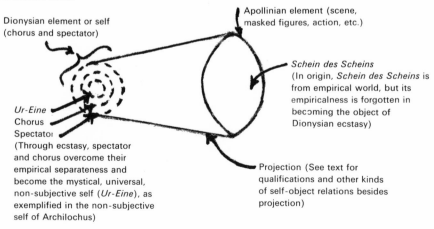

Specifically, in terms of the elements of tragedy, Nietzsche thinks of the satyr chorus and the audience as becoming a kind of self through ecstasy-evoking devices such as dithyrambic song, music, gesture, dance, and chants. The audience is drawn into the ecstasy of the satyr chorus, and the individual members overcome their individuality in a kind of mystical oneness. They feel identification with one another and with the chorus. At the same time, the actor's sense, by which he understands the meaning of every gesture, facial expression and full meaning of characterization, is developed (GT, secs. 2, 8). A mystical unity, equivalent to an expectant and perceptive self, emerges.

> In this magic transformation the Dionysian reveler sees himself as a satyr, *and as a satyr, in turn, he sees the god,* which means that in his metamorphosis he beholds another vision outside himself, as the Apollinian complement of his own state. . . . In the light of this insight we must understand Greek tragedy as the Dionysian chorus which ever anew discharges itself in an Apollinian world of images. (GT, sec. 8)

Of course, the Apollinian image is the object of attention of this ecstatic group self.[7] In the earliest forms, before there was true drama, the spectators provided their own private Apollinian images in states of vision and trance. "But now we realize that the scene, complete with the action, was basically and originally thought of merely as a *vision;* the chorus is the only 'reality' and generates the vision, speaking of it with the entire symbolism of dance, tone, and words" (GT, sec. 8). Later, with the earliest true drama, the revelers focused their ecstatic state on an actual masked figure of Dionysus appearing in form and functioning as Apollinian scene. Notice that as an element the masked god was Apollinian, but the represented content was Dionysian. Dionysus appears in Apollinian form, that is, he appears as a visual representation.[8] Given the heightened sense of the actor, the spectator and chorus understand the god's every gesture and expression. And their state of ecstacy, as we shall see, transforms the clumsy masked figure into a new reality.

The *content* represented or shown can be respectively Apollinian or Dionysian. (I shall return to differences between representing and showing later.) Music can show a character which is like the character of Apollo or like the character of Dionysus. The image on the stage can represent Dionysus; the content of the image is Dionysian even though as an element it is Apollinian. One character in a

---

[7] I emphasize that "object" here does not mean purpose or thing, but intentional object in the sense in which a *Bild* or image is the object of a state of dreaming.

[8] This does not necessarily mean that Dionysus appears Dionysian-like, so to speak. A Dionysian visual representation such as a satyr might be executed so that, though recognizably a satyr, the tone, gesture and atmosphere would be Apollinian in restraint, plasticity, etc. Of course, a Dionysian representation might also have a Dionysian air or atmosphere, and no doubt the greatest tragedies have this multilevel reinforcing of recognizable image, atmosphere and suggestive aura of the image. This multilevel reinforcing will be made clearer when the full range of symbolic powers is examined.

drama can represent the Dionysian while another can represent the Apollinian. And the elements or functional parts of tragedy, of course, can be unified with the content. The chorus is after all not only the Dionysian element but shows Dionysian character. The Apollinian element, unlike the chorus, which is a Dionysian element and shows Dionysian nature, is more content-open, so to speak. Anything can be represented, even Dionysus. Nietzsche does seem to believe the scene shows Apollinian content, but not only Apollinian content.[9] The satyr chorus, on the other hand, is less content-open. It creates the role of an ecstatic self, involving the audience. It sings, chants, and dances Dionysian wisdom or content. It does not articulate Dionysian wisdom in visual representations. The meaning of Apollinian and Dionysian as content has been thoroughly and well treated in the literature, and thus I return to my main theme of the structure of tragedy.

The mechanisms by which the self-object model operates are very important. Nietzsche clearly believes there is a causal primacy of the Dionysian. There are various formulations of this primacy: 1) There is the genuine *projective* relationship (as diagramed). The Dionysian ecstasy at first entirely generates the image. In the earliest stages of Dionysian worship, the vision of the god was like private visions in dreams, intoxication, sorrow, or ecstasies of cruelty. The Apollinian component was private and subjective and caused by the Dionysian ecstasy. (This causal primacy is parallel to Nietzsche's later claims that self-conscious motives are a mere result, a causal epiphenomenon of the will to power.)[10] How could one be sure that the Apollinian complement of the Dionysian state was true to the ecstatic state? How can one be sure that the images of the god are not entirely personal and unrelated? Nietzsche holds a version of what I call the automatism thesis. The thesis is that when one is in a state of ecstasy or trance, as in sleep, the images more truly reflect the true self than do empirical and waking states. This thesis of course is later important in Freud, and in surrealistic and automatic art. Nietzsche's version is most directly stated here:

> Though it is certain that of the two halves of our existence, the waking and the dreaming states, the former appeals to us as infinitely preferable, more important, excellent, and worthy of being lived, indeed, as that which alone is lived—yet in relation to that mysterious ground of our being of which we are the phenomena, I should, paradoxical as it may seem, maintain the very opposite estimate of the value of dreams. (GT, sec. 4)

Nietzsche no doubt thought that dreams were uninhibted, and thus truer projections in image of a universal Dionysian self.

Even more directly, Nietzsche clearly means a kind of automatism in this description of artistic ecstasy:

---

[9] Nietzsche does not, I think, use the phrase "*apollinische Weisheit*," but he does think tragedy has Apollinian content as well as Dionysian wisdom.

[10] See WM, secs. 666, 674; GM, II, sec. 12.

The *extreme sharpness* of certain senses, so they understand a quite different sign language—and create one—the condition that seems to be a part of many nervous disorders—; extreme mobility that turns into an extreme urge to communicate; the desire to speak on the part of everything that knows how to make signs—; a need to get rid of oneself, as it were, through signs and gestures; ability to speak of oneself through a hundred speech media—an *explosive* condition. One must first think of this condition as a compulsion and urge to get rid of the exuberance of inner tension through muscular activity and movements of all kinds; then as an involuntary co-ordination between this movement and the processes within (images, thoughts, desires)—as a kind of automatism of the whole muscular system impelled by strong stimuli from within—; inability to prevent reaction; the system of inhibitions suspended, as it were. (WM, sec. 811)

The thesis of automatism is clearly stated though it here seems to mean automatic correlation between various symbolic realms such as thought, images, desires, gestures and movements. Nietzsche was perhaps unaware that this sort of auto-matism in the correlation of the imagistic, ideational and vascular was a main idea of Baudelaire, deriving perhaps from Poe, and influencing the symbolic poets.[11] We also notice in the passage that artistic ecstasy heightens perceptiveness, and sensitive perceptiveness is a receptiveness and not an active projection, and we shall shortly shift to this idea.

It is because of this direct projection that the lyrical poet escapes mere subjective reverie in his images.

The artist has already surrendered his subjectivity in the Dionysian process. The image that now shows him his identity with the heart of the world is a dream scene that embodies the primordial contradiction and primordial pain, together with the primordial pleasure, of mere appearance. The 'I' of the lyrist therefore sounds from the depth of his being: its 'subjectivity,' in the sense of modern aestheticians, is a fiction. (GT, sec. 5)

Archilochus does not just express the private world of his subjective reveries. In a state of ecstasy the images projected reflect the heart of the world. The self re-flected is not the empirical self, "but the only truly existent and eternal self resting at the basis of things, through whose images the lyric genius sees this very basis" (GT, sec. 5). No doubt Nietzsche would say the Dionysian revelers manifested the same sort of lack of subjectivity in their visions. To anticipate the analysis of symbolic powers: Dionysian ecstasy, in tapping the universal self, releases sym-bolic powers of dance, music, poetry and gesture which have inter-subjective meaning. Unless the image reflected reality it could not be called the complement of the Dionysian state. Because of the causal primacy of the Dionysian and because of its control of the image, one can speak of "the Dionysian chorus which ever

---

[11] Charles Baudelaire, *Art in Paris: 1845–1862: Salons and Other Exhibitions*, trans. and ed. Jonathan Mayne (London: Phaidon Press, 1965), pp. 51, 142–43, 155–58.

anew discharges itself in an Apollinian world of images" (GT, sec. 8). The image is no mere illusion but "the Apollinian embodiment of Dionysian insights . . ." (GT, sec. 8).

2) But we must not overemphasize a free and automatic projection, for that is only one sort of self-object relation Nietzsche suggests in *The Birth of Tragedy*. A second self-object relation is that the self *shapes* or *forms* some material. We know Nietzsche, even in his later theory of dreams, conceives of dreams as not just free projections, but more as an imaginative embroidering of perceptual cues. Sounds, pressure of bed cover, and body positions can be the causes of dreams, though the dream state reverses the true cause-effect relationship and makes it seem as though the imagistic embroidering is the cause of the physical cue (G, "The Four Great Errors," sec. 4; WM, sec. 479). In this imagistic embroidering we should perhaps describe the self-object relation as a shaping, parallel to the shaping we conceptually do with scientific and other concepts.[12] Our expectations, desires, mental sets and other forms of our will to power do not have an entirely free hand when the object is a physical object or masked figure which has an inertia of its own. There is more of a sense of manipulation as mastery of a resistant stuff in the shaping relationship.

With the development of true drama, with the masked figure replacing private visions, shaping is a more accurate description than projecting. The masked figure is the focus of the Dionysian energy of the ecstatic self, but the heightened sensitivity of this expectant self implies that the state is not a complete projecting into but a partial reading out of the givenness of the figure. This active-receptive dialectic of shaping and sensing is of course inherently difficult to clarify, and the closest Nietzsche comes to it is I think in his description of Admetus.

> Consider Admetus as he is brooding over the memory of his recently departed wife Alcestis, consuming himself in her spiritual contemplation, when suddenly a similarly formed, similarly walking woman's figure is led toward him, heavily veiled; let us imagine his sudden trembling unrest, his tempestuous comparisons, his instinctive conviction—and we have an analogy with what the spectator felt in his Dionysian excitement when he saw the approach on the stage of the god with whose sufferings he had already identified himself. Involuntarily, he transferred the whole magic image of the god that was trembling before his soul to that masked figure and, as it were, dissolved its reality into the unreality of spirits. (GT, sec. 8)

We notice that the veiled figure must, in form and walk, resemble Alcestis. Apparently not just any sort of veiled figure could become the focus of Admetus' ecstatic sadness. Ecstatic states develop our perceptiveness to the meaning of the given object. The chorus provides something like an ecstatic, expectant mental set, but it is a mental set that because of perceptiveness must be sensitively represented in the image.

[12] See WM, secs. 495, 513, 602, 605, 606.

Since the Dionysian energy could not discharge itself in an inappropriate image, I suppose Nietzsche would say a dramatist could fail on grounds of characterization, gesture of the actor, logic of the scene, etc. Of course, there are Apollinian characters in Apollinian form, as well as Dionysian characters in Apollinian form, and a failure of characterization would have to be when characters did not represent one or both basic artistic drives. There also could be failures of suitability of other perceptual aspects of the scene to the meaning of the drama, failures we might call failures of sensuous logic. Perhaps sensuous logic is what Nietzsche means when he speaks of "a coloring, a causality, and a velocity" peculiar to individual arts (GT, sec. 5). But on the active and forming side, Admetus' extremely agitated and intense mental set, his intense desire to see his wife, mentally seizes the image of the actor, shapes it and gives in convincingness. (The analogies to Nietzsche's later concept of perspectivism, where the most basic scientific concepts like the atom are images and shapings responding to our will to power, are striking.)

Of course, with the introduction of the actual masked figure of Dionysus, with the development of true drama, one has the possibility of the artist's control of the Apollinian world of imagery. The spectator, excited to a state of ecstasy by the satyr chorus, still lends the image reality and convincingness, but the spectator ceases to be a complete artist who provides his own Apollinian complement to his ecstatic state. The masked figure is not just a space for him to project into. But even with true drama ecstasy excites and unleashes artistic powers. Now the artist himself, in acts of creation, needs to excite himself into states of ecstasy so that he will be able to project and sense the meaning of and determine the adequacy of his images.

> *Toward a psychology of the artist.* If there is to be art, if there is to be any aesthetic doing and seeing, one physiological condition is indispensable: frenzy. Frenzy must first have enhanced the excitability of the whole machine; else there is no art. All kinds of frenzy, however diversely conditioned, have the strength to accomplish this: above all, the frenzy of sexual excitement, this most ancient and original form of frenzy. Also the frenzy that follows all great cravings, all strong affects; the frenzy of feasts, contests, feats of daring, victory, all extreme movement; the frenzy of cruelty; the frenzy in destruction; the frenzy under certain meteorological influences, as for example the frenzy of spring; or under the influence of narcotics; and finally the frenzy of will, the frenzy of an overcharged and swollen will. What is essential in such frenzy is the feeling of increased strength and fullness. Out of this feeling one lends to things, one *forces* them to accept from us, one violates them—this process is called *idealizing.* . . . A man in this state transforms things until they mirror his power —until they are reflections of his perfection. This *having to* transform into perfection is—art. (G, "Skirmishes of an Untimely Man," sec. 8–9)

The artistic energy described here is distinctly more like shaping and mastering than like projecting. (Strictly speaking, idealizing is a third kind of self-object relation and is a concept Nietzsche does not clearly articulate in *The Birth of Tragedy*. He does vaguely hint at idealizing in suggesting that Oedipus and Prometheus are types [G, sec. 10].) There is conscious mastery, control and overpowering of his material. The artist, like the man who really loves his destiny, is able to bring a purposive order and unity into the accidental and meaningless.[13] Nietzsche unfortunately did not clarify the difference between mastery of a representation, where there is an element of correspondence with metaphysical reality, and mastery of material. One does not overcome an idea or representation in the same way as one overcomes the resistance of matter.

3) A final version of the self-object model is that the Dionysian self *infuses a sense of reality* into the image. The Apollinian imagistic vehicles as reflections of the gods were, apart from their transfusions of conviction and power from Dionysian states, becoming unconvincing and hardened into the dogmas of historical religions. Admetus' state dissolves the empirical reality of a veiled figure into the unreality of spirits. The actor and masked figure cease to be such. The veiled figure is transformed into the world of spirit. The meaning here is that the masked figures, scenery, dialogue, etc., of the Apollinian element cease to be merely what they are and become parts of the microcosm of the drama. They do not thereby become mistaken for empirical realities. Tragedy has this paradoxical unreality while yet being a higher reality. It is empirically unreal but metaphysically real. The sensuous image may be as true as the image of the atom but like any image it must be loved as a mere image, that is as a fixed picture of a dynamic and everchanging reality. "Knowledge and becoming exclude one another" (WM, sec. 517). Notice here Nietzsche agrees with Plato that knowledge is of what is stable, fixed, though of course he differs with Plato and sides with Heraclitus in saying reality is becoming. Nietzsche clearly holds that the image in great art reflects Dionysian metaphysical reality in Apollinian form. (The content of Apollo also is not foreign to Dionysian wisdom.)[14]

In sum, in the self-object or energy-object relation, Dionysian energy can project itself in an Apollinian vision or shape and transform Apollinian scene elements. These are only three (with idealizing being a fourth) of the many energy-object relations which are various forms of what later is the will to power. The energy-object model evolves from the self-object model and is I think the basic structure of the will to power. I do not here attempt to prove that the self-

---

[13] See GM, pt. II, secs. 11, 17 f.

[14] I agree with Danto that: "The radical character of Nietzsche's thought, even in its first significant expression, may be seen in the fact that he is indeed prepared to allow that art has no less a claim than sense or science to objective truth. But this is because neither sense nor science can make any stronger claim to truth than art." Arthur C. Danto, *Nietzsche as Philosopher* (New York: The Macmillan Co., 1965), p. 37. (See the following for discussions of image, appearance and fiction in art and science: J, secs. 34, 192, 296; GM, III, secs. 12, 25; G, " 'Reason' in Philosophy," sec. 6, "Skirmishes of an Untimely Man," sec. 26; WM, secs. 545 f, 553 f, 618 f.)

object model evolves to the energy-object model, for this would, of course, require extensive analysis of later work. I have only analyzed the early self-object model, with hints, mostly in the footnotes, about continuities with later energy-object models. I agree with Kaufmann that the will to power is a unification of various earlier forms of drives. "The will is not a single entity but more like a constantly shifting federation or alliance of drives."[15] Later there are unifying functions of the will to power, parallel to Dionysian drive, and there are also forming, boundary setting, specializing functions of the will to power, parallel to Apollinian drive. Instead of two drives, Nietzsche later speaks of very many different forms of the will to power. A dynamic center of energy forms, shapes, transforms, dominates, integrates, idealizes, masters, etc. Such acts are various kinds of energy-object relations.[16] My analysis of the structure of tragedy clarifies some of Nietzsche's criticisms of Euripides. The chorus ceases to play its role as the *cause* of tragedy. The causal primacy of the Dionysian part of the self-object model is destroyed by the new role which Euripides gives the chorus. Music ceases to be the substratum which discharges itself in Apollinian imagery.

SYMBOLIC POWERS

Nietzsche repeatedly refers to Dionysian ecstasy as exciting all the symbolic powers, and it is essential here to clarify what is meant by symbolic powers and thus what kind of assertion and truth various elements of tragedy can have.

> In the Dionysian dithyramb man is incited to the greatest exaltation of all his symbolic faculties. . . . The essence of nature is now to be expressed symbolically; we need a new world of symbols; and the entire symbolism of the body is called into play, not the mere symbolism of the lips, face, and speech but the whole pantomime of dancing, forcing every member into rhythmic movement. Then the other symbolic powers suddenly press forward, particularly those of music, in rhythmics, dynamics, and harmony. To grasp this collective release of all the symbolic powers, man must have already attained that height of self-abnegation which seeks to express itself symbolically through all these powers—and so the dithyrambic votary of Dionysus is understood only by his peers. (GT, sec. 2)

We notice the causal primacy of the Dionysian dithyramb, reminding us of the causal primacy of ecstatic states originally in private visions and later in transforming the masked figure of Dionysus, a transformation analogous to the transformation of the veiled figure by the grieving Admetus. But to move further, we notice that symbolic powers include a rich range of bodily and imagistic expres-

[15] WM, p. 381 n.
[16] See the following for the variety of activities which are the will to power: WM, secs. 602, 605, 658, 1050; J, secs. 36, 213; GM, pt. II, secs. 11, 17 f.

sion. There is symbolism of lips, face, speech and the whole pantomime and gesture of dancing. There is symbolism of music in rhythmics, dynamics and harmony. These symbolic powers in a state of ecstasy release still further images of symbolic power, specifically of course the symbolic realm of images, the Apollinian. Even dreams are "symbolic chains of scenes and images in place of a narrative poetic language" (MA, II, pt. II, sec. 194). Nietzsche apparently means that acts such as gesturing, dancing, movements of the face have their own kind of meaning, and thus they are symbolic; they can be kinds of "assertions." They are non-verbal languages, languages which speak in the natural symbolism of gesture and bodily movement. The meaning of such symbolic realms can be understood only by other Dionysian votaries in ecstatic states. We are reminded of the New Testament glossolalia where only others possessed of the spirit could understand the strange tongues. Nietzsche here means that Dionysian ecstasy heightens the actor's sense by which he knows the meaning of every gesture, movement and facial expression. The Dionysian not only releases a full range of symbolism but heightens the sense of gesture necessary to understand the symbolism. With the freed ranges of symbolism and the heightened actor's sense necessary to understand them, the gestures can be "assertions" which express reality, reality here being Dionysian "Ur-Eine."

When the masked god appeared in Apollinian form on the scene, replacing private visions, the full range of symbolic powers of drama were complete. "In the light of this insight we must understand Greek tragedy as the Dionysian chorus which ever anew discharges itself in an Apollinian world of images. . . . Thus the drama is the Apollinian embodiment of Dionysian insights and effects and thereby separated, as by a tremendous chasm, from the epic" (GT, sec. 8). The Apollinian definitely introduces a new realm of symbolic possibilities and a new kind of articulation. "That he *appears* at all with such epic precision and clarity is the work of the dream-interpreter, Apollo, who through this symbolic appearance interprets to the chorus its Dionysian state" (GT, sec. 10). The visual statement has some advantages over symbolism of dance and gesture and music in its clarity, precision and beauty.

> The Apollinian appearances in which Dionysus objectifies himself are no longer "an eternal sea, changeful strife, a glowing life," like the music of the chorus, no longer those forces, merely felt and not condensed into images, in which the enraptured servant of Dionysus senses the nearness of the god: now the clarity and firmness of epic form addresses him from the scene; now Dionysus no longer speaks through forces but as an epic hero, almost in the language of Homer. (GT, sec. 8)

This passage is especially significant because it tells us what would be lost without the Apollinian. The Dionysian no longer speaks just through forces or energies of the affective self aroused by ecstasy, but it now speaks in forces condensed into images. The Dionysian is still causally basic, but the Apollinian adds a distinct kind of articulation in visual imagery. Without Apollinian articulation, one merely *feels* the value of life in experiencing Dionysian energy. Apollinian imagery and representation more clearly *state* Dionysian wisdom. At the level of felt value of Dionysian energy, Dionysian "wisdom" has to be placed in qualifying quotes because it is not fully articulated. We recall, however, that visual symbolism tends to lose its convincingness and creep into historical dogmas unless infused with a sense of reality, but not entified, by Dionysian energy and ecstasy.

To sum up, "symbolic powers" seems to mean a full range of natural and conventional languages each of which has its own peculiar advantages and kind of meaning, the full range of which make various kinds of "statements" or "assertions." I place "statements" and "assertions" in qualifying quotes because there is some peculiarity about statements made by dance, facial gesture, body gesture, song and image. All these can have their kind of meaning, peculiar to their medium, and they give multi-level assertions of Dionysian wisdom. Thus they can be "true" in the sense of "asserting" the nature of reality. The highest tragedies show in dance, song, poetry, imagery, dialogue and characters the truth of Dionysian wisdom. A visual representation, as in painting, can obviously be an assertion. Given a system of projection, and given titles and names of art works, they make assertions about how things look, and what they were like as based on their looks. Likewise in viewing dance we expect to find some meaning in gestures and movement. The dance can be an assertion in that sense. Poetry obviously can assert truth, and since it is a linguistic art there is less of a metaphor in calling poetry statemental or assertive, though of course we have to emphasize that it does not assert like science. Further, there can be meaning in the interactions of characters and events. As Aristotle saw, we even look for meaning in chance occurrences when they are in a tragedy.[17] Tragedy employs a full range of symbolic powers to assert Dionysian wisdom, and the Dionysian state of ecstasy is causally basic in releasing these powers which ultimately express the truth of Dionysian wisdom. Art is metaphysical in the sense that it employs a full range of symbolic powers to "assert" the truth about reality. There are passages where Nietzsche suggests that Apollo is escapist (GT, secs. 1, 4). These lines of thought are later rejected as weak pessimism. But there are more passages where the Apollinian is a condensation into imagery of Dionysian wisdom, where Dionysian wisdom discharges itself into Apollinian images, where the image is an Apollinian representation of Dionysus.

The relation of symbolic powers to the self-object model is this: The Dionysian self drives forth all the symbolic powers. The symbolic powers are various levels of meaning which represent or show in the various parts (dance, poetry, gesture, imagery, music) of tragedy. These layers of symbolic meaning gravitate to two parts, the Dionysian self or the Apollinian scene, as shown above. Nietz-

---

[17] *Poetics*, 1452a, 6–10.

sche does not discuss how these different levels of meaning "assert" Dionysian wisdom. He does not discuss how an art which can represent Dionysus in image can assert the same meaning as an art (music) which is not representational but presumably shows a Dionysian nature or wisdom. The problem here is how arts which can *represent* subject matter harmonize with or mutually assert what non-representational arts *show*. Of course, the interrelations of representing, evoking and showing are very complex and still problematical.

THE ART OF PAINTING

The distinction above between Dionysian and Apollinian as elements versus content is helpful in understanding Nietzsche's scattered remarks about paintings. In general, of course, music, images and other elements, when experienced in themselves, apart from their role in tragedy, must have a very different nature than they have in tragedy. Apart from the drama or some other combining art, the art in question (say music or plastic imagery) naturally ceases to have the sense of some special role. When we view plastic images apart from their role in tragedy, those images cannot in the same direct sense be the focus of Dionysian ecstasy. The Dionysian cannot discharge itself into an image because one does not view paintings normally as a part of a satyr chorus. The normal museum-goer does not work himself up or have himself worked up by a satyr chorus in preparation for the image of his god. Unfortunately, Nietzsche does not, at least with regard to painting, make the transition from the role of a plastic image in drama to the nature and rich possibilities of plastic images considered as arts in themselves. To be specific, Nietzsche's few discussions of actual Renaissance paintings are, so far as I know, entirely discussions of represented content. Representational content is the role plastic imagery plays in tragedy, but there are many other levels of symbolization in painting, and Nietzsche has the equipment, so to speak, to discuss them. I think perhaps the reason Nietzsche does not make the transition from discussing the rich levels of symbolic meaning of parts of tragedy to a similar discussion of aspects of an art like painting is this: Functional parts such as chorus versus scene are relatively isolable. There is certainly a sense in which paintings have parts too, but I think the true parallel to what I have been calling functional parts in tragedy, in contrast to content, might be *aspects* of a painting. Aspects are ways we can attend to works of art (for example attending to color or line) even though that aspect cannot exist independently as a functional part can. Tragedy has a full range of symbolic powers, some easily isolable because of distinct elements of tragedy. A painting has fewer isolable elements, but it still has a wide range of aspects such as subject matter represented, color considered in a color scheme, line drawing, etc. There are here abundant possibilities for the reinforcement of various symbolic realms (say the different realms of brush gesture versus represented subject matter) though the symbolic powers now show themselves in aspects of the art work instead of isolable functional parts (such as chorus, music, scene, dance, poetry). Nietzsche could, in other words, have shown levels of aspects in painting equivalent to levels of symbolic powers which are exemplified in functional parts of tragedy. Instead of this, however, he discusses only represented content of painting, and I shall suggest some extensions of his thought. Representational content is only one aspect of painting, and to discuss it alone is not enough.

In extending the above ideas to specific paintings, I must emphasize that Nietzsche was not very interested in analyzing specific works of art.[18] A survey of Nietzsche's work for references to Renaissance painters such as Raphael and Michelangelo will turn up few references to specific paintings. Nietzsche was more interested in the phenomenon of artistic creation, more interested in the genius of Michelangelo and Raphael as phenomena of culture, than in showing how genius leaves its mark in painting. Even the references to specific works, such as Raphael's "Transfiguration," use the work mainly to tell us about Raphael. Works are looked at in terms of being symptoms or signs of Dionysian genius. Thus I realize I am extending Nietzsche's thought beyond his main interests, and in these extensions relatively few paintings cited by Nietzsche can be mentioned. Further, I only extrapolate the *terms in which* one could analyze specific paintings. I leave actual analyses to art critics and art historians.

In projecting Nietzsche's ideas to aspects of painting, one can use basically two kinds of remarks, those specifically about paintings and acts of painting and those about other arts which could have a painting analogue. To extend his comments on other arts to painting would require an examination of Nietzsche's ideas of the interrelations of various arts, a subject too large to explore here.[19] But the simpler task of collecting his remarks about paintings and painting acts will reveal the critical possibilities of Nietzsche's thought and at the same time show how various aspects of painting could be cues to the nature of the painter's genius, the latter possibility, of course, being completely in line with Nietzsche's basic intentions and interests.

The remarks about painting are more often about activities of painting than they are about aspects of specific paintings. The important exceptions to this claim are discussions of representational content, the first aspect discussed. In discussing

---

[18] See his denial of this claim: GM, III, sec. 4.

[19] For example, Nietzsche clearly thought certain rhythms and gestures in music or dance could be characterized as Dionysian or Apollinian. Perhaps one could transfer these suggestions to brush gesture, and then one could discuss how brush gestures of an Apollinian or Dionysian nature reinforced or were in tension with subject matter represented. This would enrich the critical possibilities of Nietzsche's concepts of Dionysian and Apollinian. A related suggestion is Nietzsche's claim that certain tempos were Apollinian and others were Dionysian (J, sec. 246). These perhaps also could be transferred to brush stroke and other aspects of plastic arts which could have something analogous to rhythms.

the second, third and fourth aspects, I have extended hints and suggestions Nietzsche makes about creative *acts* in contrast to actual paintings. 1) Representational content, in terms of the subjects chosen and the manner treated, can give us cues to the painter's philosophy of life or *Weltanschauung*. Representational content, as suggested in the section on symbolic powers, can "assert" in a relatively direct sense a view of life or reality. The discussion of Raphael's "Transfiguration" is in terms of representational content, the lower half of the painting representing Dionysian wisdom in suffering and the upper half representing Apollinian light and beauty (GT, sec. 4). There is the same emphasis on subject matter in the later remarks on the Sistine Madonna. Nietzsche speculates about what the beautiful maiden on the right is saying to the spectator. He discusses the Christ child's eyes in terms of expressing anticipated distress and in terms of being the eyes of a man instead of a child (MA, II, pt. II, sec. 73). Further, Nietzsche reads Raphael's philosophy of life from these paintings. Raphael's subjects are too sensual for a nay-sayer, he could not be a Christian, he is too Dionysian for that. There is a problem here of identifying Raphael's views with the nature of the represented subjects, a problem analogous to identifying Shakespeare with any of his dramatis personae, and Nietzsche is aware of the problem (MA, I, pt. IV, sec. 176). The discussion of the Sistine Madonna is called "ehrliches Malertum" and shows how Raphael could be honest and paint religious subjects, an honesty which suggests Raphael's mocking smiles at the faith of simple viewers. Similarly, the discussion of Dürer's "Knight, Death, and Devil" is in terms of the hopeless but determined, hard, iron look of the Knight, a philosophy attributed in this instance not to Dürer but to Schopenhauer (GT, sec. 20).

Nietzsche's discussions of actual Renaissance paintings are, so far as I know, all like this in being about the meaning of the represented subject matter and the inferences these allow one to draw about the painter's philosophy of life or illustrations of other philosophies of life. Such representational content may be the role plastic imagery played in tragedy, but painting considered in itself has to be analyzed in terms of richer levels of aspects. Painting can show some further fullness of reinforcing symbolic powers, as suggested below. 2) The powerful, Dionysian painter always idealizes, he never mirrors. Idealizing consists in seeing the essence, the typical, and Nietzsche admired this aspect of Greek art. Treatment of detail shows decadence. Idealizing is the confidence to seize the main features (G, "Skirmishes of an Untimely Man," secs. 8, 9). Here is an aspect of painting Nietzsche could have explored, a level of symbolic power other than representational content. To make this a critically useful concept, the critic would have to know when idealizing had taken place, and that would take knowledge of the essence of the thing represented, a rather difficult concept to employ critically with any confidence. Ruskin perhaps faces this dilemma in *Modern Painters* in looking for true nature in painting. Further, signs that a painter had idealized, assuming we could overcome the problems just mentioned, would not be signs of his view of life so much as signs of his confidence and knowledge of the kind of thing represented. Idealizing tells us only the view of the nature of what is represented, not the painter's views in some more general sense. 3) Power can be shown in dominance of material, and power in the sense of sheer technical mastery, complete control of the medium, would be a different aspect of painting which Nietzsche could have discussed. Such power would not tell us a painter's views, nor what he sees as the essence of some subject. It would simply evidence his mastery of his art. Nietzsche clearly realized the role of craft in genius.[20] Power could show in one's views, in the boldness in seizing the essence with economical means and in mastery. Raphael's views are almost stated in the subject matter represented, but his power is shown in his mastery. Nietzsche definitely shifts to emphasizing mastery of means as perhaps a necessary condition of art (MA, I, pt. IV). 4) "All art exercises the power of suggestion over the muscles and senses . . ." (WM, sec. 809). Analogously, "movement is symbolism for the eye; it indicates that something has been felt, willed, thought" (WM, sec. 492). There are two senses in which painting can speak through our muscles. We could feel the brush gesture, perhaps sensing what making that gesture would be like, and thus perhaps whether it is Apollinian or Dionysian. Painters no doubt have more of this sort of sensibility than the viewer who has never handled a brush. A second sort of appeal to our muscles, or at least to our tactile-kinaesthetic senses, would be more what the shapes or forms in the painting felt like. Are they impending, stable, about to collapse, etc.? We might summarize these two senses of speaking through our muscles by saying a picture space is sometimes a space to gesture in and at other times a space to look into, corresponding to two levels of tactile meaning. In summary, we might say that in representations and idealizations a painter states views and shows what he considers the nature of the represented subjects to be. In mastery and tactile symbolism there is more showing than stating. Body knowledge, so to speak, here manifests itself. These are four levels on which the Dionysian or Apollinian could be involved in forms of representing, idealizing and showing. Raphael's Dionysian energy manifests itself in aspects of his painting (representation, idealizing, mastery), aspects here being somewhat equivalent to elements of tragedy. Nietzsche makes many remarks about Raphael being Dionysian, a true Renaissance genius, and I have tried to show how he could give these remarks substance in analyzing Raphael's paintings. I have tried to show how Dionysian release of a full range of symbolic powers can be seen in many aspects of painting. If we developed some of the realms of symbolic powers from other arts, Nietzsche would be able to talk about a painting at a plurality of levels of aspects. He could show how Raphael's views, seizing the essence of things, and various levels of symbolism of gesture were Dionysian. This would be a more adequate discussion of Raphael's painting than any Nietzsche actually gives.

[20] See: J, sec. 188; MA, Vol. I, pt. 4, secs. 145, 155, 156, 163, 164, 165.

I give this final suggestion on how to extend the self-object model to the *act of viewing* paintings. Even though the museum spectator before a painting is not in a Dionysian state of ecstasy, that spectator has previously experienced or felt the life force of overcoming even in the face of death, and a great painting (one which articulates Dionysian wisdom) is a visual articulation of these feelings and experiences even though the self is not in that ecstatic state immediately prior to the appearance in image. One recognizes a great painting by seeing a visual articulation of life energies one has felt. It works through memory of ecstasy instead of actual states of ecstasy. A painting thus is an assertion of metaphysical truth, of the reality of life, which rings true to our memories of Dionysian experiences or states. Nietzsche does not give these arguments, perhaps because he was not clear about the difference between role and content, but he could quite consistently give these extensions of his thought.

VI

The Impact of Ancient Greece and of French Classicism on Nietzsche's Concept of Tragedy *

KURT WEINBERG

> Only as esthetic phenomena are existence and the universe forever justified. (Nietzsche[1])

Nietzsche's views on classical tragedy are closely linked to his tragic vision of life, and informed by an uncompromising aestheticism which precludes all judgments about the moral effects of tragedy on the audience. He looks upon both life and tragedy from the viewpoint of the artist who experiences the creative process which originates in chance but, paradoxically, bears the stamp of an inescapable necessity, engendered as it is by forces deeply rooted beneath the reaches of consciousness. They are brought to light by the disciplined exercise of controls, and subject to the strictures of rhetoric and poetics. The poet and the tragic hero alike must consent to their fate which leads to an act of self-destruction: *amor fati*. The poet, fervently committed to his fate, consents to an orgiastic self-sacrifice, to his self-denial in an act both intuitive (or Dionysian) and rhetorical (or Apollonian, form-giving), for the poet's creative principle is in Nietzsche's own term a "sublimation" of erotic energy (W, III, 924). *Amor fati* commands the tragic hero to obey a will to power, a frenzied instinct which, blinding his reason, controls him and drives him towards his doom. The poet's creative sublimation and the tragic hero's acceptance of his fate, their subsequent redemption and purgation, are symbolized by the seasonal immolation and resurrection of Dionysus Zagreus who, for Nietzsche, is incarnate in the heroes of tragedies enacted during the Dionysian festivals.

---

* The present chapter is a considerably expanded version of Kurt Weinberg, "Nietzsche's Paradox of Tragedy," *Yale French Studies*, 38 (1967), 251–66.

[1] Quotations, if not otherwise indicated, refer to the three-volume edition of Nietzsche's *Werke* edited by Karl Schlechta, which, although not complete, offers the advantage of not having been bowdlerized by Frau Elisabeth Förster-Nietzsche. (For key to abbreviations, see p. xvii above.) F.O. and F.N. = Carl Albrecht Bernoulli, *Franz Overbeck und Friedrich Nietzsche: Eine Freundschaft*, 2 vols. (Jena: E. Friederichs, 1908). The translations are mine. The epigraph is from (W, I, 40; I, 131).

From Heinse to Kleist, Hölderlin, Friedrich Schlegel, Schelling and Friedrich Creuzer, the figure of Dionysus had obsessed German thought and letters. It had led Gottfried Welcker to syncretic speculations on similarities between Dionysus and Christ, which Nietzsche shattered by opposing to Christianity's ascetic values the frenzies of the Dionysian mysteries, life-asserting even in the triumphant acceptance of the necessary destruction of the highest type of individual within the never-ending cycle of birth, death, and rebirth in a universe governed by the law of the conservation of energy. But Nietzsche went beyond the German obsession with the Dionysian. Even in *The Birth of Tragedy* he had limited its impact by counterbalancing it with the Apollonian: in tragedy, the Dionysian and Apollonian symbolically combine into a complex *Bruderbund*, a unity where "Dionysus speaks the language of Apollo, Apollo however, in the end, the language of Dionysus" (W, I, 120). It amounts to a critique of the Wagnerian *Musikdrama*, subversively built into a work that purports to exalt it, and written by a former disciple of Wagner who, gradually disenchanted with the master, was rapidly progressing toward a passionate rejection of the Germany of the *Gründerjahre*, its coarse *Bildungsphilister*, and its cultural emptiness. Wagner's "total work of art" will ultimately become for Nietzsche the exemplum for everything that is amorphous, excessive, pretentious, and (what I would call) *Heldenkitsch* in the newly founded *Reich:* an uncouth and plebeian mixture of genres, the very opposite of classical restraints, *bienséances, honnêteté, esprit,* sophrosyne, and aristocratic litotes which distinguish French civilization before the advent of Romanticism, and, despite Romanticism, far into the late nineteenth century. It is true, Nietzsche's attitude toward Wagner will always be ambiguous; his passion for Wagnerian music will never quite die down. Yet, the break with Wagner becomes more and more pronounced. In the end it proves irreconcilable, after the experience of Bayreuth and Germany's military victory over France, the only European country which has achieved that "unity of artistic style in all vital expressions of a nation" that, for Nietzsche, is the very essence of "civilization" (*Kultur;* W, I, 140). While the Wagnerian *Musikdrama* and the Wagnerians with their boisterous chauvinism and antisemitism are Nietzsche's warning examples of vulgarity and barbarity, he upholds the classical French civilization of the seventeenth century as an exemplary combination of self-restraint, moderation, good taste and elegance—in language, thought, manners, and art—which alone qualifies as "civilization." The civilizing lesson taught by the court of Louis XIV goes counter to the peasant instincts of the Germans from Lessing to the Wilhelmian era who clamor for a return to man's first, unpolished animal nature (not unlike Goethe's *Baccalaureus,* who proclaims: "Im Deutschen lügt man, wenn man höflich ist"—"In the German language one lies if one is polite" [*Faust II*, l. 6771]). They show little or no understanding for the French classical concept of "le naturel," i.e., the inborn natural potential, the germ of that accomplished second nature which man attains by undergoing the complex process of a humanistic education. This refining process strips him of *naïveté*, credulity and brutishness, giving him in the end a *persona* consistent with his status in life, a social mask of manners, language, gestures and ostentation—(in the seventeenth century, a gentlemanly *virtue* and *not* a vice)—apt to conceal his human, all-too-human first nature in its naïve (= native), "sincere" crudity. In a word, the aristocratic civilization of seventeenth-century France—a school of manners, taste, intellectual rigor, urbane skepticism, and wit whose indelible stamp can be found in French civilization even in an age of Romantic decadence— serves as the ideal model of an *aesthetic ethics* with which Nietzsche confronts the Philistine and inelegant grossness of his contemporary Germany, the military power that overcame the French Army while remaining far behind the cultural achievements of the nation it had vanquished in 1871.

At this point, it would seem useful to see to what extent Nietzsche might actually have read French seventeenth-century authors. One wonders, in the presence of Carl Albrecht Bernoulli's well-documented claim that "Nietzsche never mastered, even approximately, any modern foreign language" (F.O. and F.N., I, 154). In Basel, Nietzsche had taken French lessons with a student in theology. "It was pretty much a beginners' course; the dictionary was frequently referred to. Nietzsche never succeeded in reading a French text off the page, much less in following one that was read aloud to him. He often asked his friends to translate passages for him that he considered important. Orally, Overbeck . . . occasionally translated French texts for him on the spur of the moment; Mrs. Overbeck, Gersdorff, Mrs. Marie Baumgartner and others did so for him in writing" (ibid.).

What seventeenth and eighteenth-century French authors had Nietzsche actually "read"—either in this manner, or in translation? Racine is mentioned six times *en passant;* twice (W, I, 801, and again W, II, 1045) to illustrate Nietzsche's theory that music often lags behind poetry, and that a century after Racine, Mozart does for music what Racine had done for the drama. A strange compari- son; while it may apply to the melodious quality of Racine's alexandrines, the analogy leaves one perplexed when confronted with the ferocious passions and vacillations of Racine's heroines and heroes (e.g., Phèdre, Pyrrhus). Corneille appears four times in Nietzsche's works, again quite incidentally, as an example of classical excellence, worthy of his aristocratic and refined French audience, and— in the most important passage (which I shall consider in due time)—to elucidate Nietzsche's idea of classical self-sufficiency (W, II, 91). Not once does Nietzsche quote, refer to, or analyze a single Cornelian or Racinian tragedy. Nor does his criticism dwell in any significant way upon other seventeenth-century French dramatists. Wherever French classicists are mentioned, their merits are discussed in general terms to oppose the virtues of good breeding—a passion for lucidity, form, psychology, courtly manners, *esprit*, and moderation—to the blundering barbarity of Germanic "naturalizing" tendencies. For Nietzsche is actually more concerned with the French moralists than with France's playwrights of the seventeenth and eighteenth centuries. In search of a new morality "beyond good and evil," Nietzsche finds in La Rochefoucauld's *Maximes* the potential germ for an aristocratically aesthetic ethos, as he had found it in his youth in Theognis. He had admired and shared Theognis' hortatory contempt for *hoi kakoi*—in a literal and archaic sense "the ugly," and hence "the villains," the "baseborn" (cf. Theognis, *Elegeion* I, ll. 39–52; 847–50; and Nietzsche, W, II, 776). Although thoroughly Christian, La Rochefoucauld furnishes Nietzsche with a modern parallel to Theognis which, if thought through to its logical extreme, would permit the elaboration of an anti-Christian ethos where "good" would equal "beautiful" and "highborn," while "evil" would be the equivalent of "ugly," "brutish," and "baseborn." La Rochefoucauld's *Maximes* could be stretched to encompass Theognis' morality of fate (in which *lineage* is fate), goodness being *areté*, the innate virtue of being wellborn, and evil, the genetic villainy of *kakia*, base birth.[2] Within such a scheme, tragedy could experience a rebirth, mirroring the tragic fate of humanity's highest individuals in a celebration transcending all modern "Naturalism," transfigured into a ritual governed by the strict restraints of the classical genre. An aristocratic ethos would place—as does Racine's poetics —verisimilitude above "truth." It would, to use Nietzsche's terms, set "Schein" above an immoderate concern with "Sein" or (even worse) with "Werden"— the modern German disease of historicism. It could modify, in an aristocratic and Nietzschean way, Hegel's bourgeois dictum "What is, is good" to read "What is, is fated"—pointing back to a classicist sense of magnificence and of *noblesse oblige*, irretrievably lost, it would seem, since the French Revolution. For what is fated must be accepted by the hero, and lovingly so, even if it leads to his destruction.

Originally, Nietzsche's interest in La Rochefoucauld, La Bruyère and Vauvenargues was apparently aroused by a rather pejorative judgment of La

---

[2] In one of Nietzsche's less fortunate aphorisms (W, II, 775 f.), his enthusiasm for Theognis spills over into a racist praise of the blond, Aryan *Herrenrasse*. His attitude is prompted in part by his disappointment with Dr. Paul Rée and Lou von Salomé. However—as we have tried to explain—it is mainly to replace the Judaeo-Christian morality of "good" and "evil" by an esthetic ethos of "good" and "bad" ("wellborn" and "villainous"). A number of Nietzsche's inconsistencies can be traced to his sermonizing on *Herren- und Sklavenmoral*, by far the weakest and most outlived part of his philosophy. His anti-Jewish outbursts stop short of anti-Semitism. Paradoxically, they have much in common with the religious anti-Judaism of evangelical theologians like Erasmus and Luther, although they move diametrically in the opposite sense, i.e., that of paganism. They are directed against Judaeo-Christian ethics as they derive from the New Testament—not against the Jews as an "inferior race." In fact, Nietzsche loves the Old Testament and its vigorous "immoral" Jews. What he rejects is Pauline doctrine. His praise for the "blond barbarians" who "conquered the original population of Northern and Central Europe" does not extend to the "debased" modern Germans and their vulgar chauvinism. The key to Nietzsche's paradoxical views may be found in Hannah Arendt's *The Origins of Totalitarianism* (New York: Harcourt, Brace, 1951), where the author stresses that totalitarianism is by its very nature "anti-nationalist."

Rochefoucauld's *Maximes* in a letter by Rohde, dated 24 November 1868. Ironically, Frau Cosima Wagner (who had once given him Montaigne's *Essais* as a Christmas present) was among those who most enthusiastically stimulated Nietzsche's growing regard for those French authors whom he later used as weapons against Wagner and the Wagnerians. Whatever little Nietzsche may have read in La Rochefoucauld and Pascal, in particular, had left a lasting impact on his thought, and even more so on the formal aspects of his work. For it was, no doubt, the compact form of Pascal's *Pensées*, La Bruyère's *Les Caractères*, La Rochefoucauld's and Vauvenargues' *Réflexions et Maximes*—perhaps more than Lichtenberg and Paul Rée—which determined the mature Nietzsche's choice of the aphorism as his favorite vehicle of expression.

Pascal becomes Nietzsche's prime example of the most terrifying facets of the Christian faith, a faith which "resembles a perpetual suicide of reason" (W, II, 610). Pascal occupies the first place among all Christians owing to a combination of fire, spirit, and integrity (W, I, 1139); he is "the most instructive victim of Christianity" (W, II, 1088), and its "most admirable logician" (W, III, 589). At one point, Nietzsche speaks of him in nearly passionate terms: "Pascal whom I almost love, since he has taught me infinitely much; the only *logical* Christian," he admits in a letter to Georg Brandes, dated Torino, 20 November 1888. Among the moralists of the seventeenth century, Pascal is the one who truly obsessed Nietzsche's mind; his name occurs fifty times in Nietzsche's work (not to mention his correspondence). The name of La Rochefoucauld, whom he prefers to all others, and whom he admires for his passionate refusal to be duped by his own potential rationalizations, for his gentlemanly pessimism and natural nobility, occurs only seventeen times in his writings (although some aphorisms can be traced back to the *Maximes*).[3] His predilection goes next to Fontenelle's incorruptible intellectuality and stylistic urbanity. Vauvenargues' polite stoicism goes somewhat against his grain. La Bruyére's *Les Caractères* repels Nietzsche; as he sees it, it partakes of its author's middle-class baseness. And Rousseau is Nietzsche's prototype for "modern" man—half idealist, half *canaille*.

This bird's eye view may suffice to give an idea of Nietzsche's cursory but surprisingly concise knowledge of seventeenth and eighteenth-century French moralists. It is not that of a scholar, concerned with minute details that might serve as a basis for cautious conclusions. It is, on the contrary, that of a bold thinker who, founding his thought on the most sketchy "readings," sometimes blunders in details but who intuitively reaches remarkably keen and accurate insights of a general nature. For Nietzsche, at heart a somewhat reluctant Platonist, is interested in universal rather than in particular ideas. And from his unscholarly and fragmentary, yet precise knowledge, he abstracts universals which contrast the age of Louis XIV with that of Wilhelm II, classicism (i.e.,

[3] W. D. Williams has done so in his *Nietzsche and the French* (Oxford: Blackwell, 1952).

civilization) with romanticism (barbarity), an era of restraint and self-sufficiency
—ahistorical by definition—with the romantic drive toward boundlessness, the
infinite, and historical histrionics. What exactly are these universals, which, in
turn, will allow us to focus on the Nietzschean concept of tragedy as a genre and
as a cosmic law, governing the stage as a world, and, metaphysically seen, the
world as a stage for the tragic sense of life?

Classicism simplifies, omits detail, assimilates thought, plots, and myths
without concern for "historical accuracy," shows qualities of hardness, coldness,
and the unavoidable logic of fate which is grounded in the irrational. Periods of
classicism represent those very brief moments of perfection and ripeness towards
which human history slowly ascends in its ever repeated cycles of maturation and
decline. In Nietzsche's description, the classicist artist has regained that innocence
and self-sufficiency which is symbolically marked by the last stage in the three
metamorphoses of Zarathustra's first speech (*Von den drei Verwandlungen*). The
classicist author is indeed—like the child in the *Zarathustra* parable—an incarna-
tion of Nietzsche's *Übermensch:*[4] he has successfully overcome the "camel's"
burden of heaviness, slain the dragon "thou shalt" with the "lion's" "I will" and
has reached, beyond that, the "child's" innocence and liberation from the past.
In his creative self-sufficiency, he strangely combines elements of Jacob Burckhardt's man of the Italian Renaissance with those of the playwrights and *moralistes*
of the court of Louis XIV. (1) A classicist author must vanquish his potential
repressions; he must allow all his contradictory talents, emotions, and desires to
participate in his creative efforts, but in such a way that "they all move under one
single yoke"—an image for formal control under the aegis of *les contraintes*, the
restraints imposed upon the artist by the requirements of genre, style, level, taste,
the "Aristotelian" unities, the alexandrine, etc. (2) A classicist author must (and
actually can only) come at the right moment (*a*) to bring about the culmination
of a particular type of literature, art, and politics; and (*b*) to mirror in his work the
totality of a nation, a civilization at a time when this totality is still intact (for
example, in the case of both (*a*) and (*b*), Corneille, Racine, Poussin, La Rochefoucauld). (3) A classicist dramatist must write his plays without self-consciously
attempting to reconstitute with scholarly accuracy the historical scene of the
classical model he imitates. (4) The classical author must bring things to an end
and move beyond them, he must conclude rather than look back. His mind must
move forward rather than "react"—boldly transposing classical situations into
the language and world of his day. (5) The classical author must say "yes," in all

---

[4] The concept of the *Übermensch* offers many disturbing and confusing aspects. The contradictions
involved in this concept seem to resolve themselves, in part at least, if one integrates the *Übermensch*
into Nietzsche's cyclical idea of history (the Eternal Return): he would then mark those cyclical returns
of culminating points in the history of Man which coincide with periods of "classicism" (e.g., Attic
civilization, the age of Augustus, the Italian Renaissance, the seventeenth century in France).

instances; he must say "yes" even when he voices hatred, spite, negation (just as Racine, for example, depicts the passions of Phèdre, Nero, and Roxane, without passing moral judgment on his characters). Finally, (6) "moral perfection," in the Christian sense of the word, stands in absolute contradiction to everything classical (W, III, 516). For Nietzsche, these conditions coincided in the great men of sixth century (B.C.) Greece, as well as in those of the Italian Renaissance and of seventeenth-century France. Classicism is the art of the mask: "Always in disguise," is its formula: "the greater a man's superiority, the greater is his need of the incognito" (W, III, 445). The mask is our best defense against the temptation of naturalism which Lessing and Shakespeare were unable to resist: "The rigorous restraints which the French dramatists accepted regarding the unities of action, place and time, style, versification, and syntax, the choice of words and thoughts was as important a school" [as the fugue for music and Gorgian figures for Greek rhetoric]. There is "no other means to rid ourselves of naturalism"—the lowest and most primitive anti-art form—"Schein," illusion, being the highest and most civilized result of artistic endeavor (W, I, 577 f.). French classical tragedy is the "only modern form of art" which has shown European poets the way out of "naturalizing" crudeness (W, I, 578). Combining the Dionysian violence of passions with the classical restraints of Apollonian form, which the French classical dramatist imposed upon his work, he paralleled what Nietzsche had characterized as the Greek poet's ability "to dance in chains" (W, I, 932). Goethe alone among all German poets had understood the allegorical universality of classical art, and of tragedy in particular: "no new topics and characters but the old, well-known ones in continuously renewed attempts at revival and transformation: that is art such as the mature Goethe *understood* it, such as the Greeks, and also the French, *exercised* it" (W, I, 581). The same aphorism condemns German literature after Lessing, with its struggle for "liberation" from all classical restraints: "Yes, they stripped themselves of the 'irrational' fetters of French and Greek art, but imperceptibly they accustomed themselves to finding irrational all fetters, all restraints—and thus art is moving towards its *self-dissolution*, while, in the process, . . . touching upon all phases of its beginnings [in crude naturalism] . . . : it interprets, in its decline, its origins, its becoming" (W, I, 580). In *Ecce Homo,* "classical" and "German" are polemically contrasted as a contradiction in terms (W, II, 1083). By their very nature, "the French are closer to the Greeks" than the Germans ever were (W, I, 579). Nietzsche, the specialist of Greek prosody, goes so far as to assert that the quantifying principle which governs French syllabic verse far better approximates the Greek hexameter than do the emotionally stressed rhythms of German metrics (W, III, 1227). Here again, the affectively neutral versification of the French, with its relatively equal flow of syllabic verse, stands for a climax of refinement, which is contrasted with the "naturalizing" trends of the German meters' imitation of emotional tensions. Nietzsche's ever-repeated parallel praise of the ancient Greeks and the French of the seventeenth-century, to the detriment of unrestrained German barbarity (e.g., W, II, 725), strangely contradicts Elizabeth Butler's somewhat mechanical thesis, according to which Nietzsche (like other great Germans) was under the spell of "the tyranny of Greece over Germany."

To choose only one among the numerous equations of Greek civilization with that of the age of Louis XIV: "*Comparison* of Greek civilization and the French in Louis XIV's times. Determined belief in oneself. A leisure class who make things difficult for themselves and who are steadily conquering themselves. The power of form, the will to form *oneself*. Eudaemonism as an avowed goal. Much strength and energy *behind* formal essence. The enjoyment of the spectacle of life which is *seemingly* so *easy*. —The French looked upon the Greeks as though the latter were *children*" (W, III, 431).

It would become tedious to repeat Nietzsche's frequent analogies between ancient Greece and the age of Louis XIV, his constant reiterations of the superiority of French seventeenth-century civilization over the barbarian dissolution of formal restraints in German art and literature since Lessing. I shall turn instead to one major argument, Nietzsche's exaltation of myth over history, as a key to an understanding of his insistence (1) on Hellenic and French classical values, and (2) on tragedy—as a genre, as an aristocratic way of life, and as a law governing the universe.

All art is, for Nietzsche, an overcoming of things as they are. It is the will to conquer "becoming," to eternalize (W, III, 896). Since art perfects being by overcoming it, tragedy does not (as Schopenhauer suggests) teach resignation. "The representation of terrifying and problematic things is itself an instinct of power and magnificence in the artist. . . . Art says 'yes,' Job says 'yes' " (W, III, 784). The opposite of classical soundness, of good taste, of aristocratic values resides in a "sense of history": "The sense of history: an ignoble sense" (W, II, 687), is characterized by its "servilely plebeian curiosity" (ibid.). "Our great virtue of having a sense of history" stands in "a necessary opposition to our good taste" (W, II, 688). In a word, the sense of history is a modern disease (W, II, 1113) which is closely linked to the rise of that other modern sickness, Romanticism, which Goethe had already diagnosed ("Classical is what is sound, romantic that which is sick"—"Klassisch ist das Gesunde, romantisch das Kranke," (*Maxime* 863). The very spirit of Romanticism is ghostly and ghoulish, *Totenerweckung*, "ressurrection of the dead" (W, I, 218, 1122). Modern man in his lack of self-sufficiency needs history as a substitute for life; having no predetermined role, no *persona* imposed upon him by a caste, he is a protean *voyeur* and an actor constantly in search of a part to play. He vicariously masquerades in disguises which are furnished him by history, "the storeroom of costumes" (W, II, 686). History with its need to destroy illusions is the very opposite of art, the creator of illusion (W, I, 252): it exorcises all healthy instincts (W, I, 239). While historicism, even in Hegelian dialectics, sees things in the perspective of a linear progression, myth is cyclical, constantly renewing itself, eternal. The whole modern concept of progress is absurd, for "all that is essential in human development took place in primeval times," before the dawn of history (W, I, 448). The historical disease, like Romanticism, is above all a German affliction: "We Germans are Hegelians, even if there had never been a Hegel, since we . . . instinctively attribute a deeper meaning and a richer value to becoming, to evolution, than to that which 'is' " (W, II, 226 f.).

An attitude of this nature was alien to seventeenth- and eighteenth-century France: "Corneille's Frenchmen, and still those of the Revolution, seized upon Roman antiquity in a manner for which we are lacking in courage—thanks to our superior sense of history. And Roman antiquity itself: how violently and, at the same time, how naively did it take possession of everything good and superior in the still more ancient Greek antiquity!" (W, II, 91). Corneille and his contemporaries feel at ease in their century. Instead of empathizing their way into a mentality far removed in time and history, they assimilate ancient Rome and Greece to their own needs. Racine's and Corneille's ancient Romans and Greeks, their Trojans, Huns, biblical Jews, medieval Spaniards, and modern Turks are naturalized subjects of Louis XIV, indistinguishable in manners, speech, and gestures from *la cour et la ville*—and yet, they are more Roman and more Greek, etc., than for example, Wagner's *Meistersänger* are medieval, in spite of the latters' historically more accurate attire. For art is not based on (often far-fetched) "originality," or on the "realism" of portraiture; it is founded upon the verisimilitude of an illusion (*Schein*) which uses typical rather than atypical characters. For the seventeenth-century French, its foremost principles were, and for Nietzsche still are, the conventional ones of "imitation" and "invention"—in the classical sense of these words: the "imitation" of great models taken from antiquity (in myth, tragic plots, and poetics), which demands in turn the strict observance of rules (three unities, alexandrines, five acts), and limits "invention" to the domain of embellishments (rhetorical devices, imagery, *schemata verborum*, etc.). For Nietzsche, convention "is the condition of art, not its hindrance" (W, III, 754), and tragedy, in particular, is predicated upon the most basic of human conventions: upon language, both as verbal expression and gesture. Not in a confused *laisser aller* does the classical dramatist attain his ends but rather by rigidly controlling "invention"—in the traditional sense: the "finding" of, the "coming upon" striking images, rhythms, sound and rhyme patterns within the narrow confines of traditional plots, metric forms, and genres. His freedom resides in *contraintes*, in his ability to "dance in fetters," to vanquish self-made difficulties while covering them up with "the deception of facility" (W, I, 932). In so doing, he conforms in his own way to the same rules of artistic artificiality which govern the acting of the dummy-like hero of Greek tragedy (or the stylized protagonist of French classical drama). All art is serious play and as such is stylization: in the strictest meaning *play-acting*, per-*forming*, representing; in short, *histrionics* or *hypocrisy* (literally, the "playing of a part," Greek *hypocrisis*).

Hypocrisy, mimicry, an unconscious but infinitely artful cunning is the very law by which organic life seduces, for the sake of its own reproduction, the improvement and the evolutionary outstripping of the species. In this sense, the psychology of Nietzsche's Dionysian ideal of the actor—the polar opposite of the nineteenth-century artist who, in his schizophrenia, vicariously acts out his own fantasies in the characters of his novels and plays ("Madame Bovary, c'est moi!") —provides an insight into the physiology of deception, the *sprezzatura*, one might say, by which all organisms seem to plot the triumph of the strongest individuals over the mediocrity of their race.

The paradox of art as a sexual device of Nature, the procreative and fertilizing stimulus provoked by enticing colors, perfumes, sounds, and rhythmic movement as organic functions of plant and animal life demonstrate to what an extent beauty as dissimulation, as play-acting, as hypocrisy, reaches far beyond man and human consciousness: "*Dissimulation* increases, according to the ascending *hierarchy* of living things. . . . It seems to be absent from anorganic Nature: [there] power [is pitched] against power, quite crudely so—*ruse* begins with the world of organic beings; already plants are masters of ruse. . . . Cunning multipled a thousand times belongs to the *essence* of man's rise . . . problem of the actor, my Dionÿsos-ideal . . ." (W, III, 578). One and the same type of energy or "will to power," a physiological and psychological drive for intoxication, blindly animates and metamorphoses all living things. It attains its goals by devious means, by sham and deception: From plant to animal and man, all sexual activity takes place through a triumph of art. Not Nature, but productive and sexual fantasies, set in motion by the illusion of beauty, lead to procreation as well as to the creation of works of art. In man's unique case, "it is one and the same energy that is spent in the conception of art and in the sex act" (W, III, 924). For the very existence of art, "one physiological preliminary is indispensable: *intoxication*," and "above all the intoxication of sexual excitement, great cupidity, strong emotions." Idealization is no more than "a rape of things, a manner of forcing the dominant features into the open by way of that intoxication which is a feeling of increased energy and exuberance" (W, II, 995). The artist's creative instinct is closely related to "the distribution of *semen* in his blood" (W, III, 870). An inquiry into his psychology would involve a critique of his play instinct as "a pouring our of energy, the enjoyment of change" and of willful transformation, a curious pleasure taken in "impressing one's own soul upon foreign matter," the artist's boundless selfishness, the kind of "instincts he sublimates" (W, III, 867). Intoxication as a phallic experience constitutes the heightened feeling of power which brings about artistic creation. It is that inner need which drives the artist, "to make of things reflexes of his own perfection" (W, II, 995).

Against the esthetics of "disinterested contemplation, by means of which the emasculation of art tries today . . . to give itself a clean conscience" (W, II, 598), against Kant's and Schopenhauer's assertion that the contemplation of art neutralizes sexual desires, Nietzsche suggests that Stendhal comes closer to the truth with his contention that art is "a promise of happiness." All theorists of art, from Aristotle to Schopenhauer, have failed to see the essential aspects of the esthetic experience because, rather than envisaging art from the creative artist's viewpoint, they have always looked at it from the spectator's perspective. Nietzsche, turning to the psychology of the artist, points bluntly to the myth of Pygmalion (W, II, 845 ff.) as a key to the understanding of the motives behind artistic creation. Far from being disinterested, the creative instinct takes its impetus from a heightening of sensual appetites and a state of intoxication. With "the divine Plato," Nietzsche holds that "all beauty excites the procreative powers: this precisely is its property, from the most sensual to the most intellectual and spiritual" things on the ladder of being (W, II, 1003). The desire for art and beauty "is an indirect longing for sexual thrills which the procreative instinct communicates to the *cerebrum*" (W, III, 870). Just as situations which are transfigured and enhanced by our sexual and emotional fantasies will reflect our own vitality, so, inversely, if we come into contact with objects which rank high on our personal scale of sensual values and which, accordingly, show "this sort of transfiguration and enhancement, then our animal existence responds with an excitement of those spheres where such states of pleasure are imbedded—and a mixture of these very delicate dispositions for animal enjoyments and desires is the *esthetic condition*" (W, III, 535; cf. II, 995; III, 755). It can only be found in persons who are endowed with an excess of "procreative vigor" in which "always inheres the *primum mobile*" (ibid.). In short, as Freud himself acknowledges, the Freudian concept of "sublimation" preexists in Nietzsche's psychology of the esthetic experience, and so does the word itself. It originates in *Human, All-Too-Human* (1879), with Nietzsche's realization that "there is no unselfish action, nor is there such a thing as disinterested contemplation: both are but sublimations . . ." (W, I, 447). The creative act overpowers the artist, turning him into its mere tool: The *paternal patterning* "Apollonian" and the *maternal, matter*-providing "Dionysian" (cf. Aristotle, *On the Generation of Animals*) take possession and dispose of him with the violence of natural *forces majeures*, "whether he is willing or not: compelling him, on one hand, to become a visionary, on the other, to orgy. Both conditions are present in normal life too, only more weakly, as dream and intoxication" (W, III, 788). These latter, too, "unleash in us artistic powers which are at variance: dream releasing the power to see, to connect things in logical sequence, to create poetry; intoxication endowing us with the gift of mimicry, passion, song, dance" (ibid.). Rimbaud in 1871, and Nietzsche in 1872, independent of each other, enunciate the same truth about the lyrical poet as a quasi-passive instrument, a voice and mime ("*Je* est un autre") in the hands, as it were, of a creative power that works through him (Rimbaud to P. Demeny, 15 May 1871; and *The Birth of Tragedy*, W, I, 38; I, 40).

"All perfect doing, to be exact, takes place unconsciously and is not willed" (W, III, 746). For Nietzsche, the will to power is "not a being, not a becoming, but a *pathos*—the most elemental fact to begin with, from which as a consequence 'becoming' and 'producing' result" (W, III, 778). Since *pathos*, *passion*, implies passivity, a suffering, in a way a *maternal* state, the difference between "committing" one's actions and "enduring" them as they arise spontaneously from the blind "will to power" is, to say the least, negligible. In Nietzsche's world, where consciousness falsifies all values by rationalizing them, and where the individual never senses the true role he plays within the overall plans of the species, one does not "do": one is "*being done*, at every instant! Mankind has at all times confused the active and the passive: that happens to be its eternal grammatical blunder" (W, I, 1096). Wherever our ignorance begins and our vision is blocked, we "place a word, e.g., the word 'I,' the word 'do,' the word 'suffer': those, perhaps, are the horizons of our knowledge, but they are no 'truths'" (W, III, 863). In the very separation of the concept of "action" from that of "suffering," Nietzsche sees a misunderstanding which is rooted in language itself, and hence in consciousness: language and thought, in their stumbling manner, can only proceed by way of "distinctions," and only distinguish or categorize by positing "pairs of opposites" where, in truth, seeming opposites occur organically intermingled as a complex and, as it were, hermaphroditic unity. "Acting" and "suffering" are simultaneously present in artistic creation, in the Apollonian-Dionysian polarity and duplicity of *poiein*—for Nietzsche (the classical philologist) not merely a "making," but as in Hesiod a "bringing into existence" (*Works and Days* 110; *Theogony* 161, 579 etc.), in Andocides a "begetting" (1.124; 4.22), and in Plato literally a "conceiving" of children (*Symposium* 203b). Artistic creation wholly depends on a sexual stimulation which, in the final analysis, is identified by Nietzsche as an excess of procreative strength, an overflowing and sublimation of the will to power: "Without a certain overheating of the sexual system, a Raffael is unthinkable," and "music making, too, is a way of making children" (W, III, 756).

Nietzsche's erotic concept of poetry (in the broadest sense, as a "making of works") affords remarkable insights into the psychology and physiology of the artist as "the maternal type of man" (W, II, 251), who is "constantly pregnant" (W, II, 243), and far beyond that, on the cosmic level, into the self-creating nature of "the universe as a work of art giving birth to itself" (W, III, 495). The problem which, from the outset, intrigues Nietzsche, in retrospect is formulated by him in these terms: "How far does art reach into the innermost recesses of the world? And do there exist, apart from the 'artist,' other artistic powers?" To the second question, he unhesitatingly answers "yes." As to the first, he elaborates: "The world is nothing else but art!" And once more he passionately affirms the superiority of art over philosophy: "There is something contrary to nature in *wisdom* that is revealed by its hostility to art: to ask for *knowledge* where *illusion* alone gives

deliverance, salvation—this indeed is perversion, the instinct for nothingness!"
(MusA, XIV, 324): words which echo the major thesis of *The Birth of Tragedy* and
"The Pathos of Truth," one of five prefaces for unwritten books presented in
1872 as Christmas gifts to Cosima Wagner: "Art is mightier than cognition for
it *wills* life, and cognition attains as its ultimate goal—destruction" (W, III, 271).

Aisthesis, sense perception, establishes the link between art and science; it
facilitates the understanding of the artful workings of the organic and the anorganic world. Like artistic production and receptivity for art, all worthwhile
knowledge is fully dependent on the subtlety, vigor, and alertness of the senses:
"Today our science reaches exactly as far as our determination to accept the
testimony of our senses" (W, II, 958). To be meaningful at all, the "realm of
concepts" cannot be absolutely severed from "the world of the senses"; nor can
the identity of "being" and "thinking" be abolished (W, III, 394). In the final
analysis, all true cognition—in its anthropomorphic relativity—amounts to no
more (and no less) than an *esthetic* experience: it cannot transcend the organic
prison walls of the human senses. To the mind of the ancients, the esthetic
experience rated above all other forms of knowledge. The sense of taste in
particular, as the most subtle tool of *touch* and *testing*, for them was so closely
related to the idea of "wisdom" that "the Greek word which designates the *sage*
etymologically belongs to *sapio* I taste, *sapiens* the one who is tasting, *sisyphos*
the man with the keenest taste; an acute feeling out through tasting, a significant
aptitude for *distinguo* by the palate: this was the specific art of the philosopher,
such as popular consciousness saw it" (W, III, 363 f.). Where taste, sensuality,
wisdom, and knowledge are said to be interrelated, esthetics has clearly conquered
the epistemological scene, and the object of its inquiry, no matter *what* the
domain, will be art, that very force which, for Nietzsche, in all organisms
stimulates life and excites its reproduction: "Art and nothing else but art: Art is
that great power which alone makes life possible, the great seducer of life, the
great stimulus for life" (W, III, 692). Wherever art, i.e., the will to power, commands, it works through "agents" that only "act out" whatever *it* wills while
they are under the impression that they are acting of their own accord, at their
own discretion. Psychologically seen, "the concept of 'cause' is the sensation of
power we experience in the exercise of our so-called [free] 'will';—our notion
'effect,' the superstition that this *feeling* of power is the power itself which
moves . . ." (W, III, 775). When, as in Nietzsche's thought, the entire universe
determines like an organism the functions of even the smallest of its parts by the
animating and destructive force of a blind will to power, haphazardly, and
without the benefit of a guiding Hegelian *Weltgeist* (that obligingly would
become conscious of itself in the cataclysms of "world"—i.e., "human"—
history) then there can be no such things as "moral" or "immoral" acts; then
"free" and "spontaneous intentions" and the concept of "action" itself must needs
be relegated to the world of imagination and fiction (W, III, 612). In such a

scheme, nothing would remain of the mystery of the universe but the dual and pulsating lust and rhythm of a permanent self-creation and self-destruction in great things and small, a constant metamorphosis of the "actor," the mask, while the play and the role would essentially stay the same in the eternal return of the life cycle. On the largest scale, the universe itself would perform in eternal repetitions (and rehearsals) the parts of Nietzsche's Dionysian actor: "Dionysian universe of eternal self-creation, eternal self-destruction . . . this world is the will to power and nothing else! And you are yourselves that will to power—and nothing else!" (W, III, 917).

Life, in all its manifestations, would then be *one* infinite and eternal *pathos*—a suffering, a fate, a *moira*—personifying itself in countless "actors" on all ranks of its hierarchy. The theater, as a dark mirror to life, would then show the tragic hero as a *sufferer* at the hands of a power that wills and acts through him, and over which he exercises practically no control whatsoever. A determinist view of this magnitude, organic rather than mechanistic, would also lead to an idea of the "drama" and to a "poetics" in some ways different from Aristotle's. It is then not surprising that Nietzsche should deplore what he considers to be one among a number of errors in Aristotle's rather insensitive interpretation of the nature of "drama" in general, and of the tragic hero in particular. A casual footnote in *The Case of Wagner* (W, II, 921), in fact, calls into question the Aristotelian views of tragedy, pointing out that the Doric word *drama* by no means designated "action"; instead, it meant a hieratic *event*, a sacred "story"; the oldest drama enacted the holy legend on which the local religious cult was founded. Substance is lent to Nietzsche's hypothesis by more recent commentaries on the extended Attic form of "drama," *dramosyne*, "sacred service,"[5] "ceremony" (*Inscriptiones Graecae* II² 1358, ii, 34, 40: 4th century B.C.). Aristotle himself explains that Doric *dran*, the root of "drama," meant the same as Attic *prattein* (i.e., "to go through," only later "to achieve," "to accomplish," "to effect," etc.; *Poetics* 3.6). Nietzsche suggests that by mistranslating *dran* as a *doing*, the German classical philologists—who, ever since Wilamowitz-Möllendorff's violent attacks on *The Birth of Tragedy* (*Zukunftsphilologie!*) have observed a hostile silence—are guilty of spreading misconceptions on the character of tragedy. What Nietzsche seems to imply is that *dran* and *prattein* alike express a "bringing about," an "effecting" which is its own end and has no moral connotations. It turns the subject through whom it works into a *sufferer*, not into a "free" agent. Instead of *spontaneously acting*, the tragic hero in the end recognizes that he is and has been no more than a plaything in the hands of a *fate* to which he consents (*amor fati*), and which coincides with those uncontrollable forces that through his immolation, his consciously accepted sacrifice, fulfill themselves. Here again, Nietzsche's contention seems to be borne out by the derivatives of *prattein: praxis*, the mythological

---

[5] Cf. Hjalmar Frisk, *Griechisches Etymologisches Wörterbuch* (Heidelberg: Carl Winter, 1954), I, 416.

event (and *not action*) which according to Aristotle (*Poetics* 6.8), rather than the hero's character, is to be acted out through the hero's *persona; pragma* (pl. *pragmata*) —misleadingly translated as *actus*, "act(s)"—in the language of the theater: the principal divisions of the play (in Latin, originally, the role of the actor), means primarily "events," "circumstances," i.e., *happenings* rather than actions (cf. Herodotos 1.207; Thucydides 1.89; 3.82); while in Euripides' *Helena* (286), *pragmasin* "by circumstances" is expressly contrasted with *ergoisi* "by acts."

Whatever the merits of Nietzsche's reinterpretation of the concept of "drama," he makes short shrift of the meaning which, since the Renaissance, classical scholars have read into the Aristotelian idea of *mimesis* as the purported "imitation of an action," for he sees in it the representation of *suffering, passion, pathos* (pl. *pathê*), which befall the hero by a fatality that he cannot escape, and against his *conscious* will. Thus Nietzsche resolves in an ironic and tragic *coincidentia oppositorum* the age-honored antinomies of *praxis* "action," *pathos* "incident," "accident," "chance," and *pathé* "suffering," "misfortune." He can conclude: "Tragedy had in mind great *pathos scenes*—action, as it were, was precluded from it ([in time] situated *before* the beginning and [in space] *behind* the scene") (W, II, 921)—words which could stand as a gloss to Boileau's: "Ce qu'on ne doit point voir, qu'un récit nous l'expose" (*Art poétique* 3, 51)—but which ultimately touch upon what Nietzsche considers as the essence of tragedy: those poignant *pathos scenes* (Aristotle, *Poetics* 14, 9) where the tragic hero, suffering from an excess of tensions which explode into "action," moves toward his doom without conciously becoming a "culprit," a "sinner."

This idea, a major theme, a *leitmotif*, the esthetic foundation underlying Nietzsche's entire work, is expressed as early as 1864 in the student essay *Primum Oedipodis regis carmen choricum:* "The Greeks thought differently from us about the tragic effect; it was brought about by way of the great *pathos scenes . . .* where action meant little but lyricism everything . . ." (HKG, II, 375). With the exception of the seventeenth-century French, no modern playwright has understood what Nietzsche elsewhere (and without reference to the French) calls "the awesome Gorgon-head beauty of the classical" (W, III, 159), which destroys the tragic hero without "adequately" relating his misfortune to any "guilt"—for there is such a thing as "pure, innocent misfortune" (W, I, 1065).

Christianity, in particular in its Northern manifestations, where it has lost contact with its Mediterranean origins, has falsified all psychological values: it has abolished the innocence of suffering by causally linking it with the concepts of "sin," "justice," "punishment"; it has branded as "sinful," "suspect," and "seductive" all great emotions of overflowing lust and strength, such as haughtiness, pride, voluptuousness, triumph, self-assurance, temerity, self-love; it has sanctified meekness and made it desirable; it has distorted the meaning of love by interpreting it as altruism and, in doing so, demanded unselfishness, the forsaking of the "self," the "ego," its *alteration* (the true significance of "altruism"); it has made a punishment of life itself, a temptation of fortune; it has condemned the passions as diabolical, man's trust in himself as godlessness. Christian psychology, as Nietzsche sees it, is a psychology of inhibition, a walling-in against life—out of fear of life's tragic sense (W, III, 519 f.). "The doctrine of [the free] will was, on the whole, invented for the purpose of punishment" (W, II, 976; III, 822). Against the Christian exorcism of human passions by the frail dogma of the "free will," Nietzsche's depth psychology affords abysmal insights into the blind "will to power" which is impersonal and disposes of the individual, allowing—if one accepts these premises—equally terrifying apprehensions about the obscure forces which drive certain Cornelian and Racinian heroes to their orgies of destruction and self-immolation. For Nietzsche asks questions such as: "whether all conscious willing, all conscious aims, all valuations are not mere means by which something essentially different must be effected than what might appear within consciousness" (W, III, 901). Man is at the same time much more and much less than an individual; it is impossible for him "*not* to be possessed by the qualities and preferences of his parents and ancestors. . . . Provided that something is known about the parents, a conclusion is permissible as to the child" (W, II, 738). No traits of character, however small, are insignificant. Nor do they occur as a matter of chance. Everything in a "personality" obeys the iron law of an ineluctable determinism which organically extends into the past and into the future of mankind. "On the whole, everything is *worth exactly as much as one has paid for it*. . . . 'Heredity' is an erroneous notion. For what someone is, his ancestors have paid the price" (W, III, 552). If one applies Nietzsche's views to French classical tragedy, even such monsters of "will power" as Corneille's Horace, Polyeucte, Auguste, and Attila appear to be guided by an instinctive "will to power" prepared by the preceding generations: their generosity, their sense of honor, their *terribilitas*, their religious or political fervor then seem no longer matters of choice but predestined, the unique and only form which their inescapable fate can take. They represent rare culminating points where mankind, after decades or centuries of blind elaboration, produces its healthiest and strongest exemplars in whom it attains perfection: the end toward which in ever returning cycles the human race moves in its tireless and unconscious efforts to overcome itself. And yet, they are nothing more than incarnations of Nietzsche's Dionysian actor who consents to a tragic fate over which he has no control and which is acting through his mask, his *persona*, his person.

There is no escape for the individual from the fatal chain of mankind; "every human being is himself a piece of fate" (W, I, 905). Inexorably, Nietzsche demonstrates the utter vanity of everyone else's and his own attempts to break through the prison walls of fate and to seek his personal salvation: "You are yourself that invincible *moira;* in you the entire future of the human world is predestined; little does it avail you if you shrink from yourself in horror" (ibid.). From the lowest cell to the universe itself, all existence *suffers* the will to power, in the final analysis, a permanence of tensions and of constant changes. On the cosmic scale: "The world subsists, without becoming, without perishing. Or rather: it is becoming, it is perishing, but without ever having begun to become or ended perishing—it *persists* in both conditions.... It feeds on itself: its excrements are its nourishment" (W, III, 703). On the human scale: the same cycle; in the strongest exemplars, in the type of the tragic hero, a frail balance: a tension of power quanta, each striving for greater intensity, for usurpation; all competing with each other, and producing in the subject a rapid change, a pendulum movement of violent passions, an imperious desire for the total possession or (if this should prove impossible) for the total destruction of the coveted object; in other terms, an insatiable appetite for an absolute ascendency which, feeding on itself, corresponds to a maximum of pleasure or a maximum of repugnance, but which is *not* identical to a platitudinous, plebeian, Darwinian "instinct of self-preservation," nor to a sense of "order" or to a devotion to "lawfulness."

Racine's Pyrrhus, Hermione, Néron, Agrippine, Roxane, Athalie (among others) do not pursue "happiness" but absolute power over the objects of their persecution, in a spirit of total and passionate commitment, at the risk of their own immolation, and as prisoners tied to the pendulum swing of their alternating emotions. In so doing, they blindly obey their chameleon-like instincts, "they change, but they do not *evolve*," to use Nietzsche's terms which, however, do not specifically refer to Racine's characters (W, III, 725). "Every instinct is a type of despotism" and establishes its "own perspective" (W, III, 903; cf. II, 571), and since "all instincts are unintelligent," no instinct proceeds from a utilitarian viewpoint (W, III, 909). The life of the instincts is explained by Nietzsche as "a structure and a branching out" of that basic and thoroughly subconscious form of will, the will to power, whose commands are promptly rationalized by consciousness: "To the strongest of our instincts, to the tyrant in us, submits not only our reasoning but also our conscience" (W, II, 638).

When all is said, the conscious exercise of our will amounts to a delusion, a rationalization of dark instinctive forces which dispose of us on all levels of our being. Whatever we may take for our "activity" is at heart only something that comes to *pass* by way of our existence, and that we are fated to do. It is no more than a *passing*, a *passion* that we undergo; both literally, a *happening*, and etymologically (German: *Geschehen* "event," *Geschick* "fate," *Geschichte* "history"—all stemming from the same root), an *event* that by *fate* and *historically* is bound to come into being through and by our existence: paradoxically, an "act" of ours that we must *suffer* to be performed by us.

Man is *what* he is by a higher and innate necessity, and to speak of him "as he *ought* to be is as absurd as: a tree as it ought to be" (W, III, 671). In this sense, every human being is a unique and prodigious phenomenon (W, I, 287); and yet, he but exists as a necessary link in a sequence, "concretized out of the elements and influences of things past and present. . . . He cannot be held responsible:

neither for *what* he is, nor for his motives, nor for his actions, nor for their effects"
(W, I, 479 f.). The entire history of the human emotions amounts to "the history
of an error, the error of responsibility which rests upon the error of the freedom
of the will" (ibid.). Nietzsche never tires of repeating that man is totally without
responsibility for his actions and innocent of their consequences (W, I, 513; I, 544;
I, 709; I, 908; I, 912 f.; etc.). The doctrine of responsibility is founded on the
naive assumption that "only the will can be causal, and that a person must know
that he actually willed in order to be entitled to believe in *himself* as a cause"
(W, III, 745). We are as little responsible for the things we do while we are awake
as we are for our dreams (W, I, 1098 f.). If for Friedrich Schlegel "the historian is
a prophet turned backwards" (*Athenäums-Fragmente*), for Nietzsche (as for the
ancients), the past is like the voice of the Pythia, darkly but infallibly foreboding
the future: "The judgment of the past is always an oracular response" (W, I, 251).

In this manner, the fatality incarnate in Racine's Phèdre, as well as her
guiltlessness for the persecution she suffers at the hands of Aphrodite (Vénus), are
forecast and, as it were, subsumed, right from the very first scene of the play, in
Hippolyte's portentous line: "La fille de Minos et de Pasiphaé" (*Phèdre* I.i.36).
Similarly, in *La Thébaïde*, the recurrent words *sang* and *nature* (*naissance, famille,
race*) and *dénaturé* foreshadow the inescapable doom of the unfortunate children
of Oedipus who bear as little responsibility for their existence as does their father
for his incestuous marriage with Jocasta or for the death of Laius. "No one is
responsible for his deeds, no one for his nature" (W, I, 481). In speaking of
morality where all is a matter of predestination, one would risk making a mockery
of the very spirit of tragedy, which Nietzsche defines in these terms: "To understand the world from the viewpoint of *suffering:* that is the tragic essence of
tragedy" ("das ist das Tragische in der Tragödie"; W, III, 338). Would not
"moral" actions depend on the triumph of *reason* over excessive passions and
desires? Yet, any attempt to distinguish between "reason" and "passion" would
amount to a misconstruction of both: for reason is no more than "a relationship
between different passions and desires" (W, III, 648).

All intentions, all actions, as it were, are amoral, since all reasoning about
underlying motives and emotions—as we have seen—turns out to be a fabric of
rationalizations. In fact, "the healthier, the stronger, . . . the more enterprising a
man feels, the greater his amorality" (W, III, 919); any rise in vitality inevitably
brings with it "an increase in amorality" (W, III, 583). In what precisely consists
the preeminence of any great civilization, e.g., the Renaissance in Italy, over a
barbarian state of affairs? "Always in *one* thing: the great quantum of *frankly
admitted* amorality" (W, III, 572). The higher species of man differs from all lower
ones not for reasons of greater *moral* distinction but because of a more refined
esthetic organization which lies beyond "good" and "evil," enabling the higher
men to "see and hear infinitely more and to think while they are seeing and
hearing" (W, II, 176). For Nietzsche as for Baudelaire (whom he depreciates),

esthetics and bourgeois morality are diametrically opposed, ideal beauty and greatness incompatible with the meekness of a "virtue" which allows the secret showings of criminal fantasies in the theater of the mind but with feigned indignation shrinks from the admission of criminal fantasies, out of hypocrisy, cowardice, and the fear of being caught. "All great men were criminals, not in a miserable sense. . . . Crime and greatness belong together," proclaims Nietzsche (W, III, 521 f.)—always speaking from the viewpoint of esthetics and tragic knowledge, and somewhere in the neighborhood of Baudelaire's ideal beauty ("Ce qu'il faut à ce coeur profond comme un abîme/ C'est vous, Lady Macbeth, âme puissante au crime," etc.).

Seen in the perspective of life and its stimulation, the ascetic values of "virtue" *diminish* man: "One is a thoroughly small type of man if one is only virtuous" (W, III, 603); "a virtuous man: a lower species" (W, III, 604)—in fact, a living lie, a denial of human reality. Modern man in his worm-like, purely economic and social existence is striving for an even smaller meaning of life, for smaller risks, lesser dangers, perfect security. "Has not the self-diminution of man made irresistible strides since Copernicus?" (W, II, 893). In order to enjoy "security," men have declared their equality (W, I, 892). Greatness in man results from the free reins he gives to his senses, the free play of his appetites, and from "the still greater power that knows how to employ in its service these monsters" (W, III, 528): the amoral, ancestral, and tragic will to power—for "the only power which exists is equal in kind to [this] will" (W, III, 473). All great works and deeds which were not swept away by the ages—were they not, asks Nietzsche, "in the deepest sense, *amoralities?*" (W, III, 920). Morality itself, when seen from the only valid perspective, from the viewpoint of the tragic heightening of *life*, is not truly a "moral" force but merely one tool among many used in the economy of vitality: in the service of life itself, the apparent opposites of "good" and "evil" do not appear as absolutes, they merely "express *power-degrees of the instincts*, a temporary hierarchy by means of which certain instincts are kept under control" (W, III, 615).

The heroes and heroines of Greek and Racinian tragedy, driven by hybris and violent passions to their own immolation, live in a state of tension, pathos, insecurity. They approach with every step they take their imminent fall. Idealizations of the *great criminal* in his utter isolation, they are examples of a hard, cold, and tragic greatness which, for sentimental nineteenth-century man in his quest for material comfort and security, had lost its meaning. For the Greeks, even "theft, as in Prometheus' case, even the massacre of cattle as the expression of a mad envy, as in Ajax' case" could have dignity: "In their need to ascribe dignity to crime . . . they invented tragedy" (W, II, 132). The ethical background of tragedy is seen, in *The Birth of Tragedy*, in the "*justification* of human evil" (W, I, 59). In this sense, the pathos of tragedy is the life-asserting pathos *par excellence* (W, II, 1129), the very opposite of the will- and life-denying pessimism of

Schopenhauer: it accepts and gives meaning to the dual necessity of becoming and of annihilation. "The depth of the tragic artist consists in the ability of his esthetic instinct to see at a glance the farthest consequences, and not myopically to stop at the nearest point: he is capable of accepting the *economy* of the whole *on the largest scale*, which justifies, and not merely justifies, *the fearful nature of evil and all that is questionable*" (W, III, 575).

Life is illogical, hence unjust (W, I, 471; cf. I, 443; I, 229). To Aristotle's *catharsis*, Nietzsche opposes the esthetic enhancement of life by an art form which cannot be explained in moral terms (W, I, 131). The purpose of tragedy is *not* to move the spectator to fear and pity; it is to awaken in him the "poetic state"—a thought which is echoed by Valéry (*Variété* V, 138). To see in tragedy a *purgative* which releases a state of depression is to misunderstand its *tonic* effect, the stimulus it provides for life: the festive spectacle of human suffering "ignites pleasure (i.e., the awareness of strength)" (W, III, 753; III, 828 f.; cf. I, 571; etc.).

Nietzsche's Dionysian concept of tragedy as a tonic to life, an intoxication for the senses, in the final analysis is not so far removed from (and considerably more palatable than) that of Tertullian and Thomas Aquinas—who advise the believer to abstain from the sin of visiting theaters on earth, all the more to enjoy in after-life the edifying and eternal spectacle of the damned roasting in hell (W, II, 794). Nietzsche's theories on the guiltless and fated misfortune of the sacrificial tragic hero, in the end, replace all Leibnitzian and post-Leibnitzian *Théodicées* by a *Tyrannodicée* which amounts to an esthetic justification of human evil and injustice.

Finally, Nietzsche's perennial exaltation of life over intelligence, his distrust of reason and "virtuous" intentions seems to present an unexpected twist by which his abandoned Lutheran faith takes its revenge for its long inhibition. It turns out to be a variation on a traditional Augustinian theme: the corruption of man's original state of nobility by the knowledge of "good" and "evil." By leaving the noumenal for the phenomenal, ethics and consciousness for esthetics and aisthesis, intellectual knowledge for the intuition of the instincts, in short by substituting what N. O. Brown, modifying the meaning of a well-known Freudian term, has so aptly named "polymorphous perversity" for an illusory morality, Nietzsche's road to the recovery of a tragic and Dionysian innocence—as in all apocalyptic schemes of the nineteenth century—leads for modern man "down and out," through nihilism.

VII

Nietzsche in His Relation to Voltaire and Rousseau *

I. HOMMAGE À VOLTAIRE

What does Voltaire mean to Nietzsche? The first edition of the first volume of *Human, All-Too-Human*, published in 1878, was dedicated to the memory of Voltaire in honor of the hundredth anniversary of his death. And to this solemn dedication the author added, with some pathos, that "this monological book" would not have been given to the public at this time if the proximity to 30 May 1878 had not given rise to the all but irrepressible wish to render personal homage at the proper moment "to one of the greatest liberators of the human spirit."[1] Moreover, Nietzsche had planned originally to include an epilogue which would have repeated his intention to set up an "electric current" leading across a century

---

* The following essay is a revised and modified English version of pp. 277–99 in *Von den ersten und letzten Dingen: Studien und Kommentar zu einer Aphorismenreihe von Friedrich Nietzsche* (Berlin: Walter de Gruyter, 1972) reproduced by permission of the publisher. I do not pretend to exhaust the subject of Nietzsche and Voltaire, let alone the topic of Nietzsche's more problematic relationship to Rousseau, which leads directly into his perennial debate with Romanticism (see ibid., 299 ff.). The scope of the present essay thus excludes some major aspects of Nietzsche's struggle with *Rousseauism*. (Nor have I sought to determine whether or to what extent Nietzsche deals at all with Rousseau's texts rather than with an image of Rousseau.) For some further suggestions, see W. D. Williams, *Nietzsche and the French* (Oxford: Blackwell, 1952), a book with which I found myself in agreement in many respects after having arrived at my own conceptions quite independently. A rather biased dissertation on *Nietzsche und Rousseau* by Herbert Gerhard Kramer (University of Erlangen [Borna-Leipzig: Noske, 1928]) became available to me only after completion of this essay. Further references: see index to *Von den ersten und letzten Dingen* under "Voltaire" and "Rousseau.

[1] WKG, IV-2, unnumbered title page. (For key to abbreviations see p. xvii above.) For English versions of Nietzsche's texts I am greatly indebted to Walter Kaufmann's translations: *The Birth of Tragedy* and *The Case of Wagner* (New York, 1967); *On the Genealogy of Morals; Ecce Homo* (New York, 1969); *Beyond Good and Evil* (New York, 1966); *The Will to Power* (together with R. J. Hollingdale; New York, 1967) all published by Random House (Vintage); and *The Portable Nietzsche* (New York: Viking, 1958) as well as to the—far less reliable—translations of *Human, All-Too-Human*, I (Helen Zimmern); *Human, All-Too-Human*, II (Paul V. Cohn); *The Dawn of Day* (J. M. Kennedy); and *The Joyful Wisdom* [i.e., *Gay Science*] (Thomas Common); contained in *The Complete Works of Friedrich Nietzsche*, ed. Oscar Levy (New York: Russell and Russell, 1964). However, I have felt free to adapt and to modify existing translations in keeping with my own interpretation of the original texts.

from a deathbed to the birthplace of new freedoms of the spirit (WKG, IV-2, 576). Similarly, the continuation of *Human, All-Too-Human*, the *Mixed Opinions and Maxims*, were meant to conclude with another homage to Voltaire in order to pay him his "last honors" (WKG, IV-4, 301).

All of this suggests Nietzsche's worship of Voltaire, a sense of affinity, and an ambition to be Voltaire's heir, to succeed Voltaire, and to replace him. The retrospective of *Ecce Homo* summarizes characteristic features of this relationship:

> One will find the book [that is: *Human, All-Too-Human*] clever, cool, possibly toughminded and mocking. A certain intellectual temperament in keeping with *nobility* of taste seems to assert its predominance in a constant struggle against a more passionate subterranean current. In this connection it makes sense that it was actually the celebration of the centennial of Voltaire's death which the book pleaded, as it were, as its excuse for coming out as early as the year 1878. For in contrast to all who wrote after him, Voltaire was, above all, a *grandseigneur* of the spirit—precisely what I am. The name of Voltaire on one of my writings—that was truly progress—a progress on the way *toward myself*. (K, 77, 359)

However, this is what Nietzsche's former friends denied from the start, and their denial was endorsed by most of the German disciples of Nietzsche and by the bulk of German Nietzsche scholars. Perhaps Cosima Wagner made the beginning. She herself was of French descent. She contributed to Nietzsche's closer acquaintance with French literature.[2] Long after the break with Wagner, Nietzsche continued to admire her as the foremost judge ("[die] erste Stimme") in questions of taste (K, 77, 322), much as he admired her high degree of culture. Extremely irritated by *Human, All-Too-Human*, Cosima Wagner suggested to Nietzsche's sister, in an epistle attacking the author, that Nietzsche was basically ignorant in matters concerning French literature and that he scarcely knew even Voltaire (WKG, IV-4, 63). The sister—Elisabeth Förster-Nietzsche, the chauvinistically teutonic *llama*, destined to become the editor of Nietzsche's works and the chief of the Nietzsche archive—reassured the Germans concerning *Human, All-Too-Human*: "the content . . . , the ideas developed in the book have nothing in common with Voltaire" (GB, III, 584). This assertion fitted in with the standard ideology of the Germanists who ignored Lessing's acknowledgments of Voltaire's merits as a writer, but endorsed Lessing's excessive attack on French Neoclassicism as well as his specific aversion to the character of Voltaire, and combined these prejudices with a worshipful respect for the *true* (Weimar) classicism, and with a Romantic and nationalistic hostility toward the French Enlightenment. The result was a proud and carefully cultivated ignorance maintained, so to speak, on principle—not merely with respect to Voltaire—and a strong conviction that what should not be, cannot be. This attitude might well account for the fact that even Bertram, the author of a sensitive and distinguished

2 See Williams, p. 8.

study on Nietzsche, felt constrained to explain away Nietzsche's positive relation to Voltaire.[3]

And yet this kind of polemic against a *Germanistic* misinterpretation is too pat and constitutes, in turn, a simplification of a more complex reality. To be sure, Bäumler, a considerable Nietzsche scholar—and at the same time the proclaimer of a Nietzsche for National Socialists—expressed his own tendency and bias when he asserted that Nietzsche's attacks on German culture were merely *tendentious* ("sind *Tendenz*") much as the entire book (*Human, All-Too-Human*) served the expression of a tendentious bias (K 72, II, 339). Nonetheless, the name of Voltaire might be merely something like an advertisement for Nietzsche's own brand of Enlightenment, and indeed for an enlightenment characterized by tendencies contrary to those of the older Enlightenment of the eighteenth century. For even in *Human, All-Too-Human,* where Nietzsche declares that we must carry forward the flag of the Enlightenment bearing the names of Petrarch, Erasmus and Voltaire (WKG, IV-2, 43), we may suspect that the antagonists of the Enlightenment who seem to come to Nietzsche's mind in this historical context, notably Luther and Rousseau, have greater relevance for him than his presumable allies.

However, let us first confirm our impression of a positive relationship. Nietzsche's letters testify to the fact that he esteemed Voltaire in the phase of *Human, All-Too-Human.* On the occasion of his visit to Geneva in April 1876, he tells his friends that he offered "echte Huldigungen" to Voltaire, the first object of his worship, whose house in Ferney he visited (WKG, IV-4, 20 f.). In the following winter, which he spent in Sorrento, he reports with reference to the circle gathered there around Malwida von Meysenbug: "We have read a great deal of Voltaire."[4] Moreover, there is other evidence, both from an earlier and a later period.

---

[3] See Ernst Bertram, *Nietzsche* (Berlin: Bondi, 1918). Voltaire, a convinced Deist who, if religion consists of the faith in a god, was, after all, more religious than Nietzsche (or Bertram?), appears in this book only as the "spider of skepticism" ("Spinne Skepsis," p. 54). Nietzsche's "Voltairetum" is said to constitute "an intentional contrast to a religious nature" and consequently serves the true, religious essence of Nietzsche *e contrario* as a "perspective on God" (p. 144). Or: when Nietzsche says Voltaire, he really means "the Goethean type" ("den Typus Goethe," p. 189). Or again: in devaluating Shakespeare and expressing esteem for French Neoclassicism (including Voltaire), Nietzsche merely imitates Napoleon; for he wants to be Napoleonic in his tastes (p. 214). Yet ultimately the Greek principle in Nietzsche conquers the skeptical principle: Eleusis will triumph over Ferney (p. 348). For that perspective must not be admitted under which Nietzsche found the French and especially Voltaire more Greek than the Germans (including Goethe, that late convert to classicism, which went against his original bent; see WKG, IV-2, 182 ff. and below p. 114. Rather, Bertram wishes to invoke a mysterious paradox and the breakthrough of secret wellsprings in Nietzsche's innermost being when—at some point in MA—"suddenly the voice of Herodotus" is heard in the midst of Voltairean talk ("mitten zwischen Voltaire"; Bertram, p. 356).

[4] See Nietzsche's letters to Franz Overbeck, Sorrento, December 1876; and to Marie Baumgartner, Sorrento, 27 January 1877. HKG (*Briefe*) IV, 317, 327, as well as WKG, IV-4, 27.

Nietzsche became acquainted with the *Histoire de Charles XII* in school as early as 1861 (when he was 17). Among his juvenilia (up to and including 1864) there is an unpublished manuscript of thirteen pages concerning "Voltaire's life and personality" and "Voltaire as a philosopher," and there are excerpts from Hermann Hettner's *History of French Literature in the XVIIIth Century* (HKG, II, 458). *Mahomet*, a drama which, surprisingly, is recommended in *Human, All-Too-Human* for repeated reading, Nietzsche recommends even in 1881 to his sister in Paraguay for "reading in company" (GB, V/2, 446). A quote from *Zadig* ("Il maudit les savants et ne voulut plus vivre qu'en bonne compagnie") Nietzsche takes down in his notebooks in 1876. And one can assume that he does not merely quote the Voltairean "cultiver son jardin"—in contrast to Rousseau's "return to nature"—(GB, V/2, 699) but that he has actually read *Candide*. Above all, as one might expect, he seems to be fascinated by Voltaire's letters.[5]

Beyond all this one gains the impression that Nietzsche generally inclined toward an *imitatio* of Voltaire and a mythical self-identification with Voltaire. The quote "Il faut dire la vérité et s'immoler" (WKG, IV-1, 201) points in this direction; as does the "Écrasez l'infâme!" at the end of *Ecce Homo;*[6] and—in the phase of *Human, All-Too-Human*—the quote of a statement made by Goethe to the effect that Voltaire was the "general source of light" (WKG, IV-3, 408; see Goethe's conversations with Eckermann, 16 December 1828). It is as if Nietzsche wanted to exchange at one point his earlier paternal model, Schopenhauer,[7] by honoring Voltaire—an author frequently quoted by Schopenhauer—as his father's true father, and thus as his own grandfather. For Nietzsche does claim now that he had always distrusted Schopenhauer's *system* as distinct from "the live incarnate Voltairean Schopenhauer," to whom his own Romantic and meta-physical vagaries, such as the fourth book of the *World as Will and Idea*, became unintelligible (WKG, IV-3, 381 f.).[8] Later on, Nietzsche claimed that Schopen-

---

[5] *Lettres choisies* ed. Louis Moland, 2 vols. (Paris: Garnier frères, 1876); WKG, IV-4, 327. See also *Aphorisms 140* and *159* of *The Wanderer and his Shadow*. "It seems probable that [Nietzsche] read Voltaire mainly in German. His library contained *Sämtliche Schriften* (a 1786 translation), *Zaïre, Lettres Choisies* (both in French) and *Der Geist aus Voltaires Schriften* (an 1827 selection)," Williams, p. 89; see also ibid., pp. 7, 9. According to Bernoulli, Mrs. Overbeck translated for Nietzsche some essays from Sainte-Beuve's *Causeries du Lundi*, including "The Letters of Mme de Graffigny or Voltaire in Cirey." "Mme du Châtelet. Continuation of Voltaire in Cirey." "Mme de Latour-Franqueville and Jean Jacques Rousseau," as well as essays on Fontenelle, Montesquieu, Diderot, Vauvenargues, Mlle de Lespinasse, and Beaumarchais. These translations were published in 1880 by Nietzsche's publisher E. Schmeitzner in Chemnitz under the title "Menschen des XVIII. Jahrhunderts." Carl Albrecht Bernoulli, *Franz Overbeck und Friedrich Nietzsche: Eine Freundschaft* (Jena: Eugen Diederichs, 1908), I, 444.

[6] See also the aphorism in MA quoted below, p. 117; and below, p. 113.

[7] Concerning the conception of Schopenhauer as a father-figure and as the prototype of a teacher and educator, cf. the fictitious frame and the role of the Schopenhauer-figure in Nietzsche's lectures "On the Future of Our Educational Institutions" (K, 71, 391–527), as well as the essay on "Schopenhauer as Educator" in U.

[8] Similarly, he also notes earlier: "The live Schopenhauer has nothing in common with the metaphysicians. He is essentially a Voltairean; the fourth [book is] alien to him" (WKG, IV-3, 353).

hauer—like Nietzsche himself?—had been seduced by the Romantics in his youth. He had turned away from his "best instincts." Yet *au fond* he was a Voltairean, mentally and viscerally ("mit Kopf und Eingeweiden"; K, *82*, 240), an opinion which, to be sure, does not prevent Nietzsche from continuing to characterize and to reject Schopenhauer as a Romantic.[9]

Given the assumption that Nietzsche's positive relationship to Voltaire develops as *imitatio* within and out of his relationship to Schopenhauer, one is tempted to look for intimations of this development even in the earlier Nietzsche who is still loyal to Schopenhauer. Perhaps Nietzsche's annoyance at the pretension of David Friedrich Strauß,[10] the old "philistine of culture" affecting stylistic grace and ease and the attitude of the *esprit libre* in order to assume the role of a German Voltaire (K, *71*, 63–66), may be an early symptom of a similar ambition on the part of Nietzsche. More striking is a slip of mind of the fully developed *Voltaire redivivus* in a note which reads: "1778 finished the manuscript [i.e., of *Human, All-Too-Human*]" (WKG, IV-4, 41), and thus shifts the date of the completion of Nietzsche's own work back to the year of Voltaire's death. An anonymous gift from Paris presented by an admirer, the bust of Voltaire accompanied by the words "l'âme de Voltaire fait ses compliments à Frédéric Nietzsche" (GB, IV, 7), was, at any rate, in harmony with the intent of the author: "I was *quite* moved. . . . The fate of the man who remains subject to nothing but partisan judgments, even after a hundred years, stood before my eyes as a terrifying symbol: Against the liberators of the mind men are most implacable in their hatred and most injust in their love" (GB, III, 585). And finally one might even point out that in mentioning his preference "for a large, comfortable, scholarly easy chair," Nietzsche observes more than once that the French refer to this piece of furniture as "un Voltaire" (GB, IV, 248; see GB, V/2, 649).

II. THE "GRANDSEIGNEUR OF THE SPIRIT"

Yet the most important questions cannot be answered by observations of this sort, least of all in the case of Nietzsche. For Nietzsche himself was to suggest that he expressed his appreciation of a man and conferred distinction on him by opposing him. Nor would Nietzsche's tendency to self-identification with a given figure necessarily preclude opposition. What does Nietzsche admire in Voltaire? What is he interested in? And what are his disagreements with Voltaire?

---

[9] See also K, *74*, 113. The last step in the demolition of the *imitatio* of Schopenhauer which, to be sure, does away also with the *imitatio* of Voltaire, may be suggested by K, *78*, 66 where Schopenhauer is said to be merely one of those Germans who are "always late" and dependent on influences "from abroad": "Schopenhauer—Indians and Romanticism, Voltaire." For the note suggests that Schopenhauer merely combined influences of Buddhism and Romanticism with influences from Voltaire.

[10] A note in WKG, IV-2, 487 (numbered 22[72]; cf. WKG, IV-4, 436) seems to allude to the *Six Lectures on Voltaire* (*Voltaire: Sechs Vorträge*) by David Friedrich Strauß.

Nietzsche admires Voltaire insofar as Voltaire impresses him as *noble* and as a *free spirit:* Voltaire appears to have succeeded in combining nobility of mind with freedom of thought, to be, in short, a "grandseigneur of the spirit," and thus a unique exception among intellectuals.

Voltaire is noble as a poet: the last representative, as Nietzsche sees it, of a severely disciplined artistic tradition. Neoclassical art was bound by strict and compulsory rules—comparable to the discipline of counter-point and the fugue, or the rules of classical rhetorics. It was restricted in terms of the unities of action, time and place, as well as with respect to style, structure of verse and syntax, selection of vocabulary and admissible ideas. And thus art was enabled to pass beyond a "naturalizing" stage, "to learn to walk gracefully on narrow paths" in order to attain "the greatest suppleness of movement," and to produce the "semblance" (*Schein*) of freedom, which is the "highest result" of a logical, a "necessary" development in art (WKG, IV-2, 182 f.).

After Voltaire, Nietzsche writes, the French

> suddenly lack the great talents who would have continued to lead the development of tragedy from constraint (*Zwang*) to that ultimate semblance of freedom. Later on, following the German model, they also took the leap into a kind of Rousseauistic state of nature, and experimented. One need but read Voltaire's *Mahomet* from time to time in order to realize what was lost to European civilization once and for all through that crumbling away of tradition. Voltaire was the last of the great dramatists who tamed with Greek measure a multiform mind and heart equal to the mightiest tragic thunderstorms. He was capable of what no German has achieved as yet. because the French are far more akin in temperament to the Greeks than are the Germans. (WKG, IV-2, 183 f.)

What is noble is the classical Greek ideal of contained strength which the French approximated and realized in some measure, while the later Goethe merely longed for it: "Art, as Goethe later on *understood* it, and as it was *practiced* by the Greeks and indeed by the French as well" (WKG, IV-2, 186).[11]

It is not a mere accident if Nietzsche develops one of his central notions of culture and art from one of Voltaire's incidental remarks. In the course of a brilliant apology of the French language—in which he contrasts the ease of rhyming and composing verse in Italian with the difficulty of this art in French— Voltaire arrives at the aperçu: "vous dansez en liberté et nous dansons avec nos chaînes." In the context of Nietzsche this notion recurs in the definition and praise of the highest form of art and culture as a dance in chains; a conception

---

[11] See also, WKG, IV-2, 186: The later Goethe "lived . . . in art as in the memory of true art." At the same time it is worth noting that the ideal of art which Nietzsche associates with Voltaire also reflects the somewhat *fin de siècle* ideal of Gautier's poem "L'Art" (in *Emaux et Camées*) of which Nietzsche said on his journey to Sorrento that it corresponded to his own views. See Charles Andler, *Nietzsche: Sa vie et sa pensée*, 4th ed., 3 vols. (Paris: Gallimard, 1958), II, 266 f.

which, in a sense, also designates Nietzsche's ultimate goal and ideal, that is, the playful freedom or freedom to play attained by the most nearly perfect men or supermen.[12]

Even a seemingly trivial note, "Voltaire said: 'if Homer's admirers were sincere, they would confess that they are frequently bored by their favorite' " (WKG, IV-1, 103), points to the same theme which will increasingly occupy Nietzsche's mind. Even in *Beyond Good and Evil*, when he is discussing what we owe to our vulgar historical sense, to that semi-barbarian attitude toward our physical existence, desires and appetites which opens up for us "accesses in all directions" such as a noble age could never allow, Nietzsche observes:

> Thus—to give an example—we can once more enjoy Homer: perhaps this is our happiest advantage that we can savor Homer. The men of a noble [aristocratic] culture—e.g., of the French seventeenth century, as represented by St. Évrémond, who objects to Homer's "esprit vaste," or even by Voltaire who represents the fading away of this epoch—could not easily assimilate Homer and would hardly permit themselves to enjoy him. (K, 76, 147 f.)

And in this context Nietzsche also varies the dictum of Voltaire concerning the "great Barbarian" Shakespeare (WKG, IV-2, 184). For thanks to our barbarian taste, we will no more allow ourselves to be disturbed in the enjoyment of Shakespeare by the disgusting exhalations and the proximity of the English rabble in which Shakespeare's art and taste dwell, than, for example, on the Chiaja of Naples where we go our way with our senses awake, enchanted and willing, though the sewer smells of the plebeian quarters fill the air (K, 76, 148).

To be sure, this suggests a crucial area in Nietzsche's problematics. He himself enjoys Shakespeare: "we accept precisely this wild abundance, this intermingling of the most delicate, the coarsest, the most artificial, with a sense of secret intimac·· and heartfelt familiarity—we enjoy him as the very refinement of art which has been reserved especially for us" (K, 76, 148). Nietzsche himself shares "our great virtue of historical sense," even though this virtue may be necessarily opposed to "*good* taste, or at least to the best taste," in opposition, that is, to the artistic imitation of those "moments and marvels when a great force stopped voluntarily" this side of the immeasurable, the excessive, the boundless. For "*measure* is alien to us" and our "thrill is the thrill of the infinite, the unmeasured. Like a rider on a galloping horse panting ahead in its course, we drop the reins before the infinite, we modern men, we semi-barbarians, and find our bliss only where we are most *in danger*" (K, 76, 149).

We shall come back to this contradiction between noble and barbarian taste, between Voltaire and Shakespeare, or between Voltaire and Rousseau. At

---

[12] See *Aphorisms 140* and *159* of S; WKG, IV-4, 327; cf. WKG, IV-2, 232 f.; and Oehler's *Nietzsche-Register*, (K, *170*) under "Tanz"; as well as Voltaire's letter to Deodati de Tovazzi, Ferney, 24 January 1761.

this point, let us continue merely to trace the relationship between Nietzsche and Voltaire. Nietzsche's provocative admiration for Voltaire is not restricted to the epigone of neoclassical tragedy so unappealing to a modern taste. According to a more easily acceptable judgment of Nietzsche's, Voltaire is "also the last great author [*Schriftsteller*] who, in the treatment of prose speech, possesses a Greek ear, the artistic conscientiousness, simplicity and grace of the Greek" (WKG, IV-2, 184). Moreover, Nietzsche is impressed with Voltaire's elegance, *désinvolture*, and controlled aggressiveness—notably with the manner in which Voltaire deals with his opponents, e.g., in a letter to Frederick the Great or in five lines concerning his literary opponent Piron. Nietzsche speaks in this connection of the "most terrible revenge" which requires the ability to wait until one has an entire hand of truths so that the fulfilment of revenge coincides with the exercise of justice (WKG, IV-3, 297; see IV-4, 342).

Finally, Voltaire was "one of the last men . . . who were able to unite supreme freedom of spirit and an entirely unrevolutionary cast of mind without being inconsistent and cowardly" (WKG, IV-2, 184). And this observation establishes a connection between the nobility of an aristocratic style in art and life, and the nobility of the elitist, individualistic *free spirit*, the intellectual, who is the protagonist of *Human, All-Too-Human*. Voltaire thus appears to anticipate one of Nietzsche's perennial ideals: namely, a synthesis of aristocratic civilization and spiritual freedom. Indeed, supreme intellectual and spiritual freedom cannot belong to those who are enslaved, nor to the rebels and revolutionaries who protest against their own inner or external enslavement. The ultimate freedom of mind can only belong to the truly free man. It is, according to Nietzsche, the prerogative of the fewest. And even in his art and life-style, the free man must have gained that supreme suppleness of motion which, as we learned above, can only be attained through mastery and the overcoming of self-imposed fetters and restraints. In the same sense the later Nietzsche will say: "I understand by 'freedom of spirit' something quite definite: being a hundred times superior to philosophers and other disciples of 'truth' in severity toward oneself, in sincerity and courage, in the unconditional will to say 'no' where it is dangerous to say 'no' . . ." (K, 78, 326). And in this manner Nietzsche again seeks to distinguish his ideal as sharply as possible from any kind of slave rebellion in the name of the modern egalitarian principle or the instincts of the herd.

III. THE ANTI-REVOLUTIONARY

What is decisive is the juxtaposition (or confrontation) of Voltaire and Rousseau, of the aristocratic free spirit ("quand la populace se mêle de raisonner, tout est perdu" (WKG, IV-2, 295) and the "masked man of the rabble" (GB, IV, 341)—and consequently, in the phase of *Human, All-Too-Human*, to rescue (as

Nietzsche sees it) the spirit of true enlightenment from the confusion with its opposite: the egalitarian and plebeian, the optimistic and irrational faith in human nature and in the advent of utopia as a quasi-automatic and *natural* consequence of the destruction of civilization by revolution:

> *A Delusion in Subversive Doctrines.* There are political and social dreamers who ardently and eloquently call for the overthrow of all order, in the belief that the proudest temple of beautiful humanity will then rear itself immediately, almost of its own accord. In these dangerous dreams there is still an echo of Rousseau's super-stition, which believes in a marvellous primordial goodness of human nature, buried up, as it were; and lays all the blame for that burying-up on the institutions of civilization, on society, the state, and education. Unfortunately, it is well known by historical experiences that every such overthrow reawakens into new life the wildest energies, the long-buried horrors and extravagances of the remotest ages; that an overthrow, therefore, may possibly be a source of strength to an effete humanity, but never a regulator, architect, artist, or perfecter of human nature. It was not *Voltaire's* moderate nature, inclined toward regulating, purifying, and reconstruct-ing, but *Rousseau's* passionate follies and half-lies that aroused the optimistic spirit of the Revolution, against which I cry, "Écrasez l'infâme!" Owing to this the *spirit of enlightenment and progressive development* has long been scared away; let us see—each of us individually—if it is not possible to recall it! (WKG, IV-2, 309)

According to Nietzsche's view in *Human, All-Too-Human*, the Enlighten-ment was corrupted by and since Rousseau by being amalgamated and tainted with revolutionary substance:

> All the half-insane, theatrical, bestially cruel, licentious, and especially sentimental and self-intoxicating elements which go to form the true revolutionary substance, and became flesh and spirit, before the revolution, in Rousseau—all this composite being, with factitious enthusiasm, finally set even "enlightenment" upon its fanatical head, which thereby began itself to shine as in an illuminating halo. Yet, enlighten-ment is essentially foreign to that phenomenon, and, if left to itself, would have pierced silently through the clouds like a shaft of light, and thus only slowly trans-figuring national customs and institutions as well. But now, bound hand and foot to a violent and abrupt monster, enlightenment itself became violent and abrupt. Its danger has therefore become almost greater than its useful quality of liberation and illumination, which it introduced into the great revolutionary movement. Whoever grasps this will also know from what confusion it has to be extricated, from what impurities to be cleansed, in order that he may then by and within himself continue the work of enlightenment and thus squash so to speak after the event the spirit of the revolution at its point of origin, and undo its effect. (WKG, IV-3, 292)

In the same sense Nietzsche's own book was recommended—in a notice written in 1879 by Peter Gast, the intimate friend of Nietzsche, at the request of Nietzsche's publisher, Schmeitzner. To be sure, this advertisement went contrary to Nietzsche's intentions. Nor did he know who had written it. Even so, it is worth noting what Gast emphasized: as in his earlier writings, Gast pointed out, Nietzsche was again concerned with the "problem of culture." However, *Human, All-Too-Human,* enlarged this concern beyond a national sphere to global civilization, in the spirit of a "philosophy" which extends and expands the mentality of the older Enlightenment and refutes the "spirit of reaction" that manifested itself in Rousseau and continues to manifest itself in the ever more apparent machinations and movements instigated by the spirit of Rousseau. To be sure, Gast adds that Nietzsche's criticism of Schopenhauer's doctrines concerning "the saint and metaphysics" should be understood similarly on the bases of Nietzsche's enlargement of the critical mind of the Enlightenment. However, the intent of Gast's notice is unmistakable. With reference to the *Thoughts out of Season* (an earlier work of Nietzsche), he emphasizes the fact that Nietzsche's concept of (German) culture is conceived in a spirit which differs entirely "from the manner of certain subversive spirits (*Umsturzgeister*) of the past [i.e., the eighteenth] century . . . to whom one can trace certain social movements of our own time" (WKG, IV-4, 71 f.). In short: Gast underlines Nietzsche's anti-socialistic tendency.

In full agreement with the opposition to socialism, but from an opposite standpoint, Nietzsche's publisher and the *spiritus familaris* of Nietzsche, whom the publisher hired to do the job, thus emphasized an ideological intention which the Marxist critic, Georg Lukács, was to claim as the primary motive, cause and purpose of all of Nietzsche's work: the struggle against socialism.[13]

It is true that Nietzsche was innocent of, and annoyed about, this advertisement for his works which the publisher attached in an appendix to the first sequel to *Human, All-Too-Human* (the *Mixed Opinions and Maxims*). He wrote to Schmeitzner: "I am already objectionable to people. Is it in *your* interest as a publisher that I should also become *ridiculous* in their eyes? To me one is as much a matter of indifference as the other. I merely ask whether *you* will derive an advantage from this" (WKG, IV-4, 71). He fears that people might think he shared the responsibility for the "Verlags-Reklame" and that they might laugh at his "vanity." Furthermore—though he adds that the summaries of content are *"well* made"—he remarks to Schmeitzner: "From this 'appendix' I learn what you think of me—and I have my own second thoughts (*Hintergedanken*) about that" (WKG, IV-4, 72). Also, one might object that the publisher was merely trying once more in the course of the year 1879 to attract attention to Nietzsche's book which had been a "miserable failure." (For according to the records, after the Easter book fair they had sold only 120 copies instead of the 1000 copies which the publisher had expected to sell.) Schmeitzner said he wanted to sound off on behalf of Nietzsche's writings ("Lärm für Nietzsches Schriften schlagen"). Thus he sent, for example, Nietzsche's book as well as Wagner's essay on "Publikum

---

[13] See his essay on "Nietzsche als Begründer des Irrationalismus der imperialistischen Periode" in *Die Zerstörung der Vernunft* (Berlin: Aufbau Verlag, 1955).

und Popularität" (which contained an attack on Nietzsche) to the anti-Wagnerian music critic Eduard Hanslick in the hope of arousing "a useful scandal" (WKG, IV-4, 77). And hence the anti-socialistic appendix to Nietzsche's book might have been written with the thought of exploiting a prevalent climate of opinion. For after two attempts on the life of Kaiser Wilhelm I, a law had been promulgated in 1878 against the excesses of the Social Democrats. Nonetheless it is obvious that the tendency emphasized by Schmeitzner and Gast does correspond to one aspect of Nietzsche's work. And this suggests in turn that the *basic* thesis of Lukács might not be quite as untenable as it appears to be in view of his obviously untenable caricature of Nietzsche's universe of thought—which has all the characteristic of a deliberate distortion for the purpose of propaganda in the simplistic spirit of *Vulgär-Marxismus*.

What is Rousseauism for Nietzsche? A revolutionary and radically utopian *egalitarianism*. According to the later Nietzsche, Rousseauism is a modern derivative of the Judaeo-Christian ethics of the herd, the continuation of the rebellion of the slaves in the domain of morals, inspired by the *ressentiments* of the weak, ill-favored, low-born, ignoble mass, by a plebeian compulsion toward equalization, toward levelling, and thus the precursor of revolutionary and radically egalitarian socialism. For by socialism Nietzsche understands the consistent radicalization in the practice or utopia of an egalitarianism which would reduce one and all to the same level. However, it is obvious that the disbelief in *equality* pervades all domains of Nietzsche's thought, if we bear in mind that *Gleichheit* in its literal and metaphorical meanings encompasses equality, sameness, identity, conformity, uniformity, likeness, equivalence, etc. The most abstract and perhaps the most comprehensive expression of Nietzsche's disbelief in *Gleichheit* may be his denial of the principle of identity, or indeed of any kind of identity, in favor of the Heraclitean flux of becoming. And one could certainly claim that Nietzsche's polemic against *Gleichheit* (equality, uniformity) in the socio-political realms is analogous to his resistance against *Gleichheit* (equality, equivalence) as a principle of ethics, and to his rejection of the deified principle of identity "I am who I am," as well as to his denial of *gleiche Dinge* (that is, to the assumption of objects which are equal or the same in all respects), and consequently to his conception of *truths* as a species of fictions (for "truths," or allegedly true statements *generally*, assume the possibility of making valid generalizations), etc. And consequently a Marxist—that is, an ideologist who, on the basis of his doctrine, will admit as the true *movens* of all human behavior none but the *social* factors—might well claim that the true, the primary motif and motive of Nietzsche's thought was the rejection of equality in the social domain, and hence, its antisocialistic tendency—while all else in Nietzsche's thought is to be regarded as an epiphenomenon or superstructure. And yet it would be arbitrary to claim that Nietzsche denied uniformity in all realms *because* he abhorred socialism as an attempt to impose uniformity on all men or as the levelling-down of humanity.

And the attempt to represent Nietzsche's entire work as an expression of his anti-socialism would be likely to lead to distortions and to the neglect of some of the most essential and most interesting of Nietzsche's positions and movements of thought. Indeed, this would be the case even if one could argue convincingly that the antisocialistic tendency—though a minor and derivative motif in terms of Nietzsche's own explicit statements on the subject (which, incidentally, also include a few positive remarks)—was, in fact, a hidden or unconscious power inspiring Nietzsche's thought; and if one conceded what is obvious to all but some Marxists, namely, that the presence of an antisocialistic tendency does not *per se* afford a criterion with regard to the validity or invalidity of Nietzsche's ideas. Yet to come back to Nietzsche's struggle against Rousseau, it does seem to us now that this relationship, which, by the way, is by no means purely polemical (see, for example, K, *73*, 268), betrays a higher degree of interest and even of intimacy than Nietzsche's relation to Voltaire.

IV. CONCERNING ROUSSEAU'S IMPACT

Thus Nietzsche—to begin with a random example—observes in the phase of *Human, All-Too-Human* that Rousseau "naturalizes," like Epicurus in his style or Wagner in his music. That is to say, he keeps the strings of his bow less taut in order to abandon himself to nature. And yet he attains only that "nature" which has become part of his inheritance, which has been cultivated in him by habit, and thus became instinctive. And it is in keeping with this condition that Rousseau's conception of nature does not designate a primal state but describes a cultural "mythology of nature" (WKG, IV-2, 501). To be sure, Nietzsche's observation characterizes the very tendency toward naturalizing which, according to his view, the neoclassical style in art sought to overcome. And we recall that he praised the victory over naturalism as a triumph of art in connection with the recommendation of Voltaire's tragedies. Nonetheless it is clear that Nietzsche also recognizes the advantages of, and even the necessity for, regressive relaxations. For as he observes with a view to the emancipated intellectual, even the most reasonable man is occasionally in need of "nature," that is to say, he must regain his "illogical basic attitude toward all things" (WKG, IV-2, 47).

Nietzsche fully acknowledges the impact of Rousseau: The "mythical Rousseau" whom people had invented ("erdichtet") on the basis of a mythical exegesis of Rousseau's writings and in keeping with hints provided by the author (for he and his readers were continually at work on this idealized figure) was *one* source of that current of "ethical reawakening" which "flowed through Europe since the end of the eighteenth century." The other source of this moral current, Nietzsche observes, was the restoration of the Stoic ideal, whose original pro-claimers, one might add, were also *naturalizing* (though in a different sense from

Rousseau), for they also proclaimed a mythical, virtuous, and reasonable pan-cosmic Nature. However, in Nietzsche's view, the resurrection of the great Stoic Roman ideal ("[die] Wiederauferstehung des stoisch-großen Römertums") was the achievement of the French, whereby they continued the labor "on the task of the Renaissance in the worthiest fashion." For starting out with the imitative recreation of classical forms, they went on with marvellous success to recreate classical characters and thus gave—so far—"the best books and the best of human beings" to modern mankind (WKG, IV-3, 288 f.).

A confluence of Rousseau and of the classical French is held responsible by Nietzsche for the renovation of German *Bildung* (culture). The "moralism of Schiller" as well as Beethoven's "moralism in the form of musical sound" ("it is the eternal praise of Rousseau, of the classical French, and of Schiller") are derived from the same sources. Indeed, the "grandfathers" of the "deutscher Jüngling," the proverbial German youth and his "German virtue" so frequently invoked in German national literature, are to be sought for in Paris and in Rousseau's native city of Geneva (WKG, IV-3, 289 f.).

Praise and censure, praise and satire are scarcely to be separated from one another in this context. In its effect upon the Germans that "moral reawakening" inspired by Rousseau and the stoically classical French brought about "only disadvantages and regressions" as far as the "insight" into "moral phenomena" is concerned. For German moral philosophy—together with its French, English and Italian derivatives—was merely a "semi-theological attempt and attack on Helvétius, a rejection of the hard-won freedom of perspective and of the pointers in the right direction" which that theoretician of a doctrine of morality based on egoism and its sublimation "had finally brought together and expressed well" (WKG, IV-3, 290).[14]

A series of motifs is sounded here; but it is difficult to decide what value Nietzsche assigns to Rousseau and to his impact in this context. Would it not have been more beneficial to men to follow the path indicated by Helvétius rather than to experience that "moral reawakening?" Or was the moral awakening—even though it diminished intellectual insight into the moral phenomena—a gain with respect to the heightening of the human potential, a profit, so to speak, in terms of man's illogical basic position and attitude? And if so, was the moral awakening a gain only insofar as it was patterned on the reawakening of the noble Roman spirit which appeared in the guise of idealized Nature? Or was it a gain also insofar as that moral awakening was inspired by the more barbarian and plebeian ideal of Rousseau?

It seems appropriate at this point to recall the fact that Nietzsche's essay on Wagner which preceded *Human, All-Too-Human* had contained among other

---

[14] See also, WKG, IV-3, 414: "Retrogression in ethics in comparison to the last century—Hel-vétius. From thereon downwards Rousseau, Kant, Schopenhauer, Hegel."

things an expression of sympathy for what Nietzsche called the Faustian man of Rousseau—for his "avid hunger for life," his "discontent and longing," his "intercourse with the demons of the heart," his determination not to accept its compromises, conventions, restraints, nor the "arrogant [social] castes" nor the "dominance of pitiless wealth," of priests and miserable systems of education, all of which conspire to squash and deform the oppressed. And in the same context Nietzsche had acknowledged the power emanating from this mythical man of Rousseau—a force "which has urged and continues to urge men onward to violent revolution. For in all socialistic tremors and earthquakes, it is still the man of Rousseau who moves, like the old Typhon under the Aetna," and readies the souls of men to form "terrible resolutions," but who will also call forth the noblest and rarest qualities from their depths (K, 71, 234 ff.).

Surely, this perspective of thought and sentiment continues to exist as a possibility even for the Nietzsche of *Human, All-Too-Human*. And consequently even the antisocialistic tendency is not maintained as constantly or as unambiguously as it seemed to us previously. The considerations for and against Rousseau are included in the dialectic of Nietzsche, which centers on the question how to enlarge and to ennoble, to increase and to intensify, to maximize, to heighten the potential of man. Rousseau's type of man seems to have access to elemental potentialities which are lacking in the mere intellectual, the man of cognition and insight, or even in the civilized representative of an aristocratic or noble culture. Nietzsche is at no point an adherent even of the mythical Rousseau, let alone of a demythologized Rousseau—not even in the sympathetic passages quoted from *Thoughts out of Season*, even less so in *Human, All-Too-Human*, and least of all in his later works. But neither does he wish to renounce the barbaric advantages which are connected in his mind with the Rousseauistic reaction and regression. As in the case of the Protestant Reformation (which Nietzsche regards as a regressive reaction against the vital, humanistic and enlightened spirit of the Renaissance),[15] the powerful impact of revolutionizing primitivisms, of protests in the name of the suppressed—and of all that has been suppressed, oppressed or repressed by civilization—should accrue ultimately to the benefit of mankind by producing an enrichment of man's potential. A movement of reaction is to be turned into a movement of progress—not by the victory of the destructively regressive tendencies, but by way of a process in which the regressive forces are assimilated, suspended and overcome. For the progress in human self-realization is to take place, after all, in the direction of a noble culture which would prove its strength, rank, and abundance also and especially in its capacity to assimilate and to subjugate barbaric and elemental forces and to render them productive; much as such a superior culture would also be capable of utilizing pathological tendencies.

[15] This is true of Nietzsche ever since the reversal recorded in MA, in contradistinction to the early—Wagnerian—Nietzsche of GT and U (see my *Von den ersten und letzten Dingen*, pp. 272–77).

Indeed, Rousseau is to Nietzsche of great interest, and almost a model, precisely with respect to the exploitation of the pathological. For "men like Rousseau understand how to use their weaknesses, defects, and vices as manure for their talent. When Rousseau bewails the corruption and degeneration of society as the evil results of culture, there is a personal experience at the bottom of this, the bitterness of which gives sharpness to his general condemnation and poisons the arrows with which he shoots; he unburdens himself first as an individual and thinks of getting a remedy which, while benefiting society directly, will also benefit him indirectly by means of society" (WKG, IV-2, 361).

This implies a criticism of Rousseau; but it also implies a justification of Rousseau, and indeed a self-justification of Nietzsche, who is surely aware of the fact that he himself knows as well how to "sow and reap harvest" on a soil fertilized by "personal defects" (WKG, IV-2, 361), and that he too is compelled—and able—to turn his own sickness to productive use. Moreover, by generalizing this personal experience, Nietzsche arrives at the opinion that cultural progress consists in a successful assimilation of pathological elements, in "Veredelung durch Entartung," an "ennoblement through degeneration." The individuals who are less stable and less firmly bound *because* they are insecure and "morally weaker" are also prone to experiment and to try new things. And thus they have occasionally a liberating effect and may succeed in inoculating something new into the stable body of their culture which, to be sure, must be strong enough to accept and to assimilate the new ingredient (WKG, IV-2, 191 f.).

Like Luther, Rousseau thus appears to represent to Nietzsche a conjunction of the primitive and the pathological, of elemental and pathogenic regression. And with regard to both elemental primitivisms and pathological deviations (or the inoculation of pathogenic substance), Rousseau and his works—or should we say, a myth of Rousseau?—constitute a phenomenon significant in terms of Nietzsche's own "elemental" and "decadent" tendencies. Hence it is not altogether surprising if Nietzsche was more preoccupied with Rousseau than with Voltaire. He had originally intended to conclude the sequel to the first volume of *Human, All-Too-Human* with another homage to Voltaire. Instead, he concluded with an aphorism in which there is no mention of Voltaire, while Voltaire's opponent, Rousseau, appears as one of the live spirits of the dead, whom Nietzsche claims that he must ever consult and confront (WKG, IV-3, 170).

It might be objected at this point that we have gained altogether too much by the enlargement of our knowledge concerning Nietzsche's relation to Rousseau. How do we distinguish between Nietzsche's *positive* self-identification with the model of Voltaire—which may serve ultimately also to suspend and to overcome this very model—and the *negative* but more intense, more passionate self-identification of Nietzsche with his opponent or enemy, Rousseau? Can one help but suspect here and elsewhere in Nietzsche that if we would bring together all his thoughts and opinions on the subject at hand in order to gain optimal understanding, we might still be unable to say what he really thinks, since every thought seems to provoke a counter-thought, every opinion seems to elicit its contrary? And perhaps the uncontradicted or one-sided positions of Nietzsche and the idiosyncracies, which we find in his work, were allowed to stand because Nietzsche's course as a thinker was cut short too soon; because he lacked time and opportunity to arrive at a still more encompassing self-contradiction? Like an instrument which responds all too easily, Nietzsche appears to vibrate with a multiplicity of vibrations, and to find accesses everywhere, not merely by virtue of a somewhat detached historical sense but by virtue of a sensibility which is constantly irritated and impelled to imitative and, indeed, to histrionic empathy. In keeping with his own concept of our age of comparison, Nietzsche seems compelled to attempt not merely to understand, to compare, and to judge all things, but to enter by way of an emotional experiment into all feelings, and in a sense, to re-experience all things.

In a most comprehensive sense he strives to re-integrate the many-headed crowd which dwells within him. He will ultimately desire precisely the strength to extirpate and to eliminate without pity, with the "cruel" injustice of a "healthy" sense of vitality which, for the sake of self-assertion, must set limits. But again and again the synthesis will threaten to disintegrate. The suppressed voices within will not allow themselves to be silenced. The later Nietzsche confronts the "*dividuum*,"[16] which is his own self, with an abrupt dictatorial gesture and speaks against enfeebling multiplicity in a very loud voice. But perhaps he does so also because the counter-voices have become louder, in turn, and more disparate and dissonant; thus he feels compelled to shout them down. Perhaps he does so because the threat of disintegration into chaos has become ever more acute. And consequently one also feels tempted to repeat with regard to Nietzsche: "Ce grand esprit, c'est un chaos d'idées claires," a remark by Faguet[17] concerning Voltaire, which would reveal, in turn, an affinity between Nietzsche and the opponent of Rousseau. And yet, proportionate to the chaos in Nietzsche there is always Nietzsche's ever-renewed, never-surrendered attempt to overcome this chaos. And in this context the above-mentioned aphorism should be quoted, which reveals—in keeping with the relative moderation characteristic of *Human, All-Too-Human*—Nietzsche's attempt to derive a synthesis and unity of heightened and all-encompassing humanity by way of a discussion and confrontation with divergent representatives of Occidental tradition:

[16] To this conception of man as "*dividuum*" (MA, *Aphorism* 57) compare also Nietzsche's view of man as "dissonance" incarnate (K, 70, 189 f.) or as a conjunction of "several spheres" (WKG, IV-1, 257). Nietzsche deals again and again with this multiplicity of selves within the self—a theme popularized later on as (modern) man's schizophrenic state, e.g., in Hesse's *Steppenwolf*, the poetry of Gottfried Benn, etc.

[17] Quoted in Voltaire: *Oeuvres philosophiques (extraits)* (Paris: Classiques Larousse, n.d.), p. 106.

I, too, have been in the underworld, even as Odysseus, and I shall often be there again. Not sheep alone have I sacrificed that I might be able to converse with a few dead souls, but I have not spared my own blood. Four pairs did not reject my sacrifices: Epicurus and Montaigne, Goethe and Spinoza, Plato and Rousseau, Pascal and Schopenhauer. With them I must come to terms when I have long wandered alone. I will let them agree and disagree with me, and listen to them when, in proving me right or wrong, they agree and disagree with one another. In all I say, decide, or think out for myself or for others, I fasten my eyes on those eight and see their eyes fastened on mine. (WKG, IV-3, 169 f.)

It would be tempting to trace, by way of analogy and contrast, the connections which tie together the members of each of these pairs in Nietzsche's mind; e.g., Pascal and Schopenhauer, the Christian and the atheistic proclaimer of an ascetic pessimism, (see K, *78*, 666; *83*, 396); or Goethe and Spinoza, the quasi(?) pagan and the intellectualized or spiritualized pantheist (see K, *78*, 44, 235). Why Plato and Rousseau? Because one prefigures Christianity while the other introduces the secularized, modern, massively popular after-effect of Christian faith (K, *83*, 407)?[18] Or perhaps because both—the aristocrat and the plebeian—are connected with each other by the fact that they disagree with each other on a matter which is essential to Nietzsche. In a note of summer 1879, Nietzsche observes that Plato and Rousseau are in opposition to each other regarding "culture": "Plato says if we lived among natural men (savages), we would embrace even the Athenian criminal (as a civilized being). He is right, against Rousseau" (WKG, IV-3, 453).

V. THE PROBLEM OF CIVILIZATION

This brings us back to an issue so central to the later Nietzsche that it keeps alive his interest in the antagonism between Voltaire and Rousseau, both of whom he will, in turn, confront with his conception of culture and civilization— though in other respects his regard for Voltaire seems to have become rather qualified and Rousseau is treated increasingly as the pure villain. Why is it then that the antagonism between Voltaire and Rousseau concerning their evaluation of civilization causes the later Nietzsche to emphasize his respect for Voltaire and to proclaim with a passion his contempt and hatred for Rousseau's alleged advocacy of a "return *in impuribus naturalibus*" (K, *77*, 129 f.)?

The later Nietzsche strives to the point of frenzy to conjure up the ideal

---

[18] For Rousseau and Rousseauism as plebeian offshoot and heir to Christianity, see below p. 126. and K, *78*, 52 f., 671; for a summary of some aspects of Nietzsche's conception of Plato relevant in the present context, cf. my *Von den ersten und letzten Dingen*, 292.

image of the most comprehensive human being. Consequently he too seems to demand—not only, but among other things—a return to nature. All the more he feels compelled to disarm the catastrophic suspicion that he, Nietzsche, could agree at all with that pathological, inferior, sick, effeminate, histrionic Rousseau, a man inspired by the *ressentiments* of the weak, preaching morals—like Luther— out of a desire for vengeance, and glorifying his need for revenge as a moral and religious duty, that *Blasebalg* of morality, that rabble rouser, that modern hybrid between idealist and *canaille*.[19]

In their simple, bare outlines, the major positions in the conflict between Voltaire and Rousseau, as Nietzsche sees them, are as follows: Voltaire loves, praises, defends culture and civilization as a triumph over the state of nature, the natural bestiality, the rapacious animal nature of man. Rousseau, moralist on the basis of *ressentiment*, wants to give the oppressed a good conscience in their rebellion by contending that injustice, cruelty, corruption are inherent in the state of civilization and culture, and by proclaiming his utopia as the state of nature. Nietzsche repeats at this point the views he expressed in *Human, All-Too-Human*. However, his position has grown more complex because he is now criticizing both points of view with reference to the value of civilization. In opposition to Voltaire's estimate, Nietzsche opposes *Kultur* to *Zivilisation*. He reformulates the problem of civilization which, he claims, was left unsettled in the conflict between Rousseau and Voltaire. Nietzsche wants man to become more natural—but not at all in the sense of Rousseau (or in the sense which he attributed to Rousseau). For man is to become less trusting, more skeptical, stronger, more confident in himself and more self-reliant, and indeed *amoral* like Nature herself. And this amoral nature of his he will not gain via a return to some idyllic past or by a revolutionary abolition of civilization. He can only attain his amoral nature by going forward. Only in a distant future will he perhaps make the conquest of his own nature which, from the very outset of his history, he denied. For precisely in the aboriginal state, the morality and barbaric artifice of error, deception, and illusion dominated the primitive mind. Nietzsche wants man to become—in the future—amoral like Nature herself. And with this he stands in opposition also to Voltaire who, contrary to Rousseau, believed man was growing ever more perfect the greater the distance he gained from nature.[20]

The wishes and ideal images of the later Nietzsche grew increasingly more ambitious. To give an example: he dreamt of a type who would combine Napoleon—the reawakener of the true man, the soldier who resuscitated the struggle for power—and Goethe, who conceived of a Western culture that would inherit all the accumulated treasures of *Humanität*, all the civilized, enlightened, refined humanity and humane sentiments evolved in the course of civilization (K, *78*, 78).

---

[19] Cf., for example, K, *77*, 171, 265; *78*, 68 f., 234, 239, 501 f.
[20] Cf. with respect to this entire issue K, *78*, 74 f., 88 f.

And Nietzsche would intensify this synthesis and have it increase ever more in strength and *virtù* to a degree where it would become all-embracing.

As Nietzsche sees it, domestication, ennoblement, refinement, sublimation conflict with the need for the intensification, vitalization, animalization of man (K, *78*, 89). And therein lies the problem of civilization and culture which, to be sure, would deserve to be dealt with extensively in relation to Nietzsche's own dual-ideal of vitality and nobility, an ideal that finally reaches a point where it turns into a kind of sublime monstrosity, a maximal conjunction of ruthless vitality and transcendent spirituality.

However, though the later Nietzsche contradicts Voltaire's views as well as those of Rousseau, he nonetheless admires Voltaire's struggle against Rousseau to the point almost of confessing his own solidarity with Voltaire: "The fight began around 1760—the citizen of Geneva and *le seigneur de Ferney*. From that moment on, Voltaire becomes the man of his century, the philosopher, the representative of tolerance and unbelief (till then he had been merely *un bel esprit*). Envy and hatred of Rousseau's success impelled him forward 'to the heights' " (K, *78*, 75).

It is important to realize that even the later Nietzsche does not object to civilization as such and that he certainly relished himself the mitigations, refinements and subtleties, the intellectual and spiritual joys of the civilized state, which he claimed were so highly appreciated by Voltaire. He shares Voltaire's contempt for "narrowmindedness even in the form of virtue, for lack of delicacy even among monks and ascetics" (K, *78*, 74). He did not reject refinement and spiritualization as such, but he rejected civilization as enfeeblement, as "domestication of the animal"—especially in a moral sense (K, *78*, 89). Indeed, insofar as civilization does *not* contribute to the moral improvement of man (in Nietzsche's pejorative sense of that term), this is a point in favor of civilization (K, *78*, 260). For what Nietzsche fears above all is a moralization and a levelling of intensities in favor of moral norms which will result in "intolerance against the boldest men and keenest spirits" (K, *78*, 89). Nietzsche's ideal, possibly a conjunction of opposites, is to fuse and to unite the maximum of animal drive and stamina with the highest degree of cultural energy: since, after all, cultural energy and intensity are fed only by that animal driving force.

The later Nietzsche sympathizes with Voltaire, insofar as Voltaire still conceives of the comprehensive *"umanitá* in the Renaissance sense" and retains an appreciation for Renaissance virtues, that is: for *virtù* free of *Moralin*, free of the moral poison (K, *78*, 74). Indeed, Nietzsche claims now that the higher degree of *admitted* immorality constitutes the superiority of culture over the lack of culture, which is why all high points in the history of human development—including the society of Voltaire—appear to the eyes of moral fanatics as the climax of corruption (K, *78*, 501 f.). Nietzsche sympathizes with Voltaire, insofar as Voltaire appears versus the plebeian Rousseau as the "missionary of culture," the aristocrat, the representative of the victorious social classes and of their sense of values (K, *78*, 75) not because Nietzsche agrees with the ideology of these social castes but because he wants to side with the strong, the noble, the men of a fine race and of good breeding, and against the sick, the weak, the *tshandalah*. And finally: he admires Voltaire because in Voltaire an uncommon health, ease and abundant facility are as unquestionable as in the case of Rousseau the predominance of mental disturbance and the *rancune* of the sick and ailing man (K, *78*, 75).

VI. THE OVERCOMING OF VOLTAIRE

Indeed, even in the last year of his sanity, Nietzsche will quote Voltaire— notably the Anti-Christian who mocked the "immortal soul that spent nine months between excrements and urine," and said of Christ, even on his death-bed: "Do not speak to me of that man."[21] Nonetheless, the impression remains that Nietzsche's admiration for Voltaire has waned. True, he does claim, even in 1887, that it is a "criterion for judging a man's worth whether he affirms Voltaire or Rousseau." And since Nietzsche himself now likes to assume the attitude of the aristocratic immoralist, he is pleased with symptoms of amoral vitality to be found in Voltaire. Hence one may take it to be a compliment to Voltaire if Nietzsche refers to him with Galiani's couplet: "Un monstre gai vaut mieux/ qu'un sentimental ennuyeux."[22] Yet he says in the same context: "Voltaire is a magnificent, a brilliantly witty *canaille*," and thus suggests that he no longer considers Voltaire to be noble, although he will acknowledge him as the literary advocate of nobility. It is as if Nietzsche now tolerated and patronized M. Arouet after the model of the higher French aristocracy. For "Voltaire is possible and bearable only in the context and on the basis of an aristocratic culture which can *afford* the *luxury* of spiritual *canaillerie*" (GB, IV, 340 f.).[23]

Or is this to take too seriously the semi-humorous letter in which this passage occurs? The later Nietzsche who deletes the dedication to Voltaire in the second printing of *Human, All-Too-Human* (1886), considers himself "a few centuries ahead of Voltaire in matters of enlightenment" (K, *78*, 66). However, the process of *overcoming* Voltaire, that is, Nietzsche's attempt to claim for himself the position of the man of Enlightenment and of the *grandseigneur* of the Spirit, and thus to become the new Voltaire who supersedes the older Voltaire, sets in as early as *Human, All-Too-Human*. Nietzsche himself suggests this in the retrospective quoted above: "The name of Voltaire on one of my writings—that was progress—toward *myself*. . . ." And he adds: "On closer inspection, one will

---

[21] WKG, VIII-2 [1970], 10, 325.

[22] Occasionally, Nietzsche also attributes these lines to Voltaire; see K, *78*, 28, 66.

[23] Similarly, Nietzsche also speaks of Voltaire's "kind of play-acting for the benefit of society" (K, *83*, 392).

discover [in *Human, All-Too-Human*] a merciless spirit that knows all hideouts where the ideal is at home—where it has its secret dungeons and . . . ultimate safety." And obviously, this merciless spirit is of quite a different cast than the spirit of Voltaire.

Perhaps some more conclusive proof for this contention is needed. The fact that the original epilogue to *Human, All-Too-Human* was not even included in the first version of the first volume may mean little in itself. Somewhat more striking is the circumstance that the name of Rousseau appears in the concluding aphorism of the first sequel to *Human, All-Too-Human*, I, and that this concluding aphorism of the *Mixed Opinions and Maxims* replaced a final homage to Voltaire (which should have found its place in an extended version of *Aphorism 407*). And yet this last tribute to Voltaire was probably deleted because the solemn irony of its conclusion would have betrayed all too clearly the intentions of the new Voltaire.

Aphorism 407 of the *Mixed Opinions and Maxims* reads as follows: "*The Glory of All Great Men.*—What is the use of genius, if it does not invest him who contemplates and reveres it with such freedom and loftiness of feeling that he no longer has need of genius?—To make themselves superfluous is the glory of all great men." At this point the eliminated lines would have been inserted: "Let us name once more at this juncture the name of Voltaire. What will be his future *highest* honor, to be rendered to him by the freest spirits of future generations? His *last* honor . . ." (WKG, IV-4, 301). Evidently, the last honor to be rendered to the spirit of Voltaire would be the proof that his model had been surpassed. Now Voltaire's spirit could be finally put to rest to enjoy the calm of oblivion. For he had finally succeeded in making himself superfluous.

Nietzsche's claim to have overcome and superseded Voltaire, and consequently, to have gone beyond the spirit of the old Enlightenment, occurs in *Human, All-Too-Human* in conjunction with the notion that the modern mentality represents a higher stage of culture: e.g., Voltaire could still observe in a spirit of mockery that he was grateful to Heaven for the institution of marriage and the church, which had provided so well for our amusement. But for us, Nietzsche claims, all mockery on these subjects has been exhausted ("diese Themen [sind] zu Ende gespottet"). All contemporary witticisms directed against these institutions are belated and come too cheap. For the "higher the cultural level of a man," the larger the range of topics which become unavailable as objects for mockery. Hence we are living now in "the age of seriousness," in which "the differences between reality and pretentious appearance, between what a man *is* and what he wishes to represent" should no longer be an object for jokes. For the "feeling for these contrasts . . . has quite a different effect once we seek for underlying causes." "The more thoroughly anyone understands life, the less he will mock, though finally, perhaps, he will mock at the 'thoroughness of his understanding' " (WKG, IV-2, 205 f.).

Actually, Nietzsche himself was not beyond publishing some rather cheap witticisms on the subject of marriage, e.g., "*The Unity of Place and the Drama.*—If married couples did not live together, happy marriages would be more frequent" (WKG, IV-2, 276). Or, "Some husbands have sighed over the elopement of their wives; most about the fact that no one was willing to elope with theirs" (WKG, IV-2, 275). Yet these occasional and somewhat contrived lapses into mockery seem less characteristic of the author of *Human, All-Too-Human* than his intention and program to leave aside irony, mockery, laughter, and to value only the kind of spirit which is allied with seriousness, to esteem only the scarcely perceptible spiritual smile,[24] and thus to establish his seriousness in the place of Voltairean mockery as the dominant stylistic principle of the new Enlightenment. Indeed, who could ignore the keynote of irredeemable seriousness even—or especially— in the later Nietzsche, though he will wear and sanctify the crown of laughter in the name of Zarathustra!

Nor is this to claim that Nietzsche's observation is purely subjective. The Enlightenment in our age of strict and increasingly specialized sciences does differ in spirit from the semidilettante, sociable and playful *esprit* of the eighteenth-century *philosophes* by virtue of an unrelenting seriousness which has been elevated to the dignity of a method, by a thoroughness quite devoid of humorous relief, such as was scarcely cultivated in previous ages. And Nietzsche may be right that even in the critique of *moralia*, the "play" with thoughts which were once esteemed as bold sallies and paradoxes has turned into "seriousness."[25]

Nonetheless this characterization of Nietzsche's attitude—while it does correspond to one facet of his character—is altogether too unambiguous and too undialectical to do justice to the *dividuum* or multiple self of this author. For among other things, Nietzsche is also addicted to mockery; and what is more, he would like to look upon all existence as an eternal comedy.[26] With a view to the Jews—to Heine, to Offenbach—the later Nietzsche claims that ingenious buffoonery, or rather, buffoonery raised to the level of genius ("geniale Buffonerie") is "the supreme form of spirituality" (K, *83*, 406). And he himself would have been quite capable of deriding the German lack of humor which characterizes his own aphorism concerning the age of seriousness and its heavy-handed censure of the mocking and superficial Frenchman Voltaire, which is quite in keeping

[24] Cf. MA, *Aphorisms 186, 372, 553; Mixed Opinions and Maxims, Aphorism 276;* S, *Aphorism 173.*
[25] Thus Voltaire and Helvétius, arbiters of taste and *esprit* pronouncing judgment on the audacities of Fontenelle, read in his *Dialogues of the Dead* as paradoxes of a somewhat dangerous sort the very ideas which are being proven to us by solid science (K, *74*, 108).
[26] For pertinent quotes see Karl Joël, *Nietzsche und die Romantik* (Jena and Leipzig: Diederichs, 1905), 125 f. According to Joël's reading of *Aphorism 240* of MA, Nietzsche does conceive the contemporary age as the age of seriousness; but he suggests that the future may well belong to laughter, and consequently a "carnival in the grandest style," the most spiritual of high spirits and carnival laughter, may be in its incipient stage of preparation even now (pp. 125, 133).

with a well-worn German cliché.[27] What is more, the very seriousness of thorough knowledge which is to distinguish the new Enlightenment from the Enlightenment of Voltaire, is to create the prerequisite for an all-encompassing sense for the human comedy and—ultimately—for the comedy of our universe which is, in essence, pure play freed of all morality, goal, meaning or purpose. After all, Nietzsche's philosophy does culminate in a notion of creative play, much as he sees the ultimate stage of wisdom represented in the image of the innocently creative child at play.[28] And even the free spirit of *Human, All-Too-Human* has learned by virtue of his thorough genetic knowledge that in regard to their origins all human affairs deserve to be treated with irony, although he concludes that, in view of this pervasively ironical state of human affairs, irony is, in fact, quite superfluous (WKG, IV-2, 214). And the same *esprit libre* also knows that the most thorough knowledge will only enlighten him concerning the genesis of human errors and will teach him only that man is inevitably caught up in deceptive perspectives of mere semblance. That is why the "serious" free spirit will finally be inclined to make fun of only one thing: namely, of the "thoroughness" of his own knowledge and insight (WKG, IV-2, 205 f.). But this one thing, in turn, includes all others; and thus it is the hope of the later Nietzsche that the most radical insight and desperate seriousness of knowledge without hope, a most comprehensive doubt and skepticism, a profoundly traumatic insight, will give rise to Olympian laughter and the Dionysian dance.

Even in *Mixed Opinions and Maxims* Nietzsche characterizes the *progress in free thinking* by observing that Voltaire's dictum "croyez moi, mon ami, l'erreur aussi a son merite," which in his days expressed a daring thought, is reduced to an "involuntary *naiveté*" when judged in the light of our present insights (WKG, IV-3, 18). For having realized that man has developed all he treasures on the basis

[27] Cf. also Nietzsche's polemic against excessive seriousness as uglification: One deforms things by taking them seriously (see Joël, p. 105; also K, *74*, 215 (*Aphorism 327*): against taking things seriously as an expression of the prejudice of the "serious beast" *vis à vis* all "gay science"; K, *82*, 90: "There is too much seriousness in the world." As with many other things, Nietzsche also advocates a transvaluation and reversal with regard to seriousness and mirth: All that was taken seriously and weighed heavily hitherto is to be taken lightly henceforth. Yet the "great seriousness" will only "begin" with this lightness and serenity (K, *77*, 374). The *628th Aphorism* of MA (*Seriousness in Playing*) may be considered a first step toward this transvaluation.

[28] I am indebted to the comprehensive discussion of the pervasive relevance of this motif and of Nietzsche's philosophy of play in an—as yet unpublished—study by Richard Perkins (graduate student in the Department of Philosophy at The State University of New York at Buffalo). Perkins traces the thematic configuration from an essay on "Fatum und Geschichte" (HKG, II, 59), which Nietzsche wrote when he was seventeen years old, to the last year of Nietzsche's sanity. Characteristic for the early Nietzsche are the reference to Heraclitus, who compared the cosmos or cosmic force to a child at play (in the 24th section of GT) and the sections on Heraclitus in *Philosophy in the Tragic Age of the Greeks* (*secs.* 5 to 9). The best known passage in the mature works of Nietzsche is to be found in the speech "On the Three Metamorphoses" in the first book of *Zarathustra*.

of errors, we would have to say: "croyez moi, la vérité," believe me, my friend, even the truth has its merits! (WKG, IV-4, 256). As Nietzsche suggests in the *26th Aphorism* of *Human, All-Too-Human*, the older Enlightenment—though it brought about a historical approach and perspective[29]—must be corrected in an "essential" respect. What we need now is a genetico-historical insight, analysis, critique: a retrograde movement of the intellect. For only by way of a just appreciation and evaluation of archaic—notably: religious—errors (some of which greatly benefited mankind in the past), will we finally suspend and overcome these archaic errors. The Voltairean free thinker of the eighteenth century was incapable of such insight. He could confront the power of ancient errors—e.g., as represented by the church—only with defensively aggressive mockery.

According to Nietzsche, the typical protagonist of the old Enlightenment could engage in the struggle for liberation only on a somewhat superficial level. He remained bound to the ancient errors, notably to Christian morality. And this is indeed the "essential" respect in which Nietzsche believes that he has left Voltaire far behind. Beginning with *Human, All-Too-Human*, Nietzsche will engage increasingly in a polemic against Christian ethics and its derivatives, the ethics of pure *humanity* and pure *virtue*. In *The Dawn* he still disguises his conviction of superiority in the form of a quasi-objective observation: "The more men became emancipated from [religious] dogmas, the more did they seek the justification, as it were, for this emancipation in a cult of love of humanity; not to fall short in this respect of the Christian ideal, but to exceed it, if possible, was a secret ambition of all the French free-thinkers, from Voltaire to Auguste Comte" (K, 73, 117). The critical edge is more apparent in a paragraph from *The Gay Science* in which Nietzsche discusses the errors to which mankind owed the promotion of science, among them Voltaire's faith "in the absolute utility of cognition . . . , notably in the most intimate nexus between morality, knowledge and happiness" (74, 66). And this very faith he will later scorn utterly, e.g., as subordination of the free-thinker's quest for truth to the morality of humanitarian love of man: "Oh Voltaire! Oh humanity! Oh nonsense!" Concerning Voltaire, who goes about his quest for truth in a fashion that is "all-too-*human*" or all-too-*humane* ("il ne cherche le vrai que pour faire le bien"),[30] Nietzsche now exclaims: "I bet he will find nothing!" (K, 76, 47).

Generally Nietzsche holds: "Much as it was progress on the part of our fathers when finally religion as a pose offended their taste"—and this progress included "hostility" and Voltairean bitterness against religion (and everything else that formerly belonged to the gestures of free-thinkers)—it is the symptom of a further progress on our part that our taste can no longer tolerate even "the

---

[29] Also in this connection Nietzsche may be thinking of Voltaire and his achievements as a historian.

[30] Voltaire: *Épître à un homme* (1776).

solemn word and formula of virtue," that the pose and gesture of morality offend us, that puritan litanies, "moral sermons," square respectability will not harmonize with the "music in our conscience" and "the dance in our spirit" (cf. K, 76, 141).

In one of his last works, at the very end of *Ecce Homo*, Nietzsche applies Voltaire's "Écrasez l'infâme!"—that is to say, Voltaire's battle-cry in the fight against the church and the clergy—to that "morality" which, as Nietzsche puts it, by virtue of its conception of "the good man," sided with "all that is weak, sick, a failure, suffering of itself—all that *ought to perish*," a morality which consequently subverted "the principle of *selection*." This application of Voltaire's motto amounts to a transvaluation of Voltaire's anathema, or indeed to its perversion in the service of the new—anti-moralistic—Enlightenment as advocated by the later Nietzsche. And a similar, though less extreme transformation takes place in *Human, All-Too-Human*, where Voltaire's favorite curse—directed especially at the privileged and repressive rule of the Catholic hierarchy and the clerical party, and destined to become a slogan of liberal democratic *Jacobins*—is made to function as a slogan directed against the left, against the ideology of Rousseauistic, egalitarian, socialist demagogues, and opposed to the uprising of the enslaved masses (see WKG, IV-2, 309).

From Nietzsche's point of view these transvaluations are quite justified. Ultimately, he regards the moralisms of Christianity and of a secularized humanitarianism in the name of the weak and all-too-many or the revolutionary ideologies of liberals, Jacobins and Socialists as links in a single continuum. All belong to the anti-elitist, anti-aristocratic, anti-individualistic mentality and tradition of rebellious *slaves*. However, his own position—as a free aristocratic individual, convinced of the prerogatives of a superior elite—Nietzsche regards as being in keeping with the essential position of Voltaire. He thus could persuade himself that he merely continued Voltaire's struggle with greater consistency, in a different context and under other auspices. Even the author of *Zarathustra* will compare himself to Voltaire. Proudly, he assures Peter Gast: "I am one of the most terrible opponents of Christianity and have discovered a mode of attack of which even Voltaire did not have an inkling" (GB, IV, 173). No doubt, Nietzsche is right. And yet these bragging pronouncements of superiority in a struggle in which he remained, after all, both the murderer and the victim, seem feebler in their very insistence than the earlier, more restrained and more complex statements which characterize the skepticism of *Human, All-Too-Human*.

VIII

Socrates in Hamann's *Socratic Memorabilia* and Nietzsche's *Birth of Tragedy* *

JAMES C. O'FLAHERTY

Earlier I had occasion to compare the versions of Socrates presented by Hamann in the *Socratic Memorabilia* and Nietzsche in *The Birth of Tragedy*.[1] In the present article I propose to take another look at the same problem but from a different point of view. For a comparison of the differences in the two portraits of Socrates feature by feature raises the more fundamental question of the reasons for the differences. In the more than a century intervening between the publication of Hamann's and Nietzsche's treatises on Socrates there appeared, to be sure, other important interpretations of the life and work of the Greek philosopher (especially by Hegel and Kierkegaard) but it is particularly instructive to compare the Hamannian and Nietzschean versions for reasons which will become obvious in the following remarks.

I am aware that in raising the epistemological question I am proceeding in a manner which Nietzsche would disallow, for, in his own words in *The Will to Power*, he was "deeply distrustful of the dogmas of epistemology."[2] Further, as Karl Jaspers says: "Epistemology, conceived as an attempt critically to analyze man's cognitive faculty, is simply an object of Nietzsche's contempt."[3] This atti-

---

*This chapter is a reprint, slightly edited, of a *Sektionsreferat* which was read at the Fourth International Conference of Germanists in Princeton, August 1970. See *Dichtung, Sprache und Gesellschaft: Akten des IV. Internationalen Germanisten Kongresses in Princeton*, ed. Victor Lange and Hans-Gert Roloff (Frankfurt a. M.: Athenäum Verlag, 1971), pp. 554–61. For the complete study, of which the present chapter is a summary version, see my article "The Concept of Knowledge in Hamann's *Sokratische Denkwürdigkeiten* and Nietzsche's *Die Geburt der Tragödie*," *Monatshefte*, 54 (1972), 334–48. Unless otherwise indicated, all translations are my own.

[1] See "Socrates in Hamann's *Socratic Memorabilia* and Nietzsche's *Birth of Tragedy*," in *Philomathes: Essays in the Humanities in Memory of Philip Merlan*, ed. R. B. Palmer and R. G. Hamerton-Kelly (The Hague: Nijhoff, 1971) pp. 306–29. Parenthetical references in the present text by page number only are to: J. G. Hamann, *Sämtliche Werke*, ed. Josef Nadler, II (Vienna: Herder, 1950). (For key to abbreviations see p. xvii above.)

[2] *The Will to Power*, trans. Walter Kaufmann and R. J. Hollingdale (New York: Random House, 1967), sec. 410, p. 221.

[3] *Nietzsche: An Introduction to the Understanding of His Philosophical Activity*, trans. C. F. Walraff and F. J. Schmitz (Tucson: University of Arizona Press, 1965), p. 288.

134

tude is, of course, quite consistent with his view that the theory of knowledge is always in the service of a set of values, and is therefore special pleading. Hamann, on the other hand, remains within the mainstream of the Western philosophical tradition by virtue of taking the question of cognition seriously. He was a cultural revolutionary, but instead of breaking with the Christian tradition, as in the case of Nietzsche, he attained to such radically new perspectives *within* that tradition that, in his hands, it seemed to undergo a metamorphosis into something new and strange.

It is interesting that both Hamann and Nietzsche managed, for opposite reasons, to become an offense to the conventionally minded. First, we should note that for Hamann sexuality is involved in all veridical knowledge, and that abstraction is the castration of such knowledge.[4] There is neither space nor occasion to go into the details of the Hamannian epistemology (one which, paradoxically, in striving for simplicity becomes fairly complex, involving as it does his idea of language). Suffice it to say that his theory of knowledge is derived from the Biblical concept of knowing as knowing sexually. Since the rationalist inevitably becomes an abstract thinker, it follows that he also becomes in the Hamannian view eunuchoid. Thus, in the *Aesthetica in nuce* Hamann inveighs against rationalistic philologists and critics like Michaelis and Lessing:

> You desire to rule over nature and yet you stoically bind your hands and feet in order to be able to sing in a falsetto voice all the more movingly about the diamond-hard chains of fate in your miscellaneous poems. If the passions are members of dishonor, do they therefore cease to be instruments of manhood? Do you understand the letter [of the Scriptures] better than that allegorical chamberlain of the Alexandrian church [Origen] who made himself into a eunuch for the Kingdom of Heaven's sake? The prince of this age makes the greatest mutilators of themselves his favorites. . . . (208)

In the *Socratic Memorabilia* itself the doctrine of knowledge as involving eros is not *explicit* but *implicit*. Hamann accepts the homosexuality of Socrates, tending to excuse it on the grounds of the "pagan age" in which he lived (67). This fact is epistemologically indifferent in itself. However, Hamann then proceeds to generalize about friendship thus: "One cannot feel a lively friendship without sensuousness, and a metaphysical love sins perhaps more grievously against the nervous fluid than does an animalistic love against flesh and blood" (68). In speaking of an ideal or "metaphysical love," he introduces the element of understanding, hence moves with this idea onto epistemological ground. Later he cites approvingly Alcibiades' remarks concerning Socrates' teaching: "Alcibiades . . . compared his parables to certain sacred images of the gods and goddesses which were carried, according to the custom of that time, in a small case, on the outside of which only the form of a goat-footed satyr was visible" (80). The *form* which

---

[4] See my "Hamann's Concept of the Whole Man," *German Quarterly*, 45 (1972), 258–61.

the wisdom of Socrates assumed was such as to suggest sexuality, for the "goat-footed satyr" is an unambiguous symbol of the erotic. The ambivalence of man's nature—that he is at the same time a spiritual and a crudely physical creature—is a paradox which the ancients understood well and expressed cleverly in their myths until the rationalists arose and condemned such irrationality: "Through the cleverly devised myths of their poets, the heathen were accustomed to such contradictions until their Sophists, like ours, condemned such things as a parricide committed against the first principles of human knowledge" (68).

    If the doctrine of abstraction as castration is only implicit in his Socratic essay, Hamann makes it quite explicit in the *Wolken: Ein Nachspiel Sokratischer Denkwürdigkeiten* (1761). Thus he writes:

> In these latter days the eunuch [i.e., the Enlightener as "der Verschnittene"] may no longer say: "*Behold! I am a dry tree!*" Such a confession would appear modest, but would not be honest. In the case of Socrates, on the other hand, it was quite honest; nevertheless, it appeared immodest to expose the weakness of his cognitive faculties without making use of the apron of fig leaves or coats of skins. . . . (97)

That Hamann here employs a metaphor which equates the Socratic ignorance with the pudenda is unequivocal evidence of the role of sexuality in knowledge.

    Nietzsche's covert epistemology shows a marked affinity with Hamann's in regard to sexuality. For also in Nietzsche's conception genuine knowledge springs from sexuality or, to use his term in *The Birth of Tragedy*, from "Orgias-mus" (GT, sec. 21; cf. "Musikorgiasmus," ibid.). In employing this term Nietz-sche obviously has in mind that aspect of the human psyche which expresses itself in the collective excitement of the Dionysian rites. (It is to be strictly distinguished from "Orgasmus.") This kind of knowledge is, of course, the wisdom of Diony-sos, the rival of Apollo for the hearts and minds of men. One might expect then that Apollonianism would be the true conceptual opposite of the Dionysian mode. As far as artistic creativity is concerned, this is the case. The Apollonian and the Dionysian modes of creativity are basically at odds with one another, but, when they are reconciled, they succeed in producing the greatest of all works of art: Attic tragedy, which was "equally Dionysian and Apollonian" (GT, sec. 1). If, on the other hand, one looks closely at the conceptual framework of Nietz-sche's treatise from the standpoint of the idea of cognition which underlies it, the matter is quite different. For in that case *das Apollinische* turns out to be not a mode of knowledge at all, but is no more than "the beautiful illusion of the dream worlds" ("der schöne Schein der Traumwelten"; GT, sec. 1) or, to be more specific, it is "der Schein des Scheins." Hence, as illusion of illusion the Apol-lonian mode cannot, by definition, be knowledge.[5]

    [5] See my "Eros and Creativity in Nietzsche's *Birth of Tragedy*," *Studies in German Literature of the Nineteenth and Twentieth Centuries, Festschrift for Frederic E. Coenen,* ed. Siegfried Mews. UNC Studies

The genuine antithesis of "Orgiasmus," on the other hand, is Socratism, a thoroughgoing rationalism relying exclusively on logic or dialectic. Nietzsche makes it quite clear that Socratism produces knowledge, but of an aesthetically inadequate and unfortunate kind. Thus, it is important to note that he tacitly assumes *two modes of knowledge*, not three as the case would be, if Apollonianism were true knowledge. However, he slips on occasion and quite inconsistently equates it with Socratism. It was just this epistemological antithesis which was so fateful for Greek tragedy: "This is the new antithesis: the Dionysian and the Socratic; and Greek tragedy as an art form perished as a result of it" (GT, sec. 12). Socratic rationalism is not a deviant form of Dionysian knowledge but is a radically different mode. Like the latter it is simply a given fact of experience. Strangely enough, Nietzsche later on finds a term for Socratism, namely, "décadence." (He uses the French term consistently to relate Socratism to the nineteenth-century literary movement by that name, especially to Baudelaire and Wagner). This identification is of little use, however, since it raises more questions than it answers.[6] As for Nietzsche's use of the idea of castration else-where, it generally has ethical relevance only: it is significant in connection with his idea of the "good," and is a metaphor for the effect of Christianity on the normal healthy instincts of the human being.[7]

It is surely an eloquent testimony to the central importance of Socrates for Western culture that both Hamann, the ardent defender of Christianity, and

in the Germanic Languages and Literatures, No. 67 (Chapel Hill: University of North Carolina Press, 1970), p. 85. That the Socratic mode of knowledge is not simply an extension and refinement of the Apollonian is evidenced by the fact that Socrates is alleged to have seen in the tragedy of Aeschylus and Sophocles "etwas recht Unvernünftiges, mit Ursachen, die ohne Wirkungen, mit Wirkungen, die ohne Ursachen zu sein schienen . . ." (GT, sec. 14). In the dramas of Euripides, on the other hand, the precise relation between cause and effect is carefully observed (GT, sec. 14). It follows then that the tragedy of Aeschylus and Sophocles must be, despite the presence of the Apollonian element, essentially irrational and that of Euripides essentially rational. Further evidence that Apollonianism does not play a genuine epistemological role or that it is dispensable from the standpoint of knowledge is indicated by the fact that, in the course of time, it becomes completely subsumed under the category of the Dionysian. Cf. Walter Kaufmann, *Nietzsche: Philosopher, Psychologist, Antichrist* (Princeton: Princeton University Press, 1950), p. 129.

6 See "Eros and Creativity in Nietzsche's *Birth of Tragedy*," pp. 98–100.

7 Cf. Friedrich Nietzsche, *The Will to Power*, secs. 383 (p. 207), 204 (p. 122), 248 (pp. 143–44), 351 (p. 192). On two occasions, to my knowledge, Nietzsche tends to understand castration as episte-mologically significant. Thus he writes in GM apropos of asceticism: "Den Willen aber überhaupt eliminieren, die Affekte samt und sonders aushängen, gesetzt, daß wir dies vermöchten: wie? hieße das nicht den Intellekt *kastrieren?*" (GM, sec. 12); again in criticism of German classical education he writes: "Nur auf einem ganz kastrierten und verlogenen Studium des Altertums kann unsere Bildung sich erbauen" (MusA, I, 95). Only the latter quotation has purely epistemological significance, for the former is set within a consistently axiological framework. As Walter Kaufmann says, "Nietzsche never worked out an entirely satisfactory theory of knowledge, and most of the relevant material remained in his notebooks and did not find its way into a more coherent presentation in his published works." *Nietzsche: Philosopher, Psychologist, Antichrist*, p. 177.

Nietzsche, the archenemy of that faith, should have opened their respective literary careers with treatises on the Greek philosopher. The portraits presented in the two works are, however, so different that one might well question whether they were written about the same historical figure. It is not my task in this study to judge which of the two images presented accords more with the facts about the historical Socrates. It is rather my purpose to examine the chief differences which characterize the two accounts and to attempt to explain such differences as far as possible on the basis of the epistemological assumptions of the two writers.

Before considering the specific differences between the two versions of Socrates, however, we should take note of their similarities, for these also are illuminating. First, both works are indictments of their age: the *Socratic Memorabilia* (1759) is an attack on the prevailing *Aufklärung* and *The Birth of Tragedy* (1872) on the contemporary materialism and philistinism of the nineteenth century. Both are personal confessions of faith, Hamann's in Christianity, and Nietzsche's in a revived pagan Greek religion with Dionysos as the chief deity and with Richard Wagner as its high priest. Strangely enough, in both works Socrates is seen as a forerunner of Christ (but for very different reasons). Both Hamann and Nietzsche reject the Winckelmannian notion of the Hellenic spirit as characterized essentially by "edle Einfalt und stille Größe." Both writers attack the rationalistic philologists and historians of their day. Finally, the two treatises are written in a prose which is often metaphorical, even poetic, the opposite of the learned jargon of the schools, and both works bristle with allusions which call for a commentary. Undoubtedly it was these similarities which help explain why Nietzsche could write to his friend Erwin Rohde in 1873 that he had been "very edified" by reading Hamann.[8]

The very fact that these two works reveal so many opinions held in common by their authors, makes the differences all the more striking. First, it should be noted that the Hamannian Socrates is the prototypal man of faith. After Ha-

___

[8] "Sodann lese ich *Hamann* und bin sehre [sic] erbaut: man sieht in die Gebärzustände unsrer deutschen Dichter- und Denker-Cultur. Sehr tief und innig, aber nichtswürdig unkünstlerisch." GB, II, 394. Although Nietzsche had probably not read Hamann before writing *The Birth of Tragedy*, we know that he read him shortly thereafter from his reference to the *Sokratische Denkwürdigkeiten* in *Die Philosophie im tragischen Zeitalter der Griechen* (1873), where, in discussing the lost works of classical authors, he cites the Magus as his *Gewährsmann*. (See W, III, 142.) It is interesting to note that Friedrich Ritschl, in his letter to Nietzsche of 14 February 1872 dissociating himself from *The Birth of Tragedy*, confesses that in his youth he had flirted with the ideas of Schelling and the "spekulativen Phantasien des tiefsinnigen 'Magus des Nordens,' " thus evidently seeing Nietzsche's book under the aspect of those thinkers (GB, III, 142). Ritschl makes it quite clear that this was a road he could not travel. Rose Pfeffer says in her recent book, *Nietzsche: Disciple of Dionysus:* "In 1873 Nietzsche read Hamann at the suggestion of his friend Ritschl . . . ," but this is not the import of the letter cited above (Lewisburg, Pa.: Bucknell University Press, 1972), p. 113. However, it is possible that Ritschl's remark aroused Nietzsche's interest, in which case Miss Pfeffer's statement would be, in a broad sense, correct. Whatever the cause, *Die Philosophie im tragischen Zeitalter der Griechen* clearly reflects, even to the borrowing of a felicitous phrase ("philosophischen Heroismus"), the Hamannian influence.

mann's conversion to evangelical Christianity in 1758, his newly won religious faith so offended a close friend, Johann Christoph Berens, that he called on Hamann in Königsberg in the company of the young *Privatdozent* Immanuel Kant in an attempt to re-convert his erring companion to the principles of the *Auf-klärung*. The *Socratic Memorabilia* was Hamann's answer to that attempt. Since the Socratic ignorance had become a sort of talisman for the *Aufklärer*, and since a believing Christian could logically relate it to the Pauline doctrine of man's ignorance of God outside revelation, it became the main weapon in Hamann's arsenal: "The ignorance of Socrates was *sensibility* ("Empfindung"). But between sensibility and a theoretical proposition is a greater difference than between a living animal and its anatomical skeleton" (73). Thus, a conviction of one's ignorance does not arise from discursive reasoning, i.e., it is not a deduction, but is something which one senses, which one feels with complete sincerity to be true.

One should not, however, make the mistake of thinking that such *Emp-findung* is an illusion. It is no more an illusion than the conviction that we exist or that the phenomenal world around us exists: "Our own existence and the exist-ence of all things outside us must be believed, and cannot be determined in any other way" (73). The influence of Hume's epistemology on this formulation is immediately obvious. Many years later Hamann wrote to Jacobi: "I was im-mersed in Hume when I wrote the *Socratic Memorabilia*, and my statement that '*our own existence and the existence of all things* outside us must be *believed* and cannot be proven in any other way' stems from that fact."[9] Thus, the Hamannian Socrates is made into a man of faith, and therefore an enemy of all attempts to probe the mystery of existence by means of dialectic. At the beginning of his treatise Hamann had laid down the proposition that "to dissect a body and an event into its primary elements means attempting to detect God's invisible Being, His eternal power and Godhead" (64).

For Hamann, Socrates' maieutic approach to knowledge is further evidence of his anti-speculative tendency: "Socrates was, therefore, modest enough to compare his theoretical wisdom with the skill of an old woman who merely comes to the aid of the mother's labor and her timely birth, and renders assistance to both" (66). Apparently it was Hamann's conception that a Socratic procedure simply leads the interlocutor to a realization of the intuitive (not the rational) wisdom latent within him. In Nietzsche's treatise, on the other hand, maieutics is mentioned only once, and then in a philosophically indifferent context (GT, sec. 15). Perhaps Nietzsche tacitly agrees with the Hamannian idea that the maieutic method is evidence of an antitheoretical bias, in which case Nietzsche would, of course not emphasize it.

If Socrates is the prototypal man of faith for Hamann, he is the opposite for

[9] *Hamanns Briefwechsel mit Friedrich Heinrich Jacobi*, Vol. V of *Johann Georg Hamanns, des Magus im Norden, Leben und Schriften*, ed. C. H. Gildemeister (Gotha: Perthes, 1867), p. 506.

Nietzsche. Moreover, it is precisely the Socratic confession of ignorance which Nietzsche links with excessive rationalism:

> The strongest endorsement of this new and unheard of esteem for knowledge and critical insight Socrates expressed when he realized that he was the only one who confessed to himself that he *knew nothing*. While on his critical wanderings through Athens, engaging in conversation with the greatest statesmen, orators, poets, and artists, he met everywhere with the presumption of knowledge. He recognized with astonishment that all those celebrities had no proper and firm conception concerning even their profession and that they practiced them only out of instinct. (GT, sec. 13)

Opposed to the Hamannian Socrates of feeling and faith is, thus, the Nietzschean conception, namely, that Socrates is the spokesman for "this new and unheard of esteem for knowledge." To drive his point home Nietzsche says further that "Socrates is to be characterized as the perfect type of the *non-mystic*, in whom, as the result of a superfetation, the logical powers are as excessively developed as instinctive wisdom is in the case of the mystic" (GT, sec. 13). Socrates' confession of ignorance constitutes, in the Nietzschean view, an indirect confession of faith in reason. Thus, throughout *The Birth of Tragedy* he accentuates his view of Socrates as the arch-rationalist with such phrases as the following: "the antagonist of Dionysos, the new Orpheus" (sec. 12); "the foremost and supreme *Sophist*, the mirror and quintessence of all sophistical strivings" (sec. 13); "the dialectical hero of the Platonic drama" (sec. 14); "the mystagogue of science" (sec. 15); "the prototype of the theoretical optimist" (sec. 15; cf. sec. 18).

The Nietzschean Socrates has such complete confidence in the power of thought that he believes all that is amiss with human life and even the universe itself may be recognized and corrected by means of reason. In this he is the model for theoretical or Alexandrian man. We have noted above that for Hamann the attempt to penetrate the mystery of existence by means of reason "means attempting to detect God's invisible Being, His eternal power and Godhead." Accordingly, the Hamannian Socrates is not guilty of such hubris. But the Nietzschean Socrates definitely *is*, for he is committed above all to the firm belief "that thought penetrates, by means of the clue of causality, into the deepest abysses of being, and that it is not only able to comprehend being, but is even able to *correct* it" (GT, sec. 15). Intellectuals, who invariably look to Socrates as their model, will therefore easily cherish an optimistic belief in "a revision of the world by means of knowledge."

Despite the fact that the antithesis of instinct and reason as coequal powers of the human mind is basic to *The Birth of Tragedy*, an inconsistency in Nietzsche's treatment of reason arises when he deals with the historical effects of Socratism. On the one hand, Socrates is the irresistible destroyer of high culture on an epochal scale. Such destructive power is not surprising, since Socrates is represented as a "demonic power," even "a divinity" (GT, sec. 12), whose influence on future generations is like a shadow cast by the evening sun, growing ever larger (GT, sec. 15). This vast power of a Socrates accords with the basic conceptual framework of Nietzsche's essay. On the other hand, a difficulty arises when one also notes that the same Socrates serves as the prototype of the cerebral, hence sickly and feckless individual, "the eternal starveling, the 'critic' without pleasure and power, the Alexandrian man, who is basically a librarian and proofreader, miserably blinding himself with the dust of books and typographical errors" (GT, sec. 18). The true nature of the intellectual is revealed most fully, however, in his reaction to the orgiastic frenzy which periodically seizes Dionysian man: "There are people who, convinced of their own health, scornfully or deploringly, turn away, whether as a result of lack of experience or obtuseness, from such phenomena as if from 'diseases of the common people.' But such poor souls do not suspect how corpse-like and ghostly their 'health' appears when the Dionysian throng, glowing with vitality, rushes past them" (GT, sec. I). Nietzsche's inconsistent view of Socratism, that it is a powerful cultural force and at the same time helpless before the vital forces of life, is built into his portrait of Socrates. It would be unfair to suggest that Nietzsche should have solved the perennial problem of "Alexandrian man" in society. However, he seems to be unaware of his inconsistency at this point.

Hamann and Nietzsche cast the Sophists in opposite roles in their accounts of Socrates. For Hamann, they are, as we have seen, the adversaries of Socrates with whom the philosopher is sharply contrasted. Nietzsche, on the other hand, speaks of "the profound instincts of Aristophanes" in identifying Socrates as the foremost and supreme Sophist (GT, sec. 13).

Other differences, which flow naturally from the basic assumptions of the two authors, can be mentioned only briefly. For Hamann, the daemon of Socrates is the divine afflatus, the source of both artistic creativity and, as a prototype of the Holy Spirit, the source of religious inspiration (75). Thus, the influence of the Socratic daemon is essentially positive. In direct contradiction of the Hamannian conception is Nietzsche's: the daemon is the hypertrophied instinct for logic and criticism, and has an essentially negative function (GT, sec. 13). In the case of the Hamannian Socrates, beauty is conceived as irrational; symmetry, harmony, and grace of external form are not its hallmarks (though Hamann distinguishes between the Socratic ideal, which is characterized by such qualities, and the Socratic actuality, which is not).

It was Hamann's intention to write about Socrates "in a Socratic manner" (61). Consequently it is necessary to analyze the literary form of *Socratic Memorabilia*, its style, etc. in order to grasp fully the Hamannian notion of spiritual beauty which manifests itself in unlikely form. One of the leading ideas in *The Birth of Tragedy*, on the other hand, is that beauty must, according to the Socratic ideal, be rational ("verständig," GT, sec. 12). It is to the great discredit of Socrates according to this view that he infected Euripides with this notion and, as a consequence, eliminated myth and miracle from drama. In such a way Euripides, under the spell of Socrates, succeeded in banishing genuine tragedy from the Greek stage. (Hamann, as we have seen, blames the Sophists, not Socrates, for the demise of myth and miracle.) As far as the form of his work is concerned, Nietzsche makes no claim that it is written either in a Socratic or anti-Socratic manner. In the first place Socrates is not even mentioned until halfway through the treatise, and, although he thereafter becomes the central figure, the burden of the work is concerned with the origin of the Apollonian-Dionysian tragedy and its destruction by Socrates. There is great irony in the fact that the most lyrical and moving passages of the book are those which pertain to Socrates, the archenemy of impassioned beauty.

Although Hamann is not concerned with the aesthetic problem of the demise of Attic tragedy, it is true that the *Socratic Memorabilia*, in so far as it is an account of the historical Socrates, is essentially tragic. Indeed it is the tragic aspect of the life and death of the Greek philosopher which foreshadows the life and death of Christ (82), even though the Savior's death may not be interpreted as tragic. Socrates is, of course, the great destroyer of Greek tragedy according to Nietzsche, and though he recognizes the tragic element in the death of the philosopher, he nevertheless sees the Socratic influence as absolutely inimical to tragedy: "Wielding the scourge of its syllogisms, optimistic dialectics drives *music* out of tragedy, i.e., it destroys the essence of tragedy . . ." (GT, sec. 14). Finally, Hamann's crude and scurrilous humor borders at times on the sacrilegious, and is in marked contrast to Nietzsche's pervasive solemnity.

It is clear, I think, that the differences between the Hamannian and Nietzschean versions of Socrates derive from their contrasting epistemologies. Both treatises are concerned with the problem of intuitive versus abstract knowledge. Both are in essential agreement with regard to the close relationship of sexuality to intuitive knowledge, but their views diverge on the question of the status of abstract knowledge. For Hamann, abstraction as castration is a mutilated, hence a subordinate kind of knowledge. It cannot really prevail in any earnest contest with intuitive wisdom. For Nietzsche, on the contrary, abstraction is a coordinate power with intuition. (The curious notion of *décadence*, which Nietzsche later explicitly applies to Socrates, throws no light on the subject of Socratism, but is simply evidence of his feeling of uneasiness about the role in which he had cast the philosopher.[10]) It is the *coequal* relationship of the two modes of knowledge which sets the stage for the fateful, world-historical struggle between Dionysos and Socrates. Thus far in the course of Western history Socratic intellectualism has generally been triumphant, but Nietzsche anticipated its imminent end: "The age of Socratic man is past . . . Arm yourselves for a deadly struggle, but believe in the miracles of your god!" (GT, sec. 113). Yet the contest *could* go either way, for both antagonists are eternally powerful. There is no such struggle between the

10 Cf. n. 5 .

Hamannian Socrates and his Sophistical adversaries, nor could there be. True, the Sophists are deadly enemies of Socrates, but the contest is unequal, for they are mainly scheming and contemptible hypocrites. Though the Hamannian Socrates is destroyed by a hostile "Welt" (82), his cause must ultimately triumph, because God has so willed it.

In conclusion we may say that the differing epistemological conceptions which underlie the Hamannian and Nietzschean treatises (whatever their relative merits from a purely philosophical point of view)[11] serve their authors well as a background for their contrasting portraits of the father of Western philosophy.

[11] It is interesting to note, however, that the classical scholar Philip Merlan maintains that "only the interpretation of Hamann and Kierkegaard, both of whom were possessed by an eminent sense of the demonic, does full justice to the demonic element in the Platonic (and . . . even in the Xenophontic) Socrates." "Form and Content in Plato's Philosophy," *Journal of the History of Ideas*, 8, No. 4 (October 1947), 417. n. 33.

IX

The German "Classicist" Goethe
as Reflected in Nietzsche's Works *

KARL SCHLECHTA

TRANSLATED BY TIMOTHY F. SELLNER

Early in the year 1804 that astute and unprejudiced observer, Madame de Staël, made the following statement in Weimar, presumably to Böttiger: "Écoutez, il y un double Goethe, le poète et le métaphysicien. Le poète est lui même, l'autre est son fantôme."

Aside from the fact that there are certainly more sides to Goethe than this, for example, the Goethe of the Color Theory and Goethe the morphologist and evolutionist, and aside from the fact that, precisely in the case of Goethe, classicistic "metaphysics" frequently not only influenced, but even determined the nature of his writings, Madame de Staël is doubtless correct in her observation—she perceived the main idea and was quick to give it expression with the appropriate word: "metaphysics." The classicistic program does indeed have its basis in metaphysics.

To return to Goethe, Karl Reinhardt has pointed out that it is in Goethe alone that the ever-reappearing marble contours of the Greek are infused with the inner light of a transparent soul. In the case of Nietzsche, there is no evidence whatsoever of any such perceptiveness or understanding.

The classicistic program originates with Winckelmann. His conversion had obtained for him a year in Dresden free of obligations, a year which was to be a decisive one in his life. The year 1755 saw the appearance of *Thoughts on the Imitation of Greek Works in Painting and Sculpture*, which was then followed by his *Letter Concerning Thoughts on the Imitation of Greek Works. . . .* In the latter work Winckelmann allows a hypothetical opponent of his theory to have his say, so that he can then give reply in a third small pamphlet, the *Commentary on the Thoughts on Imitation . . .* , and *Reply to the Letter Concerning these Thoughts*. These

---

* In view of the fact that chronological sequence plays such a decisive role with respect to this question, I have drawn my quotations in the main from the Musarion Edition (MusA; for key to abbreviations, see p. xvii above). Both Nietzsche's works and his literary remains, each enclosing segments of the other, are arranged chronologically in this edition. The text is based largely on the Complete Edition in large octavo (GOA and GOA[2]). To the extent that critical editions exist for the passages cited, I have used these in making my additions and corrections.

three pamphlets comprise a unity and constitute a self-contained system. When Winckelmann went to Italy in 1755, he took with him this "system" in its already completed form, and even the first of these small pamphlets contains all the essential elements of the Germans' veneration of the Greeks. The basic tenor of these pamphlets is aesthetic, ethical, and above all, pedagogic. With the zeal of a reformer he advocates a rebirth of man in a sense that is almost religious. It is a question of the education to an authentic style of life. A kind of mild obsession with basic principles expresses itself in philosophical and apodictic fashion. Such statements as: "Painting is concerned with things which are not material . . ." are presented as self-evident propositions. Even before he begins his investigation, Winckelmann is already aware of the direction it will take. The serenity of his mode of expression, which would have us understand man as living out his existence quietly and peacefully as an expression of the divine within himself, is not quite able to conceal the presence of a powerful act of creation—creation in the sense of a rebirth of the *whole* man on the basis of aesthetics. The fact that for the ancient Greeks man and the divinities were separated by an abyss did not seem to bother Winckelmann. His analogies, laden with symbols, are immensely elastic—how else, for example, would the classical philologist Nietzsche have later been able to compare Richard Wagner with Aeschylus? Even Winckelmann's most important work, the *History of Ancient Art*, is a historical metaphysics, a self-conceived myth, a dream which he carried with him from the North to Rome.

Still one more factor seems significant to me in determining Winckelmann's point of view: the association with his principal acquaintances during the Dresden period, Oeser and Hagedorn. Both exerted a lasting influence on Winckelmann—Oeser as a painter, sculptor and theoretician, Hagedorn as a writer on aesthetics. Oeser's taste for the simple, the naive, and the serene had the same power of attraction for Winckelmann as it later did for Goethe in Leipzig. And especially captivating for both was his unpretentious and concerned manner of teaching. With Oeser, doctrine and criticism prevail over the productive powers. He speaks of harmony but has no genuine capacity for working with color; he speaks of "beauty" and fails to produce that which is "characteristic." Grace and dignity become *style* by means of a kind of dilution of nature. In Oeser was united the saccharine sensuousness of a Viennese academician with the ideality of a clearheaded Saxon; although somewhat languorous when it came to working with his hands, he nevertheless possessed a very nimble mind.

Hagedorn was of a thoroughly kindred spirit. He, too, preferred ideal beauty to character, and grace to charm—and more than anything he cherished serenity in nature. He, too, saw in the history of art a heuristic principle. Characterized by all the weaknesses of an admittedly noble but asthenic personality, his humane gentleness felt comfortable only in the realm of the uncommitted and the neutral. As one might expect, it is particularly the case with Hagedorn that it is not the eye or direct observation which prevail in the consideration of works of the plastic and graphic arts, but the word, elegant rhetoric with all its pretentiousness. This is an idiosyncrasy, a character trait peculiar to classicism from which even Lessing was not entirely free.[1]

When we recall Oeser and Hagedorn, we are not surprised at Winckelmann's close association with Mengs in Rome. He, as well, was an inveterate theoretician of metaphysical provenance. To be sure, Winckelmann's deep insecurity in matters of aesthetic taste did have a profound effect on the relationship between him and Mengs—one need only recall here the mischievous forgery of a work of classical antiquity by Mengs in his fresco "Zeus and Ganymede."[2] Nevertheless not only Winckelmann, but even Goethe fell victim to this rather wicked little scheme.

It is not at all surprising: the whole thing began with a theory, and all at once one found himself on a path leading to an antiquity which had never existed. There were no criteria which were convincing in and of themselves; neither did the continual references to nature afford any help, for a nature such as this had never existed. No amount of discussion could explain away the profound lack of creative power; no aesthetics, no pedagogy, no metaphysics was helpful in this regard. Even his art-loving friends in Weimar were not able to help.

We must not overlook the fact that here, too, a fundamental difference exists between the founder of the school and the school itself. In contrast to his industrious followers—literary men of all kinds—life and work were one and the same for Winckelmann. With a certain degree of necessity his remarkable life flows into his doctrine, and the whole pathos of his doctrine is not a little determined by his existence. His entire being is but an expression of an *inner* necessity, a quality lacking in his followers.

Be this as it may, the theory produced an epoch-making misunderstanding. Two things stand irreconcilably opposed to each other: Goethe's statement that "among all peoples the Greeks dreamed the dream of life most beautifully," and that of Jacob Burckhardt: "Of all civilized people the Greeks are the ones who have inflicted upon themselves the bitterest, most deeply felt suffering."

With this as our background, then, let us now consider the image of Goethe in Nietzsche's works. Schulpforta, that famous and rigorous humanistic *Gymnasium*, the pedagogical institution for the training of a middle-class elite, was thoroughly permeated with the spirit of classicistic ideals. The study of classical languages and intensive reading in the principal representatives of German Classicism were of central importance in the curriculum. In contrast to the

---

[1] Cf. No. 14 of his "Antiquarian Letters."

[2] Cf. in the excellent and extensive catalogue of the London exhibition, *The Age of New Classicism* (1972) under "Paintings," No. 198, where the pertinent texts can be found in English translation. At this point I would like to thank Professor Judith Janoska of the University of Bern for this very informative catalogue.

majority of German *Gymnasien*, the study of the former discipline was distinguished, of course, by its very rigorous philological requirements. The students not only studied Latin and Greek, they actually mastered them as well. Questions regarding textual criticism and problems in interpretation were, so to speak, the students' daily fare. Thus the educational foundation consisted not only of the exemplary understanding of classical antiquity as viewed from the perspective of Winckelmann, Goethe, and Schiller, but also of the scientific and critical study of the classical languages. This latter study was not so much one of content, but primarily one of form. Thus there existed a hiatus of sorts, or a kind of dual-track system, which was some years later to receive a great deal of attention from Nietzsche.

The first statement concerning Goethe—of any consequence at least—made by Nietzsche during his years at the Schulpforta is to be found in a composition of March 1863. Here we read: "Goethe . . . the exalted and enveloping spirit of the German nation" (MusA, I, 110). In this statement lies concealed an element of no small importance: the element of national consciousness. From its very beginnings, German Classicism was borne along by the hope for a German national rebirth. The return to the Greeks and the disregard for the Roman-French tradition had always been interpreted as the discovery of a national identity. Across the span of two millenia—people were convinced of this—kindred spirits confronted one another. The appreciation for one's remote origins, for a brilliant pre-history involved the understanding of one's own present—not the real present, but the one which was thought to lie below the surface. It was believed that one's identity as a chosen people was only to be found in the remote past. This spontaneous leap out of the continuum of European tradition, prepared by Lessing, was not without its remarkable consequences. Just as Luther in his own time had hearkened back to the pure word of Scripture, appeal was now made to pure human form, a form which had been brought forth by Winckelmann in his image of the Greeks. With that begins the history of the mythologem in German intellectual life extending all the way to Stefan George. A special role in this history was always reserved for that which was German—a procedure almost always involving violence to historical fact.

As far as this interpretation of the content of classical literature is concerned—an interpretation quite in the spirit of the German humanistic *Gymnasium*—we find in Nietzsche's valedictory essay in Latin, "De Theognide Megarensi," the following revealing quotation from Goethe: "We are accustomed to giving an author's statements of whatever kind a universal interpretation and adapting them however possible to our own circumstances" (MusA, I, 230).

This is a methodical program which leaves nothing to be desired in the determination of a subject matter for a universal education—we are accustomed to giving statements a universal *interpretation*, to adapting them however possible to our own circumstances. And indeed, this is just the way it was done. On one

particular occasion, when a certain passage from the "adapted" version of Sophocles refused to be disposed of in this manner, no less a person than Goethe expressed the wish that a philologist demonstrate that the passage in question was
an interpolation. It is possible that the German character could have been helped
by such exegetical artifices; the reality of the Greek became lost in Germanic
mists.

Just to define the limits of our theme: in the spring of 1868, during an inter-
lude in his work, Nietzsche planned a philosophical treatise with the title "Teleology since Kant." In the notes for this work he speaks only in passing of Goethe as
a natural philosopher.[3] Goethe the evolutionist does not appear at all—he is
simply not perceived as such. Classicism is averse to all movement and energy—
it is static.

On a level with this wilful disregard for the very important non-classicistic
side of Goethe is a notation in the literary remains on *Human, All-Too-Human*, I,
which thus dates from the year 1876 or 1877. Here we read that "Goethe, in his
Color Theory, . . . was wrong." Goethe was, of course, "wrong" in his controversy with Newton. Now while this judgment does correspond to the prevailing
communis opinio of that time, and to a great extent of the present time as well, it is
somewhat surprising to find it presented as a self-evident proposition among the
formulations in a work which contains some very interesting—and for this period
unusual—rudimentary ideas of a scientific and critical nature. It is not possible to
speak of "right" and "wrong" as between Goethe and Newton. Goethe speaks of
qualities infused with feeling and meaning—perceptual qualities, and thus precisely that which Newton dispensed with as the first step in his scientific procedure. "Sense" and "meaning" play no part whatsoever, and the question
concerning their importance is never even raised.

From the time of his inaugural address ("Homer and Classical Philology")
at Basel in May 1869, to the year 1872, the conceptual twins "*Deutschtum*" and
"*Hellenentum*," "authentic *Deutschtum*" and "authentic *Hellenentum*" predominate in Nietzsche's mention of Goethe, for they are complementary concepts. At
the outset he still confines himself in gentler tones to the diction of Winckelmann,
for example, when he addresses "the passionate admirers of Hellenic beauty and
noble simplicity." In the address mentioned above, however, "ideal antiquity"
figures as "the most beautiful flower of passionate Germanic longing" (MusA,
II, 8). We are, of course, indebted above all to Winckelmann and Goethe for the
concept of "ideal antiquity." In the lecture which he held in the summer of 1871
entitled "Introduction to the Study of Classical Philology," he strongly urges
that one "become intimately acquainted" with the writings of just these two men
(MusA, II, 343). They alone—occasionally together with Schiller—provide
access to the sanctuary. "The German spirit" has struggled more forcefully than

---

[3] Cf. MusA, I, 411; 414 ff.

any other to learn from the Greeks, Nietzsche says, and it has done this through the noblest strivings of Goethe and Schiller toward educational development (MusA, III, 135). These words are to be found in *The Birth of Tragedy from the Spirit of Music* (1872). That we are dealing here with what is basically a pedagogical program of national scope can be seen from the fact that both in the preliminary studies to the lecture series "Concerning the Future of our Educational Institutions," as well as in the lectures themselves (held in the early months of 1872 under the auspices of the Basel "Academic Society"), Nietzsche apostrophizes Winckelmann and Goethe—here and there Schiller as well—as the pioneers of a new and decisive understanding of the ancient Greeks. "The German character," he says, has attained through them a "level of culture and education" no one had thought possible before (MusA, IV, 47). And always it is "the Greek homeland" which refreshes and restores the Germans. Here is the place of pilgrimage for the German spirit, for the innermost German being, and for the best representatives of the German nation. The members of his audience as well as posterity in general merely have the task of continuing that which had already experienced such a grandiose beginning (MusA, IV, 133).

Information concerning the methods by which this projected canon was to be brought about, or according to which it could have been brought about, can be found in a passage from only a few years later (1874–75)—a passage which Nietzsche delivered as part of a university lecture entitled "The History of Greek Literature." It reads: "We must imagine Plato as an old man in the process of revising his rough drafts—just as, for example, Goethe did. Through collation, and not without a certain amount of arbitrariness, a complete work is put together" (MusA, V, 146). In other words, the unevenness of his earlier, spontaneous thoughts is smoothed out, contradictions are eliminated, "a whole" is "put in order." One needs closed horizons, and within these a pervasive sense of order—in short, and once again, one needs "a whole."

What this means in reference to Goethe can be illustrated by several passages from his posthumously published studies and preliminary sketches to the second of the *Untimely Meditations*, viz, *On the Use and Disadvantage of History for Life*. To cite the most important: "As a stylized human being, Goethe has ascended higher than any other German. . . . Let one read Eckermann and ask himself whether there ever was a human being in Germany who has come so far in such noble form" (MusA, VI, 340). And here we come upon a very significant catchword for German Classicism: "stylized." True, artists stylized continuously, and this was true for their lives as well as their artistic production. But this was not all; whatever did not conform to this "style" was condemned, and not infrequently this involved one's own powers of spontaneous creation—in poetry, in the plastic arts, and also in music. Models were set up and absolute standards were to be adhered to; on the other hand, however, support was given to mediocrities who submitted to these demands. All this was not accomplished without tremendous cost, for one had lost contact with the concrete reality of the present. This cost had to be borne by the generations which followed. Nietzsche recommends that Eckermann's "Conversations with Goethe" be read "in order that one remain protected in this way from all fashionable teachings of the legionaries of the moment" (MusA, VI, 300). In the treatise which he planned called "Philosophy in Distress," Nietzsche blusters at "the tyranny of the press" (MusA, VII, 20), and points out emphatically that Goethe was to be furnished only with periodicals which appeared serially or in weekly issues—and thus with nothing immediately current. That was tedious, and distracted one from elite stylization.

Nietzsche could not have found a better example for this hymn of stylization than Eckermann's conversations with Goethe, for they provide a classical example of classicistic self-description. Goethe speaks like Eckermann, and Eckermann like Goethe. All the retouchings and stylizations had the blessing of the Master. The notes for the work arose in large part under his supervision, and the elderly gentleman spent more than a little time working on their correction. With some justification Nietzsche later speaks of "Goethe's feat in idealizing his own life" (Human, All-Too-Human, I; 1876–78; MusA, VIII, 244). We have here a treasure chest of sayings for every conceivable occasion, and at the same time a carefully cultivated terrain surrounded entirely by prohibitory markers. In short, we are dealing here with the first Goethe-novel, produced under the aegis of the Olympian himself, in which he gives himself a classicistic interpretation. To what extent manipulation took place here—not to say falsification—is clear to everyone who compares, for example, Eckermann's description of 23 and 24 February 1823 with the notes of Chancellor von Müller from the same two days. Reality and the "ideal" stand here irreconcilably opposed at a very critical point. Eckermann relates the event as a witness in the first person—this same Eckermann who had met Goethe for the first time at the beginning of June that same year. *Sapienti sat!*[4] Nietzsche's recommendation of Adalbert Stifter's *Indian Summer* (*Nachsommer*) arises out of the same misunderstanding (cf. MusA, IX, 245), the only difference being that this prose has been diluted to an even thinner broth; the "stylization" can no longer be surpassed.

From about 1874 on a slightly critical tone is introduced into this theme of "stylization," a tone which visibly intensifies, however, when reference is occasionally made to that which is truly Greek. Nietzsche makes the remark that Goethe the man is an example of "the contemplative man in the grand style," but not of the active man; the Goethean man was of "a noble gentleness." This quotation stems from the third of the Untimely Meditations: Schopenhauer as Educator (MusA, VII, 74 and 79). We find an even more radical formulation in the preliminary studies to this "Meditation": The "Goethean conception of the

---

[4] Cf. the splendid analysis by Josef Hofmiller in *Wege zu Goethe* (Hamburg-Bergedorf: Strom Verlag, 1949), pp. 59–78.

Greeks is, in the first place, historically incorrect, and moreover, too weak and unmanly" (ibid., 145).

We also have preserved for us from that same period, the years 1874–75, certain notes—presumably for a further "Meditation" with the title "We Philologists"—which make his position quite clear. Here we read, for example: "Misunderstanding of the Greeks . . . Goethe-Schiller" or "Our education can find edification only in an utterly castrated and mendacious study of antiquity" (WKG, IV-1, 195). He even goes so far as to say: "Our attitude toward classical antiquity is really the basic reason for the unproductivity of modern culture" (ibid., 129).

What has happened here, and why this change of opinion? Several causes can be imagined: the vehement awakening of a critical consciousness with regard to the classicistic content of the curriculum of the German *Gymnasium*, as well as in relation to the pedagogical goals of classical philology in general. Such expressions as "the philologist as schoolmaster of the upper classes (Goethe-Schiller)" (MusA, VII, 153), provide evidence for this. Even the social factor makes a fleeting appearance! Further, the inner confrontation with Schopenhauer and Wagner, both of whom were treated as main topics in the *Untimely Meditations*. In contrast to both of these men, Goethe has something soft, gentle, and comfortable about him (cf. MusA, VII, 260), which can be said for neither Schopenhauer nor Wagner.

However, I suspect that yet another factor is involved. On 6 May 1872 Jacob Burckhardt began to lecture for the first time on the "Cultural History of Greece." Nietzsche attended these lectures—how often and for how long is not known, but his protégés Adolf Baumgartner and Louis Kelterborn each presented him with a transcript of them. I am acquainted with both of these transcripts; they were written down very conscientiously. Since Nietzsche was still in continuous communication with Burckhardt during these years, we must assume that there was a good deal of talk between them about this particular topic. Otherwise how could Nietzsche write the following to his friend Carl von Gersdorff as early as the first of May 1872 (thus before the lectures even began): "The summer lectures by Burckhardt will be unique: you will be missing a lot by not hearing them" (W, III, 1066). These magnificent lectures have long since been posthumously published. The image of the Greeks which, with all its details, is projected here, stands in stark contrast to the shadowy figures of the German dream of Greece prevailing at the time. Personally, I am of the opinion that something in the way of necessary corrections could have been discovered before that time from August Böckh's *The Public Economy of the Athenians*.[5]

Jacob Burckhardt had already caused Friedrich Nietzsche to do an about-face

---

[5] (Berlin: G. Reimer, 1817). English translation of the title is from the 2nd German edition (Boston: Little, 1857).

once before, and that was in connection with the evaluation of the victory in the war with the French in 1870–71 and the cultural consequences of that victory. The letters and notes of Nietzsche from this period, not yet very far in the past, furnish unequivocal proof of this change of mind. In this matter, too, it was the elder of the two who opened the eyes of the younger. Why not, then, in the case described above? The high level of the dispute was assured in any event.

Even in the rough draft of an essay on "the possibility of a German culture" (1873), this question of style is brought up again and again: "Enormous labor of Goethe and Schiller to develop a German style" (MusA, VII, 228); and at another point: "Attempt on the part of our great writers to arrive at a convention" (ibid., 231).

Is not all of German Classicism such a remarkable attempt as this—an attempt apparently arising from the extraordinary notion that style could be created merely through proper execution? That captious word "labor" stands in the first sentence. What is the vacuum out of which the demand for a "convention" arises—for a convention within what specific limits, or even for a convention at all? We must assume that they felt themselves to be in a state of oppressive uncertainty and insecurity, where their freedom was a threat. They were afraid in the same way that Goethe—according to Nietzsche—had been "afraid" of Heinrich von Kleist (ibid.). Actually, this feeling of anxiety is in itself not very surprising; they had intentionally disengaged themselves from the entire European tradition —the naive, great Wieland, in spite of all his coquetry, is the significant exception —and they had rejected the real world, the given world in all its unclassifiable details. Where did that leave them then? Presumably, in a literary cloister which was surrounded by high ramparts, where fresh breezes no longer penetrated. Only the "cultured" were allowed inside, and even they soon turned into "cultural Philistines." They were among their own kind, and the lack of immediacy and of any permanent contact with the unpleasant—but vital—outside environment was compensated for by the conviction that they constituted an elite society. They had completely shoved aside the long-overdue reckoning with the natural sciences, indeed with critical scholarship in general. One need only think of Nietzsche's later efforts to make up for lost time in this area—a nearly hopeless undertaking, in view of his humanistic provenance. In the first part of his *Human, All-Too-Human*, we find the characteristic remark: Goethe sees nature as "the best means for pacifying the modern soul" (MusA, VIII, 115). This is nature as seen from within the confines of the cloistered walls of classicism.

The problem of tradition, that is, the problem of assigning the correct place to Goethe the classicist in the total history of European culture, occupied Nietzsche's mind again and again during these years.[6] In the fourth of the *Untimely Meditations*, entitled *Richard Wagner in Bayreuth*, is to be found a clear formulation

[6] Cf. MusA, VII, 172, 209; WKG, IV-1, 350.

of the crucial idea: Goethe is to be interpreted as one of the "last great camp-followers in the ranks of the Italian poet-philologists" (MusA, VII, 325). Thus, for example, his Tasso has its origins in the Renaissance model.[7] The catalogue of models and standards of the Renaissance is known to us. It stems from the Alexandrian philologists and historians of literature, is constructed on the basis of canonically interpreted concepts of genre, and still today lingers on in the German humanistic *Gymnasien*. Nietzsche characterizes the philologist-poet in the following way: "no new subject matter or characters, but only those we have long been acquainted with in everlasting re-animation and transformation." He continues: "this is art as Goethe later came to understand it."[8] In contrast to this stand the pithy sentences: "Classical writers . . . become classical in terms of their capacity to serve as models and be imitated . . . , while great writers cannot be imitated. In classical writers language and the word are dead; the mollusk is dead in his shell."[9] But can we then entirely believe, after such a determination, his concluding sentence: "But it is still alive in Goethe"? Much more convincing is the statement: "The ideal in Schiller and Humboldt: a false antiquity . . . somewhat too glossy, soft, . . . refined in manner . . . but no life, no real blood" (MusA, IX, 448 f.).

In 1879 the vocabulary applied to Goethe was something like this: moderation, gentleness, level terrain, and harmonious manner of living. He also speaks of "Schiller's and Goethe's fields of tender fruit."[10] To be sure, he does not hesitate to add that, as a thinker, Goethe embraced the clouds more intimately than was proper (MusA, IX, 195).

From the time of *The Dawn* (1880–81) on, Nietzsche's mode of expression becomes more aggressive once again—he even comes to the point of an outright dispute with German classicism in general, with German education, and again and again, with Goethe the classicist. This dispute continues—although not without interruption—all the way into Nietzsche's final period of creativity. But more about this later.

The attack begins with the statement: "those silly 'classicists' have deprived us of all honesty."[11] In reference to German education he says: "boneless generalities . . . 'beautiful' in terms of an inferior and dulled sense of taste, which prided itself, nonetheless, on its Greek origin. It is but a weak, mild-mannered, silvery idealism, which more than anything else wishes to possess the voice and gestures of a feigned grandeur—a thing as harmless as it is presumptuous, inspired by the heartiest repugnance toward 'cold' or 'barren' reality" (ibid., 170 f.). One has the impression that Nietzsche by this time has a good grasp of the main problem;

---

[7] From the notes to MA, II; cf. MusA, IX, 450.
[8] MA, I; MusA, VIII, 193.
[9] Notes to MA, II; MusA, IX, 451.
[10] Cf. MusA, IX, 54 ff., 90, 242.
[11] M; MusA, X, 152.

not infrequently he is overcome with impatience and anger in the face of this sort of "niaiserie allemande." In *The Twilight of the Idols* (1888), he simply concludes: "Goethe did not understand the Greeks" (MusA, XVII, 157). In large parts of his literary remains from the eighties—later compiled as the so-called *Will to Power*—one can find now and again such turns of phrase as, for example, the statement that even the noble ardor of such friends of antiquity as Goethe and Winckelmann had something "illicit and almost immodest" about it.[12] Nietzsche is convinced—with regard to Winckelmann's and Goethe's image of Greece—that some day the entire farce was going to be discovered (MusA, XIX, 233); indeed, that "only now are we finally learning to laugh" at them (ibid., 245). Thus it seems clear enough: his general reckoning can hardly be surpassed in its severity.

I spoke previously of interludes. First of all, the question of style does, to be sure, recede into the background; nevertheless, it continues to remain virulent. Furthermore it is narrowed down to the person of Goethe; thus, he, Goethe, "in a subtle and artful way entrenched and disguised" his own culture.[13] At the same time, however, this was done with such a lack of assurance and resolution that the question arises; "In what light will he later appear?" (MusA, XVI, 355). As a summation one could take Nietzsche's words from the poem "To Goethe": "The immortal is but the symbol of Thee."[14] In regard to the problem of style, Goethe is also several times brought face to face with Beethoven. Notes concerning this confrontation can be found as early as the period of *The Dawn* and *The Gay Science*.[15] Beethoven figures in these works as the "untamed mortal"; Nietzsche welcomes Goethe's "cautious stance toward music," and even expresses the regret that a "music of equal rank" to Goethe had not yet been produced.[16] This is a frightening thought, when one recalls on the one hand Karl Friedrich Zelter, and on the other the rising maestro Peter Gast. What a disastrous misjudgment of potencies, in spite of the fact that he had become acquainted with a musician of genius in Richard Wagner, and in spite of the fact that he had once done some composing worthy of note himself—and what is more, not at all in the "classicistic" style!

In my opinion, the enduring virulence of the problem of style is related in a very fundamental way to Nietzsche's latent quest for disciples. Even with all his emphatically expressed pride in his solitude, the hope of attracting like-minded followers never died. This hope necessarily required restraint, and this restraint in turn led to occasional false conclusions—for example, after his unsuccessful endeavors to obtain the love of Lou von Salomé, and after his friendship with Paul Reé was shattered. These two attain the status of deeply disappointing, and

[12] Cf. MusA, XIII, 265; XIX, 363.

[13] The quote is from the literary remains of the eighties, MusA, XIX, 206; XVI, 355.

[14] 1882–84. MusA, XX, 107.

[15] 1881–82. Cf. MusA, XI, 89, 112; XII, 132.

[16] Cf. also MusA, XVIII, 82, from the literary remains of the eighties.

therefore hated "disciples." And to whom does Zarathustra preach, if not to an imaginary group of disciples? The note which had been sounded did not die away in vain; they came later, the disciples, and how they looked the part, too! Zarathustra went along in the knapsacks of a youthful generation setting out joyously on the road to death. Nietzsche states quite correctly in *Ecce Homo* "that a Goethe . . . would not be able to breathe for a single moment in this gigantic passion and at this altitude."[17] It only remains for us to say that this Goethe also certainly would not have wished to do so; this kind of feeling for style was utterly alien to him.

Second, and in a way which is parallel to these interpretations, the name of Goethe appears from time to time on a list alternating with other great names of modern history as well as of German intellectual history. Napoleon, Beethoven, Schopenhauer, and Wagner come and go, appear and disappear, and are exchanged for other names. Goethe appears in the obligatory contours, divested of all specific characteristics.[18] In these works we find something like a chessboard on which the above-named, as well as other great names are set up and moved by Nietzsche according to the rules which happen to prevail at any given time. They are trumpet flourishes in a battle of spectres. But this is really not so new; we have already encountered similar things in *The Birth of Tragedy*. I remind the reader here of the juxtaposition of Aeschylus and Wagner, of Socrates and Euripides. But not a word, for example, about the fact that Euripides, through Seneca, permanently influenced the entire European theatrical tradition. On the contrary, in regard to both past and present Nietzsche stuck to the sources, thereby remaining outside the great tradition. And not to mention Socrates!

In conclusion, I would like to say once again that I have not spoken of the whole Goethe, nor even of the whole poet Goethe—neither have I spoken of the whole Nietzsche. I have, to the best of my ability, held to the question as stated, and such precise questions involve a relatively limited perspective. We necessarily see but a single side.

[17] 1888. MusA, XX, 255.
[18] Cf. J, 1886; GM, 1887; MusA, XV, 123 f.; from the literary remains of the eighties, XVIII, 82.

X

The Reluctant Disciple: Nietzsche and Schiller

HELMUT REHDER

Not too many decades ago when Thomas Mann had skillfully negotiated the transition from the relatively serene satire of *Lotte in Weimar* (1939) to the stark tragedy of *Doktor Faustus* (1947) some young German critics, rooted deeply in their classical tradition, were tempted to argue about the elasticity of Mann's power of artistic adaptation: "He *is* like Schiller but *would love to be* like Goethe." Evidently literary emulation is more than a matter of artistic will and skill; often it springs from some unexplored obsession or tradition. For Thomas Mann, as for many other writers of his day, Schiller's essays represented the indispensable means of self-orientation—books one had to read to be properly initiated into the community of literature and criticism. But beyond that and below the surface of mere learning and academic nomenclature, there is a similarity of thought structure, of poetic theory and practice, that reveals a surprising parallel between the two writers. The *Zauberberg* would scarcely have been written without the precedence of the *Betrachtungen eines Unpolitischen*. By the same token, Schiller's great poems and later plays would not have matured without his *Briefe über die aesthetische Erziehung des Menschen*. Between the *Betrachtungen* and the *Briefe* there exists a striking similarity of purpose and even of method: with a degree of dedication which has rarely, if ever, been equalled, both probe into the cultural conscience and responsibility of the writer and come up with an answer of broad validity. Steeped in reflection, they reveal the faith of the reformer. The one reflects the singularity of personal decision and fate in one writer's—Mann's—historical and political situation; the other reflects Schiller's stand before the timelessness of reason. Defining the position of creative mind ("Geist") between such extremes as the aesthetic and the political aspects of art, both works turn out to be the most demanding, wearing, consuming books on literary criticism in German literature—unbending prerequisites for the genuine understanding of their authors' art.

Thomas Mann's fundamental bondage to Schiller, with all its latent correspondences and disparities, finds further though somewhat indirect support in his attitude and sentiment toward the one mind to whom he professed a lifelong spiritual indebtedness and infatuation—Friedrich Nietzsche. Throughout his literary career, Mann liberally acknowledged, modified, expanded, reinterpreted Nietzsche's philosophy. In his younger years he practically claimed exclusive privileges of such interpretation; his last major work grew into an ominous "twilight-of-the-gods," a gloomy intertwining of Germany's and Nietzsche's decline and fall. Doubtless Mann was aware that Nietzsche, too, in spite of his repeated declarations of faith in Goethe, manifested a fundamental sentiment and structure of mind which linked him to the beliefs and precepts of Schiller.

As for Nietzsche himself, the inveterate sceptic and growling solitary, there were but few minds for whom he harbored genuine regard—Hölderlin, for example, and Spinoza, or Goethe, and Socrates. Vastly distinct from one another. these men had widely different impacts on human civilization. What they had in common was a kind of immunity from illusions, a firm and downright faith and will-to-truth that put them in direct touch with reality, a simple and basic "wisdom" and an understanding of its forms and functions, and an unqualified approval ("Ja-Sagen") of existence. Significantly, Schiller is not among them, for obvious reasons. Schiller was a homiletic personality, a preacher and interpreter and monologist who would develop doctrines for the conduct of life rather than new forms symbolic of life itself. Nietzsche's appraisal of Schiller ranges over a spectrum of widely different images—from scorn to deference; in a way, all of these images bear a resemblance to the philosopher with the hollow, penetrating look. One of them—the "Moraltrompeter von Säckingen"—is so grotesque and cumbersome that it requires more effort at explaining than the intended humor justifies. Another designation—"unser Schiller"—would even sound a bit philistine if it did not reflect the pride of the eager and conscientious student of Schulpforta, celebrating the memory of genius lingering in the valley of the Saale. Intrinsically, this word echoed Goethe's memorable dictum, from his epilogue to Schiller's "Glocke"—"Denn er war unser"—which must have set the tone at Schulpforta for the study of Schiller's works under the sensitive guidance of Professor Koberstein. It must have been at the "Pforte" that Schiller, the eighteenth-century classic, ceased to be an object of mere "Bildung" for Nietzsche and became a challenge, a threat, a force, a desirability in his existence—a kind of mythical mirror of his own intellectual situation.

At an early time Nietzsche must have sensed that Goethe's poem provided a symbolism of fundamental relevance: it pictured Schiller on that narrow threshold between the material and the ideal, the earthly and the cosmic, which has characterized German thinking ever since the days of the Reformation. Schiller's image contained a latent paradox in that it had dynamic and static aspects, suggesting restlessness suspended and an enormous tension resolved. But it also summoned the messianic ambition of the youth to conquer the "resistance of an obtuse world" ("Widerstand der stumpfen Welt")—an almost impossible challenge that could result, if taken seriously, in a lofty misunion of idealism and obstinacy or in a monstrosity composed of aspiration and contempt. Later on a more articulate Nietzsche would cast this symbolism into an almost eschatological vision:

> Wer viel einst zu verkünden hat,
> schweigt viel in sich hinein.
> Wer einst den Blitz zu zünden hat,
> muß lange Wolke sein.[1]

And behind the image of the future there looms the figure of Dionysos, intimately joined to the fate of his mother, Semele, who was consumed by the lightning of Zeus. In Nietzsche's writings the connection between lightning and Dionysos occurs with increasing frequency. Is it surprising that the young Nietzsche, sophisticated in matters of myth, might have suspected that Schiller, in writing a dramatic sketch on Semele, his only play on Greek mythology, might be revealing a latent kinship to the Dionysian element even though he is generally connected with the opposite stylistic principle, the Apollinian?

It is not clear what medium of poetic expression Nietzsche originally associated with Schiller's poetic temperament. In his early writings the customary praise of Schiller the dramatist is non-existent; after a mandatory report on Schiller's plays during the extensive Schiller centennial in Pforta in 1859, Nietzsche did not express himself on Schiller's plays or dramatic characters again (as he repeatedly did in the case of Shakespeare). Perhaps, he did not feel at ease with any of them. For Schiller's critical essays, including those which eventually took on considerable significance for his own aesthetic theory, he had occasional if caustic comments. No word was lost about Schiller's lyrics: this is surprising and perhaps an indication of impatience or unfairness or indifference on Nietzsche's part. For it is on the level of the lyrical that Schiller's hymns gained an enormous importance for the development of Nietzsche's moral and aesthetic judgment. This is not to say that Nietzsche derived any particular insight from the reading of Schiller's hymns; quite the contrary. But they seem to reveal a kinship in the structure of lyrical temperament between the poet and the philosopher. As a choral chant, supported by the strains of Beethoven's music, Schiller's "Hymn to Joy" becomes a prime exemplar of the Dionysian experience, projected onto the background of the Eleusinian Mysteries:

> Ihr stürzt nieder, Millionen?
> Ahnest du den Schöpfer, Welt?[2]

To the reader of *The Birth of Tragedy* it may be something of a surprise to find

---

[1] (The translations in notes 1–6 are by the author.)

"Whoever is destined someday to proclaim great words, will have to swallow much in bitter silence; whoever is destined to kindle the lightning must long be content with being a cloud" (K, 77, 505).

[2] "Do you sink before him, millions?/ World, do you sense your Creator?" ("An die Freude").

a poem generally considered a late offshoot of the allegorical Baroque tradition—and hence not without artificiality—re-interpreted by Nietzsche as a token of Dionysian ecstasy. Insofar as music is considered by Nietzsche the cohesive, unifying, mass-merging medium, he does not hesitate to claim Schiller's well-known statement concerning the musical mood ("Stimmung") preceding poetic expression as Dionysian. It does not really matter whether he is consistent at this point. The important thing is that the two stylistic principles or psychological drives—the Apollinian and the Dionysian—not be considered as opposite and contradictory to one another but rather as correlated and complementary, like day and night. In their mutual harmony and coalescence they produced the ancient tragedy; their separate pursuits caused its downfall, particularly in the reflective reasoning of the Apollinian temperament, the medium of the intellect—and the intellect is always prone to separate, divide, alienate, destroy.

Historically, Nietzsche's hypothesis of the psychological interplay between the Apollinian and the Dionysian drives is but another stage in the long tradition of complementary concepts attempting to solve the problem of "reality." Ever since the "querelles des anciens et des modernes" demonstrated the relativity of historical judgment, the question of surpassed standards and outdated models has disquieted literary criticism. These quarrels of criticism are not responsible for the birth of romanticism or the genesis of classicism. The age of these concepts and what they stand for is as old as human memory and consciousness. Somehow they owe their rise to the tendency of the human mind to discriminate and to establish characteristics of the "individual," the irreplaceable and unique in nature, art, history, justice—and before God. Nietzsche's complementary concepts only give a novel, unexpected, expressive twist to an age-old problem which, in the eighteenth century, was solved by Wieland or Friedrich Schlegel or, in the twentieth century, by Spengler and Worringer. Their "solutions" were not real solutions; and often they merely introduced new and interesting perspectives to established and traditional outlooks. Behind the Apollinian and the Dionysian there still glow the well discussed polarities of the Classical and the Romantic or, *mutatis mutandis*, those of Antiquity and Christianity. The spiritual derivation of these concepts is difficult to determine. It seems unlikely that Nietzsche was indebted to Kant's analysis of the Beautiful and the Sublime, insofar as Kant, instead of coordinating or juxtaposing these concepts, assigned them to different levels of consciousness. Nietzsche may have derived his ideas from Schiller's famous essay on naive and sentimental poetry; he clearly saw certain limitations of these notions in literary criticism: while the "sentimental" allows manifold applications, the meaning and use of "naive" is strictly limited. "Naive" does not denote by any means the simple, initial condition of man at the beginning of time and culture—such as was suggested by Rousseau and his nature worship. Whenever the "naive" appears in art, as it does in Homer for example, it is the manifestation of Apollinian perfection. Indeed, often the "naive" is useless as a stylistic criterion because it will appear as a concealed variation of the sentimental. While it is difficult to establish a direct correspondence between Schiller's and Nietzsche's treatises, the two may be viewed quite close together in the parallelism of eighteenth-century rationalism and irrationalism—or of Lessing and Hamann.

When we apply these distinctions to poetry, more specifically to the lyrics of Schiller's philosophical poems and Nietzsche's "Dionysos-Dithyramben," we find that a remarkable resemblance of their intellectual physiognomies presents itself. We may suspect that both writers found the way to their writings through some sort of compensation for the "resistance of the obtuse world." Schiller may have been a thwarted diplomat; Nietzsche, a frustrated artist. Schiller's lyrics are like a blueprint for a human commonwealth. Expressive and visionary, they exhibit a fundamentally abstract structure. Variously described as reflective or didactic or demonstrative, they aim to persuade or even to convert. By and large, they may be called "Denk-Gedichte"; their main thrust is in the direction of the intellect. Still, in direction and degree their cerebral appeal involves a massive charge of rhetorics, pathos and emotional tension which, transcending personal experience, empties out into a vast system of ideas that now appears as art, now as culture, now as religion. The origin of these poems cannot be traced back to any one of these fields; it lies in all of them and each of them in an uncompromising struggle between life and mind, "Leben" and "Geist," a struggle which is never resolved except by the acceptance of tragedy and the recognition of the heroic: in the worlds of both Schiller and Nietzsche, an un-heroic, middle-class society seeks a way out of a metaphysical dilemma where Life and Change become acceptable only at the risk of timeless knowledge:

> Nur der Irrtum ist das Leben,
> und das Wissen ist der Tod.[3]

In a similar perspective, the rich imagery, which Schiller developed in his elegy on the primeval and its undivided harmony of existence, received its impetus from the concepts of "Leben" and "Tod," permeating the theme of his "Götter Griechenlands."

> Was unsterblich im Gesang soll leben,
> muß im Leben untergehn.[4]

Thus Schiller's perspective anticipated the concepts of the Dionysian as life and the Apollinian as death, except that in Nietzsche the two no longer share the transcendental viewpoint of Schiller's closing stanza.

A similar panegyric on Life, at the expense of "Geist," reflection, rationali-

---

[3] "Only in erring is Life and in knowing is Death" ("Kassandra").

[4] "Whatever is to live immortally in the sphere of song must perish in the sphere of Life" ("Die Götter Griechenlands").

zation, and death is found in Nietzsche's *Zarathustra* and the poems and fragments surrounding it: "Where life grows rigid, laws grow tall and towering"; "You perish if you always seek to comprehend the bottom of things" ("Man geht zugrunde, wenn man immer zu den Gründen geht"); "Divine is the art of forgetting." And it seems significant that the Apollinian image of "Heiterkeit," "serenity," which perfects Schiller's concept of the changeless ideal reappears in Nietzsche's vision of the inescapable gateway to death: "One is certain of his own death; why shouldn't one be serene?"

On a background such as this the cycle of Nietzsche's "Dionysos-Dithyramben" fulfills a function comparable to that of Schiller's philosophical lyrics. A century after Schiller they seem to have arrived at a point where they express the suffering of the isolated individual self. Written in the first person, they appear to be voicing Nietzsche's personal experiences in the discovery of the notion of the Eternal Recurrence; and the ego of the poet, reduced to the function of fool—"Only a fool! only a poet!"—is unmasked in the role of the intellect that knows itself and torments itself: "Knower of self! Hangman of self!" Behind this psychological self-portrait there emerges the mind of modern man, tortured by its own consciousness, and yearning to immerse itself wholly in the lust of life. Nietzsche's poems are "Denk-Gedichte" no less than Schiller's philosophical lyrics; like them they are facing ultimate possibilities of mankind in the realms of art, culture, religion. In their intense anti-Christian temper, these poems, like Schiller's "Götter Griechenlands," may even be suspected of having sprung from a sublimated Christian ethos or, as Nietzsche himself might have called it, "versetztes Christentum."

Nietzsche would have been the first to deny most vehemently even the possibility of such a thought. His irony would have had a field day. In regard to Schiller, he was more tolerant—or indifferent—in this respect. He scarcely protested Schiller's commitment to religious problems even though more than half of Schiller's plays and many of his poems dealt with spiritual themes. Obviously Schiller's Swabian Protestantism was sufficiently guided by his aesthetic empathy to achieve authenticity in religious or clerical matters. All this scarcely mattered to Nietzsche although he sharply denounced Wagner for precisely the same reasons. On the other hand, as a classical scholar, Nietzsche had no reason to restrain himself in acknowledging Schiller's devotion to the classical ideal: his preoccupation with the Homeric, Trojan image of the world; his lofty thoughts on the first human community; his pilgrimage through the evolution of human culture; his faith in the persistence of human values—"die Sonne Homers"—throughout the history of the human race. Some feel that Schiller too readily adopted Winckelmann's conception of an idealized and simplified antiquity to suit Nietzsche's taste. Such a view, which blames even Goethe's "classicism" on his association with Schiller, is compensated for by the expression of human compassion which Schiller read out of the ancients, as for example his elegy on the passing of greatness, the death of Achilles:

> Siehe, da weinen die Götter, es weinen die Göttinnen alle,
> daß das Schöne vergeht, daß das Vollkommene stirbt.
> Auch ein Klaglied zu sein im Mund der Geliebten ist herrlich,
> denn das Gemeine geht klanglos zum Orkus hinab.[5]

Perhaps it was in perspectives such as this that Nietzsche found his own views on "das Gemeine" corroborated and his faith in future human perfection, indeed in the possibility of the Superman, confirmed and strengthened. Nietzsche did not reject Schiller's complex theory of the aesthetic education of man. He approved of many views that Schiller held. He approved of his interpretation of the chorus in ancient tragedy—as a kind of protective wall maintaining its natural and pristine grandeur; unconditionally he defended Schiller's stand against raw naturalism; and without reservation he supported Schiller's absolute idealism although it was miles removed from his own point of view. "It is not enough to practice the *good*," he wrote, "you must want it and . . . receive the godhead into your own will. [At this point he was quoting Schiller verbatim!] You must not merely *want* the beautiful; you must be *able to do* it, in innocence and blindness and without Psyche's curiosity." Such words were simple and sincere and testified to Nietzsche's ability to project himself into the complexities of Schiller's thinking.

There were other occasions on which Nietzsche exhibited a notable affinity with Schiller's views. Those were the moments in which he expressed his notions on time. The personal, pathological aspects of time during periods of illness and suffering which taxed Nietzsche's patience beyond the tolerable sometimes resembled violent outcries:

> Aus deinem Munde,
> du speichelflüssige Hexe Zeit,
> tropft langsam Stunde auf Stunde.
> Umsonst, daß all mein Ekel schreit:
> "Fluch, Fluch dem Schlunde
> der Ewigkeit!"[6]

In his human miseries, Schiller must have given vent to his feelings in equally convincing though less expressionistic fashion. What concerns us here is the

---

[5] "Lo and behold, all the Gods and Goddesses weep since the beautiful passes and all perfection succumbs. It is great to be even a funeral dirge in the mouth of the loved ones for the common descends to the nether-world silent, without even a sound" ("Nänie").

[6] "From your mouth,/ you spittle-flowing witch of time/ slowly drips hour on hour./ It's useless that all my aversion shouts:/ Cursed, cursed be the gorge/ of eternity!" ("Rimus remedium"; W, II, 269).

manner in which both writers are experiencing the time perspective which Kant described as the "inner sense," the medium of consciousness which transcends the limits of instinct and the present. For both writers the time perspective becomes evident in the theme of waiting: Zarathustra is often portrayed as waiting—for his friends, for high noon or deepest midnight, for the fulfillment of his fate, the realization of the Eternal Recurrence. For Nietzsche, waiting is merely another aspect of loneliness, of empty space, a form of the basic existence of the human soul that is left to its own devices at an utter loss of communication. —"Were there listening ears?" . . . In Schiller's works likewise, waiting and loneliness become a matter of extreme urgency. *Don Carlos, Wallenstein, Maria Stuart, Die Jungfrau von Orleans, Die Braut von Messina*—none of these plays can be imagined without the theme of waiting, waiting for the decisive act in the decisive hour, waiting for the realization of fate. The poem "Erwartung" intensifies the theme to such a degree that from now on it becomes a lyrical and dramatic requisite for the composition of romantic opera from Weber to Wagner—and to Nietzsche's own "Ariadne."

The time component in individual consciousness leads to another consideration which is of enormous importance in the ultimate evaluation of Nietzsche and Schiller: both writers agree in the critique of their age which they unanimously denounce as an age of decadence. Latecomers to their respective eras, both voice the pathos of the moralist and the reformer. Schiller, imbued with the ideal of freedom, which he placed higher than its realization in the French Revolution, chose the path of the artist and "aesthetic education" as the sole way to human liberation and spiritual independence. On the other hand, Nietzsche, wary of human nature, entrusted the future possibilities to man's natural institutions and to gigantic slogans, such as the Will to Power, Transvaluation of Values, Eternal Recurrence, or the defeat of moral ideologies, Schiller endowed his "artist," selective as he had to be, with certain substantial qualities: as the son of his age he should be above his age and receive his mandate from the ageless ideal. Strangely, in the pursuit of this ideal Schiller seemed to anticipate the image of Nietzsche:

> But not everyone whose soul glows with this ideal was granted either the creative tranquillity or the spirit of long patience required to imprint it upon the silent stone, or pour it into the sober mould of words, and so entrust it to the executory hands of time. Far too impetuous to proceed by such unobtrusive means, the divine impulse to form often hurls itself directly upon present-day reality and upon the life of action, and undertakes to fashion anew the formless material presented by the moral world. The misfortunes of the human race speak urgently to the man of feeling; its degradation more urgently still; enthusiasm is kindled, and in vigorous souls ardent longing drives impatiently on towards action. But did he ask himself whether those disorders in the moral world offend his reason, or whether they do not rather wound his self-love? If he does not yet know the answer, he will detect it by the zeal with which he insists upon specific and prompt results. The pure moral impulse is

directed towards the Absolute. For such an impulse time does not exist, and the future turns into the present from the moment that it is seen to develop with inevitable Necessity out of the present.[7]

A century later, Nietzsche reflected a fundamentally different cultural situation. He was no longer confronted, as Schiller was, with an alternative between materialism and idealism. Capital, industry, technology had long since replaced the idyllic existence pictured in Schiller's "Glocke." Rousseau, who had been Schiller's inspiration, had been pushed aside—and Nietzsche did not regret it—and Hegel, Marx, Richard Wagner had taken the place of the revolutionary of the mid-eighteenth century. Nietzsche no longer acknowledged the absoluteness of a moral law, nor did he understand or appreciate the totality of reason, of a system, of the state. In the place of such concepts or idols—"Götzenbilder," as he called them—Nietzsche attempted to establish a relativity of values, or rather of emotional contents which uncounted individuals—the masses—sought to express in many forms, figures, and moods. The historian of literature and literary criticism will find it provocative to observe how Nietzsche's psychological individualism evolves from Schiller's concept of the sentimental ("sentimentalisch") and its variety of characteristic differentiations. In his poems and plays Schiller often placed the common spirit ("Gemeingeist") over the expression of singularity. Steeped in the exposition of pathos, tension, and dramatic inexpectancy, Schiller was a master in the rousing of psychological shock ("Erschütterung"). His works are filled with countless emotional situations which illustrate his purpose: "den tiefen Grund der Menschheit aufzuregen" ("stir up the deep foundation of mankind"). Frequently this mood accompanied his serious interest in the reasons for human culture, the beginnings of the state, the human commonwealth—a problem he shared with other great thinkers of his century. For Nietzsche this problem has ceased to be acute. For him, it sank to the bottom of consciousness a long time ago and only in rare moments does it rise to the surface again. Those are the moments when the ideas of Schiller, almost timeless like myth, stir the imagination of his unruly disciple, Friedrich Nietzsche.

[7] Friedrich Schiller, *On the Aesthetic Education of Man*, ed. and trans. Elizabeth M. Wilkinson and L. A. Willoughby (Oxford: Clarendon Press, 1967), Ninth Letter, p. 59.

XI

Nietzsche and the Tradition of the Dionysian

MAX L. BAEUMER

TRANSLATED BY TIMOTHY F. SELLNER

When we speak of the "Dionysian" today, we are referring to the semantic context which was given to it by Nietzsche.[1] Modern authors have derived their knowledge of the Dionysian from Nietzsche's first book, *The Birth of Tragedy*, published in the year 1872. The Apollonian and Dionysian are herein depicted as physiological and psychological phenomena occurring in dreams and ecstatic states, whose dual nature as artistic drives is necessary for the further development of art.[2] In Nietzsche's later writings and in the criticism of his early work, *The Birth of Tragedy*, included in *Ecce Homo* (1888) the Apollonian hardly plays a role at all. In this latter work we read: "The two decisive *innovations*[3] of this book [*The Birth of Tragedy*] are, first, the understanding of the *Dionysian* phenomenon with respect to the Greeks—it gives the first psychological interpretation of it, and sees it as the root of the whole of Greek art. The second is the understanding of

---

[1] Melvin Maddocks, "The New Cult of Madness: Thinking as a Bad Habit," *Time Magazine*, 13 March 1972, pp. 51–52: "The new cult of madness, the far-out wing of Dionysus, has passed its judgment on reason more harshly than Nietzsche could have foreseen, but the time is coming when judgment must be passed on the Dionysiacs themselves." Stefan Brecht closes his review of Richard Schechner's famous nudity-play *Dionysus in 69*, a liberated version of Euripides' drama *The Bacchae*, with the remark: "The end of this production presents a Dionysiac spirit in something like Nietzsche's sense." Brecht terms the philosophy of the play "Dionysianism"; *The Drama Review*, 13, No. 5 (1969), 156–69. Norman O. Brown, *Life Against Death: The Psychoanalytical Meaning of History* (Middletown, Conn.: Wesleyan University Press, 1959), p. 175: "But the Greeks, who gave us Apollo, also gave us the alternative, Nietzsche's Dionysus."

[2] W, I, 21. (For key to abbreviations see p. xvii above.) The newest treatment of the Dionysian in Nietzsche's works, Rose Pfeffer's *Nietzsche : Disciple of Dionysus* (Lewisburg, Pa.: Bucknell University Press, 1972), is based mainly on *The Birth of Tragedy* and on Nietzsche's concept of the tragic. The author confronts Nietzsche's concept of the Dionysian uncritically and equates it with the Faustian in Goethe's works. She overlooks Martin Vogel's philologically and historically precise investigation *Apollinisch und Dionysisch: Geschichte eines genialen Irrtums*, Studien zur Musikgeschichte des 19. Jahrhunderts, Forschungsunternehmen der Fritz Thyssen Stiftung, No. 6 (Regensburg: Bosse, 1966). Vogel provides clear proof for the fact that Nietzsche's Dionysus and his antithetical concepts "Apollonian-Dionysian" are completely un-Greek. Also E. R. Dodds, in *The Greeks and the Irrational* (Berkeley and Los Angeles: The University of California Press, 1951), pp. 68–69, rejects the antithesis Apollonian–Dionysian.

[3] The emphasis is Nietzsche's own.

Socratism: Socrates as the instrument of Greek disintegration, recognized for the first time as a typical *décadent*" (W, II, 1109). In the next section of the book Nietzsche asserts that he himself thus became "the first to comprehend the marvelous phenomenon of the Dionysian," and on the basis of his innermost experience, he had "*discovered* it to be the only parable and equivalent which history possesses." In *The Twilight of the Idols* he speaks of himself as "the first to take seriously that marvelous phenomenon which bears the name Dionysus" (W, II, 1030). In this work (1032) he also carries over into his self-criticism of *The Birth of Tragedy*, mentioned above, his own definition of the Dionysian: "The affirmation of life even in the face of its most unfamiliar and difficult problems; the will to life, rejoicing in the sacrifice of its highest types to its own inexhaustibleness—is what I called Dionysian, *this* is what I interpreted as a bridge to the psychology of the tragic poet" (W, II, 1110). Just as Nietzsche concludes *The Twilight of the Idols* with the remark, "—I, the last disciple of the philosopher Dionysus—," so he also asserts of himself in *Ecce Homo:* "Before me no such transformation of the Dionysian into a philosophical pathos existed" (W, II, 1111).

Nietzsche's assertions that he was "the first to comprehend," "discover," and "take seriously" the Dionysian, and that he was the first to describe it in its "psychological" significance and to have "transformed" it into a philosophical system, are intentional rhetorical exaggerations. Winckelmann, Hamann, and Herder had already discovered, comprehended, and formulated the concept of the Dionysian long before him. Novalis and Hölderlin united it with Christian elements in the form of poetic inspiration; Heinrich Heine and Robert Hamerling, a much-read novelist in Nietzsche's time, anticipated his famous antithesis "Dionysus versus the Crucified One"; and in the research of the German Romantics in the areas of mythology and classical antiquity the antithesis Apollonian-Dionysian had been employed for decades. Friedrich Creuzer and Johann Jakob Bachofen had written voluminous works in which they placed the Greek, Egyptian, and Indian mysteries under the sway of Dionysus, and approximately sixty years before Nietzsche, Friedrich Schelling, in the *Philosophy of Mythology* (*Philosophie der Mythologie*) and the *Philosophy of Revelation* (*Philosophie der Offenbarung*), had described the development of the Greek spirit on the basis of his concept of a threefold Dionysus and had formulated the concept of the Dionysian, in contrast to the Apollonian, as an unrestrained, intoxicated power of creation in the artist and the poetic genius. One can grant Nietzsche the primacy he asserts for himself only with relation to his "transformation" of the Dionysian into a "philosophical pathos," that is, into a rhetorical cliché. He accomplished this so brilliantly and propagandized it so effectively, however, that we hardly remember anything more about the long and significant prehistory of the Dionysian in the nineteenth century, or the mighty epiphany of Dionysus[4] in early German Romanticism.

[4] Cf. Max L. Baeumer, "Die romantische Epiphanie des Dionysos," *Monatshefte*, 57 (1965), 225–36;

I

Aristotle had traced Western tragedy back to the dithyrambic myth of suffering, and comedy to the glorification of the sexual element and its tradition in divine ritual.[5] While Nietzsche, it is true, does not base his interpretation on that of Aristotle, he does proceed from an identical conception in *The Birth of Tragedy* and in his formulation of the Dionysian. In the eighteenth century as well, this dual relationship of the god of ecstasy to poetry, which Aristotle had expressed by means of his "poets of the dithyramb" and his "poets of phallic hymns," led, in the case of Johann Joachim Winckelmann, to an idealized conception of beauty drawn from the figures of Apollo and Bacchus, and in the case of Hamann and Herder, to the first Dionysian aesthetics and literary criticism.

In connection with the definition of the Dionysian cited above, Nietzsche reproaches Winckelmann and Goethe for not having understood the Greeks, since they had found intolerable that particular element "out of which Dionysian art grows," that is, "Orgiasm" and "the mysteries of sexuality" (W, II, 1031). To ferret out "beautiful souls," "tranquil grandeur," and "noble simplicity" among the Greeks, he rails against Winckelmann and the classicists, to fall prey to this "niaiserie allemand" was something which the psychologist within him ever prevented him from doing (W, II, 1029). "For in the Dionysian mysteries and in the psychology of the Dionysian state is expressed for the first time the *fundamental fact* of the Hellenistic instinct—its 'will to life' " (W, II, 1031). In reality, Winckelmann had formulated his classical maxim "noble simplicity and quiet grandeur"—a fact which remained forever concealed from Nietzsche and the proponents of an art and literary criticism based on the psychology of ecstasy who followed him—in opposition to the Dionysian, that is, to the "parenthyrsus" of "gigantic passions," which were "much too fiery and wild,"[6] and in his *History of Ancient Art* (*Geschichte der Kunst des Alterthums*) he set up both Apollo and Dionysus as the two highest types of "ideal beauty"; Apollo, "the highest conception of Ideal Manly Youth, in which the strength of mature years is united with the tender form of the most beautiful springtime of youth. . . . The second type of Ideal Youth taken from castrated natures is to be found, united with this Manly Youth, in the figure of Bacchus, . . . in the most beautiful figures of all times, with their fine, rounded limbs, and with the full and bulging hips characteristic of the

---

Joachim Rosteutscher, *Die Wiederkunft des Dionysos: Der naturmystische Irrationalismus in Deutschland* (Bern: Francke, 1947).

[5] "It [the tragedy] arose out of improvisations, just as the comedy did, the former through the dithyrambic poets, the latter through the poets of the phallic hymns, such as are still sung in many of our cities during religious ceremonies." *De arte poetica*, 1449a.

[6] *Sämtliche Werke*, ed. by Joseph Eiselein (Donaueschingen: Im Verlage deutscher Klassiker, 1825), I, 33.

female sex."[7] Winckelmann sees the raging God of Wine as a boyish, dreamy, and effeminate catamite, and as the ideal of both homosexual and heterosexual beauty:

> The image of Bacchus is that of a beautiful boy, entering upon the threshold of the springtime of life and adolescence, in whom the stirrings of passion, like the tender shoots of a plant, are just beginning to appear, and who, as between sleeping and waking, half submerged in a delightful dream, begins to gather the images of this dream and to apprehend himself; his features are full of sweetness, but his joyful soul is not yet entirely apparent from his face. (160–61)

Winckelmann's obviously homoerotic disposition of mind, which also later determined his tragic fate, leads him to derive his over-elevated conception of beauty from the statues of youths, and he imputes this disposition, in idealizing fashion, to the Greeks in the figures of Apollo and Bacchus. "In their contemplation of ideal beauty, such as in the representation of the face, as well as in the youthful body structure of a number of gods like Apollo and Bacchus, the artists of antiquity elevated themselves to the realm of the ideal." Winckelmann was the first, even before Schelling and Nietzsche, to give expression to the aesthetic definition of the Dionysian.[8]

When Nietzsche demands the development of a new art form from the Dionysian "mysteries of sexuality," he is preceded in doing so by Johann Georg Hamann. Although it is disguised in a profusion of Dionysian quotations, images, and concetti from Horace, Tibullus, and the treatises of the apologetic Church Fathers on mysteries, Hamann proclaims in his *Aesthetica in nuce*, in his *Writers and Critics (Schriftsteller und Kunstrichter)*, in the *Hierophantic Letters (Hierophantische Briefe)*, as well as in his treatise on mysteries entitled *Konxompax*, a new poetry arising out of the senses and passions, out of the wine-blood-*topos* of the Graeco-Roman, Jewish, and Christian mysteries, and out of the Dionysian phallic symbol as the mark of the generative "creative spirit."[9] In his *Aesthetica in nuce* Hamann

---

[7] *Geschichte der Kunst des Alterthums* (1764; facsimile rpt. Baden-Baden and Strasbourg: Heitz, 1966), pp. 158–60. Cited hereafter by page number in the text.

[8] Winckelmann's *Anmerkungen* of 1767 to his *Geschichte der Kunst des Alterthums* are added in the form of an appendix to the edition cited in footnote 7; here, p. 36.

The fact, however, that even the formulation of the Apollonian-Classical ideal is bound up with his sexual-psychic attitude, and that even the aesthetic maxim "noble simplicity and quiet grandeur" arose out of the antithesis to the Dionysian could very well be a surprising conclusion for many an enthusiast of Winckelmann's classicism. In this regard, cf. Max L. Baeumer, "Winckelmanns Formulierung der klassischen Schönheit," *Monatshefte*, 65 (1973), 61–75.

[9] *Johann Georg Hamann. Briefwechsel*, ed. Walther Ziesemer and Arthur Henkel, Wiesbaden: Insel, 1955–59), II, 415. The most important Dionysian quotations in the historical-critical edition of Hamann's works edited by Josef Nadler (Vienna: Herder, 1949–57), are in volume II, pp. 203–4, 336–37, 409–10, volume III, pp. 141, 217, 215–28; volume IV, p. 376. This is the edition cited in the text. Cf. James C. O'Flaherty, "The Concept of Knowledge in Hamann's *Sokratische Denkwürdigkeiten* and Nietzsche's *Geburt der Tragödie*," *Monatshefte*, 64 (1972), 334–48. (Cf. also Chapter VIII of the present work.) O'Flaherty refers here and in his article "Socrates in Hamann's *Socratic Memorabilia* and Nietz-

described his "poetry"—using no less than ten quotations referring to Dionysus and the mysteries—in the psychological terms "senses and passions," of which "the whole wealth of human knowledge and happiness" consists (I, 197). These quotations culminate in the powerful challenge to the writers of his time:

> Do not venture into the metaphysics of the fine arts without first having attained perfection in the orgies [Latin: which tolerate neither a Pentheus nor an Orpheus] and the Eleusinian mysteries. The senses, however, are Ceres, and Bacchus the passions—ancient foster-parents of "beautiful nature." [Latin: Appear, O Bacchus, encircle thy head with clusters of ripened grapes, and Ceres, adorn thy brow with a garland of corn ears.] (201)

The immediate effect of Hamann's Dionysian aesthetic of passion and sexuality is difficult to determine. One of Hamann's direct influences can be seen in Johann Gottfried Herder. For Herder Dionysus becomes the embodiment of a new, ecstatic, dithyrambic poetry, the theory for which he develops in his *Königsberg Scholarly and Political Journal for the Year 1764* (*Königsberger Gelehrte und Politische Anzeigen auf das Jahr 1764*), his *Fragments Concerning Recent German Literature* (*Fragmente über die neuere deutsche Litteratur*) of 1767, and his *Critical Forests* (*Kritische Wälder*) of 1769. Herder formulates: "The truly dithyrambic descends perhaps the farthest of all forms of poetic expression to animal-like sensuality in order to attain its heights; it addresses itself only to the eye, the ear, and to the sense of taste—it always speaks to the emotions, rarely to the intellect, and never to the power of reason."[10] Concerning the supposed state of ecstasy in which the first Greek poets were said to have composed their dithyrambs, he writes: "Their hymns were full of the animal-like and sensual language of wine, and the wine in turn rose to the level of a certain mystical-sensual language of the gods" (I, 310). The essence of this poetry, Herder says, is "that extension of the soul which consists in the *parenthyrsus* of intoxication and the contemplation of heavenly things" (I, 311). Here Herder gives us the first explanation of literary motivation in terms of the psychology of affects to be found in the history of German literary theory. What is essential is that Herder looks at this animal-like and mystical-sensual Dionysian as the origin of, and touchstone for, a new national poetry intoxicated with inspiration. He addresses himself to the poets:

sche's *Birth of Tragedy: A* Comparison," *Philomathes: Studies and Essays in the Humanities in Memory of Philip Merlan,* ed. Robert B. Palmer and Robert Hamerton-Kelly (The Hague: Nijhoff, 1971), pp. 306–29, to the significance of sexuality for Hamann and Nietzsche, especially in connection with their concept of knowledge. This is in accordance with the fact that Nietzsche himself does not mention Hamann when he refers to the Dionysian or *The Birth of Tragedy,* but only for the first time in a printed manuscript from the year 1873 entitled "Philosophy in the Age of Greek Tragedy" (W, III, 359), and with the fact that he was in the process of studying Hamann's works at this time (W, III, 1364).

10 *Herders Sämtliche Werke,* ed. Bernhard Suphan (Berlin: Weidmann, 1877–1913), I, 69. Cited hereafter in the text by volume and page number.

Geniuses, you who draw everything from the abysses of your souls, what need is there for me to relate to you that intoxicated hymns of a sacred inspiration for religion and the state, moving hymns and paintings of human emotions and situations—which even show disdain for the very altar of Bacchus himself—can also be evoked from the innermost part of our religion, our nature, our education, and our conception of the world? (I, 180)

Like Hamann, Herder traces Dionysian poetry back to the frenzy of wild dances (I, 310), and characterizes them as affects from the abyss of the soul (II, 180). "In the Dionysian state," Nietzsche writes, "the entire affective system is aroused and intensified, so that it discharges all of its means of expression at one time, simultaneously driving out the power of representation, transformation, and every type of mimicry and play-acting" (II, 996). One could continue indefinitely to make comparisons between Herder's irrational-ecstatic view of poetry under the banner of Bacchus and Nietzsche's conception of the Dionysian in terms of the psychology of intoxication. It is very doubtful whether Herder, whom Nietzsche often cites, and Hamann, whose name appears in his works only in connection with the *Socratic Memorabilia* (*Sokratische Denkwürdigkeiten*) and the lost works of the ancients, exerted any direct influence on Nietzsche. The fact that he takes Winckelmann so severely to task in connection with his own conception of the Greeks could signify for Nietzsche a kind of influence in the sense of an inducement to contradiction. Nietzsche has, as a matter of principle, this irrational conception of poetic production based on genius in common with the writers of the *Sturm und Drang*—a conception already encountered in the dry versification of the German Anacreontics Hagedorn, Gleim, and Uz, for whom, after the model of Horace and Ovid, Bacchus-Dionysus was the appropriate symbol for the poetry of ecstasy.[11] In the course of just such a tradition the youthful poet Goethe, in his "Wanderer's Storm Song" ("Wandrers Sturmlied") of 1772, elevated Dionysus, under his sobriquet "Bromius" (the "Roaring One"), to the poetic "genius of the century": "Thou art, what inward fire/ to Pindar was." At a later point, however, he characterizes the passionate outburst contained in this poem as "half nonsense."

It is in the writings of the German Romantics, however, that the *topos* "Dionysus" first receives its full significance.[12] Independently of each other, both

[11] I have shown elsewhere that Nietzsche's and Wilhelm Heinse's statements on the Dionysian often are identical, even in terms of their wording—nevertheless, in this case, too, no direct influences have been established. Cf. Max L. Baeumer, "Heinse und Nietzsche. Ausgang und Vollendung der dionysischen Ästhetik," *Heinse-Studien* (Stuttgart: Metzler, 1966), pp. 92–124; Otto Kein, *Das Apollinische und Dionysische bei Nietzsche und Schelling* (Berlin: Junker and Dünnhaupt, 1935).

[12] A coherent examination of the Dionysian as it relates to the Romantic period, or to literature in general, does not exist. Joachim Rosteutscher, in the work cited above, gives a depth-psychological interpretation of possible Dionysian attitudes in the writings of Hölderlin, Novalis, Schopenhauer, Bachofen, Wagner, Nietzsche, George, Rilke, and others; Louis Wiesmann, in *Das Dionysische bei Hölderlin und in der deutschen Romantik* (Basel: Schwabe, 1948), investigates the Dionysian character of

Hölderlin and Novalis celebrate the return of the Greek deity, summoned by "the Wine-God's holy priests" ("Bread and Wine") and by inspired poets "in enthusiasm and Bacchic intoxication" (paralipomena to *Heinrich von Ofterdingen*). The same religious-ecstatic inspiration which Hamann derived from the mysteries and Herder from Greek dithyrambic poetry, and which they require from the poets of their time in the name of Dionysus, this inspiration is now kindled, like a fire in the soul of the poet, in the form of a new symbol for Hölderlin in the poem "As on a Holiday" ("Wie wenn am Feiertage"). It is described as identical to the fire of lightning by virtue of which, Hölderlin maintains, divinely struck Semele gave birth to holy Bacchus, and whose ray the poets now hold in their very hands and offer to the people as a heavenly gift veiled in song. This pure ray does not burn the poet, but violently shaken, he is compelled to share the sufferings of Dionysus. In the hymn "To our Great Poets" ("An unsre großen Dichter"), these poets appear in the retinue of the God of Joy, young Bacchus, who returns all-conquering from India in triumphal procession, waking the nations with his holy wine:

> O, ye poets, too, waken them from slumber,
> Those who yet sleep; give us laws, give
> Us life, O triumph, heroes! Ye alone,
> Like Bacchus, have the right to conquer.

The *topos* Dionysus has the same function in the odes "The Poet's Vocation" ("Dichterberuf") and "Chiron." This function becomes even more apparent in the later poems of Hölderlin in the form of the return of the "heavenly" and in the attempted unification of Dionysus and Christ. Also in Novalis's *Christianity or Europe* (*Christenheit oder Europa*) the new Savior, "at home among the people, . . . is consumed as bread and wine, embraced as a loved one, breathed as air, comprehended as word and song, and finally received, amid the greatest sufferings of love, as death into the innermost part of the failing body." But Novalis is not actually using the *topos* Dionysus here, in the *Hymns to the Night* (*Hymnen an die Nacht*), the *Novices of Sais* (*Lehrlinge zu Sais*), and in his Ofterdingen-novel; rather he is merely making use of Dionysian metaphors, with which he elucidates his

the language and some of the imagery in *Hyperion*. Isolated references are to be found in Walther Rehm's *Griechentum und Goethezeit: Geschichte eines Glaubens* (Leipzig: Dieterich, 1936), and in Richard Benz's *Die deutsche Romantik: Geschichte einer geistigen Bewegung* (Leipzig: Reclam, 1937). Momme Mommsen, in an article entitled "Dionysos in der Dichtung Hölderlins mit besonderer Berücksichtigung der *Friedensfeier*," *Germanisch-Romanische Monatsschrift*, NS 13 (1963), 345–79, intends mainly to show that the "Prince of the Feast-day" ("Fürst des Fests") in this poem is Dionysus. More precise references can be found in Max L. Baeumer, "Die zeitgeschichtliche Funktion des dionysischen Topos in der romantischen Dichtung," *Gestaltungsgeschichte und Gesellschaftsgeschichte*, Literatur-, Kunst- und Musikwissenschaftliche Studien, ed. Helmut Kreuzer in collaboration with Käte Hamburger (Stuttgart: Metzler, 1969), 265–83.

ecstatic love-death conception and his idea of unification with nature.[13] His
translation of the ode by Horace (III, 25), "Quo me, Bacche, rapis tui,/ Plenum?",
which Hamann before him had used in his formulation of the *topos* of the poetry
of intoxication, is a reworking of the theme, which precisely by virtue of its
deviations from the original makes apparent its transformation into the Romantic
topos of a new poetic transfiguration of the world.

> Whither carryest thou me,
> Fullness of my heart,
> God of intoxication,
> Through which woods and chasms
> Do I roam, with courage not my own.
>
> .   .   .   .
>
> Of things powerful, things unheard,
> Things never before uttered by mortal lips,
> Of these will I speak.
> As the ardent sleepwalker,
> The Bacchic maiden
>
> .   .   .   .

In the ode "To our Great Poets" from the years 1797 and 1798, and in the
hymn "As on a Holiday," stemming from about the year 1800, Hölderlin equates
the inspired poets with Dionysus himself. They are to arouse the people from
sleep, conquer "like Bacchus," and "ignited by the holy ray," proclaim to men
"the fruit born of love, the work of gods and men. . . ." Also in both of his later
significant poems, the elegy "Bread and Wine" (first called "The God of Wine"
["Der Weingott"]) and the hymn "The Rhine" ("Der Rhein"), Hölderlin
equates the poets with Dionysus. In the Rhine-hymn, the Dionysian characterizes
the content and form of a new, unrestrained, and divine priesthood, expressed
here of Rousseau: "that he, from holy plenitude/ As the God of Wine, divinely
foolish/ And lawlessly gives it away, the language of the most pure." In "Bread
and Wine," Dionysus performs the function of expressing the poetic goal of the
older Hölderlin: the return of the gods and their unification with Christ. Here
Hölderlin develops, in a way similar to Novalis, the image of the night of holy
intoxication as the matrix of the Dionysian life, and, like Novalis, intensifies it to
the point of a nocturnal appearance of Dionysus himself: "Thence has come and

---

[13] In the *Hymns to the Night*, in which the poet lies "intoxicated in the bosom of love," and feels
"death's rejuvenating stream," Novalis describes the night in Dionysian and generally ecstatic symbols,
e.g., with the expression "the golden flood of the grapes" and the "brown juice of the poppy." In his
novel-fragment *The Novices of Sais* the Dionysian character of the pleasurable submersion in the
universal is depicted merely in the imprecise images of "procreative po·ver," "the desire to procreate,"
and of "surging waves of passion." In Klingsohr's wine-song in *Henry von Ofterdingen* the wine, "the
golden child," and "the god who brings us heavenly pleasures" are identical.

back there points the god who is to come." The answer to the question "Wherefore poets in impoverished times?" is placed in the mouth of Wilhelm Heinse: "But they, sayest thou, are like the Wine God's holy priests,/ Who proceeded from land to land by hallowed night." Here, too, the poets have become identical to the restless god and his expeditions to India and back to Thebes.

Christ, the Silent Genius, Hölderlin says, appeared as the last in the heavenly chorus of gods, and, as a divine consolation, left behind gifts as a sign of His return: "Bread is the fruit of the earth, yet it is blessed by the rays of the sun,/ And from the god who thunders issue forth the pleasures of wine . . ./ Thus the poets, too, sing in serious praise to the god of wine." The gifts of bread and wine left by Christ to his disciples are originally the gifts of Dionysus and Ceres. The return of the gods of antiquity and their unification with Christ is to be brought about as a function of Dionysus, speaking through the mouths of the poets. When Christ then comes as the "Torchbearer, the Son of the Highest, the Syrian," He is appearing with the same symbol and in the same manner as Dionysus in the *Bacchae* of Euripides: "Bacchus swings in his dance the torch smelling of Syrian incense, startling the revelers with his rejoicing, his long locks disheveled by the wind." In the words "Syrian" and "Torchbearer," Hölderlin is assigning metaphors of the Dionysian *topos* to Christ in order to express the blessed unification of Christ and Dionysus, in which the world is to find a new harmony. In the hymn "The Only One" ("Der Einzige"), Christ is called the brother of Heracles and Dionysus:

> And I confess, Thou
> Art brother also to Evius, who
> To his chariot harnessed
> The tigers and down
> As far as the Indus
> Commanding joyful service,
> First the vineyard planted and
> Tamed the rage of the nations.

In the third version of this hymn Dionysus is characterized as the "common spirit," and in the elegy "Stutgard" as the "common god," since "each" sacrifices "what is his" for the fatherland. Hölderlin is referring here to the secret society of Swabian republican conspirators and poets who were gathered around him, all inspired by the French Revolution. It is in the same sense that Hölderlin's letter from Nürtigen to his brother in December 1800 speaks of a "common spirit." In his conception of Dionysus Hölderlin unites mythological occurrences with contemporary political and religious events in a Romantic unity.

In keeping with his destruction of the Romantic picture of the world, Heinrich Heine also dissolves the tenuous Romantic unification of Christ with Dionysus. For Heine, Dionysus is the "god of vitality," and, in the tradition of later Romanticism, a pernicious seducer, the greatest of the dethroned gods who live on in concealment while they deceive their Christian subjugators and strike terror into their hearts. In his work *Gods in Exile* (*Götter im Exil*) from the year 1836, Heine has Bacchus play the role of a Superior in a Franciscan monastery in the Tyrol. A meddlesome fisherman is forced to view with terror the midnight Bacchic procession of the wan gods, "who have arisen from the sarcophagi of their tombs or the hiding-places of their temple ruins in order to celebrate once again the triumphal journey of their divine liberator, the Savior of the Senses, and to dance once more the joyful dance of heathendom, the cancan of the ancient world, . . . utterly without hypocritical disguises, utterly without any intervention by the police of a spiritualistic morality, with the utterly uninhibited frenzy of days gone by, rejoicing, raging, exulting: 'Evoe Bacche!' " In Heine's pantomime "The Goddess Diana" ("Die Göttin Diana") Bacchus appears with Diana and his own raging retinue in a German Gothic castle of the Middle Ages. Only the knight in love with Diana and his fool are seized by the wild and obscene carryings-on and proceed, under the guidance of Bacchus, to the wanton festival of pleasure in the *Venusberg*, the "seat of all voluptuousness and lasciviousness." The knight is slain in a Christian duel with the old and awkward "Faithful Eckhardt" in front of the *Venusberg*, so that the soul of the knight, at least, can be saved. Apollo, with his music of "peace and harmonious beatification," is unable to awaken the knight, lying in state in the *Venusberg*. Bacchus, however, in his "all-powerful inspiration as the god of vitality" causes the knight to be resurrected to a new life of love with Diana. After everyone is crowned with the heathen rosary of the goddess Venus, the pantomime ends in a "glory of transfiguration."

For Heine, the Dionysian has an exclusively negative connotation. Every one of the late Romantic images of a terrifying Bacchus is brought forth by him for the purpose of a biting satire on the classical German image of Greece: Eduard Mörike's seductive, Dionysian nature-spirit in "Autumn Celebration" ("Herbstfeier"); Wilhelm Hauff's lascivious Bacchus-knave in *Phantasies in a Bremen Rathskeller* (*Phantasien im Bremer Rathskeller*); and Joseph von Eichendorff's dream-like figure of the moonlight, Donati-Bacchus, who appears "pale and disorderly" in his work *The Marble Image* (*Das Marmorbild*). The ecstatic passion expressed by Bacchus in Heine's works is more base sensuality than anything else. Its function is not the Romantic rejuvenation and poeticization of the world, rather the demythologization and the zestful destruction of the moral and social order; not the ecstatic exaltation and deification of life, but rather an anguished lust for life; not the unification of religion and poetry, antiquity, and Christendom, rather their separation into mutually hostile camps. The synthesis Dionysus-Christ is transposed to the antithesis Dionysian-Christian, which corresponds to Heine's antithetical formulation Hellenic-Nazarene. While Hölderlin describes Christ using Dionysian metaphors in order to express the unity between Him and the God of Wine, Heine conversely describes Dionysus as the "Savior of the

Senses." The Bacchic celebrations of the mysteries have become the "cancan of the ancient world," the Olympian Parnassus has turned into the *Venusberg* of "voluptuousness and lasciviousness," and the creative frenzy of the poets has changed into the "unrestrained frenzy of ancient times." Just as the Dionysian *topos*, because of its ecstatic character, had become the appropriate form for thought and expression for the early Romantics, so it is for Heine, writing at the close of the Romantic period, the favorite *topos* of the period's rapturous dissolution and destruction. Nietzsche then attempts somewhat later to unite the positive and Romantic function of the Dionysian with Heine's cliché-like, deprecating utilization of the *topos*. Heine's antithesis Dionysian-Christian becomes in the case of Nietzsche the slogan "Dionysus versus the Crucified One."

Even more strongly than Heine, the Austrian *Gymnasium* professor Robert Hamerling, an epigonic classicist, propagates in his great epic poem *Ahasuerus in Rome* (*Ahasverus in Rom*) the idea of Dionysus as the embodiment of "boundless passion." Gothic Romanticism resplendent with color, genius-like pretension, and uninhibited pleasure in morbid decadence are all united in Hamerling's best-seller, which, after six years and during the very same year which saw the first publication of Nietzsche's *Birth of Tragedy*, was flooding the market of the more cultivated middle-class reading public with its eleventh printing. In the figure of Ahasuerus,[14] the Wandering Jew, utter denial of life and a longing for death are contrasted with the ruthless greed for life and pursuit of sensual pleasure symbolized by the person of "Nero-Dionysus," the prototype of the Caesar-craze in the popular tradition of the nineteenth century. In the second of the six "hymns," entitled "The Bacchanal," the tyrant, under the double title "Nero-Dionysus," is proclaimed by the wild multitude of maenadic followers as the ruler of a new age in which man will not first be compelled to earn his right to Elysium by the sweat of his brow, but will possess this right in pleasure and happiness from the very beginning.[15] An old Silenus proclaims in an anti-Winckelmannian manner that the "world of beauty" of a peaceful, boring Olympus is past, and that the new god "Nero-Dionysus" is in the process of founding a more beautiful and more joyful epoch (45). Here, in the person of the tyrant, Dionysus becomes the advocate for the oppressed people, the Roman proletarians. In the year 1848 the *Communist Manifesto* had first appeared, and one year after Hamerling's conclusion of the Ahasuerus poem the first volume of Karl Marx's *Das Kapital* was published. In a grotesque perversion of the socialistic appeal of the time for the emancipation of the oppressed Third Estate, Hamerling has his Dionysus, as the initiator of a new epoch, proclaim to the proletarian class of Rome a participation

[14] Patterned after the main characters in the late Romantic writer Joseph Christian von Zedlitz's epic *Die Wanderungen des Ahasverus* which appeared in 1832, and in Eugène Sue's ten-volume, best-selling novel, *Le Juif errant* of 1844.

[15] Robert Hamerling, *Ahasverus in Rom: Eine Dichtung in sechs Gesängen* (Hamburg and Leipzig: Richter, 1866). Cited hereafter by page number in the text; here, p. 49.

in material pleasure in its most sensual form. As the high point of the proclamation from "the Bacchic destroyers," Hamerling stages a confrontation between his "Nero-Dionysus" and the God of the Christians amid the flames of Rome:

Yet another new god! calls Nero. Ha!
A new god, crucified on a cross?
In truth, a rival of terrible power
For a Nero-Dionysus! . . .
Give up this madness, and before
Ye too are nailed to the cross, like
The god whom ye so strangely revere,
Join in the jubilation of my faithful!
Join in the *evoe* of the Corybantes! (124)

Shortly thereafter, "the new god" Nero-Dionysus is overthrown, and meets his end, in Hamerling's version, in the catacombs of the Christians through suicide.

Hamerling, who had been schooled in the classical tradition, unites the entire literary tradition of the Dionysian myths in all of their possible ecstatic and negative aspects in his image of this one magnificently wicked sensualist and man of power. In spite of, or better yet, because of its obviously trashy and inartistic character, this bombastic piece of inferior craftsmanship was, precisely during the years of the origin and dissemination of Nietzsche's first Dionysian work, *The Birth of Tragedy*, one of the most popular and most-read books of the semi-educated upper middle-class. We know that Hamerling was indebted to the patriotic and pessimistic lyrics of the classically-trained Italian poet Giacomo Leopardi, whose poems, together with a highly regarded introduction on Leopardi's life and work, Hamerling published in a translation of his own (Hild-burghausen, 1866), which was well received at the time. Nietzsche was intimately acquainted with Leopardi's work, and designated the poet, along with Goethe, "as the last of the great stragglers in the ranks of the Italian philologist-poets" (W, I, 428); he twice refers to him, together with Byron, Poe, Kleist, and others, as "these great poets . . . and the so-called higher types of men in general." Nietzsche held the "philologist-poets," to which group the widely-read Hamerling surely also belonged, in especially high esteem, and regarded them as equal in rank to himself. Moreover, he was surprisingly well acquainted with the sensational and semi-or pseudoscientific literature of his time, as we can see from his *Untimely Meditations*, as well as from other of his works. Thus, we must assume that he was acquainted with Hamerling's most successful work—all the more so, since we know that it was customary for him to remain silent intentionally in matters concerning such literary relationships and sources. In view of his claim to have been the first to recognize and formulate the Dionysian, it is not surprising that Nietzsche would also keep hidden all possible influences on the part of Winckel-mann, Herder, Novalis, Hölderlin, and Heine, all of whose works he knew well and, except in the case of Winckelmann, held in especially high regard.[16] Therefore, in examining and evaluating the concept of the Dionysian in Nietzsche's works it is all the more important to set forth the instances in which he is in obvious conformity with the works of these writers, which has been demonstrated here for the first time.

II

The actual Dionysian tradition prior to Nietzsche is to be found for the most part in obscure, semi-scholarly works reflecting what is basically a Romantic philosophy and mythology, carried on as it was in the circles of classical philologists oriented toward the fields of philosophy and literary criticism. We must not forget that Nietzsche, as a professor of classical philology (officially until 1878), belonged to this professional group. I believe it can be shown that he was influenced in his conception of the Dionysian to an exceptional degree by several authors who stood outside the field of classical philology and were advocates of an imaginary Romantic mythology.

Friedrich Schlegel's Romantic philosophy and aesthetics of literature are based on his study of classical philology and his early philological writings. In these, he considers Dionysus, more than any other figure, to be the origin and content of dithyrambic poetry, and recommends the Dionysian nature-myths of Eleusis to contemporary scholars and poets for the creation of a new Romantic mythology. Dionysus is for him "immortal joy," "wonderful abundance," and the "abundance of nature."[17] Nietzsche uses similar expressions to define the Dionysian at the beginning of his *Birth of Tragedy*. His notes from the years of the creation of *The Birth of Tragedy* contain many quotations from the work of

[16] For Nietzsche, Herder possessed to the greatest degree "the sense for determining the turn things would take" ("den Sinn der Witterung"), and had "a foretaste of all the intellectual dishes which the Germans brought together during the period of a half-century from all ages and places" (W, I, 924–25). He praises Novalis for proclaiming with naive happiness "the association between sensual pleasure, religion, and cruelty" (W, I, 543). He declares Hölderlin to be his "favorite poet" (W, I, 148), who because of his tender nature is destroyed by the civilization of the Philistines (W, I, 148). Nietzsche says of Heine that the poet gave him "the loftiest conception of the lyric poet," and that he possessed "that divine malice without which I would not be able to imagine perfection." He especially appreciated in Heine the fact that he was capable of conceiving "the god as inseparable from the satyr" (W, II, 1088–89). Thus, one could perhaps read into Nietzsche's judgments of Heine and Winckelmann concealed references to their preoccupations with Dionysus.

[17] Cf. *Friedrich von Schlegels sämmtliche Werke*, 10 vols. (Vienna: Klang, 1822–1825), IV, 27; V, 272, 281; above all his short essay *Die griechische Mythologie* from 1803–1804, and the well-known Dionysian-Apollonian quotation from his essay of 1795, *Über das Studium der Griechischen Poesie:* "In the soul of Sophocles were blended in equal proportions the divine intoxication of Dionysus, the profound resourcefulness of Athena, and the quiet reflectivity of Apollo."

Friedrich Schlegel, even if there are none which refer directly to Dionysus.[18] Schlegel unites the Dionysian with the feminine, as do Schelling and Bachofen after him, and the figure of Dionysus with oriental mysteries, as a short time later do the writers Schubert, Görres, and Creuzer.

In 1808, in his *Views Concerning the Night-Side of Natural Science (Ansichten von der Nachtseite der Naturwissenschaft)*, the Romantic-mystical natural philosopher Gotthilf Heinrich Schubert traced the Dionysian mysteries back to Indian mythology and an Egyptian origin, and extolled these and all mysteries as the "union of that which destroys and that which creates, of death and love."[19] Schubert lectures: "Phallus—worship, which existed in all mysteries, was altogether and everywhere bound up with symbols of decline and death" (72). This same union of love and death, decline and rejuvenation is expressed, Schubert says, in Indian mythology by the god Siva, whose symbol of the eternal lotus blossom is identical to the Bacchic lingam—the grain-shovel and cradle of the child Dionysus in the Greek mysteries (76–77). In identical fashion, the prematurely deceased "Balder, the most beautiful and best of all the sons of the gods," lives on in Teutonic legend with the immortal ring of Odin, the "symbol of a new procreation out of its own being, and the symbol of death" in nature (78–79). "The destruction of that which is individual resulting from the most noble strivings of the soul" is, then, the main content of most of the mysteries and sacred legends (79). But above all it is essential to note here that Schubert is offering the perceptions and conclusions resulting from his Dionysian view of the mysteries to his Romantic contemporaries as a new religion of the longing for death, rebirth, and immortality (81).

Two years later, Joseph Görres, in his *History of the Myths of the Asiatic World (Mythengeschichte der asiatischen Welt)* from the year 1810, describes the mythical origin of the world and the development of its different nations as a single Dionysian epiphany of procreation and birth: "Heaven is the embracing, bestowing, essentially igneous, masculine principle; the earth, on the other hand, is the embraced, receiving, dark, moist, feminine principle—out of the combination of these two principles all things have issued forth" (24). Görres goes on to explain that the Dionysian lingam-worship is the oldest form of the veneration of the divine, and, as Schubert had done two years before, he declares it to be the symbol of a unification in love and of a renewal of life. "Sensual life-strength, rapid, highly inflamed ecstasy and wantonness, unrestrained raging of the life-spirits in orgies and Bacchanalian frenzy, and Asiatic hospitality in the form of sexual submission at the festivals and in the temples"—so runs his Romantic and animated description of the cult during this epoch. In the following universal age

---

[18] GOA(2), IX, 452.

[19] *Ansichten von der Nachtseite der Naturwissenschaft* (1808; facsimile rpt. Darmstadt: Wissenschaftliche Buchgesellschaft, 1967), p. 77; hereafter cited in the text.

of the heroic gods Heracles, Dionysus, Vishnu, Belus, Osiris, Odin, and Huang Ti which follows, a higher procreative drive awakens in the male and expresses itself in a rule of justice and benevolence (25). The victorious procession of Dionysus from India to Greece is for Görres evidence for, and the symbol of, the spread of all religions from East to West through the propagation of the mysteries. Even in the work of his mature years, *Christian Mysticism* (*Die christliche Mystik*), he sees Dionysus, Mithras, Krishna, and Osiris as "emanations, procreations, and incarnations of the good" in the pre-Christian "dualistic antithesis of the two principles light and darkness, good and evil, life and death."[20]

Görres had dedicated his *History of the Myths of the Asiatic World* to the classical philologist and mythologist Georg Friedrich Creuzer. In 1807, three years previously, Creuzer had published a treatise in Latin on Dionysus, which then appeared two years later in Heidelberg in expanded format with the title *Dionysus, or Learned Commentaries on the Origins and Causes of the Bacchic and Orphic Mysteries* (*Dionysus sive Commentationes academicae de rerum Bacchicarum Orphicarumque originibus et causis*). In it he attempts to trace the Greek Dionysian religion and the Orphic mysteries back to the Orient, to India, and to Greece, and to give evidence for a kind of Romantic longing for death as their most profound subject matter. "The blessedness of death was a tenet of the Bacchic mysteries," Creuzer writes in his German-language *Studies* of 1806.[21] In his most important work, the four-volume *Symbolism and Mythology of the Ancient Nations, Especially the Greeks* (*Symbolik und Mythologie der alten Völker, besonders der Griechen*), which appeared during the course of twenty-six years in four editions and a French translation, he views the oldest, that is, the Oriental myths as "unqualified symbols," whose function it is "to give limits to the limitless and to fathom the unfathomable,"[22] and he tries, in light of the cults of Dionysus and the mysteries, to trace back the mythological symbolism of the Occident, and above all of the Greeks, to the myths of India, Asia Minor, and Egypt. The original Dionysus, Creuzer maintains, revered in India as "Dewanishi" with "phallagogias and phallophoria," came to the Greeks with the primordial Priapus, and had already existed in Asia for thousands of years before Alexander (582–84).

In the second volume of his *Symbolism and Mythology* Creuzer unites his primal Indian Dionysus with the Phrygian Cybele-cult and the Egyptian solar bull. The comprehensive third volume is totally dedicated to the "Bacchic religion." It purports to be the all-encompassing description of the various Asiatic myths of Dionysus. Here they all become one: the Egyptian "solar bull Dionysus," the Theban "radiant fire-god Bacchus" (III, 93), the Dionysus from

[20] *Die christliche Mystik*, 4 vols. (Regensburg and Landshut: Manz, 1836–42); here, III, 21.

[21] *Studien*, ed. Carl Daub and Friedrich Creuzer (Frankfurt a. M. and Heidelberg: Mohr and Zimmer, 1806), II, 312.

[22] *Symbolik und Mythologie der alten Völker, besonders der Griechen*, 2nd ed. (Leipzig and Darmstadt: Heyer and Leske, 1819–23), I, 94. Hereafter cited in the text.

Nysa (101), the "Indian Dionysus" (119), the post-Hesiodic Dionysus, the Dionysus falsified by Homer (117), and the "Phrygian Dionysus" (349). The "Bacchic myth," he maintains, unites all these figures into a single wild syncretism.[23] Here we see anticipated, nearly sixty years before Nietzsche, the supposed "antithesis of the Apollonian and Bacchic religions" (160) and their unification in the Orphic mysteries, brought forth out of the antithetical application of the (Dionysically) provocative flute and the soothing cithara (151–69). Because of its preference for the cithara, Creuzer calls the older "Orphic school" an "Apollonian school" (151), "in which the reformed doctrine of Dionysus was united with the old light-theories of Upper Asia into a single great theological system—a system which "combined within itself probably all the sacerdotal wisdom which had at that time found its way to the Greeks" (168–69). The antithesis and unification of Apollo and Dionysus are then treated further by Creuzer in that third volume of his *Symbolism*. The same Dionysus-volume was borrowed by Nietzsche from the library of the University of Basel on 18 June 1871, at a time when he was still at work on *The Birth of Tragedy*.[24]

Creuzer's "orientalization" of Greek mythology and his devaluation of classical Greece did not long remain without reply from the camp of the classicists. Of the countless refutations published, Johann Heinrich Voß's *Antisymbolism* (*Antisymbolik*) of 1824 had the greatest effect among his contemporaries.[25] As Creuzer's *Symbolism and Mythology* had dealt mainly with the Dionysian, so Voß,

---

[23] The legend that Semele, "a human girl," gave birth to Dionysus is rejected by Creuzer as a usurpation by the Greeks (III, 88). He maintains instead that the Theban Dionysus arose from the sea as an "equinoctial bull" just like the Egyptian Osiris (pp. 102–6). The sea, the bull, the birth out of fire, and the ivy are for Creuzer the Egyptian-Oriental attributes of Dionysus, while the phallus, orgies, and the triumphal procession from the East form his Indian characteristics. The Greeks, Creuzer states, have partly concealed these origins, and only in his own time will they appear in their true light by virtue of the new symbolic understanding of the myths (pp. 119–20).

[24] Cf. Karl Meuli's concluding remarks to Bachofen's *Unsterblichkeitslehre* in volume VII of Bachofen's *Gesammelte Werke* (Basel: Schwabe, 1943–48) pp. 510–15; likewise the above-cited work by Martin Vogel, pp. 97–98.

[25] Johann Gottfried Jacob Hermann, *Briefe über Homer und Hesiodus* (Heidelberg: Oswald, 1818); *De mythologia Graecorum antiquissima* (Leipzig and Heidelberg: 1818); *Ueber das Wesen und die Behandlung der Mythologie* (Leipzig: Fleischer, 1819); Johann Heinrich Voß, *Antisymbolik* (Stuttgart: Metzler, 1824), hereafter cited in the text; Christoph August Lobeck, *Aglaophamus, seu de theologiae mysticae Graecorum causis*, 2 vols. (Königsberg: Bornträger, 1829). Cf. also Goethe's letter (No. 7951) of 16 January 1818 to Sulpiz Boisserée: ". . . one was compelled now to suffer continuously from these wretched Dionysian mysteries"; his letter (No. 263) of 25 August 1819 to Johann Heinrich Meyer on the "miserable Egyptian-Indian mist-visions" ("*Nebelbilder*") in Creuzer's *Symbolik*; and Goethe's journal entry for 10 March 1826: "Voß vs. Creuzer in *Hermes*, vol. XXV, no. 2"; likewise the "lively discussion on the Symbolists" with Boisserée on 19 May 1826 (Eduard Firmenich-Richartz, *Sulpiz und Melchior Boisserée als Kunstsammler* [Jena: Diederichs, 1916], p. 429), and the part of Goethe's letter (No. 1332) to Reinhard of 12 May 1826, where he states that the Symbolists are "basically anti-classicists," who have produced nothing worthwhile in art or the study of antiquity (*Goethes Briefe*, Hamburg edition, IV, 189 and 584).

too, concerns himself in the first volume of his *Antisymbolism*—the volume directed at Creuzer—almost exclusively with Dionysus. It has been little noticed up to now that the famous argument between the Romantic symbolists and their classical opponents—an argument into which Goethe also felt himself drawn—was decided in reality on the issue of the mythical origin and the symbolic meaning of the figure of Dionysus. The very sub-headings for the first chapter speak for themselves: "Creuzer's Theory of the Bacchic Religion"; "The Illusion of the Theban Dionysus"; "The Spurious Indian Dionysus"; "The Phantom Dionysus of Calcutta"; "How the Calcutta Phantom Claims to Have Passed through India." At the same time, behind these satirical titles is concealed the systematic criticism to which the rationalistic classical philologist subjects Creuzer's indiscriminate syncretism and his muddled symbolic and mystical interpretation of mythology. In every chapter he singles out another of the Dionysian myths treated by Creuzer—always in the form of a couple of especially unscholarly and tenuous quotations from the latter—so that he can then pillory with biting sarcasm the fantastic exegesis of the author in all its dubiousness. In the second part, Voß inquires especially into the matter of the sexual character of the Dionysian mysteries, and criticizes Creuzer's attempts at conciliation and comparison between the Dionysian religion and the rites of Christianity, as well as the equation and fusion of this religion with other mysteries. He marshals all of the well-known accusations and suspicions of lewdness against Dionysus which had been raised from the time of Hesiod and Euripides up to those of the Church Fathers and directs them against Creuzer and the mystical Romantics.

Goethe had also taken part in the argument "Voß vs. Creuzer" with "lively" interest, and had also just as decisively dismissed the "Symbolists" as "Anti-Classicists" (cf. n. 25). As early as 16 January 1818, Goethe writes resignedly to Sulpiz Boisserée of "the wretched Dionysian mysteries." Voß's *Antisymbolism* is the "Anti-Dionysus" of the classicists, and at the same time, their last, and no longer entirely effective, bulwark against the Romanticists. The well-known argument "Classical-Romantic" ends in the controversy "Classical-Dionysian." Nietzsche stands on the side of the Romantics. To be sure, he makes no direct references to Voß's *Antisymbolism*, but when he boasts, as we have cited above, about being the first to have taken the Dionysian phenomenon seriously, he does fail to point to the argument between the Dionysian Symbolists and to dismiss the work *Aglaophamus*—written by Christian August Lobeck (cf. n. 25) and directed against Creuzer—as the "contemptible babble" of a "worm dried up between the leaves of books" who understood nothing of the Dionysian orgies (W, II, 1030–31).

This new Romantic conception of the Dionysian is likewise maintained in the handbooks of Greek archaeology which appeared around the middle of the nineteenth century, even in cases where their authors intentionally keep their distance from Creuzer. The eminent archaeologist Karl Otfried Müller sees the

Dionysian as a natural force which shakes man out of his peaceful, rational condition of awareness and enraptures him. In his *Handbook of the Archaeology of Art* (*Handbuch der Archäologie der Kunst*) of 1830 he states at the beginning of his discourse on the deities of the "Dionysian Circle":

> The nature which lies at the base of all Dionysian images, and which is most perfectly symbolized by wine, is a nature which overwhelms human feelings and shakes man out of the repose of a clear self-awareness. The circle of Dionysian figures which, as it were, form their own separate Olympus, depicts this life of nature with its effects on the human spirit—conceived of as existing on different levels—sometimes in noble, sometimes in ignoble form; in the figure of Dionysus himself there unfolds the purest flower, combined with an *afflatus* which enraptures the emotions without disturbing the peaceful flow of perceptions.[26]

Müller is the first to apply the adjective "Dionysian" consistently and with far greater frequency than "Bacchic," after Goethe had introduced the word "Dionysian"—probably as the first to do so, even though only in passing.[27] Schelling had also played a part in the introduction of this term, but he, too, uses it only occasionally, and never in one of his most important works. Müller speaks of "Dionysian" festivals, figures, processions, and formations. The adjective derived from the name of this god led to a special kind of conception—to that of the general attribute "Dionysian." This attribute was abstracted from the Greek god himself, from his being and his myths, and was generalized in psychological terms by Müller, aestheticized philosophically by Schelling, and finally made by Nietzsche into the substantive "the Dionysian," whereupon it attained the status of a legitimate ancient and modern phenomenon.

Two other important handbooks of Greek antiquity from around the middle of the century are Ludwig Preller's *Greek Mythology* (*Griechische Mythologie*) in two volumes (Berlin, 1854–55), and Friedrich Gottlieb Welcker's *Myths of the Greek Gods* (*Griechische Götterlehre*) in three volumes (Göttingen, 1857–62). Preller's *Greek Mythology*, along with Erwin Rohde's *Psyche*, form the main basis of the article on Dionysus by Otto Kern in Pauly-Wissowa's *Real-Encyclopädie der classischen Altertumswissenschaft*, a work which is still valid today. In his early treatise *Demeter and Persephone* (Hamburg, 1837), Preller complains—in quite the same fashion as the elderly Voß—of the "repulsive nakedness" and the "obscenity" of the mysteries (48–49); nonetheless he prepares the ground for Bachofen's views of Dionysian sexuality, and is responsible for the differentiation which has existed since that time between the Olympic and chthonian deities in mythology.

---

[26] Hereafter cited in the text in the third edition (Breslau: J. Max, 1848); here, p. 594.

[27] Goethe writes in the year 1808 in his notes for the plan to continue his festival play *Pandora:* "Dionysian. Complete obliviousness." On 16 January 1818 in the above-mentioned letter to Boisserée, he speaks of the "wretched Dionysian mysteries" (cf. n. 25).

As early as this, Welcker speaks of the "conception of the entire Dionysian essence," and differentiates between "two main tendencies"; an aesthetic-festive one, "in which Dionysus sometimes appears spiritualized in a new and broad circle of the arts, and at other times as the patron of a gay and dissolute enjoyment of life, in contrast to Apollo Musagetes"; and on the other side, "the chthonic," especially as it is manifested in the mysteries (574–75). By bringing the "chthonic" into prominence, Welcker gives credence, just as Preller did, to the Dionysian conception of Bachofen and Rohde. On three separate occasions he treats systematically the antithesis—important for Nietzsche—between Dionysus and Apollo, as well as the "convergence and merging of their natures" (610). It is important to note that he hereby applies the terms "Apollonian" and "Dionysian" for the first time in mythology and archaeology, just as Schelling had done shortly before in the area of philosophy. As Creuzer before him had done, Welcker contrasts the "Dionysian" festivals with the "Apollonian cithara" (611). "Here and there debaucheries have attached themselves to the Dionysian as well as the Apollonian religion," he states (650). Welcker characterizes the more festive of the main tendencies of the "Dionysian essence" in its later development as the "Dionysian carnival" in the country and "Dionysian passion" in its urban refinement (579), and maintains of the "Dionysian orgies" that they were "a prologue for the Christian hypocrisies as well" (619).

The tradition of the Dionysian in Romantic philosophy, that is, in the work of Hegel and Schelling, is closely bound up with the development and significance of the Dionysian in contemporaneous classical philology and mythology. Friedrich Wilhelm Joseph Schelling himself appeals expressly to Creuzer in establishing the foundation for his philosophy of the threefold Dionysus. Georg Friedrich Wilhelm Hegel addresses his early poem "Eleusis" from the year 1796, in its superscription as well as in its content, "To Hölderlin," when he relates the mysteries of Ceres to the secret society of his Tübingen friends and their concern for the political matters of the time. Hölderlin, Hegel, and Schelling, friends from their student days at the Tübingen Theological Seminary, are all at the same time also special disciples of Dionysus. When Hegel in his *Phenomenology of the Spirit* (*Phänomenologie des Geistes*) of 1807 explains the manifestation of the spirit in its pure self-consciousness as existing at the level of "artistic religion," he is describing the masculine principle of the self-propelling force of self-conscious existence as "the many-named celestial being of the East and its delirious life, which . . . roams about as a swarm of raving women (Bacchantes), the unrestrained delirium of nature in a self-conscious form."[28] In the mystery of the bread and wine, of Ceres and of Bacchus, this self-conscious life of the absolute spirit still possesses its living unity, Hegel says, in the "stammer of Bacchic ravings" (552). In being banished

---

[28] Volume II of the 4th edition of the Jubilee Edition of Hegel's *Sämtliche Werke* in 20 volumes. (Stuttgart: F. Fromann, 1927–40). Hereafter cited in the text.

to the otherness of the material world, this self-consciousness divides into a nature consisting of higher and lower powers. Hegel designates the higher power as "the celestial side," "Phoebus Apollo"; the lower power he does not call Dionysus, however, but "the Erinys who keeps herself hidden," and who is hostile to the higher power (560–63). In the "simple figure of Zeus" the dialectic of the Apollonian-Erinnic antithesis of consciousness is overcome (564). Apollo, "the many-named celestial being," is for Hegel not separated at the primitive level of delirious, Bacchic life from the figure of Dionysus. Bachofen, in his *Discourse Concerning Tomb Symbolism of the Ancients (Versuch über die Gräbersymbolik der Alten)*, later reworks the Hegelian antithesis as a procreative, Dionysian "earth and sun power," contrasted with "Apollo, holding sway in the higher purity of light,"[29] while Schelling represents the development of the consciousness of self in the form of the dialectical antithesis of a threefold Dionysus.

For Schelling, Dionysus and the Dionysian form an essential part of his entire mythological philosophy. His "Dionysiology"—to anticipate his own technical term—which in various treatises spans several hundred pages, can only be outlined here in a few sentences, even if for the first time. In his treatise *The Ages of the World (Die Weltalter)* from the year 1813, Schelling, by means of his dialectical theory of "potencies," or powers of nature working against one another within the being of God, explains Dionysus as a symbol and an example of the blind and unconscious power of creation, and (falsifying Plato[30]) equates him with the "divine madness" of the ancients, which "even yet is the innermost part of all things . . . the real power of nature and all of her creations," and without which "no one can accomplish anything great."[31] Noteworthy here, and evident in the case of all the Romantic writers on Dionysus previously discussed, is the conscious association of the Dionysian with the present, the "even yet" of the Dionysian ecstasy and madness, and the assertion that it is a creative force. In his lecture and treatise of 1815 entitled *Concerning the Deities of Samothrace (Über die Gottheiten von Samothrake)*, Schelling attempts—with the help of vague etymological comparisons of names and objects after the syncretistic manner of Creuzer, on whom he bases his work—to show that Dionysus is one and the same demiurgic (world-creating) and transforming principle in the various religions (161–74; 202–3). The lectures on the *Philosophy of Mythology (Philosophie der Mythologie)*

---

[29] *Versuch über die Gräbersymbolik der Alten*, volume IV of the *Gesammelte Werke*, ed. Karl Meuli (Basel: Schwabe, 1943–48), pp. 70–82. This edition of Bachofen's works cited hereafter in the text by volume and page number.

[30] In the forty-eighth chapter of his *Phaidros*, Plato differentiates between the prophetic madness of Apollo, the ritually atoning madness of Dionysus, the poetic madness of the Muses, and the love-madness of Eros and Aphrodite.

[31] *Friedrich Wilhelm Joseph von Schellings sämmtliche Werke* (1856–61; rpt. Darmstadt: Wissenschaftliche Buchgesellschaft, 1966–68). This edition is hereafter cited in the text; here, *Schriften von 1813–30*, pp. 23–24, 82, 142–43, 254–56, 294–309, 365–77, 626–42.

of 1828 and 1848 contain long expositions concerning Schelling's concept of the Dionysus of the three potencies, each acting upon the other dialectically, of the divine consciousness which causes its own development, and the way in which these potencies become manifest in the various phases of Asiatic and Greek mythologies (II, 254–377; 626–42). Moreover, Schelling maintains here that Apollo and Dionysus are closely tied together, that in the Greek mind Apollo is superior to the threefold Dionysus, and that he has already passed through the latter's stages of destruction and beatification and unites these stages within himself at the highest stage (667–69).

Schelling begins his last work, the obscure *Philosophy of Revelation* (*Philosophie der Offenbarung*) by renewing the explanation of his dialectical thesis concerning the development of the divine in the form of three potencies, and preaches their utilization and transference from his "Dionysiology" to a "Christology" which is to be discussed in detail at a later time (I, 332–33). Before he does this, however, he depicts once again, in the eighteenth to the twenty-third lectures, the transitions, in the three forms of Dionysian manifestation, from unconsciousness to consciousness and then to the spiritual in pre-Christian man and his history as the first three steps of the self-identification of the absolute spirit. Human consciousness stands at the same level of development as that at which the absolute manifests itself. Among the Greeks, this development manifests itself in the three stages of Dionysus: in the wild, orgiastic, raving, utterly-beside-himself Dionysus-Zagreus; in the Dionysus-Bacchus of pleasure and the fermented juice of the grape, who overcomes and transforms this earlier, unspiritual Dionysus; and in the third Dionysus-Iacchus of the mysteries and a higher spiritual consciousness, who again withdraws into his spiritual being-in-itself (391–482). Schelling then contrasts this masculine trinity of Dionysus as the concept of overcoming with the trinity made up of the feminine deities Persephone, Demeter, and Core—all of whom are occasionally connected with Dionysus in Greek mythology—as an expression of a substantive, quiescent, and maternal primal principle basic to the ever-changing forms of marriage, procreation, and birth (486–92). In the case of Bachofen, these connections between Dionysus and Demeter are interpreted even more fantastically.

Schelling draws three conclusions from his "Dionysiology." First, he states his opinion that "The world of these many gods is actually made up of the plurality of divinities begotten and established by Dionysus in which the vanquished and transformed, exclusive principle now appears—it is the world of Dionysus" (399). The ancient world, which since Winckelmann had been exclusively classical for the Germans, will appear from now on for many, and especially for Nietzsche, to be simply Dionysian. Second, Schelling not only explains the Christian trinity as having the same functionality and cosmic interpretation as his Dionysian trilogy of Zagreus, Bacchus, and Iacchus, but he also views Christianity as the completion of, and transition from, the pre-Christian religions elevated in the Dionysian mysteries. "The Greek mysteries are truly the natural transition from heathendom to Christianity, i.e., to complete revelation" (410). Like Hölderlin, Schelling still advocates the Romantic union of the Dionysian with the Christian; a few years later Nietzsche will follow the lead of Heine and place Dionysus *in opposition* to Christ. Third, Schelling concludes in the additional and final book of his *Philosophy of Revelation* that the theogonic process of self-identification of the divine spirit in revelation could, even in man, only be the work of a free will, which, according to Johann Georg Hamann, unites the affirmative and simultaneously the negative creative powers as creative genius (II, 9–25). Out of this latter conclusion Schelling formulates the first true definition of the Dionysian as the unrestrained, intoxicated power of creation in the poetic genius, and the Apollonian as the reflective power of form which negates the Dionysian. Schelling sees the unification of these two powers in the consummate work of art:

> Indeed, not only in God, but even in men—to the extent that they have been blessed with the slightest glimmer of creative power—the same relationship is to be found, this same contradiction: a blind creative power, by its very nature unrestrained, opposed by a reflective, and thus in reality a negative power, residing in the same subject, which restrains and forms this blind power. . . . To be intoxicated and sober not at different times, but simultaneously—this is the secret of true poetry. It is this which differentiates between Apollonian inspiration and the merely Dionysian. An infinite content, and thus a content which actually resists form and appears to destroy all form—to depict such an infinite content in its most complete, that is, in its most finite form, is the highest calling of art. (26)

Nietzsche's later definition at the beginning of *The Birth of Tragedy* (W, I, 21) of the Dionysian and Apollonian as opposing creative powers agrees largely with that of Schelling. Nonetheless, it is possible that Nietzsche was not acquainted with this definition of Schelling, hidden as it was in the relatively unknown *Philosophy of Revelation*, or with the latter's obscure "Dionysiology."[32] Also in the case of the lawyer from Basel, Johann Jakob Bachofen, no direct influence can be traced. On the other hand, it can be shown that Bachofen, like Schelling and Nietzsche, is also dependent on Creuzer's *Symbolism*, as is confirmed by the page-long excerpts from this work in his literary remains. Bachofen's theory of the Dionysian can also be given here only in its essential points. In his

---

[32] As the title of the work and the year of publication indicate, Otto Kein's *Das Apollinische und Dionysische bei Nietzsche und Schelling* (Berlin: Junker and Dünnhaupt, 1935) deals mainly with Nietzsche's concept of the Dionysian, and only incidentally—in terms of a few unconnected comparisons—with that of Schelling. It is Kein's opinion that Nietzsche was not aware of Schelling's definition of the Apollonian and Dionysian (pp. 14 and 18). Nietzsche himself only gives Schelling, as he does Hegel, adversely critical mention in his works—and this in terms of fleeting wholesale judgments, avoiding any and all positive references.

first mythological work, the *Discourse Concerning the Tomb Symbolism of the Ancients* (1859) mentioned above, he sets the Dionysian phallus over against the egg of the mysteries, the symbol of the "substantive primal motherhood."[33] His thesis reads: "The union of the sexes is always the fundamental Dionysian principle, and γάμος [marriage], its realization" (40). "Dionysus in the form of a terrestrial and solar power" is not to be found solitary and sexless like Apollo, "holding sway in the higher purity of light," but rather always in connection with female beings (74–82). This relationship to female divinities of all sorts is described by Bachofen in detail in the next chapter, "Dionysian Women" ("Dionysisches Frauenleben"). He concludes his Dionysian exposition in the *Tomb Symbolism* under the political title "Dionysus as the promoter of freedom and equality." As "Liber" and as bearer of the purely material creation Dionysus gives men indiscriminate "freedom" with relation to the state:

> If the political, civil viewpoint everywhere erects barriers, separates peoples and individuals, and expands the principle of individuality to the most complete egotism, Dionysus, on the other hand, leads everything back to unity, to peace, and to the φιλία of primal life. Slaves as well as free men take part in all mysteries, and all barriers fall before the god of material lust, barriers which political life would raise in time to ever greater heights. (238–39)

Here Bachofen draws a parallel between Dionysus and the realization of the ideas of freedom and equality of the French Revolution, and between Dionysian and political-revolutionary utopias. Even more clearly than this, he is in full agreement with Hamerling's proclamation of the unbridled sensual desire which the lower classes would obtain through Dionysus. And Nietzsche, too, was not the last to proclaim a few years later in *The Birth of Tragedy*—in words identical to Bachofen's (but appealing to Schopenhauer)—the Dionysian as a shattering of the "principle of individuality," and as "the unification" of all mankind with the "primal life." On 18 June 1871, as he was occupied with the conclusion of the manuscript of *The Birth of Tragedy*, Nietzsche borrowed from the library, along with Creuzer's *Symbolism and Mythology*, Bachofen's *Tomb Symbolism*, in which he was able to find a word-for-word preview of his negative association of the Dionysian with the "principle of individuality."[34] Also from the works of his colleague and sometime friend Bachofen he was able to glean any number of different versions of the distinction between the Apollonian and the Dionysian.

"Dionysian gyneocracy" (rule by women) and "Apollonian paternity" are the true opposing themes in Bachofens *Matriarchal Rights* (*Das Mutterrecht*) of 1861. In the main part of the work he attempts to show the difference between phallic-procreative "Dionysian paternity" and a pure and lucid "Apollonian paternity" in the religious congregations of Egypt, India, Crete, Asia Minor, and

---

[33] Cf. note 26; here, IV, 37; hereafter cited in the text.
[34] Cf. note 25, Karl Meuli and Martin Vogel.

Greece, as well as in the Minoan civilization. "If Dionysus merely regarded
fatherhood more highly than motherhood, Apollo, on the other hand, frees
himself completely from any and all association with the female" (III, 61).
Finally, Apollo and Dionysus are united in the Greek mysteries: "The Apollonian
mystery becomes a Dionysian one, and Orphic mysticism fully identical in
meaning to the Dionysian" (570). Bachofen's biographer, Karl Meuli, says of the
former's third and last book, *The Doctrine of Immortality of Orphic Theology as
Depicted on the Tombs of Antiquity* (*Die Unsterblichkeitslehre der orphischen Theologie
auf den Grabdenkmälern des Altertums*) of 1867, that it contains "the most brilliant
and moving description of the religion of Dionysus" (1076). Bachofen begins
with the wholesale assertion that the principle of inner unity in all cosmic life has
passed over to Dionysus in the secret Orphic religion and united in him the entire
host of deities of the mysteries. At the same time, however, the spiritualized conception of religion has been rendered sensual in Dionysus, so that, as he says, "now
the passionate life of the tiger and the luxuriousness of tropical nature, every
fetter removed, every inhibiting barrier withdrawn, appear as the true manifestations of this deity" (96–97). The second chapter again treats the exaltation and
spiritualization of Dionysus in union with the celestial nature of Apollo. Here it is
not a mutual antagonism which divides them; rather they are distinguished from
each other only by the degree of purity: "Apollo becomes Dionysus' supple-
mentation upwards, Dionysus Apollo's continuation in a downward direction.
Out of this coupling arise a Bacchic Apollo and an Apollonian Dionysus, and
these restore once again in twofold embodiment the unity of the principle of
light" (111).

The many-sided Dionysian tradition ends with Bachofen, and with him the
connection is established with Nietzsche's alleged discovery of the Dionysian and
the Apollonian. In summation, it can be said that for Bachofen the Dionysian
represents the degrading, sexual, and all-leveling democratic principle; the
Apollonian manifests itself as a pure, spiritualized, and sexless principle of light.
The unification of both these principles in impure union signifies the sensual and
spiritual totality of life. Only the Dionysian is at times a destructive power which
dissolves the *principium individuationis* and equalizes everything in aphrodisiac
desire; at other times, however, in connection with regulated maternal culture,
it is a constructive principle, bringing joy and peace. In the realm of the mysteries
the Dionysian effects the elevation of the earthly to the spiritual, and its own
unification and equation with the Apollonian. Bachofen does not transfer the
Dionysian and Apollonian, as do Schelling and Nietzsche, over to the realm of
aesthetics and philosophy; rather he extends it from the area of religion to that of
biology. In the case of Nietzsche, too, the Dionysian possesses a biological significance in addition to its aesthetic one, and, being an utter degradation of the
feminine, it is the expression of a Romantic idealization of the ecstatic life.
Nietzsche himself stood in rather close association with Bachofen during the

years in which he was writing *The Birth of Tragedy*, and frequently was a guest of the latter's patrician family at Basel. Since both of them were intensively occupied with the Dionysian among the Greeks at the same time, it is very probable that they touched upon this theme in their conversations. Bachofen was "quite delighted" with *The Birth of Tragedy*.[35] In his formulation of the concept of the Dionysian, as well as in his writing during the genesis of his *Birth of Tragedy*, Nietzsche was influenced not only by Bachofen, but also by his friends Richard Wagner and Erwin Rohde. In the writings of Wagner from the years 1849 and 1850—which were available to Nietzsche—the subject of Dionysus in art and music had already been discussed. In like manner, we also find here a notation of Wagner's which, in terms of content and form, largely corresponds to the theme of Nietzsche's early work: "Birth out of music: Aeschylus. Decadence—Euripides." Only recently has it been shown that Nietzsche, Rohde, and Wagner, during the period 11 to 13 June 1870, entered into a lively discussion at the Tribschen residence on "the theme of the Apollonian and the Dionysian," and on Nietzsche's essay "The Dionysian World-View" ("Die dionysische Weltanschauung")—his preliminary work to *The Birth of Tragedy*—and that this conversation took place while the three were viewing the painting "Bacchus among the Muses," by the painter Bonaventura Genelli (1797–1868).[36] The tradition of Dionysus and the Dionysian in German literature from Hamann and Herder to Nietzsche—as it has been set forth for the first time from aesthetic manifestoes, from literary works, and from what today are obscure works of natural philosophy and mythology—bears eloquent witness to the natural-mystical and ecstatic stance of the German Romanticists which reached its final culmination in the works of Friedrich Nietzsche.

[35] Carl Albrecht Bernoulli, *Johann Jakob Bachofen und das Natursymbol* (Basel: Schwabe, 1924), p. 593.

[36] Cf. here, and with regard to details previously mentioned, Martin Vogel's work *Apollinisch und Dionysisch*, pp. 115–20, 147–48.

XII

Nietzsche, Byron, and the Classical Tradition

RALPH S. FRASER

At the time of Nietzsche's birth in 1844 Lord Byron had been dead for some twenty years. He and Napoleon were, of course, the dominant personalities in Europe as the nineteenth century opened, and their influence upon life and thought had become incalculable long before the century had reached its halfway mark. One need refer only to Goethe and Heine to realize the importance that Byron's contemporaries ascribed to him. Their writings and conversations offer ample evidence of their interest in him and the phenomenon of Byronism.

Many studies have been made of the nature and extent of Byron's influence, both in a general and a particular sense.[1] Curiously enough, while Nietzsche scholars have alluded to his interest in Byron, no comprehensive analysis has yet been made of the subject.[2] In the present study I shall examine the several references to Byron in Nietzsche's writings with a twofold purpose: to assess the nature of the relationship, particularly with respect to Nietzsche's development as a thinker and poet, and to ascertain the attitude of the two writers concerning the classical tradition in the Western heritage.

Briefly stated, Nietzsche's view of Byron undergoes a considerable change, moving from youthful enthusiasm and adulation to a strong disenchantment that ultimately leads to the expression of mixed favorable and unfavorable comments having to do with Byron both as a man and a poet. It seems best generally to follow Nietzsche's remarks in chronological order so that this triple pattern may be seen in its proper perspective within the development of his thought. His comments, while frequently expressed in extreme terms, nevertheless accurately and pertinently portray a particular stage in his own evolution as a philosopher.

---

[1] Typical are such works as the following: Cedric Hentschel, *The Byronic Teuton: Aspects of German Pessimism 1800–1933* (Folcroft, Pa.: The Folcroft Press, Inc., 1940, rpt. 1969) and Peter L. Thorslev, Jr., *The Byronic Hero: Types and Prototypes* (Minneapolis: University of Minnesota Press, 1962).

[2] The 1960 *International Nietzsche Bibliography*, ed. Herbert W. Reichert and Karl Schlechta (Chapel Hill: University of North Carolina Press) contains only two entries under "Byron." Since this essay was written an essay "Nietzsche and Byron" by David S. Thatcher has appeared in *Nietzsche Studien*, 3 (1974), 130–51.

Nietzsche's initial enthusiasm for Byron is reflected in various incidental comments and notations made during the period of his schooling at Pforta, from 1858 to 1864. The first such reference is found in a letter of November 1861 to his sister Elisabeth, in which Christmas wishes are discussed: "Do you want an English book? If I were you I most certainly would read Byron in English."[3] In the following month Nietzsche delivered to the "Germania" society of the school an address, "On Byron's Dramatic Works."[4] Like other youthful writings of Nietzsche (an essay on Hölderlin, for example, also written in 1861) this address reveals in embryonic form several attributes that were to be more fully developed by the mature writer: a sound sense of literary standards and qualities and, importantly, the ability and willingness to submit even an admired personality and artist to close examination and, where necessary, a good degree of skepticism.

Nietzsche discusses three of Byron's plays here, *Manfred*, *Marino Faliero*, and *The Two Foscari*. Although the last-named play is the principal object of analysis, Nietzsche is especially drawn to the character of Manfred. He calls him "this superman who controls spirits," speaks of "his superhuman despair," and concludes that the play "is almost to be called a superhuman work."[5] There is a double significance in this: it is the first recorded instance of Nietzsche's use of the terms "Übermensch" and "übermenschlich," and it emphasizes the importance that this play and its protagonist were to assume as particular symbols in Nietzsche's writings.

In 1862 Nietzsche lists the books in his personal library, and the list includes three Byron entries: two individual volumes in German and one complete set in English.[6] And another letter to Elisabeth in December 1862 asks for the Tauch-

---

[3] HKG (*Briefe*), I, 167. (For key to abbreviations see p. xvii above.) The translations from this edition are mine; in other instances, unless noted otherwise, the translations are those of Walter Kaufmann.

[4] "Über die dramatischen Dichtungen Byrons" HKG (*Werke*), II, 9–15.

[5] Interestingly enough, in these three plays Byron followed his version of the Aristotelian unities of time, place, and action. Nietzsche correctly characterizes this as subtracting from their effectiveness as dramas. Since Nietzsche's thinking at this period was concentrating on theories of the evolution of the drama, his comments are quite pertinent. *Manfred* is the one work by Byron to which Nietzsche makes repeated reference. Byron himself called it "a mad Drama" and "a Bedlam tragedy" in a letter of 25 March 1817 to Thomas Moore. It may be profitable to compare Nietzsche's use of "Übermensch" and "übermenschlich" here to Manfred's own words: ". . . my sciences, my long-pursued and superhuman art" (Act II, scene 3); ". . . whate'er I may have been, or am, doth rest between Heaven and myself.—I shall not choose a mortal to be my mediator" (Act III, scene 1); and ". . . I disdain'd to mingle with a herd, though to be leader—and so am I." (Act III, scene 1). Many have quoted Nietzsche's words in *Ecce Homo*, "I must be profoundly related to *Byron's* Manfred: all these abysses I found in myself; at the age of thirteen I was ripe for this work. I have no word, only a glance, for those who dare to pronounce the word 'Faust' in the presence of Manfred. The Germans are *incapable* of any notion of greatness . . ." (Kaufmann, *Basic Writings of Nietzsche*, p. 701).

[6] HKG (*Werke*), II, 67.

nitz edition of Byron's works, adding that Nietzsche hopes to begin the study of English the next year: "... my favorite English poet will be the greatest incentive for me."[7]

The passage of ten years brings about a radical change in Nietzsche's opinion of Byron, or at least of *Manfred*. While it may seem at first glance nothing more than maturity's abandonment of the enthusiasm of adolescence, there is considerable significance to such a change in attitude. A letter of 29 October 1872 to Hans von Bülow, the eminent conductor and critic, makes short shrift of Robert Schumann's music, including his "Manfred Overture." Nietzsche moreover turns upon himself, expressing an aversion for Byron's play; in the spring of 1872 he had attempted to replace Schumann's Manfred music with a "Manfred Meditation" of his own and asked Bülow's opinion of his efforts. Bülow's comments were unfavorable and Nietzsche, acknowledging their correctness, suddenly realized that his long-standing admiration for *Manfred* itself was replaced by a new found dislike: "... I cannot see in Byron's *Manfred*, which I almost venerated as my favorite poem when I was a boy, anything but a madly formless, dreary absurdity."[8]

The reversal of Nietzsche's opinion has its basis not only in aesthetic considerations, but in ethical ones as well. In 1872 he was professor of classical philology at Basel and was seeing his first book into print. This was *The Birth of Tragedy*, which contains Nietzsche's distinctive application of the concepts of the Apollonian and Dionysian. There is a distinct and direct correlation between Nietzsche's work on this book and his rejection of *Manfred* (and of Byron). That is, since the Apollonian represents harmonious form and control while the Dionysian exemplifies uninhibited energy and passions let loose, it is more than merely probable that Nietzsche saw in Byron and *Manfred* what may be termed the dangers of excess. In Nietzsche's view the Apollonian and Dionysian must merge into one to produce art; such had been the case, he says, when Greek tragedy originated; such was the case in the late 1800s in Germany when Wagner's music began to predominate. In the light of his later renunciation of Wagner and his second thoughts about the validity of his conclusions in this early work, it is not difficult to understand his new aversion to Byron that appears in the letter to Bülow. *Manfred* is "mad" ("toll") and "formless" ("formlos") and a "dreary absurdity" ("ein monotones Unding"). The use of such harsh descriptive terms is by no means haphazard on Nietzsche's part; although he occasionally indulged in hyperbole in applying epithets and descriptive phrases to one-time idols with newly-discovered feet of clay (Wagner and Schopenhauer, for instance), in the

---

[7] HKG (*Briefe*), I, 202–3.

[8] HKG (*Briefe*), III, 310–11. For a discussion of Nietzsche's musical compositions see Curt Paul Janz, "Die Kompositionen Friedrich Nietzsches" in *Nietzsche-Studien*, I (1972), 173–84.

present case his characterization seems sincerely meant. It is a result of his writing *The Birth of Tragedy* and is a direct reflection of his preoccupation with the concepts of the Apollonian and Dionysian. Byron's drama very fittingly illustrates Nietzsche's point about the excesses of the Dionysian, for that is exactly what it suggests. The failure of Manfred to establish self-control, to bring order out of chaos, and to strike a balance between melancholy emotionalism and a sound intellect must have alarmed Nietzsche in a way that the adolescent Pforta student could not yet grasp.

It is of more than passing interest to note that Nietzsche makes no reference to works of Byron other than the three dramas mentioned above and a few scattered poems. He does not mention *Don Juan*, for example, although the change in his opinion of Byron is somewhat parallel to the changes in Byron himself that may be seen when one proceeds from *Manfred* to the more mature work. The latter represents a poet whose attitude is quite different from the Byron whose gloomy Manfred sought the end of his unsatisfactory existence in the menacing grandeur of the Alps. Moreover, there is in *Don Juan* an obvious maturity of characterization, a clear controlling of intensity that is due to a balance of extremes within the protagonist. Byron, in his maturity as an artist, at least makes some attempt to synthesize extremes, and his effort in this direction suggests Nietzsche's synthesis of the Apollonian and Dionysian.

The thesis and antithesis of Nietzsche's attitudes toward Byron are now followed by a third stage. His final judgment is expressed in a variety of comments over several years that refer to Byron's personality and way of life as frequently as they do to his poetry. Of particular interest is his speculation that a combination of impatience and disease (specifically, epilepsy) occasioned Byron's restless activity and his need to undertake striking or astounding projects. In "Flight from the Self," which is section 549 of the fifth book of *The Dawn* (1881), Nietzsche explores this idea:

> Those men of intellectual convulsions who are impatient and darkly brooding where they themselves are concerned, such as Byron or Alfred de Musset, and who resemble runaway horses in everything they do, truly realize no profit from their creativity except for a short-lived exultation and a fire that almost bursts their veins; but they realize an even greater bleakness and grief—how can they stand themselves! They thirst for a union with something "beyond the Self"; if the man with such a thirst is a Christian he yearns for a union with God, for "becoming entirely one with Him"; if he is Shakespeare, only his merging himself into portraits of the most passionate kind of existence will satisfy him; if he is Byron, he thirsts for *deeds*, because deeds draw us away from ourselves more so than our thoughts, feelings, creations. Perhaps, then, the urge to action is basically a flight from the Self? Pascal might ask us. It is indeed! The rule may be confirmed by considering the most prominent examples of the urge to action: let one judge with an alienist's knowledge and experience how proper it is that four of those who throughout history most

needed action were epileptics (i.e., Alexander, Caesar, Mohammed, and Napoleon), just as Byron too was subject to this illness.[9]

This theory is further developed in *Beyond Good and Evil* (1886), when Nietzsche discerns the true nature of various writers:

> Those great poets, for example—men like Byron, Musset, Poe, Leopardi, Kleist, Gogol (I do not dare mention greater names, but I mean them)—are and perhaps must be men of fleeting moments, enthusiastic, sensual, childish, frivolous and sudden in mistrust and trust; with souls in which they usually try to conceal some fracture; often taking revenge with their works for some inner contamination, often seeking with their high flights to escape into forgetfulness from an all-too-faithful memory; often lost in the mud and almost in love with it, until they become like the will-o'-the-wisps around swamps and *pose* as stars—the people may then call them idealists—often fighting against a long nausea, with a recurring specter of disbelief that chills and forces them to languish for *gloria* and to gobble their "belief in themselves" from the hands of intoxicated flatterers—what *torture* are these great artists and all the so-called higher men for anyone who has once guessed their true nature![10]

Nietzsche's view of European intellectual history leads him inevitably to liken Byron to Rousseau, a figure for whom he had very little regard. He cites the "likeness" on several different occasions, and in each comment Byron appears in an unfavorable light. His writing seems outdated and a failure when compared with the music of Beethoven, who really grasped the significance of the days of freedom at the end of the eighteenth century: ". . . how strange to our ears sounds the language of Rousseau, Schiller, Shelley, Byron, in whom, taken *together*, the same fate of Europe found its way into words that in Beethoven knew how to sing!"[11] And two jottings from the 1880s offer a similar judgment; in the first Nietzsche deplores the influence on modern times of what may be termed Byron's "pathetic stance" as a man: "The *sickly* about Rousseau most admired and *imitated*. (Lord Byron similar; also screwed himself up to an exalted posturing, to the rankest resentment; a sign of 'vulgarity'; later, restored to equilibrium by Venice, he grasped what *eases* and *comforts* more: *l'insouciance*.)"[12] And he particularly castigates what he defines as "the *romantic* outlook of modern man":

> . . . —the noble man (Byron, Victor Hugo, George Sand); noble indignation; sanctification through passion (as true "nature");—sponsorship of the oppressed and downtrodden: motto of historians and writers;—the Stoics of duty;—"selflessness" as art and knowledge;—altruism as the most depraved form of egoism (utilitarianism), the most sentimental egoism.

[9] W, I, 1269; my translation.
[10] Kaufmann, *Basic Writings of Nietzsche*, pp. 408–9.
[11] Ibid., pp. 370–71.
[12] W, III, 508; my translation.

All of this is eighteenth century. What has *not* come down to us from that time: *insouciance*, gaiety, elegance, intellectual brightness. The tempo of the mind has altered; pleasure in intellectual refinement and clarity has given way to pleasure in color, harmony, mass, reality, etc. Sensualism in things of the spirit. In short, it is *Rousseau's* eighteenth century.[13]

Surely such comparison or arbitrary alignment with Rousseau would have not appealed to Byron, who protested at his contemporaries' doing much the same thing.[14] If one here takes Nietzsche at face value and grants that there may be some justification for his so comparing Byron and Rousseau, the question arises as to why he singled out the latter as an expression of that dislike that led to his own rejection of Byron. The answer to the question lies in the stance that Nietzsche took concerning contemporary romanticism and the classical tradition.

In *The Gay Science* (1882, with additions in 1887) he seeks to define romanticism by distinguishing two types of suffering: that which arises from "overfulness of life" and its opposite, arising from "impoverishment of life." Goethe exemplifies the former, Wagner and Schopenhauer demonstrate the latter:

... The desire for *destruction*, change, and becoming can be an expression of overfull, future-pregnant strength (my term for this is, as one knows, the word "Dionysian"): but it can also be the hatred of the misdeveloped, needy, underprivileged who destroys, who *must* destroy, because the existing, and even all existence, all being, outrages and provokes him. ... The will to *eternize* ... can come from gratitude and love: an art of this origin will ever be an art of apotheoses ... bright and benign with Goethe, and spreading a Homeric light and glory over all things. But it can also be that tyrannic will of one who is seriously ailing, struggling, and tortured ... who as it were revenges himself on all things by impressing on them ... and burning into them *his* image, the image of *his* torture. The latter is *romantic pessimism* in its most expressive form, whether as Schopenhauerian voluntarism or as Wagnerian music: romantic pessimism, the last *great* event in the fate of our culture. (... there *could* still be quite another kind of pessimism, one that is classical ... only that the word "classical" antagonizes my ears—it is far too trite. .... I call this pessimism ... *Dionysian* pessimism).[15]

Briefly, Nietzsche's antidote to romanticism and the flawed Byron (and Rousseau) is found in the classical ideal embodied in Goethe, who expressed the spirit of self-control and harmony, of the sublimation of potentially harmful

---

[13] Ibid., p. 529; my translation.

[14] Byron's objection to being likened to Rousseau is based in large part on the fact that ". . . he was of the people, I of the Aristocracy. . . . Altogether, I think myself justified in thinking the comparison not well founded. I don't say this out of pique, for Rousseau was a great man, and the thing if true were flattering enough, but I have no idea of being pleased with a chimera." (Cited from "My Dictionary: Detached Thoughts," entry of 15 October 1821).

[15] The translation is by Walter Kaufmann and is taken from his *Nietzsche: Philosopher, Psychologist, Antichrist* (New York: Random House Vintage Books, 1968), pp. 374–75.

energies.[16] Self-overcoming and restraint are necessary components of the will to power as Nietzsche formulated it, and he was moving on the road to this concept even as he was developing the types of the Apollonian and Dionysian.

It is evident in light of the above that Nietzsche would put Byron into the second category (those who suffer from impoverishment of life). The basis of his doing this must be found in the latent aversion to the Byronic attitude that made itself felt during the writing of *The Birth of Tragedy*.

And yet there is some evidence that Nietzsche's opinion of Byron both as poet and man was not completely one-sided. For instance, in order to substantiate his conclusion that the classical (or Goethean) ideal of form and restraint offers the only alternative to the destructive tendencies of romantic excess (as seen in Rousseau) Nietzsche cites Byron's words on the state of poetry in his day. To be sure, there is some irony in Nietzsche's choice of expressions, but his position and Byron's seem to be quite similar. He says:

> One of the great ones, whose instinct we can trust and whose theory lacked nothing more than thirty years' practice, Lord Byron, once said: "With regard to poetry in general, I am convinced, the more I think of it, that we are all in the wrong, one as much as another. We are all following a wrong revolutionary system—the present or the next generation will be of the same opinion."
>
> This is the same Byron who says: "I consider Shakespeare the worst example, even if he is the most remarkable poet." And does not Goethe's mature artistic vision in the latter half of his life say basically the same thing, that vision that so leaped over a whole succession of generations that by and large we may say that Goethe has not yet exercised an influence, that his time is yet to come?[17]

Nietzsche sustains this "classical" thought of the need for self-control and disciplined form over the next three years, until the publication of *The Dawn* in 1881. In this work he lists six ways in which one may combat the violence that his drives may bring him. The six ways are: submission to the drive; the imposition of some kind of regularity upon it; its over-indulgence to the point of loathing; the association of it with some sort of intellectual trick that ties it in with mentally painful memories; diverting one's energies to quite other things; the total suppression of it in the manner of the ascetic. In Byron Nietzsche claims to have found an illustration of the fourth way:

> This is the case when a man's pride, as with Lord Byron and Napoleon, revolts and makes him consider the primacy of any one emotional state over his total behavior and the ordering of his reason an insult; from which there consequently derives the

[16] Nietzsche makes a distinction between the Goethe who wrote *Faust* and the "other" Goethe. *Faust* drew a mixed reaction from him.

[17] W, I, 577–81. Nietzsche here merely approximately quotes Byron; the full text of the passage is found in Byron's letter of 15 September 1817 to John Murray. The translation is mine.

habit and desire to tyrannize the drive and make it grovel, so to speak. ("I do not intend to be the slave of any appetite," Byron wrote in his diary.)[18]

Nietzsche's ultimate judgment of Byron fails to take into account several points that are worth noting. For one, Byron was by no means such a child of his age that he could summarily dismiss as outmoded and irrelevant the classical heritage of the West. His unease concerning the state of poetry in his day is testimony to this, suggesting, as it does, a feeling that there has been too radical a departure from the classical roots of the poetic tradition. Byron's dissatisfaction in this regard parallels Nietzsche's conviction that his times also were out of joint and needed to be set aright. Thus a fundamental similarity between the two becomes discernible, expressed by each one just a few decades apart. Byron's words did take some root among his contemporaries, but Nietzsche's reputation was of course not solidly established in his day. And in another respect Nietzsche found in Byron the words that best expressed his own feelings when he quoted in 1878 the well-known lines from *Manfred* about knowledge and its melancholy dangers:

> Sorrow is knowledge; they who know the most
> Must mourn the deepest o'er the fatal truth,
> The Tree of Knowledge is not that of life.

Indeed, Nietzsche's position frequently was closer to Byron than he may have wished to admit.

Throughout his life Byron made constant reference to the writers of classical antiquity and to the neo-classicists of modern times; his defense of Alexander Pope is an obvious case in point. Byron shared with Nietzsche an admiration for Horace and a particular antipathy toward Friedrich Schlegel, one of the leading figures of German romanticism.[19] Again, Byron would surely have protested Nietzsche's linking him so closely to Rousseau. In his dramas he followed Aristotle's unities as interpreted by the French classicists, and he spoke well of Voltaire's efforts in the drama. He admired and respected Goethe as Nietzsche did, and perhaps for many of the same reasons; his drama *Sardanapalus* is dedicated to Goethe. Certainly the man who revered Greek art and deplored its pillage by Lord Elgin, who swam the Hellespont in tribute to Leander, and who gave his life for Greece had a sure sense of the nobility and value of the classical tradition.

Ironically, it is Carlyle (whom Nietzsche detested) who is allowed the last word here. When he says "Close thy *Byron:* open thy *Goethe*" he states what

---

[18] Ibid., p. 1082; my translation.

[19] Cf. Kaufmann's discussion of Nietzsche and Schlegel in reference to Lessing (*Nietzsche*, pp. 137–39). Byron's letter of 28 January 1821 to Teresa Guiccioli contains the following: "He [Schlegel] is like Hazlitt, in English, who talks pimples—a red and white corruption rising up (in little imitation of mountains upon maps), but containing nothing, and discharging nothing, except their own humors."

Nietzsche must have considered his own final judgment of Byron to be. That his interest in Byron was of benefit to his own development is certain. He was willing to submit Byron to examination and question, and in this sense the English poet was as much his teacher as Hölderlin or Plato. In formulating his opinions of Byron Nietzsche thus grew by outgrowing.

XIII

Parody and Parallel:
Heine, Nietzsche, and the Classical World

SANDER L. GILMAN

I

A vituperative debate has been raging for the past decade in the Federal Republic of Germany concerning the position of Heinrich Heine in the pantheon (or rogues' gallery) of German letters, a debate initiated by a suggestion to name the new university at Düsseldorf after the poet. Marcel Reich-Ranicki, in a *feuilleton* in *Die Zeit*, summarized the tenor of the present discussion as well as the history of Heine's reception in Germany with the observation that "whoever writes about Heine in Germany either defends him or attacks him."[1] The accuracy of Reich-Ranicki's conclusion for Heine criticism in Germany can be best judged on the basis of the two most often represented views of Heine. Historically, he has been presented either as one of the "unfortunate cases in the development of a truly German culture" or placed on the same plane as Goethe: "Germany has produced only one poet in addition to Goethe: Heinrich Heine."[2] While these contradictory views are not unexpected, given the radical positions usually taken by critics of Heine's works, what is astounding is that one man wrote both quotations. That man is Friedrich Nietzsche.

Nietzsche's view of Heine (and of the latter's works) has been the subject of numerous references in major studies, learned articles, and, most recently, an American dissertation.[3] Not only do most of the attempts to link the works of the

[1] Marcel Reich-Ranicki, "Eine Provokation und eine Zumutung," *Die Zeit*, 22 September 1972, pp. 16–17.

[2] All references to Nietzsche's works are to the Musarion edition (hereafter MusA). (For key to abbreviations see p. xvii above.) Wherever possible, the available volumes of the new critical edition edited by Giorgio Colli and Mazzino Montinari (WKG) have been used for comparison. Here MusA, VII, 233; MusA, XVII, 344. All translations are by the author.

[3] The most important studies which raise this question are Walter Kaufmann, *Nietzsche: Philosopher, Psychologist, Antichrist* (Princeton: Princeton University Press, 1967), esp. pp. 376–81; Ernst Bertram, *Nietzsche: Versuch einer Mythologie* (Bonn: Bouvier, 1965 [critical edition]); Hans Landsberg, *Friedrich Nietzsche und die deutsche Literatur* (Leipzig: Hermann Seemann, 1902), pp. 58–60; Ingeborg

two men fall into the pro/contra syndrome of Heine (and most of Nietzsche) scholarship, but their authors tend to oversimplify the relationship between the two men. It is neither sufficient to illustrate Nietzsche's knowledge of Heine's works, nor is it permissible to underscore the parallels in their thought. The former leads to unwarranted conclusions; the latter to polemical hyperbole. The potential goal of such a study should be threefold: first, an understanding of Nietzsche's individual reception should be obtained by examining his views of Heine; second, the greater contexts of these views should be comprehended; finally, the development of Nietzsche's image of Heine must be understood within the total development of Nietzsche's character and thought. Such a model would provide a basic approach to the question of the interrelationship of the two men, while supplying, at the same time, fruitful conclusions which may serve as the basis for further philological investigations.

II

Nietzsche's first written reference to Heine placed the latter in a specific aesthetic context in that he challenged Heine's presentation of the classical myth. Opening the (unpublished) introduction to a planned, expanded version of *Die Geburt der Tragödie*, which he composed in 1870–71, Nietzsche makes common cause with Wagner in prefacing his attack on Heine:

> I know that you, my dear friend, share with me an ability to distinguish between the true and false concept of Greek serenity, even while meeting the latter—the false concept—in its harmless comfort everywhere. I also know that you believe it to be impossible to achieve insight into the true nature of tragedy from this false concept of serenity . . . To take an aesthetic problem so seriously is indeed offensive to all sides, for our aesthetic-sensitive nature and its nauseating softness as well as for that robust or popular rabble, which is able to see art only as an amusing hobby or

Beithan, *Friedrich Nietzsche als Umwerter der deutschen Literatur*, Beiträge zur Philosophie, 25 (Heidelberg: Carl Winter, 1933); Elrud Kunne-Ibsch, *Die Stellung Nietzsches in der Entwicklung der modernen Literaturwissenschaft*, Studien zur deutschen Literatur, 33 (Tübingen: Niemeyer, 1971); Dolf Sternberger, *Heinrich Heine und die Abschaffung der Sünde* (Hamburg: Claasen, 1972), 301–8, 390–95. The basic articles remain: Arno Carl Coutinho, "Nietzsche, Heine und das 19. Jahrhundert," *PMLA*, 53 (1938), 1126–45; Georg Lange, "Heine und Nietzsche," *Österreichische Rundschau*, 64 (1920), 190–202; Helmut Prang, "Heine und Nietzsche," *Die Erlanger Universität: Beilage des Erlanger Tageblattes*, 9, No. 2 (1956), 53; Karl Quenzel, "Heine und Nietzsche," *Das literarische Echo*, 19 (1917), 599–603; Anon., "Heinrich Heine im Urteil Nietzsches und Karl Kraus'," *Psychologische Monatshefte*, 9 (1960), 49–50. The most extensive single study is the dissertation by R. J. Floyd, "Heine and Nietzsche: Parallel Studies in Paradox and Irony" (Diss. University of Washington, 1969). Recently, Hanna Spencer, "Heine and Nietzsche," *Heine Jahrbuch*, 11 (1972), 126–61, offered a summary of the earlier literature. The most striking omission in this regard is to be found in Charles Andler's *Les précurseurs de Nietzsche*, Vol. I of *Nietzsche: Sa vie et sa pensée* (Paris: Bossard, 1920), in which Andler does *not* devote any space to Heine (even though there are references to Heine in the later volumes).

as the missing fools' bells which introduce the "seriousness of existence." As if no one knew what was implied with this juxtaposition of the "seriousness of existence." Since the term "Greek serenity" rings out into the world from so many different sources, we should be content if it is not interpreted as placid sensualism: which is the sense in which Heinrich Heine usually used the term, always exclaiming it with longing emotion. (MusA. III. 167–268)

Thus Nietzsche places Heine on a specific plane, separate and distinct from the fools (his reference to the fools' bells [*Schellengeklingel*] is echoed in the verb "rings out" ["*hineinklingt*"]). While the fools do not see the vital importance of art in life, Heine has reduced art to placid sensualism. This interpretation of Greek culture is, for Nietzsche, an even more destructive one than that of the "robust" fools. Here Nietzsche reveals yet another category for his analysis of Heine. The fools are presented as "robust" and Heine as "*sehnsüchtig.*" This image of Heine as the prototype of German decadence was widely accepted throughout Europe in the nineteenth century.[4] Yet Nietzsche's classification has its roots in his own presentation of the Greek myth. For Nietzsche, the wellspring of Greek art was the presence of Dionysian ecstasy beneath the seeming order of Apollonian art. The illusion of order is present in the apparent harmony of Apollonian art only as the crust which eventually gives way, revealing the rushing undercurrent of Dionysian force. Both forces were vital for the existence of art, which is itself the synthesis of dissonance.[5] Nietzsche presents the apotheosis of these two forces early in *Die Geburt der Tragödie:*

> Apollo again appears as the divine embodiment of the *principiium individuationis*, in which the eternally achieved goal of primal unity, its redemption through appearances, is achieved: he indicates with regal gestures how this entire world of suffering is necessary, so that the individual is forced by it to produce a redeeming vision. (MusA, III, 37)

> "Titanic" and "barbaric" were the effects of the Dionysian as conceived by the Apollonian Greek, without, at the same time, being able to deny that he was internally related to the deposed titans and heroes. Indeed he had to feel even more: his entire being, with all its beauty and restraint, rested on a disguised basis of passion and knowledge, which was revealed to him by the Dionysian. And look! Apollo could not live without Dionysus. (MusA, III, 38)

It would be too crass to follow these categories literally and place Heine in the camp of the Apollonian and Nietzsche in that of the Dionysian. Yet such a comparison springs readily to mind. For Heine remains, with his concept of

---

[4] In this regard see esp. Sol Liptzin, *The English Legend of Heinrich Heine* (New York: Bloch, 1954).

[5] Cf. Peter Heller, *Dialectics and Nihilism: Essays on Lessing, Nietzsche, Mann and Kafka* (Amherst: University of Massachusetts Press, 1966), pp. 69–148, and Otto Kein, *Das Apollinische und Dionysische bei Nietzsche und Schelling.* Neue deutsche Forschungen, 16 (Berlin: Junker and Dünnhaupt, 1935).

placid sensuality, in the realm of *Schein* (in Nietzsche's rather than Schiller's sense of the term), creating a closed, compact world based on personal suffering. While this may be Nietzsche's initial presentation of Heine's concept of the classical world, is it indeed Heine's projection?

In the biographical essay *Ludwig Börne*, Heine chooses the image of the classical world as the metaphor through which to present to the reader the dichotomy between two seemingly antithetical forces. He seeks the basis for Börne's criticism of Goethe in the juxtaposition of Nazarene and Hellene:

> Börne reveals his Nazarene limitations in his judgments concerning Goethe as well as in his comments on other authors. I say "Nazarene" in order to avoid the terms "Jewish" and "Christian," even though both of these terms are synonymous to me and are used, not to indicate a religion, but a natural occurrence. "Jews" and "Christians" are, for me, semantically related terms in contrast to "Hellenes," by which I do not mean a specific people but an inherited as well as an acquired intellectual posture and manner of observation. In this regard I would like to note: all people are either Jews or Hellenes, people with ascetic, iconoclastic, spiritually dependent drives or people with joyful, proudly developing and realistic beings.[6]

Here Nietzsche's interpretation of Heine's concept of "Greek serenity" seems far from accurate. Indeed, the polarity between Nazarene and Hellene seems to prefigure, in at least general form, Nietzsche's own dialectic. For the Apollonian, like the Nazarene, seeks the closed, comprehensible system, while the Hellene, like the Dionysian, presents the undercurrent. Such a parallel would seem all too superficial, if Heine did not also present a synthesis of Nazarene and Hellene in the second book of *Börne:* "Shakespeare is at one and the same time Jew and Greek, or rather elements of both spiritualism and art have been reconciled in him, have illuminated him and developed in him a higher synthesis. Is perhaps the harmonious synthesis of both aspects not the goal of European civilization?" (*HH*, VII, 37). For Heine, the synthesis of the two discordant strains of civilization is the true European, a concept which, of course, plays a major role in Nietzsche's later thought.

The parallels as well as the divergences between Heine's and Nietzsche's dialectic are apparent. However, Nietzsche's refusal, at least in his early writings, to acknowledge these parallels reflects his general rejection of any personal, intellectual rapport with the dead poet. Yet, if Heine's understanding of the classical heritage is investigated even further, this rejection takes on an even more unusual color. For within Heine's presentation of the classical myth are the very concepts, the Apollonian and the Dionysian, which comprise the basis of Nietzsche's dialectic.[7]

---

[6] All references to Heine are to the edition of Ernst Elster, 7 vols. (Leipzig and Vienna: Bibliographisches Institut, 1887–90), hereafter referred to as *HH*; here *HH*, VII, 24.

[7] Heine's own source for this dialectic is questionable. It is possible that it stems from the Saint-

Heine had presented a classical dialectic in *Ludwig Börne;* in his ballet scenario, "Die Göttin Diana," he introduced the prototypes of the Nietzschean categories. The banal plot of the ballet, a distant relative of the Tannhäuser legend, culminates in the death of the central figure, a knight, at the hands of the true Christian, *der treue Eckardt.* Diana attempts to resurrect her beloved, calling upon her fellow gods for succor. Venus, the first summoned, can do nothing. The power of love has no hold over death. Apollo, the embodiment of ordered art, has little more effect: "The music changes and announces peace and harmonic bliss. At the head of the muses Apollo appears at stage left. . . . Apollo tunes his lute and playfully dances at the side of the muses about the corpse of the knight. The sound of these notes arouses the knight as from a heavy sleep, he rubs his eyes, looks about in a puzzled manner, and falls almost immediately back into *rigor mortis*" (*HH*, VI, 110). The absolute failure of Apollonian art is intensified by the appearance of Dionysus, for while ordered art can create the illusion of life, it has no power over the reality of life. Only the primordial force of Dionysus possesses the ultimate power:

> The music again changes; noteworthy is its transition to a joyful affirmation of life and Bacchus appears at stage right with his bacchanalian troop . . . Now Bacchus takes a hand-drum and, accompanied by his excited band, dances about the knight. A powerful sense of enthusiasm seizes the God of Joy; he almost destroys the tambourine. These melodies awaken the knight from his sleep of death and he sits up slowly, with his mouth longingly opened. Bacchus fills a cup with wine and pours it into the knight's mouth. He has hardly had time to enjoy the drink when he springs up, newly born, from the stage. (*HH*, VI, 110)

Dionysus, resurrector and resurrected, stands increasingly at the center of Heine's new mythology. In *Die Götter im Exil*, he becomes "the savior of the senses" and "the divine liberator" (*HH*, VI, 83).[8] Dionysus as Christ is not that far removed

Simonian contrast between pagan sensualism and Christian spiritualism. Cf. L. A. Willoughby, *The Romantic Movement in Germany* (Oxford: Oxford University Press, 1930), p. 144. The influence of Heine's concept, however, is not limited to Nietzsche and Germany. With the acceptance of Heine into the forum of world literature by Matthew Arnold, Heine's influence also became a major factor in nineteenth-century English letters. It was Walter Pater who continued to develop these concepts until they assumed a form strikingly similar to Nietzsche's thought (cf. esp. his essay "The Marbles of Aegina" [April, 1880] rpt. in his *Greek Studies* [London: Macmillan, 1910], pp. 251–68). The relevant studies are: John Smith Harrison, "Pater, Heine and the Old Gods of Greece," *PMLA*, 36 (1924), 655–86; R. T. Lenaghan, "Pattern in Walter Pater's Fiction," *Studies in Philology*, 58 (1961), 69–91; David J. DeLaura, *Hebrew and Hellene in Victorian England: Newman, Arnold and Pater* (Austin: University of Texas Press, 1969), pp. 253–55; David S. Thatcher, *Nietzsche in England 1890–1914: The Growth of a Reputation* (Toronto: University of Toronto Press, 1970).

　8 See A. I. Sandor, *The Exile of the Gods: An Interpretation of a Theme, a Theory and a Technique in the Work of Heinrich Heine.* Anglica Germanica, 9 (The Hague: Mouton, 1967) and Alexander Schweikert, *Heinrich Heines Einflüsse auf die deutsche Lyrik 1830–1900.* Abhandlungen zur Kunst-, Musik- und Literaturwissenschaft, 57 (Bonn: Bouvier, 1968). The recent study by Peter Koester, *Der*

from the Nietzschean image of Dionysus. For as E. M. Butler so succinctly stated, "Dionysus, who came late into Greece, came late into Germany. Heine ushered him in and then left it to Friedrich Nietzsche to see that he got his rights."[9]

III

The parallels between Nietzsche's and Heine's views of the classical world, as well as the disparities, tend to force a reassessment of Nietzsche's general condemnation of Heine. One other major aspect of Heine's presentation of the classical myth warrants examination in the light of Nietzsche's thought. Nietzsche is generally held to be the promulgator of the concept of the death of God. In *Die fröhliche Wissenschaft* he presents the often quoted anecdote of the madman who, seeking God, finds him not, but rather becomes aware of the death of the deity: "Don't we smell the divine decay?—even gods rot! God is dead! God remains dead! And we have killed him! How can we comfort ourselves—the murderers above all murderers" (MusA, XII, 157). For the madman, the symbol of the dead God is the fossilized institution of religion: "It is said that the madman broke into various churches on the same day and sang his *Requiem aeternam deo*. Led out and asked to explain, he only answered: 'What are these churches, if not the tombs and monuments of God?' " (MusA, XIII, 157). While the madman uncovers the death of God, accusing mankind as his murderers, it is only in *Also sprach Zarathustra* that Nietzsche fixes the actual cause of death: "God is dead: he died through his sympathy with man" (MusA, XIII, 114). The death of God is, for Nietzsche, a direct result of the human situation. His death, however, makes little impression on the forms of human action, such as religion, for mankind is, by nature, self-contained. The forces of this world transcend the death of God, as Zarathustra proclaimed: "I even love the churches and tombs of God, when the sky shows its pure eye through their broken roofs. I enjoy sitting, like the grass and the red poppies, in destroyed churches" (MusA, XIII, 193).

Nietzsche's indebtedness to Heine's image of the death of God has been widely acknowledged, as Georg Siegmund observed: "It was Heine who translated the philosophical speculation of his time into visual images in order to make the ideas more easily comprehensible."[10] Indeed, Heine's images are most striking, as in his lyric cycle *Heimkehr:*

sterbliche Gott: Nietzsches Entwurf übermenschlicher Größe. Monographien zur philosophischen Forschung, 103 (Meisenheim am Glan: Hain, 1972) offers a summary of Nietzsche's views as well as a new interpretation.

[9] *The Tyranny of Greece over Germany* (1935; rpt. Boston: Beacon, 1958), p. 300. Miss Butler's study remains the best discussion of German classical thought. For this present study the following two investigations were of interest: Maria Filtso, *Heinrich Heine und die Antike* (Diss. Munich, 1928; Munich: privately printed, 1928) and Karl Schlechta, *Der junge Nietzsche und das klassische Altertum.* Universitas (Mainz: Kupferberg, 1948).

[10] Georg Siegmund, *Nietzsches Kunde vom Tode Gottes* (Berlin: Morus, 1964), p. 128.

Das Herz ist mir bedrückt, und sehnlich
Gedenke ich der alten Zeit;
Die Welt war damals noch so wöhnlich,
Und ruhig lebten hin die Leut'.

Doch jetzt ist alles wie verschoben,
Das ist ein Drängen! eine Not!
Gestorben ist der Herrgott oben,
Und unten ist der Teufel tot.

Und alles schaut so grämlich trübe,
So krausverwirrt und morsch und kalt,
Und wäre nicht das bißchen Liebe,
So gäb' es nirgends einen Halt. (*HH*, I, 114)[11]

"Time past," the antiquity of his own myth of Greece, was, for Heine, the age of the gods; modern philosophy and theology sounded its death knell. The confrontation began with the confrontation between Hebrew and Hellene, between Christ and the pagan gods as described in *Die Stadt Lucca:* "Then suddenly a pale Jew, dripping blood, enters panting, a crown of thorns on his head and a large wooden cross on his shoulder. He threw the cross on the high table of the gods, so that the golden cups trembled and the gods became silent. They grew pale and then even paler until they vanished into a mist" (*HH*, III, 394). Christianity is a somber replacement for the gods of Greece, and the temples of the new religion a source of superstition (as in Heine's depiction of the Cologne cathedral in *Deutschland: Ein Wintermärchen*) and morbidity, as in Heine's answer to Schiller's *Die Götter Griechenlands:*

. . . .
Die Götter sind, die euch besiegten,
Die neuen, herrschenden, tristen Götter,
Die schadenfrohen im Schafspelz der Demut—
O, da faßt mich ein düsterer Groll,
Und brechen möcht' ich die neuen Tempel,
Und kämpfen für euch, ihr alten Götter,
Für euch und eu'r gutes ambrosisches Recht. . . . (*HH*, I, 188)[12]

---

[11] My heart is sad and filled with longing/ I think of the past;/ the world was then so comfortable/ and everyone lived so peacefully.

And everything is now as if displaced./ Such crowding! such need./ Lord God is dead above,/ And below the devil is dead.

And everything looks so peevishly sad,/ so confusing, so rotten, so cold,/ And if it were not for the bit of love,/ there would not be a foothold anywhere.

[12] It is the gods who conquer you,/ the new, ruling, sad gods,/ who, maliciously, in a sheepskin of modesty—/ O, a melancholy anger appears within me,/ I wish to destroy the new temple,/ and fight for you, you ancient gods,/ for you and your good, ambrosian law.

Nietzsche's vision of the churches in which the madman reads his memorial masses, his placing of natural forces above the artificialities of religion both find their presentations in Heine's works. If Heine stands as the promulgator of the death of God in the nineteenth century, he felt that its roots were to be traced back to Kant. In Heine's *Zur Geschichte der Religion und Philosophie in Deutschland*, published in 1834, it is Kant who is made responsible for the death of the murderer of the ancient gods:

> We shall speak of this catastrophe, the January 21st of Deism, in the next chapters. A strange dread, an unusual piety will not allow us to write any further today. Our heart is full of overwhelming pity—it is the old Jehovah who is preparing himself for death. We knew him so well, from the cradle in Egypt, as he was born among the divine calves, crocodiles, holy onions, ibixes and cats. . . .
>
> Don't you hear the bells ringing? Kneel, they are bringing the sacrament to a dying God. (*HH*, IV, 246)

Heine and Nietzsche rejected the intrusion of the concept of the omnipotent deity into the human sphere. Emphasizing a religion of this world (a *Diesseitsreligion* of "love" or "grass and red poppies"), they relegated the role of the conventional representation of God to a negative position. For Heine, however, the death of the gods was a continual process. With the advent of Christianity they underwent a series of metamorphoses. These changes merged them into the development of Western religious thought. For Nietzsche, the death of God in modern times is an absolute. There is no question of the perpetuation of the religious tradition of the past for it no longer has any validity in the contemporary sphere. Thus Heine's image of the death of the gods and Nietzsche's view of the death of God, while similar in overall structure, are radically different in their final conclusions. Heine is able, at the conclusion of his life, to find solace in a simplified version of the Judaeo-Christian God; Nietzsche ends his philosophy, which strives for the realization of a world without the need for God, in the unfulfillable desire for God:

> Was bandest du dich
> mit dem Strick deiner Weisheit?
> Was lockest du dich
> ins Paradies der alten Schlange?
> Was schlichst du dich ein
> in dich—in dich? . . .
>
> . . . .
>
> Und jüngst noch so stolz,
> auf allen Stelzen deines Stolzes!
> Jüngst noch der Einsiedler ohne Gott,
> der Zweisiedler mit dem Teufel,
> der scharlachne Prinz jedes Übermuts! . . .
>
> . . . .

> O Zarathustra! . . .
> Selbstkenner! . . .
> Selbsthenker! . . . (MusA, XX, 200–202)[13]

IV

It was not solely the content of Heine's works which attracted the interest and opprobrium of the young Nietzsche. In the spring of 1876 Nietzsche observed that:

> The influence of Hegel and Heine on German style! The latter destroys the barely finished work of our great writers, the barely achieved feeling for the uniform texture of style. He loves the variegated fool's cloak. His inventions, his images, his observations, his *sentiments*, his vocabulary are not compatible. He controls all styles like a virtuoso, but uses this mastery only to confuse them totally. With Hegel everything is an unworthy gray; with Heine, an electric fountain of color, which however, attacks the eye as much as the gray dulls it. As a stylist Hegel is a *factor*, Heine, a *farceur*. (MusA, VI, 225)

Heine's style appears to Nietzsche as the formalistic equivalent to the placid sensualism of his classical world. Yet Nietzsche uses specific references to Heine as an actor: he wears his style like a clown's cloak, he is a *farceur*. This approach to Heine reveals the basis for much of Nietzsche's antipathy towards Heine. For as early as Schubert's musical interpretations of Heine's poetry, the importance of the mask in Heine's aesthetic vocabulary had been known and appreciated.[14] Nietzsche, in the period reflected in the above quotation, assumed that Heine was but a poseur, putting on that mask which struck his fancy at any given moment. Thus the ego of the poet, his inner being, was not present in his work.

In reality, the importance of disguise and the altered presentation of personality in Heine's "ironic" *Weltanschauung* is not so easily dismissed. S. S. Prawer, in what is without a doubt the best modern book on Heine, illustrates this subtlety by comparing two passages in *Atta Troll*: "An early draft of Caput II has been preserved in which the poet tries to introduce himself into the poem as the sick man he really was. Atta Troll has just broken away from his keeper:

---

13 What binds you/ with the chains of your wisdom?/ What tempts you/ into the paradise of the ancient snake?/ What steals into you from you—to you? . . ./ But recently so proud,/ On all the stilts of your pride!/ But recently a hermit without a God,/ a compatriot of the devil/ the scarlet prince of pride . . ./ O Zarathustra! . . ./ Self-knowing/ Self-destroying!

14 Jeffrey L. Sammons, *Heinrich Heine, the Elusive Poet*, Yale Germanic Studies, 3 (New Haven: Yale University Press, 1969).

Dies geschah den zweiten Juli
Achtzehnhunderteinundvierzig
Und ein kranker deutscher Dichter
Der vom sicheren Balkone

Diesem großen. . . .

At this point Heine broke off, crossed out the last two and a half lines and substituted:

Und ein großer deutscher Dichter
Der dem großen Schauspiel zusah

(Von dem sicheren Balkone)
Seufzte tief: O Vaterland. . . ."[15]

With this glimpse into the author's working method, it becomes quite clear that the "ironic" mask does not merely disguise the poetic ego but serves to mitigate it. Thus the pathos of the "ill German poet" is altered to that of the ironic "great German poet" so that the immediacy of the effect is avoided. This avoidance creates an ambiguity concerning the reference to the irony. Does it stem from the ego of the poet, from yet a second mask (the poet as ironist), or merely from the most superficial and immediate use of irony as a rhetorical device?

It was only with Nietzsche's own development of the understanding of the role of the mask (or *Schein*) in all personality that he was able to come to terms with Heine. He became aware that the relationship between mask and ego was not merely one of armor to the defenseless spirit. The mask and the ego are so closely intertwined so as to make them inseparable. This fact has its clearest presentation in the Preface to the second edition of *Die fröhliche Wissenschaft:*

> Those who could, would attribute to me more than foolishness, exuberance, "gay science,"—for example the handful of poems which have been added to the present edition of this book—poems in which the poet mocks, in a manner which is difficult to forgive, all poets. Oh, it is not merely poets and their pretty "lyrical emotions" against which this resurrected one vents his malice; who knows what monster of parodic material will tempt him in the future? "*Incipit tragoedia*"—thus reads the end of this thoughtful-thoughtless book—take care! Something extraordinarily evil and malicious is being announced: *incipit parodia*, without a doubt! (MusA, XXI, 2)

---

[15] S. S. Prawer, *Heine, The Tragic Satirist* (Cambridge: Cambridge University Press, 1961), p. 65. "This took place on the second of July/ Eighteen hundred and forty-one/ As a sickly German poet/ who, from a secure balcony/ this great . . ." "And a great German poet/ who observed the great spectacle/ (from a secure balcony) sighed heavily: O Fatherland . . ."

It is Nietzsche himself who serves as the object for the parody of the poems, the *Lieder des Prinzen Vogelfrei*. The mask he presents to the reader of the parodist as "malicious" and his ironic defense of lyric emotionality shows that he has come to an awareness of the omnipresence of the mask and its necessity in self-reflective art. For like Heine's, Nietzsche's mask serves not to conceal but to reveal. He has come to the realization of the falseness of his earlier statement that "Hartmann and Heine are unconscious ironists, rogues against themselves" (MusA, VI, 343). On the contrary, Nietzsche and Heine are both conscious parodists, with their parodic source their own masks and egos.[16]

In the *Lieder des Prinzen Vogelfrei* Nietzsche set a monument to his new-found understanding for Heine. Written after Nietzsche's serious illness of 1879, the poem, "Rimus remedium," subtitled "Oder: Wie kranke Dichter sich trösten," parallels his illness to Heine's "Mattress Tomb":

> Aus deinem Munde,
> Du speichelflüssige Hexe Zeit,
> Tropft langsam Stund auf Stunde.
> Umsonst, daß all mein Ekel schreit:
> "Fluch, Fluch dem Schlunde
> Der Ewigkeit!"
>
> "Welt—ist von Erz:
> Ein glühender Stier,—der hört kein Schrein.
> Mit fliegenden Dolchen schreibt der Schmerz
> Mir ins Gebein:
> "Welt hat kein Herz,
> Und Dummheit wärs, ihr gram drum sein!"
>
> Gieß alle Mohne,
> Gieß Fieber! Gift mir ins Gehirn!
> Zu lang schon prüfst du mir Hand und Stirn.
> Was frägst du? Was? "Zu welchem—Lohne?"
> —Ha! Fluch der Dirn
> Und ihrem Hohne!
>
> Nein! Komm zurück!
> Draußen ists kalt, ich höre regnen—
> Ich sollte dir zärtlicher begegnen?
> —Nimm! Hier ist Gold: Wie glänzt das Stück!—
> Dich heißen "Glück"?
> Dich, Fieber, segnen?—

---

[16] Cf. Beda Allemann, *Ironie und Dichtung* (Pfullingen: Neske, 1969) and Charles I. Glicksberg, *The Ironic Vision in Modern Literature* (The Hague: Nijhoff, 1969).

Die Tür springt auf!
Der Regen sprüht nach meinem Bette!
Wind löscht das Licht, — Unheil in Hauf!
— Wer jetzt nicht hundert *Reime* hätte,
Ich wette, wette
Der ging drauf! (MusA, XX, 117–18)[17]

While this is evidently a *Rollengedicht*, it is in no way clear exactly who is speaking;
the striving after "Glück" is no more a leitmotif of Nietzsche's poetic fantasy than
it is of Heine's. For Nietzsche has incorporated the image of the suffering poet
into the model of his relationship with Heine. Heine had given sufficient material
for this parallel in his poem "Frau Sorge":

In meines Glückes Sonnenglanz
Da gaukelte fröhlich der Mückentanz.
Die lieben Freunde liebten mich
Und teilten mit mir brüderlich
Wohl meinen besten Braten
Und meinen letzten Dukaten.

Das Glück ist fort, der Beutel leer,
Und hab' auch keine Freunde mehr;
Erloschen ist der Sonnenglanz,
Zerstoben ist der Mückentanz,
Die Freunde, so wie die Mücke,
Verschwinden mit dem Glücke.

An meinem Bett in der Winternacht
Als Wärterin die Sorge wacht.
Sie trägt eine weiße Unterjack',
Ein schwarzes Mützchen, und schnupft Tabak.
Die Dose knarrt so gräßlich,
Die Alte nickt so häßlich.

[17] From your mouth/ you salivating witch, time,/ hour drips on hour,/ Needlessly I cry with
revulsion:/ "Damn, damn the abyss/ of eternity!"

"The world is made of brass:/ a glowing steer,/ which hears no cries of anguish./ With flying
daggers pain inscribes/ on my limb:/ "The world has no heart./ And it would be foolish to be angry
with it for that reason."

Pour opium,/ pour fever/ poison into my brain!/ And you who have been checking pulse and
brow/ What do you ask?/ What? "For what—reward?"/ Ha! Whore's curse/ as well as her mockery!

No! come back!/ Outside it is cold, I hear rain—/ I should approach you more gently?/ Here! Here
is gold: how the coins glisten!—/ To call you "joy"?/ To please you, fever?—

The door springs open!/ Rain sprays towards by bed!/ Wind extinguishes the light—disaster *en
masse!*/ He who does not have at least a hundred rhymes,/ I would wager,/ that he would come undone.

> Mir träumt manchmal, gekommen sei
> Zurück das Glück und der junge Mai
> Und die Freundschaft und der Mückenschwarm—
> Da knarrt die Dose—daß Gott erbarm',
> Es platzt die Seifenblase—
> Die Alte schneuzt die Nase (*HH*, I, 424–25)[18]

A further parallel to Nietzsche's poem may be found in the *pointe* in the last verse of Heine's "Böses Geträume," in which the poet awakes from an ironically idyllic dream to find himself still chained to his bed:

> Was sie zur Antwort gab, das weiß ich nimmer,
> Denn ich erwachte jählings—und ich war
> Wieder ein Kranker, der im Krankenzimmer
> Trostlos daniederliegt seit manchem Jahr— (*HH*, I, 428)[19]

The mask of the ill poet permits Heine (and later Nietzsche) to achieve distance from the reality of suffering. All illness and torment are transferred to the mask, which becomes a separate reality in which the ego is mirrored. This division of personality, the escape from the mask of the ill poet which is present in both of the Heine poems quoted above, is revealed in the *pointe* to be but a false mask for the true mask of suffering. Nietzsche takes over this structure in "Rimus remedium" with, however, a substantial alteration. "Frau Sorge" becomes transmuted into the image of time, the cause of the poet's suffering. The dialogue which results between time and the poet, like the dream sequences in both Heine poems, bridges the appearance of one mask with that of the other. Yet the culmination of the poem, the sudden presence of death in the form of the intrusion of the external world into the sickroom, is handled in an ironic mode quite unknown in Heine's poetry. For it is the rhymes of the poet which protect him from ultimate dissolution. Indeed, Nietzsche's attack on Heine's style seems here reversed. For Nietzsche, writing his own defense as well as Heine's, presents the fantasy, the mask, through which all sick poets comfort themselves. They view themselves as

[18] In the sunny glow of my joy/ the dance of the mosquito buzzing/ lingers happily./ Loving friends loved me/ And in brotherhood shared with me/ my best roasts and my last ducats.

Joy is past, my wallet empty/ And I have no friends anymore;/ The sunny glow has disappeared,/ vanished has the mosquito dance,/ vanished, the friends, like the mosquito, with the joy.

Sorrow, my attendant, watches/ at my bedside during the winter nights./ She wears a white undershirt,/ a black cap and dips snuff./ The snuff box squeaks dreadfully,/ the old woman nods so grotesquely.

Sometimes I dream,/ that joy and May have returned/ And friendship and the swarms of mosquitos/ the snuff box squeaks—God have mercy,/ The bubble vanishes—the old woman blows her nose.

[19] What she answered, I don't know/ For I awoke suddenly—and was/ once again an invalid, having lain/ without solace in a sickroom/ for many a year.

immortal through their works. Nietzsche is, however, quite aware that this is but a mask, and thus the final parodic *pointe* establishes the nature of the mask as mask, without negating its vital role in the expression of the poet's ego.[20]

Nietzsche's identification with Heine reached its height in his final major work *Ecce Homo*. In the sophomorically entitled section "Warum ich so klug bin" Nietzsche confesses:

> Heinrich Heine gave me the highest concept of the poet. I have looked in vain in all of the kingdoms of the centuries for an equivalently sweet and passionate music. He possessed that divine malice without which I cannot conceive of perfection. —I regard the value of men, of races in the light of how much they do not isolate the god from the satyr. In the future it will be said that Heine and I are by far the primary artists of the German language—an inconceivable distance from everything created by mere Germans. (MusA, XII, 199–200)

Here the "malice," which Nietzsche attributed to his own parodic attempts in *Die fröhliche Wissenschaft*, forms the bridge between his personality and that of Heine. Indeed, Nietzsche, who emphasized the Slavic source of his family, isolates himself, with the Jew Heine, from the stylistically banal camp of the Germans. It is the awareness of that godly "malice" as the bond between the two men which forms Nietzsche's final judgment of Heine. He became aware that Heine's greatest talent was the use of his linguistic facility to probe and present his own ego.

With this understanding of the development of Nietzsche's appreciation for Heine, the question of the image of Heine's classicism, as reflected in Nietzsche's works, can be examined in a new light. Nietzsche sought and found, in Heine, a poet whose prime consideration was the presentation of internal reality in artistic form. This preoccupation extended even to the presentation of a classical world which mirrors the basic human desires of the poet. The masks which Heine created in the search after the classical myth, those of Hellene and Hebrew, of the exile and death of the gods, are but extensions of the poet's ego. Thus Nietzsche began his debate with the shadow of Heine by rejecting an ego-oriented image of the past. As he came more and more to the awareness that his image, too, was determined by his own desires, his opinion of Heine altered. By the end of his creative period, Nietzsche assumed a sense of modified autoscopy, in which Heine became his historical *Doppelgänger*, a figure in which he found himself recapitulated. His awareness of the parallels between his fate and that of Heine led to this total identification with the poet. Thus the question of Heine's "influence" on Nietzsche is one which can be answered only to the degree that this dramatic

---

[20] Cf. my essay, " 'Braune Nacht': Friedrich Nietzsche's Venetian Poems," *Nietzsche Studien*, I (1972), 247–60 and "Incipit parodia: The Function of Parody in the Poetry of Friedrich Nietzsche," *Nietzsche Studien*, 4 (1975), 52–74.

alteration in Nietzsche's acceptance of Heine is taken into consideration. Even the more moderate question of the parallels between Heine's thought and Nietzsche's philosophy must be treated carefully. For Nietzsche knew Heine well even when he sought to reject him. What remains is the internal biography of Nietzsche's relationship with his own image of Heine, a biography which sheds much more light on Nietzsche's personal evaluation of the artistic process than on the more banal questions of indebtedness and influence.

XIV

Nietzsche and the *Finis Latinorum*

MARK BOULBY

Nietzsche's work, in particular that of his final years, comes into existence as a continuous process of excited interaction with selected luminaries of previous ages and, to a lesser extent, with his own contemporaries. This process is, of its very nature, one-sided; frequently, however, it impresses us as self-enclosed to the point of solipsism, an activity in which the imagination appears to cannibalize its own flesh. Sucked into this vortex, philosophers and poets become the victims of a subjectivity so intense that it quickly reduces them to little more than marionettes in Dionysus the Crucified's world drama, and dream, of history and ideas. The eclecticism of this procedure is partly a result of the thinker's isolation, his periods spent in lonely retreats, his dependence upon a few newspapers such as the *Journal des Débats*, and his book-shop browsing—by which means he discovered Dostoevsky as late as 1887, just as he had stumbled upon Schopenhauer in 1865 and Stendhal in 1879. For the rest, it is a selectivity induced by the obsessional quality of Nietzsche's mind, returning time and time again to the same battle with the same minotaurs, Pascal, Rousseau, Kant, St. Paul, Gotama Buddha and, of course, innumerable Greeks.

Among scholars there has been a tendency—both explicable and in some degree justifiable—to place but little stress on the importance of Nietzsche's encounter with the imaginative literature of his own period. Nonetheless it is clear that towards the end of his career the creative writers—poets and novelists— of his own day and age come increasingly within the range of his philosophical activity. Much of Nietzsche's reading in contemporary literature was in French— German had little enough to offer him at this time. It was a reading that seems to have been quite extensive but unsystematic. Certain questions about it still remain unresolved—even unposed. A good deal of it—Flaubert, Bourget, Baudelaire, a little Barbey d'Aurevilly—gave Nietzsche an acquaintance with the literature of decadence, on which topic he had of course developed his own comprehensive theories. Though much has been written on these, the problem of their relationship—or lack of it—with the writings of the decadents themselves, as they developed their style and peculiar conventions in France, England, Germany and elsewhere has actually been little examined. Not much has been pointed out save Nietzsche's obvious dependence, for a few of his concepts, upon Paul Bourget's *Essais* (and *Nouveaux Essais*) *de psychologie contemporaine* (1883 and 1885). It is curious but true that an attempt to do something to remedy this deficiency can profitably place at the center of discussion what might at first sight appear to be an entirely different problem, namely that of the classical tradition and Nietzsche's response to it. That there was a certain connection, certainly in France and England, between decadence and some forms of neo-classicism is however not difficult to show,[1] and it can be demonstrated that, especially in Nietzsche's later years, his manipulation of Roman and Greek material is something of a touchstone of his relationship to the so-called Decadent Movement.

A necessary prolegomenon, however, is the consideration of a pair of deep-seated paradoxes, which seem to me to underlie very much of Nietzsche's thinking on this subject. These may be called, for the sake of convenience, the paradox of the primitive-organic, and the paradox of the artificial man. Now it is generally and persuasively held that what Nietzsche gleaned from contemporary French literature and thought did not affect the development of his theories on decadence in any fundamental way; at the most (and this is true even in the case of Bourget) it merely confirmed them and greatly helped him to make them explicit.[2] That Nietzsche's ideas might themselves have influenced decadent writers in France or England before 1890 is quite improbable, although the suggestion has recently been made that Stefan George may conceivably have first heard of the philosopher at one of Mallarmé's soirées.[3] Certainly there is nothing in European literature at this time to compare with the exhaustive and passionate analysis to which Nietzsche subjects the idea of decadence and what he calls its "logic"— that is to say, nihilism. His arguments probe more deeply into it than do those of French and English commentators, not to speak of German. But his perspectives, while they do pick on similar substantive issues, are often peculiar to him. This is especially obvious in regard to his fulminations against Christianity, about which the French decadents showed themselves sometimes indifferent, sometimes cynical, and sometimes perversely aroused to blasphemy or belief, but against which they never mounted a consistent and determined campaign. No doubt it would have seemed to them quite old-fashioned to do so.

---

[1] Though the classical tradition in the authentic sense is scarcely reflected in the work of the French decadents proper, many of them—even Baudelaire ("Lesbos")—use at least some classical motifs. Neo-classicism is however a conspicuous feature of the literature of the 1880s and 1890s—for instance Jean Moréas and his "École romane." The Roman Emperors had intrigued writers such as Gautier and the young Flaubert. In England the decadents were commonly regarded as dissolute neopagans. Cf. the article "Neopaganism," *The Quarterly Review*, 172 (1891), 273–304, which commences with Goethe and traces the tradition through Leconte de Lisle, Gautier and Baudelaire to Walter Pater and J. A. Symonds.

[2] Thus W. D. Williams, *Nietzsche and the French* (Oxford: Blackwell, 1952), p. 156.

[3] Cf. Peter Pütz, "Nietzsche und Stefan George," in *Stefan George Kolloquium* (Cologne: Wienand, 1971), pp. 49–66.

Confronted, as were these decadents themselves, with what seemed to be the exhaustion of European man, the collapse of his vital instincts, Nietzsche bears down upon the Christian ethic as the very root of the disease. The symptoms are many; weariness, a general "morbidity" in social life,[4] a nervous passivity, a disassociated intellectuality, the absence of "force"; and Nietzsche sees these manifestations as in part the result of heredity, in part however the consequence of environmental factors, aided by the gross suggestibility of people—he speaks of "acquired exhaustion" (W, III, 806).[5] There is a striking passage in a letter to Gast, on the appearance of the second volume of the *Journal des Goncourts*, with its description of the famous "dîners chez Magny":

> . . . that brought together twice a month the cleverest and most sceptical band of Parisian intellects of those days (Sainte-Beuve, Flaubert, Théophile Gautier, Taine, Renan, the Goncourts, Schérer, Gavarni, occasionally Turgenev, etc.). Exasperated pessimism, cynicism, nihilism, alternating with a lot of exuberance and good humor; I myself would fit in pretty well there—I know these gentlemen by heart, *so much so* that I've really had my fill of them already. It is necessary to be more radical: basically they all lack the chief requirement—"la force." (W, III, 1269)

This deficiency is of course an essential burden of Nietzsche's entire campaign against decadence. As early as *On the Use and Abuse of History* (*Vom Nutzen und Nachteil der Historie für das Leben*, 1874) he employs an image not only relevant here but in fact central to his whole philosophy: "This is an analogy for each one of us: he must organize the chaos within himself, by reflecting upon his genuine needs" (W, I, 284). Wise beyond subsequent overstatements, Nietzsche here distinguishes the true self from the false, and insists passionately upon the possibility of the "genuine." Later pronouncements make clear that the "organization of the chaos" of impulses is to be the work of the will, the "inner tyrant" (W, III, 472). The really important point is that for this thinker form and organization are ideals from the outset and never cease to be. His work must be regarded as being dominated by an intense commitment to hierarchy, order and structural cohesion. As a celebrated section in *Beyond Good and Evil* makes clear, it is just such principles which are always subverted or abandoned by the decadent, with his lack of "force," his preference for passivity, for repose, for a corrupt Epicureanism:

> Man in an age of dissolution, in which the races are jumbled together, in whom therefore there is a multiple heredity, that is to say antagonistic and often not even merely antagonistic impulses and standards, which fight one another and seldom allow one another any peace—such a man of cultures that are old and lights that are broken will on the average be a rather weak man: his profoundest yearning is that the war which he *is* should come to an end; happiness appears to him, in accordance

---

[4] "Morbid" is a favorite epithet of Nietzsche's. Cf., e.g., W, II, 1010, 1071; III, 708, 787, etc. (For key to abbreviations see p. xvii above.)

[5] All references in the text, in my own translation, are to the Schlechta edition.

with a comforting (for example Epicurean or Christian) physic and mode of thought, principally as the happiness of repose, of being undisturbed, of satiety, of ultimate unity, as a "sabbath of sabbaths," to use the words of the saintly rhetorician Augustine, who himself was such a man. . . . (W, II, 656)

The distinction is clear enough, and it is carried consistently through Nietzsche's later writings, including the so-called *Will to Power*.[6] Nevertheless Nietzsche's theory of decadence remains, viewed as a whole, profoundly enigmatic and in some ways self-contradictory, like so much of the rest of his thought. In this particular case the difficulties arise in part from the fact that the categories in which he formulates the problem are themselves a function of it. The well-known paragraph in *The Case of Wagner* which so closely echoes the words of Bourget in his essay on Baudelaire will eventually help to bring this point out:

What is the characteristic feature of all *literary decadence?* The fact that life no longer adheres to the whole. The word becomes sovereign and jumps out of the sentence, the sentence spills over and obscures the sense of the page, the page gains in life at the expense of the whole—the whole no longer is a whole. But that is a metaphor for every *décadent* style: always anarchy of the atoms, disaggregation of the will, "freedom of the individual" if we speak morally—if we expand it to a political theory it becomes "*equal* rights for all." Life, the *identical* living quality, the vibration and exuberance of life, forced back into the smallest entities, the rest *impoverished* of life. Everywhere paralysis, fatigue, petrifaction *or* hostility and chaos: both of these become more and more apparent the higher the forms of the organization one penetrates. The whole lives no longer; it is composite, computed, artificial, an artifact. (W, II, 917)

A detailed examination of this enigmatic and highly debatable passage would lead, in every direction, into the monstrous labyrinth of Nietzsche's later works. Let us note merely a few points. Though Bourget himself begins with the analogy of the social organism he goes on very quickly to the issue of literary style; the highly tendentious social and political extensions in *The Case of Wagner* are a Nietzschean polemical outgrowth, but even in Nietzsche they are not turned into the essence of the matter. The aspersion upon "freedom of the individual" does perhaps have interesting implications, in view of the common notion that Nietzsche was a fanatical individualist. What is significant above all else, however, is that the philosopher seizes upon the organic metaphor used by Bourget and intensifies it, and that in his manipulation of it the independent animation of the disaggregated parts is seen to result in the destruction of hierarchy and the transformation of the living whole into an artificial pseudo-entity, a lifeless "artifact." The work of art is a common Nietzschean metaphor for the self of man, and the decadent process is often regarded—as Bourget regarded it too—primarily in

---

[6] This title is used for convenience, to characterize the notebook material of the years 1883–88, in preference to some German term like *Nachlaß*.

aesthetic terms as a derogation from unity or sovereignty of style. The metamorphosis of organism into artifact is very expressive of the decadent mentality,
as frequent instances in the literature of the period of such devitalization of
Romantic organic imagery suggest. Vegetable often becomes mineral, and *soma*
becomes machine; flowers are confined to the conservatory, while transcendental
bliss is replaced by the enclosed "paradis artificiel" of the opium-eater. One of
the foundations of Nietzsche's critique of decadence is self-evidently an organic
vitalism in which the whole is always greater than its parts. And it is, as a number
of passages in *The Will to Power* clearly show, the will which, in its integrating and
cohering power, is the mainstay of such organic identity.

At this point, however, we enter the realm of paradox. On the one hand that
very will which, according to Nietzsche, is a necessity if the cosmos of the living
organism is to resist dissolution also appears in his later writings as the sole true
generator of the artificial, autonomous in its organization of chaos into art or
"man": "The greatness of an artist is not measured by the 'beautiful feelings' he
arouses: that's a woman's notion. But by the degree in which he approaches the
great style, in which he is capable of the great style. This style has in common with
great passion that it disdains to please; that it forgets to persuade; that it commands; that it *wills*. . . . To be master of the chaos that one is; to compel one's
chaos to become form: to become logical, simple, unambiguous, mathematics,
law . . ." (W, III, 782). The vital will prevents degeneration into artifact, but the
will is also the force which creates form and brings the artifact into being. On the
other hand it is precisely something organic, something physiological, "the
décadence-instinct" (W, II, 988) which induces the disaggregation of the will and
the dissolution of the living entity. Or, to put the antinomy exceedingly bluntly:
the organic is both life and its decay, the artificial is both the paralysis and petrifaction of life, a sham, and also the surmounting of this disintegration, a *creatio ex
nihilo* by the will, in which the individual imposes his form on chaos and replaces
Natural Law with his own artificial principle.

In this manner the categories in which Nietzsche thinks about decadence do
disclose a fundamental unresolved polarity of this entire period in the history of
the Western artistic sensibility, which is as much a part of him as it is of decadence:
this is the tension between hypersensualism on the one hand and extreme cere-
bralism on the other, which resulted, in certain typical works of the day, in what
Mario Praz has called "that extraordinary conflagration of cerebral lechery."[7]
As far as the sensualist extreme is concerned, we should note that decadence,
though he may define it variously, is for Nietzsche as physiological a thing as it
was for Huysmans, coming in the wake of Zola and the Naturalists. Here and
there we find him pointing directly or indirectly to the biological factors: "erotic

---

[7] Mario Praz, *The Romantic Agony*, 2nd ed. (London and New York: Oxford University Press,
1970), p. 395.

precocity: the curse of French youth in particular, Parisians first and foremost: who emerge from the lycées into the world already ruined and defiled—and never free themselves from the shackles of contemptible inclinations, ironic and vile towards themselves—galley-slaves, with all their refinements . . ." (W, III, 806). It is not certain, but quite probable, that "contemptible inclinations" ("verächtliche Neigungen") implies perversions, and the question of Nietzsche's attitude to perversion is, as will be indicated further, an important one. The passage reminds the reader irresistibly of Rimbaud, of whom the writer had surely never heard. It shows us that Nietzsche, with remarkable perception, saw in the primitive the seed-bed of the decadent flora, in the instinctual and the organic the sure threat to the autonomous will. The sophisticated decadent is in fact a "galley-slave," the most primitive of prisoners. Modern analysis of this whole literature would generally endorse the nexus: decadents such as Baudelaire and Huysmans, or for that matter Wilde and d'Annunzio, deliberately revolted against the Romantic cult of Nature, without however abandoning the covert belief that such an ideal and norm did indeed exist and remained valid: "the decadents, even when they refused to live by Rousseau's gospel, never denied its truth . . . They accepted Nature as the norm, primitivism as synonymous with virtue."[8]

At this stage in the argument the question of the influence of de Sade must be raised, ingrained as it was in the entire development of decadent literature in France. It is strange that Nietzsche, who is so often accused of cruelty and sadism in his thought, never mentions the divine marquis, although (as I shall make clear later) there is one possible explanation of this omission which might have a wider significance. It could well be, of course, that Nietzsche never read a word of de Sade, but he must have known of him, if only because Bourget, whom he had closely perused, refers to him. De Sade was important for the decadents not only because he provided them with a mine of suitable materials, but also because he appears to make of the deliberate outraging of Nature a kind of philosophy of life. The abnormal and the artificial are supposed to demonstrate the totally anarchic individual's superiority to Natural Law. From such a position it is only a step to begin to reason that the perverse itself is natural, since, as Arthur Symons remarks: "I affirm that it is not natural to be what is called 'natural' any longer."[9] Nietzsche expresses an almost identical view when he declares: "*Not* 'return to nature': for there never was a natural man. The scholasticism of un- and *anti*-natural values is the rule, the beginning; man comes to nature after a long struggle —he never 'returns' to it. . . . Nature: that is, to dare to be immoral like nature" (W, III, 616). This paradox is meant to subvert thoroughly the notion of a

---

[8] A. E. Carter, *The Idea of Decadence in French Literature, 1830–1900* (Toronto: University of Toronto Press, 1958), p. 4.

[9] *The Symbolist Movement* (New York: Dutton, 1908), p. 134.

morality of natural conduct. Nietzsche employs a similar argument to distinguish his blackest *bête noire*, Rousseau, who believed that man was more complete the closer he was to Nature, from Voltaire, who thought the reverse. Here again however it is surely significant that he adduces the latter, and not de Sade or Baudelaire, as his example of the applauded "unnatural" man. At heart Nietzsche was, of course, moralist enough. In denouncing what he calls the "Romantic" morality of "tout comprendre, c'est tout pardonner" as well as the objectivity of art for art's sake (W, III, 882), he is seeking to transcend all forms of nineteenth-century Epicureanism in favor of some set of new, but "moral," principles. However there are, in his opinion, two ways of rejecting or transcending the cult of the Natural: if this is done with a sidelong acknowledgement that Nature, precisely while being violated, remains the norm, then the outcome is the decadent; if however, the denial of the ideal of the primitive, natural man is genuine and total, then there emerges a wholly new type, the true savage as distinct from the ideal one, "the 'savage' man (or, in moral terms, the *evil* man) . . ." (W, III, 742), for whom what is natural is exclusively what his will may dictate. The man himself is then artificial, for he is the creation of his own artistic power.

To understand the late writings of Nietzsche it is necessary to see that this artificial creature of adventitious will, whose reality is self-generated, is joined in these paradoxical philosophizings to a vitalistic primitive, like a highly dissimilar Siamese twin. The two do not understand one another—worse, they hardly notice that they are bound together. A recognition of this situation gives us insight into a number of typical Nietzschean contradictions, including his puzzling discussions of the actor and of the histrionic principle. Wagner who, in his one-time disciple's view, subsumed in himself the whole of French and German decadence (W, III, 647), is presented as the most grandiose example of this histrionic temperament. The "actor-spirit" is associated with the "demagogue-spirit" and the "beaver and ant-spirit" of scholars (W, III, 472), as all being characteristic of the decadent age. Opera is the concrete symbol of decadence in art, and as such, despite or rather because of its conspicuous artificiality, is associated with that Romantic idealism which Nietzsche believes he is overcoming and refuting: " 'Return to nature' more and more decisively in the opposite sense to Rousseau's;—*away from the idyll and the opera!*" (W, III, 532)—and let us note the conjunction! "*Wagner*—French cult of the ghastly and the grand opera" (W, III, 872). Wagner's showmanship, his exoticism, his sensuality, his *fin de siècle* passivity are all symptoms of the disastrous degeneration into that kind of dishonesty, sham and paralytic artificiality which is produced when the will has become disaggregated and life has receded from the calcified whole into the parts. Wagner is the complete opposite of that other species of artificial man adumbrated above, the man of creative will, the evil man, the superman. He is of course the *exemplum horribilis* of the correctness of Bourget's central perception about decadence.

But in Nietzsche's lengthy drama there is a whole crowd of actors. There is, for instance, the Emperor Augustus. Nietzsche tells us in *The Joyful Wisdom* (*Die fröhliche Wissenschaft*) that, when at the point of death, Augustus, "that terrible man . . . let his mask fall for the first time, when he made clear that he had worn a mask and had acted a comedy, had acted that father of the Fatherland and wisdom upon the throne, good to the point of illusion! *Plaudite amici, comoedia finita est!*" (W, II, 63). Augustus has in him, it would appear, elements of a type of actor different from the Wagnerian, the existential actor in good faith not bad, the creator *ex nihilo*, the virtuoso of indispensable illusion. In that he demonstrates something of the art of living in a void, and of true self-mastery, he points away from decadence, but he remains a somewhat paradoxical figure in Nietzsche's imagination. And, after all, the *comoedia* itself is paradoxical, as is the artificial life per se. For is it the sole authentic, self-created existence in a chaotic world, or could it be that it is, commonly at least, merely a perverse sham?

It is only when such ambiguities are kept in mind that the special features of Nietzsche's relationship with the European cult of decadence can be properly understood. A most useful standard of comparison in these matters is Stefan George, whose emergence as a poet is almost exactly contemporaneous with Nietzsche's intellectual demise. The question of when, precisely, and how deeply, George may have been influenced by Nietzsche is unsettled, and this is likely to remain a matter of controversy.[10] It is in any case not germane to the argument I wish to proffer here. What is relevant in this case is that George can provide a point of departure for an examination of the connections between decadence and the classical tradition. Furthermore there are, quite apart from problems of influence, a number of deep-seated affinities between his early poetry and the later writings of Nietzsche, especially the preoccupation with will, with artifice and form, and with *creatio ex nihilo*. In George's *Algabal* (1892) a figure takes the stage, emerging simultaneously from the ornate wings of French decadence and of Roman history of the Decline who, somewhat like the Emperor Augustus, imposes his *comoedia* upon "reality" by an act of tortured will. The characteristics of such a tormented act of solipsistic egoism do however differ in important respects from the *modus vivendi* of Augustus, which latter does specifically fulfill a certain social role. The nature of such an act as Algabal's had, as we shall see later, already been quite precisely defined by Nietzsche, as a typically decadent phenomenon. George's Heliogabalus-figure belongs, of course, to the central tradition of decadence, in a way in which Augustus does not. Interest in the third-century emperor-priest and his brief but vicious reign goes back at least to de Sade.[11] There is a reference to him in Poe, and in Gautier's *Mademoiselle de Maupin* (1834), which Praz calls "the Bible of the Decadence."[12] Barbey d'Aurevilly describes Baudelaire as "un

---

[10] Pütz ("Nietzsche und Stefan George," *George Kolloquium*) has concluded recently that the influence was in fact deeper, and earlier, than has been commonly assumed.

[11] See *La nouvelle Justine et Juliette.*

[12] Praz, pp. 332–33.

Héliogabale artificiel,"[13] and was not the only one to make the comparison. Bourget remarks on the manner in which "l'étrange rage qui a produit les Néron et les Héliogabale" gnawed at Baudelaire's heart.[14] French literature of the 1870s and 1880s teems with Heliogabali and sub-species thereof, and it is not unlikely that George knew Jean Lombard's glisteningly sadistic novel *L'Agonie* (1888), which dwells on the androgyne aspects of the Heliogabalus theme. The German poet, of course, also possessed a remarkably rich knowledge of classical literature, especially the Latin poets,[15] and with his customary intellectual rigor he went beyond French literary re-creations to the primary historical sources, such as Dio Cassius, Lampridius and Herodian.[16]

George's portrait of Heliogabalus in *Algabal* has certain psychological analogies with the shadowy figure of the superman that ghosts through Nietzsche's post-Zarathustran works. It also discloses specifically decadent nuances in regard to the treatment of artifice, perversion and will.[17] The French decadents, George, and Nietzsche, are all inclined to take from classical literature and history models for their visualization of man. As George reveals in his eulogy of Mallarmé,[18] his concern with ancient civilization was especially, like that of so many of his contemporaries, an interest in the era of the Decline. In choosing the figure of Heliogabalus he also accepted by implication one of the most established conceits of decadent literature, the comparison between the final years of the Roman Empire and the later nineteenth century. The best known expression of this is no doubt Verlaine's sonnet, "Langueur" (1885):

> Je suis l'Empire à la fin de la décadence,
> Qui regarde passer les grands Barbares blancs
> En composant des acrostiches indolents
> D'un style d'or où la langueur du soleil danse.
>
> (I am the Empire at the end of the decline,
> Watching the great white barbarians come past
> While composing indolent acrostics
> In a golden style wherein dances the languor of the sun.)

---

[13] Quoted by Carter, p. 13.

[14] "The strange madness which produced the Neros and the Heliogabali"; *Essais de psychologie contemporaine* (Paris: Plon, 1916), I, 18.

[15] Cf. the evidence in H. Stefan Schultz, "Stefan George und die Antike," in *Studien zur Dichtung Stefan Georges* (Heidelberg: Lothar Stiehm, 1967), pp. 90–124.

[16] Cf., e.g., Victor A. Oswald, "The Historical Content of Stefan George's 'Algabal,' " *Germanic Review*, 23 (1948), 193–205.

[17] Cf. Mark Boulby, "Nietzsche's Problem of the Artist and George's *Algabal*," *Modern Language Review*, 52 (1957), 72–80. I would no longer suggest that the motif of the will is sufficient to differentiate *Algabal* clearly from the decadent tradition.

[18] Stefan George, *Gesamtausgabe der Werke* (Berlin: Bondi, 1927–34), XVII, 53.

The picture of the Roman intellectual in his exhausted passivity and physical satiety working out acrostics as the barbarians ride in is a central symbolic statement of the decadent sense of their particular moment of history and its psychological content. In a similar vein is Mallarmé's comment: "La littérature à laquelle mon esprit demande une volupté sera la poésie agonisante des derniers moments de Rome, tant, cependant, qu'elle ne respire aucunement l'approche rajeunissante des Barbares . . ."[19] Bourget speaks of "la décadence latine" and specifically adduces the later Roman Empire as the best example available of a decadent society, sterile, with a falling birth-rate and no will to fight, surrendered to pleasure, to nervous titillation, to dillettantism and scepticism. In a long passage he puts into the mouth of an amateur psychologist the assertion that decadence is preferable to barbarism, the Emperor Hadrian debauching (presumably with Antinous, another favorite allusion of the day) had more to contribute to culture than "un chef germain du II*e* siècle." Though decadent ages always end with the inrush of barbarians, is it not "le lot fatal de l'exquis et du rare d'avoir tort devant la brutalité?"[20]

Neither Nietzsche nor George ever saw the issues quite so straightforwardly, but the latter may in fact be found using the analogue as late as a work published in 1919, and probably influenced by Spengler.[21] It is an analogue which proliferated in the second half of the nineteenth century, and in the 1890s "cette antiquité héliogabalique" (Edmond de Goncourt) gradually merged into a dream of corrupt Byzantium—indeed these two are confused, so that Karl-August Klein, in George's *Blätter für die Kunst*, could make a (deliberate?) error of several hundred years and call Heliogabalus a Byzantine emperor. It was tempting, in France, to see in the "raffish gloss"[22] of the Second Empire all the distinguishing marks of the ultimate agony of civilization, the *Finis Latinorum*. In England the comparison between late Rome and the Victorian era was also made, sometimes in considerable detail. A pupil of Walter Pater's, T. H. Escott, published in 1875 an article entitled "Rome and London. A.D. 408–1875."[23] Pater himself, in *Marius the Epicurean* (1885), drew an elaborate comparison between his own day and the age of the Antonines, which has been called "a straightforward analogue,"[24] and a rather similar line was followed by novelists such as Thackeray,

---

[19] "The literature from which my mind demands sensual delight will be the dying poetry of the final moments of Rome, just so long, however, as this does not betoken remotely the regenerative approach of the barbarians . . ."; "Le Phénomène futur" (1864).

[20] "A German chieftain of the second century. . . ."

"the fatal destiny of the exquisite and the rare to be in the wrong in the confrontation with brutality?"; *Essais*, p. 22.

[21] "Der Brand des Tempels," *Blätter für die Kunst*, 11–12.

[22] Carter, p. viii.

[23] *MacMillan's Magazine*, 32 (1875).

[24] Anthony Ward, *Walter Pater: The Idea in Nature* (London: Macgibbon & Kee, 1966), p. 148.

Shorthouse and Lord Bulwer-Lytton. The suggestion has also been made that, in a rather different fashion, the perverse world of George's *Algabal* might be regarded as a mask for Imperial Germany.[25]

At first sight we do not find the basic analogy in Nietzsche, despite occasional references to contemporary German civilization as a culture of decline (III, 872), some allusions to Roman decadence and, of course the insistence that it was Christianity that insidiously undermined and sapped the vitality of the Roman Empire. Nietzsche's thoughts on the coming barbarians, however, do come close to implying the analogue. All the same, his fundamental model for the decadent process is a different one, though also classical—namely pre-Socratic and post-Socratic Greece. *The Birth of Tragedy*, in 1872, already of course establishes this paradigm. Karl Joël long ago argued that we should see Nietzsche as a Romantic, who romanticized everything, including Greece, and that his so-called classicism is merely incidental, since he always turned his back upon the truly classical, Periclean age.[26] This opinion seems to me difficult if not impossible to reconcile with the hostility to the Romantics and all their works found throughout Nietzsche's middle and final periods. It is also not really compatible with his pursuit of the overall style, the "great" or "grand" style, that of form and whole-ness. Dionysiac pessimism, as Nietzsche adamantly declares, is not Romantic, it is rather "classical" (cf. W, II, 246)—and the vision of such a *classical* pessimism is his *"proprium* and *ipsissimum"*; *"greatness of soul,"* moreover, *"has nothing Romantic about it"* (W, III, 609). Wagner, after all, was a Romantic, perhaps the ultimate one. So Nietzsche did not, as Joël mistakenly supposes, create a Romantic myth about the history of Greece. What rather occurred was that his vitalistic primiti-vism, which has some similarities to types of Romantic idealism, led him to establish this particular historical paradigm, the most prominent feature of which is the indictment of the Socratic and Alexandrine intellectualism which is sup-posed to have put an end to the Dionysiac age.[27] If we consider this model, from *The Birth of Tragedy* right through to *The Will to Power*, we shall see that what is really posited is an organic degeneration, the disintegration of the will, the fatigue, paralysis and petrifaction of the exemplary cultural entity—namely, the πόλις,—all of which phenomena can be described in aesthetic terms, and often are, as the loss of the integrated sovereignty of style and the replacement of a living and unified identity by a sham wholeness, a Wagnerian theatrical façade:

---

[25] Cf., e.g., Richard Hamann and Jost Hermand, *Impressionismus* (Berlin: Akademie, 1966), p. 26.

[26] Karl Joël, *Nietzsche und die Romantik* (Jena: Diederichs, 1905), pp. 279–81.

[27] It is not possible to go into this question here. It may well be that in insisting on relating Socrates to nineteenth-century decadence Nietzsche made a serious error. For this view see J. C. O'Flaherty, "Eros and Creativity in Nietzsche's *Birth of Tragedy*," *Studies in German Literature of the Nineteenth and Twentieth Centuries. Festschrift for Frederic E. Coenen*, ed. Siegfried Mews, UNC Studies in the Germanic Languages and Literatures, No. 67 (Chapel Hill: University of North Carolina Press, 1970), pp. 83–104.

The philosophers are in fact the *décadents* of Hellenic culture ["Griechentum"], the revulsion against old, aristocratic ["vornehm"] taste (—against the instinct for struggle [i.e., ἀγών], against the *Polis*, against the value of race, against the authority of tradition). The Socratic virtues were preached *because* the Greeks had lost them: irritable, nervous, unstable, actors through and through, they had a few reasons too many to have morality preached at them. Not that it would have helped at all: but grand words and attitudes suit *décadents* so well. . . . (W, II, 1030)

What emerges as an essential element in Nietzsche's paradigm is the Greek "actor," *graeculus histrio* (cf. W, II, 224), who is said to have subverted the Roman Empire as well, in the end. *The Joyful Wisdom* alleges that some similar process is now occurring in modern Europe. Everything becomes inauthentic, becomes *comoedia*, as all men turn into actors. A chronic and dissolute individualism wrecks all chance for communal effort. An Epicurean preoccupation with the sensation of the moment precludes great works of the spirit, prevents the realization of human achievements spread over long periods of time. *Organizational* geniuses, Nietzsche maintains, great builders and architects, no longer appear on the scene, and here again, in this thought of building for the ages, we may detect the same fundamental desire for cosmos and hierarchy, which however is seen currently succumbing to the insurgent anarchy of the disparate parts (cf. W, II, 224–25). In such passages as these Nietzsche's notorious individualism and anarchism are certainly cast in a very dubious light.

It is in fact a serious error to regard Nietzsche's thought as essentially anarchical, or to overstress his commitment to the individual ego. "Freedom of the individual," as we have noted, was not one of his slogans. Community and cultic unity were more important to him. The "great style" always presupposes the hierarchical subordination of parts to whole, whether that whole be conceived of as an ideal and undegenerated primitive, a natural organism, or as its alternative, the artificial but nonetheless authentic self created by the existential act of will. Now when Nietzsche searches for models, not of decadence but of this kind of coherent and fully-formed organization, he finds one in the Roman Empire, which he depicts therefore in a manner antithetical to its treatment by decadent writers. It is worth noting that in his last books Nietzsche is increasingly interested in Rome and the Romans and markedly less than previously in the Greeks. Thus in *The Twilight of the Idols* he writes: "My sense of style, for the epigram as style, was aroused instantly by the encounter with Sallust. . . . Concentrated, severe, with as much substance as possible at its base, a cold malice against 'beautiful words,' also 'beautiful feelings'—I found myself in that. In my style, up to and including my *Zarathustra*, you will find a very serious ambition for *Roman* style, *aere perennius*. . . . I do not owe the Greeks anything like such strong impressions; and, to put it bluntly, they *cannot* be what the Romans are to us" (W, II, 1027–28). Roman literature is aristocratic ("vornehm"), and Nietzsche stresses an ideal of urbanity which Rome possessed supremely, and which he also finds in the seventeenth and to some degree in the eighteenth century, though not in that Rousseauistic tradition which issued in Romanticism. What Nietzsche admires in that latter century is exactly what the Romantics (and therefore the decadents) did not inherit, that is, "the *insouciance*, the serenity, the elegance, the intellectual brightness" (W, III, 529). The term *imperium Romanum* conjures up for him not at all a vision of decay but one of self-realization of the will in an integrated cultural style, "unity of the artistic style in all the expressions of life of a people" (W, I, 140), as he put it very early. The urbane patina was perhaps immune, at least for a generation or two, to the pernicious seepage of the Christian slave-ethic and its poisonous egalitarianism. What, *The Antichrist* asks, is *imperium Romanum* but:

> the most magnificent form of organization under difficult conditions that has ever been achieved, in comparison with which every Before and every Afterwards is fragmented, botched, dilettantist—those holy anarchists made a "pious act" out of destroying "the world," *that is*, the *imperium Romanum* . . . Christian and anarchist: both *decadents*. . . . The *imperium Romanum* . . . this most admirable work of art in the great style, was a beginning, its construction was calculated to prove itself through millennia—until today no one has built like this nor ever even dreamed of building in such a degree *sub specie aeterni!*—This organization was strong enough to survive bad emperors: the accident of individuals can have nothing to do with such things— *first* principle of all great architecture. (W, II, 1229)

The architectural or building metaphor recurs here. The artistic will which hews and piles in stone, refutes the centuries and defies the corruption of the organic, is Nietzsche's prerequisite for that style which can overcome decadence and nihilism. Its classical mould, its unity of surface actually negates the individualistic or particular. If we think now of the world of George's Heliogabalus, mineral and metallic, an artificial underworld created by the Emperor's own will, we must needs recognize a distinction between these two forms of artifact. Their quality is quite different. Their presuppositions are also quite different. The "unnaturalness" of Algabal's underworld is based, in conventional decadent fashion, on the notion that Nature is still the norm. Thus Algabal is in the end inevitably found wanting, indeed he finds himself so; the activities of George's hero are as pathetic as those of Ludwig II of Bavaria, one of the models for him (and of course the patron of Bayreuth). The "unnaturalness" of Nietzsche's empire of the will is something quite other than this, since it presupposes no valid Nature from which it has departed; there is for it, and can be, no other authentic "nature" but that of the will, and when this situation is given the universal or at least communal value of cult and myth there arises Dionysiac, or classical, pessimism. Now of course it is most hazardous to generalize about Nietzsche. His entire output is characterized by what may be called, at best, flashes of consistency. However in this case there are enough of these for us to establish the argument, as will emerge from a brief consideration of the philosopher's comments upon individual Romans and Greeks. But inconsistencies and side-steps inevitably do occur. On the one hand a brief note—"Primitive jungle creatures, the *Romans*" (W, III, 851)—shows a typical Nietzschean reversal, from evaluation in terms of urbanity to evaluation in terms of the primitive. On the other hand Nietzsche cannot deny that the Empire was eventually successfully attacked, from without, and this brings him, in his inner play-writing, quite close at times to Verlaine's dénouement, the unresisted inrush of the barbarians. By and large, however, his Roman models (and some Greek) are exploited in the service of a conspicuously non-decadent ideal.

Nietzsche never refers to Heliogabalus, rarely to Nero. The latter with his *qualis artifex pereo!* (whom Flaubert revered when a young man) is compared with the dying Augustus, in a passage in which both are said to have demonstrated "histrionic vanity! histrionic garrulity!" They are then contrasted with the Emperor Tiberius, who was "genuine and not an actor" (W, II, 63). It is worth noting that here, in *The Joyful Wisdom*, Nietzsche still maintains a clear-cut distinction between the genuine and the invented (or acted). In fact he never really managed to expunge the notion of "genuineness" from his thought. But as the apotheosis of the artificial man develops, a more important distinction for him is that between the two kinds of artifice, between the Wagnerian histrionic type and the superman-artist. The early origins of this latter character, as well as his culmination, may be found for instance in the references to Prometheus, with his "necessity of crime" (*The Birth of Tragedy;* W, I, 60) and his barbarian quality (*The Will to Power;* W, III, 846), while in *Beyond Good and Evil* we find an honor roll of heroes of the will, who overcome and "outwit" their inner conflict instead of surrendering to the yearning for the "sabbath of sabbaths" and a motionless placidity: here we find Julius Caesar cited, and Alcibiades. The latter was also of potential interest to decadents, as Praz indicates.[28] And even Nietzsche mentions him somewhere in some such terms as well, as one who abandoned the instinct for struggle—the ἀγών, which was the real source of Greek vitality (W, III, 299).

Among Romans, Petronius is probably the best instance of a figure in the discussion of whom Nietzsche demonstrates decisively the distance between himself and the decadents. The author of the *Satyricon* was an attractive example, of course, for decadent poets. Verlaine, for instance, mentions as authentic images of decadence Sardanapalus in the midst of his women (Délacroix), Seneca reciting poetry as he bleeds to death, and Petronius "masking his agony with flowers."[29] The anonymous article in *The Quarterly Review*, already cited, suggests that the decadents derive their inspiration from "Catullus, Apuleius of the 'Golden Ass,' Petronius Arbiter, and the host of Greek lyrical singers whom Cicero could never, as he observes, find time to read."[30] Nietzsche has no doubts about the decadence

---

[28] Cf. Praz, pp. 295 and 369.

[29] Joanna Richardson, *Verlaine* (London: Weidenfeld & Nicholson, 1970), p. 190. The flower motif, which is persistent in decadent literature and is found in *Algabal*, is strikingly un-Nietzschean.

[30] *The Quarterly Review*, 172 (1891), 293.

of Délacroix (cf. W, II, 1091), but he shows no interest in Catullus or Apuleius. Particularly in view of the remarks he makes about Sallust (and also Horace), we may suppose that "the putrescent hues of Apuleius"[31] were uncongenial, that this writer's bawdy absurdities and sensual fantasy (so attractive to Huysmans) held little appeal for Nietzsche, and this despite the latter's insistence that he esteems "buffoonery." In the case of Petronius, significantly enough, the feature he stresses is health. Petronius, stylistically, is declared to be "the master of the *presto*" (W, II, 594)—hence impossible to render well in German! Petronius "makes everything run." Just as Domenico Boccaccio wrote to the Duke of Parma about Cesare Borgia, Petronius is "tutto festo," "immortally healthy, immortally serene and felicitously made ["wohlgeraten"]" (W, II, 1210). What a contrast is the *Satyricon* to that appalling *New Testament* in which "not a single buffoonery is to be found" (W, III, 527). Nietzsche's praise for Petronius's novel is a rare case in which we find him admiring a work which specifically and centrally treats sexual perversion.

Plato and Socrates were of course major figures in Nietzsche's tragedy of decadence. Though to discuss their significance in this context would lead much too far afield, there is another Greek thinker to whom attention should be drawn, since he is also indicted directly, and perhaps more aptly, as a progenitor and excellent illustration of the decadent morality the philosopher thinks to find in his own day. This is Epicurus, whose importance among Nietzsche's *dramatis personae* until recently has been somewhat neglected.[32] Epicureanism in some form or other may be said to underlie many of the manifestations of decadence. The preoccupation with the moment, with the senses and with pleasure (in a wide sense), the essential passivity of this outlook, its static quality—all this already shows the connection. Among French writers of the period, however, there is not much interest in Epicurus himself—no doubt because he did not provide an obvious enough example of the overcultivated life. Behind him, of course, stands the shadowy figure of Heraclitus, whom Nietzsche much admired. The Heraclitean flux—"the world forever needs the truth and it forever needs Heraclitus" (W, III, 380)—is a fundamental preconception of Nietzsche's entire philosophy, although, true to his subjective dramatic method, Heraclitus is sometimes alleged in it to have played a role for which there is little or no evidence.[33] It is in English literature, not French, that these ancestors of late nineteenth-century Epicure-

[31] Ibid., p. 302.

[32] The *International Nietzsche Bibliography* (1968) notes only one study: G. Barkuras, *Nietzsche und Epikur* (Diss., Kiel, 1962). Nietzsche's great interest in the work of the contemporary sceptic Marie-Jean Guyau (*La morale d'Épicure, et ses rapports avec les doctrines contemporaines.* 1874) is worth bearing in mind.

[33] Knight accuses Nietzsche of insincerity in this connection (see A. H. J. Knight, *Some Aspects of the Life and Work of Nietzsche* [Cambridge: Cambridge University Press, 1933], p. 106). This criticism really misses the point, since it overlooks the nature of the imaginative monodrama in which Nietzsche is involved.

anism find their outstanding disciples, especially in Walter Pater. Though, in a few ways, Pater and Nietzsche are uncannily close, it is once again the differences which really count. Like Nietzsche, Pater is preoccupied with the integrated whole, and especially with the achievement of a personal cosmos, a state of order which the cosmoplastic moment of "insight" imposes upon an inchoate world.[34] As far as his lecture on Dionysus—"A Study of Dionysus: The Spiritual Form of Fire and Dew" (1876)—is concerned, this seems so near to *The Birth of Tragedy* both in its date and its dualistic explanation of Greek art that the argument that Pater must have known Nietzsche has been put forward with confidence. But the weight of the evidence is really all the other way—that Pater, even in his later years, had never heard of the German writer.[35] Pater's view of life is consistently different from Nietzsche's. In one way it is much more oriented towards the cult of the self, in another it compromises far more with conventional moral ideas. Pater dropped, from the second edition of *The Renaissance*, the famous preface which was supposed to have corrupted the morals of young people—a most un-Nietzschean concession to make. In *Marius the Epicurean*, that much misunderstood novel, he transcends, as does Nietzsche, the Epicurean solution, and asserts a morality of willed action. He is still divided from Nietzsche, however, by his altruism, and by his tentative approach to a Christian solution.

Nietzsche's criticisms of Epicurus epitomize his theory of decadence as a failure of the will and a flight from life. They help to confirm that his thinking never really led him to an introverted cult of the self, nor to the manipulation of experience for its own sake; in this respect he never endorses, even temporarily, the position with which Pater's *Marius* begins. The architectural metaphor brought out above is a more accurate indication of the general direction of Nietzsche's idealism. Nietzsche believed that the Epicureans, and also the Stoics, had lost the original "innocence" possessed, as he thought, by the early Greeks—for they did not approach life actively. Epicurus fenced himself in his garden and monitored his responses to stimuli, seeking to achieve a steady state. Aristippus, Nietzsche admitted, was a trifle more active, but Pyrrho, decidedly "weary," was even more decayed. Epicurus is called "a *typical décadent*, first recognized as such by me" (W, II, 1192). He may be commended for having denounced Plato, but he is nonetheless "the opposite of a dionysiac pessimist." Moreover, the Christian is just a kind of Epicurean, and both, according to Nietzsche, are Romantics. The highly significant passage in *The Joyful Wisdom* entitled "What is Romanticism?"

---

[34] Barbara Charlesworth, *Dark Passages: The Decadent Consciousness in Victorian Literature* (Madison: University of Wisconsin Press, 1965), pp. 45–46.

[35] Arthur Symons, among others, followed the early fashion which asserted a close kinship between Nietzsche and Pater. Several modern scholars have repeated this assertion. But for the negative evidence see David S. Thatcher, *Nietzsche in England* (Toronto: University of Toronto Press, 1970), and Patrick Bridgwater, *Nietzsche in Anglosaxony* (Leicester: Leicester University Press, 1972).

(W, II, 244–46) distinguishes two types of suffering. There is that positive type which comes from "excess of life," and that negative kind which comes from its impoverishment. Those whose suffering is of the latter variety seek "peace, silence, smooth sea, liberation from themselves through art and knowledge . . . or else intoxication, spasm, narcosis, insanity." This is the "dual need," the dual face of the Romantic longing. Though Nietzsche does not point it out here, the connection with decadent feeling is self-evident, the proximity, for instance, to Baudelaire's opium paradise and to his "luxe, calme et volupté." Another paragraph in the same book, headed "Why we seem to be Epicureans" (W, II, 250–1) stresses the hesitancy of contemporary men, their avoidance of hard decisions, their obsession with speculation. As for the Stoic, he too is in reality a decadent. Seneca is a bad actor—an ostentatious "toreador of virtue" (W, II, 991). Marcus Aurelius—much discussed in the mid-nineteenth century and a central character in Marius the Epicurean[36]—is criticized by Nietzsche for the fact that he did not know how to affirm (not, as he is by Pater, because he is unresponsive to human pain). Nietzsche confronts the Stoic-Heraclitean doctrines of Aurelius with his own affirmation of Recurrence: "My comfort is that everything that was is eternal—the sea washes it up again" (W, III, 680).

"What is Romanticism?" is a statement of great importance. Here, in his analysis of the Epicurean pursuit of the steady state of being, aiming at "making eternal" ("verewigen") rather than destroying and transforming, Nietzsche once more, as in the case of suffering itself, subdivides into two possible types. There is first of all this "will to make eternal" which, because it implies the creation of great works that overcome time, almost makes the negative kind of suffering positive again; and secondly there is the tyrannical, tormented struggle to imprint one's own pain upon the flux of life, which leads to something very different, in fact a denial of *true* cosmos, an egocentric sham and façade:

> It can however also be that tyrannical will of a deeply suffering, struggling, tortured man, who would fain stamp what is most personal, individual, near to himself, the essential idiosyncrasy of his sufferings into a binding law and compulsion, and who as it were takes revenge on everything by impressing upon it, forcing it into, branding it with, *his* image, the image of *his* torture. This last is *romantic pessimism* in its most expressive form, be it Schopenhauerian will-philosophy or Wagnerian music. . . .

Here, in *The Joyful Wisdom*, is Nietzsche's precise definition of the solipsistic act of the tortured will that is so characteristic of the decadent—Baudelaire, Huysmans,

---

[36] For Matthew Arnold on Marcus Aurelius see *Essays in Criticism* (1865). Taine was a great admirer of the Emperor, and Renan wrote both about him and about the Empress Faustina, who in *Marius the Epicurean* takes on some of the allures of a decadent femme fatale. Pater was aware of the tragedy of the man, and Nietzsche too seems to have felt something of this: "The popular ideals: the good man, the selfless man, the saint, the wise man, the just man. O Marcus Aurelius!" (W, III, 482).

Bourget, Barbey d'Aurevilly and their many precursors and followers, including George in his *Algabal*. Of the two variations upon the Epicurean attitude described in this passage the former is, to use Nietzsche's own terms, "classical" or "dionysiac" pessimism and its meaning is not purely limited to the individual, while the latter, here called "romantic" pessimism, is quite evidently the monstrous perversion of Heliogabalus modernized by de Sade. It now appears more explicable why Nietzsche should have had no interest (that we know of) in de Sade. The admiration for the *Satyricon* notwithstanding (which is clearly founded on quite other factors) Nietzsche must be read throughout his works as unsympathetic to all forms of sexual perversion. Though this conclusion is based on a negative, an absence, it is of some importance in a thinker writing, as Nietzsche was, in the period of the Decadent Movement and whose sexual attitudes are otherwise of explicit relevance to a deeper understanding of his books. On the philosophical level we can say that Nietzsche's disapproval of perversion reflects *inter alia* his basic rejection of acts of the will which lack a more general framework, or even a cultic validity.

Sadism, as Praz points out,[37] was one of the most distinctive hallmarks of decadent literature, and perversion one of its deepest thoughts. Nietzsche's work is never sadistic or perverse in this fashion. In establishing the distinction between the artifice of the superman and that of the decadents he sees the latter as sexually and organically degenerate ("sister-marriage"[!], W, III, 872). Their acts of will are nothing but exotic, tormented throws of egoism. They are—as the logic of "What is Romanticism?" shows—at least incipiently perverted. That their excesses should frequently dissolve, as they did for example in Huysmans' case, in the embraces of a sensual Catholicism would hardly have surprised Nietzsche. Such a result is all but required by his arguments. It is consistent with this that Nietzsche scarcely touches on the androgyne motif, which is so common in the literature both of the classical world and of the decadents, as *Algabal* bears witness. According to Joël, a proposed course on Sappho at Basel was never given.[38] The subversive influence of the female principle seems to Nietzsche an established cause of decadence; hermaphroditic features, if encountered, are to be spurned. Women, he implies, have infiltrated the male preserve and have destroyed "natural" relationships: "*Continuation of Christianity* through the *French Revolution*. The seducer is Rousseau: he unshackles woman again, who from then on is portrayed as more and more interesting—as *suffering*. Then the slaves and Mistress Beecher-Stowe. Then the poor and the workers. Then the vicious and the diseased. . . . Then comes the curse upon sensual pleasure (Baudelaire and Scho-

---

[37] Praz, p. 394.

[38] Joël, p. 363. By itself, of course, this signifies little. In Basel Nietzsche lectured almost entirely on the earlier periods of Greek literature and thought, avoiding the Alexandrines and hardly touching on Latin authors.

penhauer) . . ." (W, III, 431). Baudelaire, who in *Les Fleurs du Mal* had composed what amounted to a series of awesome imprecations upon sexuality, had, like the other decadents, in his cerebral lechery perverted Nature. Good examples among literary persons were Sainte-Beuve and George Sand: "It betrays corruption of the instincts [i.e., organic decadence]—apart from the fact that it betrays bad taste—if precisely a woman appeals to Madame Roland or Madame de Stael or Monsieur George Sand . . ." (W, II, 699). George Sand specifically exemplifies that condition of decadent unnaturalness in which the organism has become an artifact and what life there is is only in the parts: "She wound herself up like a watch—and wrote. . . . Cold, like Hugo, like Balzac, like all the Romantics, as soon as they composed poetic works! that fertile scribbling cow, who had in her something German in the bad sense, as Rousseau himself, her master, had . . ." (W, II, 994).

Shooting out barbs of flame in all directions, Nietzsche's fiery wheels thus spin devastatingly through the easily combustible literature of his own age. In command of the chariot, in the passages just quoted, is once again the truculent primitivist, trumpeting that "natural" masculinity he adored. Europe, he cries, is threatened by a "marasmus femininus" (W, III, 471). "*Feminism:* Rousseau, dominance of *feelings*, witness to the sovereignty of the *senses*, lies" (W, III, 510). What are artists nowadays but "hysterical little women?" Though of course this "speaks against 'nowadays' and not against the 'artist' " (W, III, 755). The *femme fatale* of the decadents, the Heliogabalus, the androgyne possess no status here. The *lycéens* of Paris, as we saw, must perforce have their "contemptible inclinations" denounced. This obsessional cerebralist thus deplores the cerebral frigidity of degenerate Romantic primitives. Hierarchy has been swept away by them, organism has dissolved in deliquescence, creative will has succumbed to titillation, all that is left is the Wagnerian opera of the sham *imperium Germanum*, founded in 1871. But yet: there are presumably still the barbarians. For the poets of the nineteenth-century *Finis Latinorum*, resident in Eternal Paris, those barbarians were not that far to seek: to some it must have seemed that after the defeat of Sedan they had really passed through, complete with spiked helmets.[39] Such a notion would of course have appeared an absurd anomaly to Nietzsche. For his own presumptive "new" barbarians, "the cynics, the tempters, the conquerors" (W, III, 449) were to combine *intellectual* superiority with physical health and excess of energy. The "wild animal" in man, the barbarian, was to be simultaneously the artificial man, organic but invented, a mask but not a sham, and *classical:*

---

[39] "Il y avait aussi l'idée que les Prussiens de 70 avaient été les barbares, que Paris c'était Rome ou Byzance." "There was also the notion that the Prussians of 70 had been the barbarians, and that Paris was Rome or Byzantium." Gustave Kahn, *Symbolistes et décadents* (Paris: Vanier, 1902), pp. 37–38. Cf. Carter, p. 108.

General view of the future European: he will be the most intelligent kind of beast of slavery . . . a cosmopolitan chaos of feelings and intelligence. How could a *stronger* species emerge from him? One with *classical* taste? Classical taste: that is the will to simplification, to strengthening, to the visibility of happiness, to awesomeness, the courage for psychological nakedness. . . . In order to struggle out of that chaos to this *form*—for that there has to be some *coercion:* one has to have the choice between being destroyed or *fighting through.* . . . Problem: Where are the *barbarians* of the twentieth century? (W, III, 690)

The will to form is reasserted against the process of dissolution. The paradoxical twinship of primitive and artificial emerges as dominant. These "classical" barbarians, by that very *contradictio in adjecto*, would be a rejuvenation, a restoration of the empire of the western mind now in decay. Democrats, Nietzsche sneered, were always afraid of barbarians from below. But in his dramatic imagination he himself rides against Rome with another kind of company, of unimpeachable classical lineage: "they come from above: a species of conquering and ruling natures, *who search for a material that they can form.*[40] Prometheus was such a barbarian" (W, III, 846).

[40] My italics.

XV

Nietzsche and the Death of Tragedy: A Critique *

WALTER KAUFMANN

I

The idea of "the death of tragedy" goes back to Nietzsche. He did not only proclaim, first in *The Gay Science* and then in *Zarathustra*, that "God is dead"; in his first book, *The Birth of Tragedy*, we read:

> Greek tragedy met an end different from her older sister-arts: she died by suicide, in consequence of an irreconcilable conflict; she died tragically.... When Greek tragedy died, there rose everywhere the deep sense of an immense void. Just as Greek sailors in the time of Tiberius, passing a lonely island, once heard the shattering cry, "Great Pan is dead," so the Hellenic world was now pierced by the grievous lament: "tragedy is dead! Poetry itself has perished with her! . . ." (sec. 11)

In the first half of the twentieth century, it was Nietzsche's discussion of the *birth* of tragedy, and of what he called the Apollinian and the Dionysian, that established the fame of his first book. The so-called Cambridge school in England developed his ideas on this subject, and a host of scholars accepted them by way of Jane Harrison's and Gilbert Murray's books. But Gerald Else has contested their theories and argued for a different hypothesis.[1]

Since World War II, Nietzsche's discussion of the death of tragedy has become more influential, and his ideas have become almost a commonplace. It will be one of the central points of the present chapter to show that these popular ideas are untenable, regarding the death of both *Greek* tragedy and tragedy in our time.

One of the systematic flaws of the popular argument is that one type of

---

* The present chapter consists of passages excerpted from Walter Kaufmann, *Tragedy and Philosophy* (New York: Doubleday & Company, 1968), sections 34, 37, 38, 40, 48 and 50, reprinted by permission of the publisher. All translations from the German and the Greek are by the author, excepting several instances from Homer's *Iliad* where the translation is by E. V. Rieu. In such cases, the reference given first is the page number from his Penguin translation (Harmondsworth, Middlesex, 1950), then the book and verse numbers of the original Greek version.

[1] Gerald F. Else, *The Origin and Form of Early Greek Tragedy* (Cambridge, Mass.: Harvard University Press, 1965).

tragedy is treated as if it were the only one; when writers speak of the death of tragedy they usually mean that no tragedies like *Oedipus Tyrannus* were written after the fifth century B.C., or are being written in the twentieth century. But Sophocles himself, once he had written *Oedipus Tyrannus*, wrote no more tragedies like it: neither *Philoctetes* nor *Oedipus at Colonus* ends in catastrophe, and *Electra* ends on a note of triumph. Even in *Ajax* the hero's suicide occurs at line 805, and most of the remaining 555 lines are concerned with the question of whether he is to receive a hero's burial or not, and in the end he does. In other words, of Sophocles' extant tragedies, only three end tragically.

My argument might be countered as follows. Although Sophocles was older than Euripides, both died in 406—Euripides a few months before Sophocles. If Euripides was responsible for the death of tragedy, or if he at least embodied the spirit of a new age in which tragedy was no longer possible—and this is Nietzsche's thesis—it stands to reason that Sophocles, particularly in his old age, during the last twenty years of his career, was infected, too.

Nevertheless, the admission that Euripides' tragedies were not really tragedies and that Sophocles, too, wrote only three bona fide tragedies would reduce the whole notion of the death of tragedy, either around 406 B.C. or in our time, to the absurd—unless we could introduce Aeschylus at this point, saying that *he* was the creator of tragedy and that we must turn to his plays if we want to know what real tragedies look like. This is what Nietzsche clearly implies, and if this point could be sustained his argument would not be absurd. For in that case we could say that Aeschylus' seven extant tragedies are the paradigm cases of the genre to which Sophocles contributed three great masterpieces before he, like Euripides, succumbed to the essentially untragic outlook of the dawning fourth century.

The facts of the matter are, however, quite different. Perhaps in large part because so much philology is microscopic and pedestrian, those who aspire to deal with our subject philosophically go to the opposite extreme and take it for granted that it would be sub-philosophical to dwell on particular Greek tragedies. As a result, the philosophical dimension of Aeschylus and Sophocles remains unexplored—in *The Birth of Tragedy* no less than in the *Poetics*. Hence it never struck Nietzsche, or those who have refurbished his thesis in our time, that the very attitudes they associate with the death of tragedy are found preeminently in Aeschylus.

Nietzsche's account of the death of Greek tragedy is diffuse, flamboyant, and shot through with interesting ideas. Instead of offering a detailed summary and lengthy polemics, let us stress three central themes. Nietzsche repeatedly calls the new spirit of which tragedy died "optimism"—and this he professes to find not only in Socrates but also in Euripides, along with a delight in dialectic and an excessive faith in knowledge. The passage in which he attributes "the death of tragedy" to optimism and rationalism will be quoted and discussed below; for the moment, it will suffice to link these two motifs with a third that helps to clarify the other two: the faith that catastrophes can and ought to be avoided. If men would only use their reason properly—this is the optimistic notion of which tragedy is thought to have perished—there would be no need for tragedies.[2]

I will argue that this was the faith of Aeschylus. Euripides, far from being an optimist, was indeed, as Aristotle put it, albeit for different reasons, "the most tragic of the poets." Aeschylus was, compared with Sophocles and Euripides, the most optimistic: he alone had the sublime confidence that by rightly employing their reason men could avoid catastrophes. His world view was, by modern standards, anti-tragic; and yet he created tragedy.

On this perverse fact most discussions of this subject suffer shipwreck. How can we resolve the paradox? We should cease supposing that great tragedies must issue from a tragic vision that entails some deep despair or notions of inevitable failure and, instead, read Aeschylus with care.

One point may be anticipated: tragedy is generally more optimistic than comedy. It is profound despair that leads most of the generation born during and after World War II to feel that tragedy is dated; they prefer comedy, whether black or not. Tragedy is inspired by a faith that can weather the plague, whether in Sophoclean Athens or in Elizabethan London, but not Auschwitz. It is compatible with the great victories of Marathon and Salamis that marked the threshold of the Aeschylean age, and with the triumph over the Armada that inaugurated Shakespeare's era. It is not concordant with Dresden, Hiroshima, and Nagasaki. Tragedy depends on sympathy, ruth, and involvement. It has little appeal for a generation that, like Ivan Karamazov, would gladly return the ticket to God, if there were a god. Neither in Athens nor in our time has tragedy perished of optimism: its sickness unto death was and is despair.

II

Gilbert Murray said of Aeschylus: "He raised everything he touched to grandeur. The characters in his hands became heroic; the conflicts became tense and fraught with eternal issues."[3] After World War I it became fashionable to contrast our own paltry and unpoetic time with the great ages of the past, lamenting that the modern writer lacked that store of myth on which an Aeschylus and Sophocles could draw.

The Greeks did have many myths, but if Aeschylus and Sophocles had not brought off this feat, nobody could have said that these myths furnished good

---

[2] The last motif is more prominent in the twentieth century than it was in Nietzsche, though he did associate tragedy with the incurable.

[3] Gilbert Murray, *Aeschylus: The Creator of Tragedy* (1940; rpt. Oxford: Clarendon Press, 1962), p. 205.

material for great tragedies or for serious literature of any kind. In his own genre, Homer could not be surpassed; hence it was pointless to retell what he had told. There were stories on which he had barely touched, like that of Oedipus; and one might well have thought that this tale would lend itself to treatment as a horror story or a comedy—certainly not to tragedy. Yet by the time Sophocles composed his masterpiece, he even had the added disadvantage that one of the greatest poets of all time—none other than Aeschylus—had preceded him in writing a tragedy on Oedipus, which was first performed the year after Sophocles had first defeated him in the annual contest, barely more than forty years before. Moreover, Sophocles wrote *Oedipus Tyrannus* in a city at war, its population decimated by the plague, its policies adrift in the contention among demagogues, its spiritual climate saturated with both superstition and enlightenment, its many moods including both an optimistic faith in reason and deep disillusionment. Had he not succeeded in becoming a great poet, he could easily have said that "the damage of a lifetime, and of having been born in an unsettled society, cannot be repaired at the moment of composition."[4]

It may be objected that Sophocles was born long before the devastations of the Peloponnesian War. But when he was a child the Persians invaded and pillaged Greece before they were stopped at Marathon, about twenty miles from Athens; and ten years later they sacked Athens before they were beaten at Salamis—and the following year, they sacked Athens again, before their defeat at Plataea. After that, to be sure, Athens was rebuilt along with the temples on the Acropolis whose ruins we still admire, and she enjoyed unexampled prosperity—and precisely the well-being and smugness that are often considered the worst climate for artistic achievements and above all for tragedy. Yet it was in those years that Aeschylus created his extant tragedies and Sophocles, too, his early works, including *Antigone*.

Great art comes into being in spite of the age to which it is linked by its weaknesses. And Aeschylus triumphed not on account of the myths he could use but in spite of them.

Gilbert Murray has shown in detail "what raw material Aeschylus found to his hand when he set to work" on his *Prometheus*.[5] First, there was a local cult in Athens "of a petty daemon called Prometheus, who was a trade patron of the potters and the smiths"; and what was related about him was "just the sort of thing for a cunning fire-dwarf to do; and so, of course, Zeus punished him." But there was also another poet who had dealt with this material some time ago: the great Hesiod. Murray cites the relevant passages from Hesiod before asking: "Now what does Aeschylus make of this very trivial and unimpressive story? He drops the undignified quarrel about the dividing of the burnt sacrifice. He drops the

---

[4] T. S. Eliot, *After Strange Gods: A Primer of Modern Heresy* (London: Faber and Faber, 1934), p. 26.
[5] Murray, pp. 19–26.

rustic wit about Pandora."[6] And he answers his own question in part by finding in the tragedy "the will to endure pitted against the will to crush."[7]

What we have found in Homer about the slaying of Agamemnon and Orestes' revenge is certainly far from being trivial and unimpressive. Neither, however, is it fraught with eternal issues. What makes it impressive is more Homer's poetry than the plot. But that might have served as a warning against picking this theme: why choose an essentially unpromising tale that a previous poet whom everyone knows has already told and varied several times?

Aeschylus changed the story, feeling quite free to create his own myth. Without contradicting Homer he added what Homer had not said: that Orestes killed his own mother. He moved the mother into the center in the first play of his trilogy in which he dealt with the murder of Agamemnon. In the second play he let Orestes kill both Clytemnestra and Aegisthus at the express command of Apollo, but let the Furies pursue the matricide. And in the third play he presented the rival claims of Apollo and the Furies, showed them unable to come to terms, and brought them to Athens where Athene finally founded a new court and cast the decisive vote for Orestes' acquittal. Most of this has no basis whatever in Homer, and the plot of the last play may be almost entirely Aeschylus' own invention.

In *Agamemnon* Aeschylus does what many critics of modern playwrights consider a sign of bankruptcy and a warrant of second-rate literature: he takes a story already told by a very great poet and makes some changes in it. These will be considered in a moment. In *The Libation Bearers* he takes a terrible deed, matricide, not mentioned by Homer, and makes it the crux of the play. One can imagine a critic exclaiming, "First a pastiche and then outright decadence!" In *The Eumenides*, finally, we encounter in absolutely climactic form that rationalism and optimism of which tragedy is said to have died—and find them at the culmination of the greatest work of the so-called creator of tragedy.

A court is founded in Athens not only to adjudicate the case of Orestes, who is acquitted, but also to sit on all capital cases henceforth so that future tragedies like that of *The Libation Bearers* may be prevented; and the action closes with hymns of jubilation. In heroic times Orestes' vengeance was justified, but in civilized Athens a man in such a dilemma needs only to come to the Areopagus, and all will be taken care of without catastrophe. Men have only to learn to employ their reason properly, and their most terrible moral problems can be solved. In this respect, as in others, Athens has led the way, and the joyous choruses in the end celebrate the great triumph of reason and, patriotically, Athens.

One can imagine the outcry of intellectuals in our time at any poet's concluding a tragedy with such a show of patriotism, glorifying his own society

[6] Ibid., p. 26.
[7] Ibid., p. 31.

instead of exposing its dry rot—of which there was plenty in Athens, along with so much conceit and self-satisfaction that most citizens of the other Greek cities hated her. And Aeschylus sang her praises because he thought that she had an institution by means of which tragic dilemmas could be avoided!

A modern writer has said, voicing the common sense of his generation in his uncommonly vigorous prose: "Any realistic notion of tragic drama must start from the fact of catastrophe. Tragedies end badly. The tragic personage is broken by forces which can neither be fully understood nor overcome by rational prudence. This again is crucial. Where the causes of disaster are temporal, where the conflict can be resolved by technical or social means, we may have serious drama, but not tragedy. More pliant divorce laws could not alter the fate of Agamemnon; social psychiatry is no answer to *Oedipus*. But saner economic relations or better plumbing *can* resolve some of the grave crises in the dramas of Ibsen. The distinction should be borne sharply in mind. Tragedy is irreparable."[8]

A page earlier we are told that, while "in the *Eumenides* and in *Oedipus at Colonus*, the tragic action closes on a note of grace," "both cases are exceptional." We have already seen that the conclusion of *Oedipus at Colonus* was not exceptional for Sophocles; none of his later tragedies ends "badly." We have also seen in the first section of the present chapter that the whole theory of the death of tragedy depends on Aeschylus.

It is not enough to say of *The Eumenides* that it "closes on a note of grace." It exemplifies the very view held to be incompatible with tragedy, namely that the conflict can be resolved by reason, by social means, by sound institutions like those at Athens.

A play like *The Eumenides*, if written in our time, would not be called a tragedy. Nor did Aeschylus write many, if any, tragedies in the modern sense of that word. Like most of his plays, six of his seven extant tragedies were parts of connected trilogies, and not only the *Oresteia* voiced the very temper of which tragedy is supposed to have died a few decades later, but the trilogies of which *The Suppliants* and *Prometheus* were the first plays gave expression to the very same experience of life. Scholars agree that both of these trilogies ended happily, not in catastrophe.

Only in *Seven Against Thebes* is catastrophe final, but Aeschylus goes out of his way to tell us that all of it, including Oedipus' tragic fate, could have been avoided but for Laius' "folly" (745 ff.); he had been told by the oracle to save his city by not having children. This version of the oracle seems to have been original with Aeschylus,[9] and its introduction (or repetition) at this point in the final play

---

[8] George Steiner, *The Death of Tragedy* (New York: Knopf, 1961), p. 8. Similar statements by Nietzsche (much briefer) and Max Scheler (much less eloquent) are cited in secs. 58 and 59 of *Tragedy and Philosophy*.

[9] H. W. Parke and D. E. W. Wormsell, *The Delphic Oracle* (Oxford: Blackwell, 1956), I, 299. Neither Sophocles nor Euripides retained Aeschylus' version.

of the trilogy tells us a great deal about Aeschylus' outlook.

In the case of *The Suppliants*, too, we need not go beyond the play that has survived to find that "as in *The Eumenides*, reason and persuasion are put forward as the proper principles of civilized life."[10] In fact, the parallel is striking and extends to the crucial point: no sooner has the poet stressed the tragic dilemma of the king of Argos who must either deny asylum to the suppliant maidens, thus outraging Zeus, the patron of suppliants, or plunge his city into war with the Egyptians who pursue them, than he cuts the knot by having the king announce that he knows an honorable solution. Being a king of free men with fine institutions, he needs only to bring this matter before them, take counsel, weigh both sides, and take a vote. Once the citizens have voted to protect the suppliants, the issue is clear. And when the Egyptian herald says in his last speech but one, "the judge is Ares," the good king reminds him that, if the maidens were willing or could be persuaded, he would let them go with the Egyptians, but the unanimous vote decreed that they must not be surrendered to force. And what has thus been resolved by vote is the law and the voice of freedom.

In the *Oresteia* we gradually move from the Homeric age to the founding of the supreme court of Athens. In *The Suppliants* the spirit of Athens is boldly projected into the heroic past by a poet who clearly felt, having fought at Marathon, that if a free people resolved to resist aggressive force this was not morally problematic. In the Prometheus trilogy the same ethos is projected on a cosmic scale: in the surviving first play, the titan with whom we cannot help sympathizing defies naked force and threats; and to remove any doubt about this he is crucified by two demons, Might and Force. The crescendo of the last hundred and fifty lines in which Prometheus hurls his defiance of Zeus into the face of Hermes, the messenger of the gods, is indescribable. But when Zeus thereupon casts him into Tartarus that is the end only of the beginning; two more plays follow: *The Unbinding of Prometheus* and *Prometheus the Fire-Bearer*. On the basis of surviving fragments and many references in ancient literature, at least the outlines of the plot can be made out. Prometheus knew that Thetis' son was destined to be greater than his father, and if Zeus had followed through his plan of having a son with her this would have been his undoing. But Zeus and Prometheus come to terms: the titan reveals the secret and is set free—and then a great festival may have been founded in the titan's honor in the third play. If Gilbert Murray's reconstruction is right,[11] the analogy to *The Eumenides* is very close.

In any case, we may here recall a sentence from the *Iliad:* "Why do we loathe Hades more than any god, if not because he is so adamantine and unyielding."[12] Pride wins Aeschylus' admiration, and he finds words for it more majestic than

---

[10] Philip Vellacott in the preface to his Penguin translation.

[11] Murray, pp. 99 ff.

[12] IX.158 f.; sec. 29, *Tragedy and Philosophy*.

almost anyone else; but what must be learned, not only by men but also by titans and Furies and gods—Apollo in *The Eumenides* and Zeus in *The Unbinding of Prometheus*—is the willingness to reason with one's opponents and to come to terms. It is violence that makes for catastrophes that prudence could prevent; and in democratic institutions such prudence is embodied.

Plainly, Aeschylus himself embodied the very spirit of which tragedy is said to have died first in the ancient world and later, after its rebirth in Shakespeare's time, again in modern times. And yet Gilbert Murray voiced a view shared by scholars and critics generally when he subtitled his book on Aeschulus: "The Creator of Tragedy."

It might seem as if no more than Aeschylus' reputation were at stake. Suppose we simply said that most of his plays were not tragedies; that *The Persians* and *Seven* represent two early forerunners of tragedy, while the works of his maturity that we know—*Suppliants, Oresteia,* and *Prometheus*—represent an altogether anti-tragic spirit. Who, in that case, did write tragedies? We have already seen that Sophocles' last three plays were not tragedies in the narrow, modern sense either, and that only his *Antigone, Women of Trachis* and *Oedipus Tyrannus* end in complete catastrophe. And according to Nietzsche, tragedy died under Euripides' violent hands.[13] Clearly, Nietzsche's reputation, too, is at stake; for from what we have found it appears that he was utterly wrong both about Aeschylus and about the alleged death of tragedy. And yet more is at stake. It has been said that it was "not between Euripides and Shakespeare that the Western mind turns away from the ancient tragic sense of life. It is after the late seventeenth century."[14] What becomes of the ancient—or any—"tragic sense of life?" If the Greek tragic poets lacked it no less than Ibsen and the moderns, was it merely an Elizabethan phenomenon? And if some few of the so-called tragedies of the Greeks really were tragedies in the more exacting sense of that word, can poets without a tragic sense of life write great tragedies, if only occasionally? In that case, is there any close connection between the tragic sense of life and tragedy, and are there any good reasons for saying that tragedy is dead?

III

What Aristotle did to some extent, modern critics have done with a vengeance. He thought that tragedy had "found its true nature" when Sophocles wrote *Oedipus Tyrannus*, and in many passages of the *Poetics* he made this tragedy the norm. But this did not prevent him from arguing in chapter 14 that, other things being equal, the best type of plot was one that involved a happy ending.

[13] GT, sec. 10, final paragraph.
[14] Steiner, p. 193.

Most critics, as we have seen, have balked at this conclusion and tried to show, albeit unsuccessfully, that he did not really mean it. But there is every reason for believing that he did mean it, and that the great Greek tragic poets would not have taken offense at this preference.

Modern critics go much further than Aristotle in their single-minded admiration for Sophocles' *Tyrannus*. They postulate this one play, for the most part quite unconsciously, as the standard of true tragedy and feel uncomfortable with all Greek tragedies that are not very similar to it. They want a tragic hero, but *The Persians, Suppliants, Eumenides*, and even *Agamemnon* do not have one (four out of the master's seven); and in *The Women of Trachis*, in *Antigone*, in *Philoctetes*, and to some extent even in *Ajax* there is a dual focus. The same is true not only of *Romeo and Juliet* and of *Antony and Cleopatra* but also, very strikingly, of *Julius Caesar* and, in a different way, of *King Lear*.

Tragedies, alas, are not what they're supposed to be. Aristotle, living so much closer to the evidence, came far closer than recent writers to doing justice to the wide range of Greek tragedy when he said that tragedies are plays that evoke *eleos* and *phobos* but provide a sobering emotional relief. Such relief is obviously quite compatible with non-tragic conclusions. What is decisive is not the end but whether we participate in tremendous, terrifying suffering.

No poet before Aeschylus and hardly any after him equalled either his majestic, awe-inspiring poetry or the immensity of human misery he captured in it. His belief in progress through the use of reason has no parallel in Homer and seems basically untragic. His preoccupation with moral issues, which concern him more than individuals, points in the same direction. He is not interested in Agamemnon and Clytemnestra beyond what is relevant to what one might call philosophic issues; he does not dwell on Agamemnon's life or his adventures, on the queen's relation to him, her upbringing; he does not raise the question what it felt like to be the sister of the most beautiful woman in the world, Helen; nor does he care what became of Orestes. Aeschylus does not approach Homer's interest in his heroes, in their deeds of valor, and in hundreds of details: he is centrally concerned with justice. Yet it would be utterly absurd to say that Homer wrote a tragic poem and Aeschylus destroyed the tragic spirit. Aeschylus is more tragic than Homer and everyone else before him in his determination and ability to show *how* tragic life is without reason, compromise, and sanity.

Homer's radiant appreciation of the countless aspects of human experience distracts from the tragic element—that is irremediable, but there is so much that is beautiful and interesting; there remains the possibility of leading a short but glorious life; and telling and hearing of men who covered themselves with glory is exhilarating. For Aeschylus the tragic is remediable and represented as a foil for progress through the use of reason. But misery is no less great for having been avoidable. One might even argue that the belief in necessity spells comfort, while the sense that a catastrophe was not inevitable heightens our suffering. But at this point Aeschylus does not insist on being metaphysical; he simply pictures suffering with a concentrated power, piling image upon image, overwhelming us with the whole weight of human grief, leaving a mark on our minds that no eventual insight, institution, or joy can wipe out. All the glory of the triumph at the end of *The Eumenides* cannot silence Cassandra's cries: they stay with us, like Prometheus' defiant anguish; they echo through the centuries and change world literature.

Tragedy is not what the philosophers and critics say it is; it is far simpler. What lies at the heart of it is the refusal to let any comfort, faith, or joy deafen our ears to the tortured cries of our brothers. Aeschylus believed, like Hegel, that though history was a slaughter bench, the monstrous sacrifices of men's happiness and virtue had not been for nothing. But the founding of the Areopagus does not erase Cassandra's anguish any more than the establishment of the state of Israel wipes out the terrors of Auschwitz.

To call the poet who created Cassandra an optimist would be grossly misleading; but to call the author of *The Eumenides* and *Suppliants* a pessimist would be worse. Admittedly, the Cassandra scene alone is not conclusive, although it ranks with Lear on the heath and Gretchen in the dungeon as one of the most magnificent and heartrending dramatic creations of all time. Nothing is more moving than a noble mind gone mad; and Aeschylus was the first poet to realize this. (The author of the First Book of Samuel did not depict the madness of King Saul in a comparable scene.) But if one had to call Goethe either an optimist or a pessimist, one would surely have to choose the former label, in spite of the dungeon scene; and Aeschylus' case is similar.

Optimism and pessimism are simplistic categories, and Nietzsche did us a disservice when, as a young man under Schopenhauer's influence, he introduced them into the discussion of tragedy. Unfortunately, others have accepted the suggestion that tragedy perished of optimism and faith in reason; but we have said what needs to be said about this as far as Aeschylus is concerned.

IV

We are brought back to Nietzsche and the death of tragedy. The step Aeschylus took from Homer's world toward the realm of the Platonic dialogue was far bigger than the further step in that direction taken by Euripides. It is even arguable that Aeschylus' interest is more purely philosophical than Euripides', considering the later poet's more intense concern with character and with psychology. Parts of Euripides' plays are certainly closer to Plato than anything in Aeschylus; for example, the scenes in which Clytemnestra in *Electra* and Helen in *The Trojan Women* are confronted with the charges brought against them and permitted to try to defend themselves. But no Euripidean tragedy as a whole is as close to Plato as the *Oresteia*, taken as a whole, or *The Eumenides* in particular. *The*

Trojan Women, for example, is far from being a particularly philosophical play.

The *Oresteia*, on the other hand, is preeminently about justice. Not only are Agamemnon and Orestes incidental to this larger theme, even the house of Atreus is. As the trilogy ends, the house of Atreus is out of the picture. The joyous conclusion celebrates neither Orestes' acquittal nor the passing of the curse from Atreus' house; both are forgotten when Orestes leaves the stage (777). The whole final quarter of the drama is concerned with the very matter that modern critics consider most incompatible with tragedy: the founding of an institution that will resolve conflicts by eliminating the causes of disaster, namely a court of justice.

I love and admire *Agamemnon* more than its two sequels, and Cassandra's scene above all; but this cannot change the plain fact that the first play merely sets the stage for Orestes' dilemma, which in turn allows the poet to pose problems about justice and to weigh different conceptions of justice. In no sense is the conclusion merely tacked on: like Homer and Sophocles and the builders of the Greek temples, Aeschylus was a master craftsman with a superb sense for architectonics. In retrospect it becomes perfectly clear, if it was not at the time, that Cassandra, too, confronted us with a conception of justice—not, of course, her own.

All this is as foreign to Homer as the conception of Cassandra as a prophetess; in the *Iliad* she is merely Priam's most beautiful daughter (XIII, 365) and the first to see Hector's remains brought home by her old father (XXIV, 699 ff.). Justice is of no central concern in the *Iliad*, and the question whether the Trojan or the Achaean cause is just does not agitate Homer. The vague poetic notion that there is some balance in human affairs suffices him. When Hector, having killed Patroclus, who had been wearing Achilles' armor, strips the corpse and puts on the armor, the Homeric Zeus says:

> . . . For now I grant you your moment of power,
> recompense for your not coming home from the battle
> to Andromache—not she will take from you
> Achilles' glorious armor. (XVII, 206 ff.)

The free rendering of Rieu puts the point as we usually do, "But you must pay for it" (321)—and falsely suggests that Hector has become guilty of hybris.

A more precise conception of justice is encountered in another passage, where Acamas, a Trojan, taunts the Achaeans: "Look at your man Prómachus, put to sleep by my spear, in prompt repayment for my brother's death. That is what a wise man prays for—a kinsman to survive him and avenge his fall" (269; XIV, 482 ff.). Any argument about this notion of justice would be totally out of place in the *Iliad;* but Aeschylus examines this very idea in the *Oresteia*.

Here, finally, is a passage from the *Iliad* in which justice is mentioned expressly. When Menelaus is about to take Adréstus, a Trojan, alive, as a prisoner to be ransomed, Agamemnon reproaches him: " 'No; we are not going to leave a single one of them alive, down to the babies in their mothers' wombs—not even they must live. The whole people must be wiped out of existence, and none be left to think of them and shed a tear.' The justice of this made Menelaus change his mind" (118; VI, 57 ff.). Or more literally: "he turned the heart of his brother, for he urged justice." One cannot imagine Aeschylus letting such a conception of justice pass unchallenged. Euripides later presented its inhumanity in his *Trojan Women*. But we have already noted that this play is less philosophical than the *Oresteia;* and we have found ample reasons for rejecting Nietzsche's notion that tragedy died at the hands of Euripides, as well as the popular variant that it was destroyed by the currents of thought and feeling that Euripides represented to Nietzsche's mind.

The question remains how in that case tragedy died, for it remains a striking fact that the fourth century evidently did not produce tragedies that could be ranked with those of the three masters, nor is Roman tragedy in the same class with fifth-century tragedy. Indeed, no tragedy at all was, for two thousand years after the death of Euripides and Sophocles in 406 B.C. What, then, happened in the fourth century?

At first glance, it may seem easier to say what did not happen. The demise of tragedy was not due to a changed attitude toward the gods. To be sure, Aeschylus had used the myths and figures of traditional religion, but not in order to shore up its ruins, and least of all to counter the iconoclastic spirit of the Greek enlightenment with miracle, mystery, and authority. On the contrary, he had attacked tradition. Even as Homer had found the language of polytheism ideally suited to a poem about war, Aeschylus, sublimating Homer's contests into moral collisions, had found that he could side against Apollo with Athene, and that he could blast Zeus through Prometheus.

A critic whose eloquence and erudition "almost persuade" has said that "tragedy is that form of art which requires the intolerable burden of God's presence. It is now dead because His shadow no longer falls upon us as it fell on Agamemnon or Macbeth or Athalie."[15] This comes close to being an inversion of the truth. Did His shadow really fall on Macbeth? And are there not millions of believers today? And if one were a believer, what further evidence could one possibly require that His shadow has indeed fallen upon us?

Nietzsche, incidentally, associated precisely our age with His shadow.[16] But more to the point, *Oedipus Tyrannus* does not require "the intolerable burden of God's presence"; neither does *Antigone*, nor *Philoctetes*. Indeed, in *Philoctetes* the outcome would be tragic but for the sudden appearance of a *deus ex machina*. And while the Delphic oracle is involved in the tragedy of *Oedipus*, the presence of the gods—not to speak of God—is not, and at the very least it is not indispensable. The

[15] Ibid., p. 353.
[16] FW, sec. 108—included in my edition of GM (New York: Vintage Books, 1967), p. 191, and in my *Basic Writings of Nietzsche* (New York: Modern Library, 1968).

situation in which Oedipus finds himself at the outset is preeminently tragic, and neither its genesis nor the development to the final catastrophe requires the supernatural. That adds a note of inevitability, but the keen sense that great calamities were not inevitable can be just as tragic. The gods can add great weight; but this can be achieved without "the intolerable burden of God's presence": witness *Lear*, *Othello*, or—the critic's own example—*Agamemnon*.

Tragedy requires no reverence for the gods, and it is doubtful whether Aeschylus had much of that. It would certainly be difficult to name many great poets who composed blasphemies to match Prometheus'. No less than in the *Iliad*, belief is out of the picture. Indeed the great tragic poets experienced traditional religion as an intolerable burden. Obviously, most poets during those twenty centuries when tragedy was all but dead had more religious beliefs than Aeschylus did—or Shakespeare.

To understand what happened after Aeschylus, we will have to consider Sophocles and, above all, Euripides. To wind up our consideration of Aeschylus and the death of tragedy, it will almost suffice to quote a remarkable but all too little known passage from Goethe's conversations with Eckermann. On 1 May 1825, not quite fifty years before the publication of *The Birth of Tragedy*, Goethe contested "the widespread opinion that Euripides was responsible for the decay of Greek drama." His remarks are worth quoting at length:

> Man is simple. And however rich, manifold, and unfathomable he may be, the circle of his states is soon run through. If the circumstances had been like those among us poor Germans, where Lessing wrote two or three passable plays, I myself three or four, and Schiller five or six, there might have been room for a fourth, fifth, and sixth tragic poet. But among the Greeks with their abundant productivity, where each of the Big Three had written over a hundred, or close to a hundred, plays, and the tragic subjects of Homer and the heroic tradition had in some cases been treated three or four times—given such an abundance, I say, we may suppose that material and content had gradually been exhausted, and a poet coming after the Big Three did not really know, what next.
>
> And when you come right down to it, why should they? Wasn't it really enough for a while? And wasn't what Aeschylus, Sophocles, and Euripides had produced of such quality and depth that one could hear it again and again without making it trivial or killing it? After all, these few grandiose fragments that have come down to us are of such scope and significance that we poor Europeans have been occupied with them for centuries and will yet have food and work enough for a few more centuries.

Amen.

Or is Goethe too serene? Was Nietzsche not right after all that there was a somewhat sinister development from Aeschylus to Euripides? He was. With the loss of the great war that had lasted almost thirty years, and the passing of Euripides, Sophocles, Thucydides, and Socrates, all within less than ten years, a great age ended. The new generation that was born during and after the war had a different attitude toward life and suffering. War was no longer the glory of Marathon and Salamis, heroism seemed futile, and Euripides' skepticism became much more popular than it had been during his lifetime. Aeschylus came to appear somewhat archaic, Sophocles old-fashioned, while Euripides' mistrust of convention and pretension, his social criticism, and his pioneering tragicomedies (*Ion*, for example, and *Alcestis*) became paradigms for the new age. Gradually the confidence that had grown in the wake of Marathon and found its ultimate expression in Pericles' great funeral oration gave way to doubt and increased self-consciousness, and eventually the New Comedy replaced tragedy.

V

No other poet of the first rank has been underestimated as much as Euripides. It was his great ill fortune that nineteen of his plays survived, compared to seven each by Aeschylus and Sophocles.

The extant tragedies of the two older poets represent selections of what were considered their best plays. There is reason to suppose that most of their lost plays were no better than, if as good as, *The Suppliants* and *Seven*, or *Ajax*. Suppose Aeschylus and Sophocles were each represented by another dozen of such dramas, while Euripides were known to us only through *Alcestis* and *Medea; Hippolytus, The Trojan Women, Electra, Ion,* and *The Bacchae!*[17]

Like his two predecessors, and other major poets, Euripides should be ranked according to his best works. And we should also be grateful to him for his share in making possible Sophocles' best plays. All but two of Sophocles' seven were

---

[17] Of these seven, *Hippolytus* won first prize, as did *The Bacchae* posthumously. *Alcestis* and *The Trojan Women* won second prize. *Medea* placed third in a contest in which Euphorion, Aeschylus' son, won first prize and Sophocles placed second. For the way in which the judges were chosen by lot, see Gilbert Norwood, *Greek Tragedy*, rev. ed. (1920; rpt. New York: Hill and Wang, 1960), p. 61. It is also noteworthy that the extremely wealthy and popular Nicias was often choregus, paying for the production, and he was never defeated (Plutarch's *Life of Nicias*, p. 524).

In antiquity ten of Euripides' plays were selected for school use, along with all of the surviving plays of Aeschylus and Sophocles: *Hecuba, Orestes, Phoenician Women, Hippolytus, Medea, Alcestis, Andromache, Rhesus, Trojan Women,* and *Bacchae*. Five of these are surely inferior to some of the other nine extant plays, which survived purely by accident, as they were close to each other in an alphabetical arrangement: *Helen, Electra, Heracleidae, Heracles, Ion, Suppliants, Iphigenia in Aulis, Iphigenia in Tauris,* and *Cyclops*, the only satyr play that has survived in its entirety.

For the history of these manuscripts see Ulrich von Wilamowitz-Möllendorff, *Einleitung in die griechische Tragödie, unveranderter* [sic] *Abdruck aus der ersten Auflage von Euripides Herakles I Kapitel I-IV* (Berlin: Weidmannsche Buchhandlung, 1906), chapter III; Norwood, ibid., 21; Bruno Snell, "Zwei Töpfe mit Euripides-Papyri," *Hermes,* 70 (1935), 119 f., and Denys L. Page in the introduction to his edition of *Medea* (1938; rpt. Oxford: Clarendon Press, 1952), xli ff.

written in competition with Euripides, whose influence is often striking. But the point is less that this influence is writ large in *The Women of Trachis, Philoctetes,* and elsewhere, than the infinitely more important fact that the younger rival, who was a great innovator, kept the older poet from getting into a rut. Sophocles repeats himself a good deal even in his extant plays; the marvel is that he did not copy his own successes even more, considering that four or five of his seven were written after he was seventy. Not only did the competition of Euripides and the presence of a master poet whose critical powers were second to none force Sophocles to be satisfied with nothing less than his very best, Euripides was also one of the most original dramatists of all time, and his new ideas provided never-failing stimulation.

The myth that tragedy died at Euripides' hands is thus almost the obverse of the truth; only one of Sophocles' masterpieces, the *Antigone*, antedates his influence. Nor was this influence what Nietzsche thought it was when he charged Euripides with an anti-tragic optimism. If there is a sense in which Aeschylus is more tragic than Homer, and Sophocles more tragic than Aeschylus, Euripides is indeed "the most tragic of the poets."[18]

Nietzsche's point is clear but nonetheless mistaken:

> Socrates, the dialectical hero of the Platonic drama, reminds us of the kindred nature of the Euripidean hero who must defend his actions with arguments and counter-arguments and in the process often risks the loss of our tragic pity; for who could mistake the *optimistic* element which, having once penetrated tragedy, must gradually overgrow its Dionysian regions and impel it necessarily to self-destruction— to the death-leap into the bourgeois drama. Consider the consequences of the Socratic maxims: 'Virtue is knowledge; man sins only from ignorance; he who is virtuous is happy.' In these three basic forms of optimism lies the death of tragedy. For now the virtuous hero must be a dialectician; now there must be a necessary, visible connection between virtue and knowledge, faith and morality; now the transcendental justice of Aeschylus is degraded to the superficial and insolent principle of 'poetic justice' with its customary *deus ex machina*. (GT, sec. 14)

Here the relationship of Euripides to Socrates and Plato is inverted, and both the poet's historical significance and his philosophical dimension are totally misapprehended. There is no evidence that Euripides was under the spell of Socrates, as Nietzsche claimed, and there is every evidence that he did not accept the three Socratic dicta of which Nietzsche says: "in these three basic forms of optimism lies the death of tragedy."

An intense interest in arguments and counterarguments *is* present in Euripides, but there is not the slightest reason to attribute it to the influence of Socrates, that of the Sophists will do. It should also be recalled how much of this is found in

---

[18] Aristotle's *Poetics* 13: 53a.

The Eumenides and, not quite to the same extent, in *Antigone*. While the super-abundance of dialectical fireworks in some Euripidean tragedies dissipates our tragic emotions, it usually illustrates the futility of reason, its inability to prevent tragedy.[19] At this point, Aeschylus is infinitely more optimistic than Euripides.

Aristotle says that Euripides was criticized for having more tragic endings than the other poets.[20] To have had more than Aeschylus cannot have been difficult, but evidently the surviving nineteen plays give a misleading picture of the way most of his tragedies ended. Of the seven that most critics would probably agree in calling his best, four end in catastrophe; the two earliest, *Alcestis* and *Medea*, are, however, no less relevant. The former ends happily, but was performed in lieu of a satyr play. While it provides some laughs at the drunken Heracles, it was, no doubt, incomparably more tragic than any satyr play. The portrait of the king is anything but optimistic, the less so if we recognize it as a cutting attack on the men of that, and not only that, time. His wife, Alcestis, belongs with Antigone and Deianeira and foreshadows Euripides' later heroines who die for others—few critics question that the Sophoclean Deianeira was profoundly influenced by her. Admetus needs someone to die for him, or he will have to die; he eagerly accepts his wife's self-sacrifice, and then feels that others should feel sorry for him because he has lost his wife. Eventually, Heracles brings her back from the underworld, but it is difficult to find any optimism in this play; rather is it a bitter tragicomedy, perhaps the first one ever written, and quite possibly the best. It is doubtful whether anybody before Shakespeare wrote a tragicomedy that merits comparison with *Alcestis*.

Medea, Euripides' earliest surviving tragedy, ends with a *machina*, but hardly with "poetic justice." Having killed her husband's new wife and slain her own children, because they were also his, the triumphant sorceress flies off, unscathed. Where is virtue? Where happiness? Where optimism? What makes the play great, apart from the poetry, is, once again, the telling attack on the callousness of men, the poet's subtle understanding of the feelings of a woman, his insistence that barbarian women wronged suffer no less than other human beings, and his probably unprecedented portrait of impassioned jealousy. *The Women of Trachis* might well show the influence not only of *Alcestis* (438 B.C.) but also of *Medea* (431 B.C.) and possibly even of *Hippolytus* (428 B.C.). We cannot be certain whether Sophocles meant to counter the younger poet's Phaedra and Medea, or whether Euripides felt provoked by the idealized portrait of Deianeira and resolved to show the Athenians how a jealous woman really feels. Either way,

[19] Cf. John H. Finley, Jr., "Euripides and Thucydides," *Harvard Studies in Classical Philology*, 49 (1938), 43: "Both Thucydides and Euripides lost faith in debate, although both, it must be added, were molded intellectually by it." Also E. R. Dodds's introduction to *Bacchae* (Oxford: Clarendon Press, 1944), p. xliii: "There never was a writer who more conspicuously lacked the propagandist's faith in easy and complete solutions."

[20] *Poetics* 13:53a.

one might say that Sophocles portrayed people as they ought to be, Euripides as they really are.[21]

We have previously discussed *Hippolytus* and *The Bacchae*:[22] neither they nor *The Trojan Women* fit Nietzsche's account of Euripides' untragic optimism. The point is not that Nietzsche was devoid of insight; he scarcely ever wrote on any subject without noting something interesting. The few exceptions are comprised by cases in which he repeated the prejudices of earlier writers, for example, about women. The opinion, widespread at one time, that in *The Birth of Tragedy* Nietzsche vilified Socrates cannot be sustained, and it is odd how regularly those who have made this charge have simply ignored the vehemently anti-tragic outlook of Socrates' most famous pupil, Plato. But Nietzsche *was* exceedingly unfair to Euripides, falling in with an old prejudice against that poet, which Goethe already had attacked. The most relevant passage from Goethe's conversations with Eckermann has been quoted above; here is another: After noting that classical philologists have long ranked Aeschylus and Sophocles far above Euripides, Goethe said: "I have no objection to the view that Euripides has his flaws." But he felt outraged by August Wilhelm Schlegel's treatment of Euripides: "If a modern man like Schlegel should have to censure flaws in such a grand old poet, decency demands that he should do it on his knees" (28 March 1827).

A passage in Goethe's diaries (*Tagebücher*, 22 November 1831) is more extreme. Exactly four months before his death, he jotted down these words: "I reread the *Ion* of Euripides to be edified and instructed again. It does seem odd to me that the aristocracy of the philologists fails to grasp his merits and, putting on traditional airs, subordinates him to his predecessors, feeling justified by the buffoon Aristophanes. . . . Have all the nations since his day produced a dramatist who was even fit to hand him his slippers?"

---

[21] Aristotle ascribes this remark to Sophocles himself (*Poetics* 25: 60b).

The date of *The Women of Trachis* is utterly uncertain. Cedric H. Whitman, *Sophocles: A Study of Heroic Humanism* (Cambridge, Mass.: Harvard University Press, 1951), p. 48, stresses its "unmistakably Euripidean flavor" and the influence of *Alcestis*, but dates it rather early, between 437 and 432 (p. 55). His argument that "the immense technical superiority of the *Oedipus* [*Tyrannus*], however, seems to demand that we allow a few more years to elapse between the two" (p. 257, note 40) carries little weight, as Sophocles' last two plays do not approximate its perfection either. G. M. Kirkwood, *A Study of Sophoclean Drama* (Ithaca: Cornell University Press, 1958), p. 293 f., devotes a whole appendix to the question; he concludes that "the evidence for early dating is not really strong," but favors "a date after *Ajax* and before *Antig.*" In the end he acknowledges that H. D. F. Kitto, *Greek Tragedy: A Literary Study*, 3rd rev. ed. (1939; rpt. Garden City: Doubleday Anchor Books, n.d.), placed the play "about 420" and Gennaro Perrotta, *Sofocle* (Messina and Milan: Principato, 1935), "at the end of Sophocles' career." Wilamowitz argued at great length in his 162-page introductory essay in his edition of Euripides' *Herakles* (2nd rev. ed., 1895) that the influence of *Heracles* (after 425 B.C.) was writ large in *The Women of Trachis* (I, 152–57), and Gilbert Murray was of the same opinion (*The Literature of Ancient Greece*, 3rd ed. [1897; rpt. Chicago: University of Chicago Press, Phoenix Books, 1956], p. 246).

[22] Sec. 42, *Tragedy and Philosophy*.

The fact that *Ion*—a magnificent tragicomedy—is quite generally considered Euripides' most anti-clerical play throws a good deal of light on the old Goethe who had just finished his *Faust* (writing Act IV after Act V). Goethe's implicit slur on Shakespeare is surely unintentional; his many references to Shakespeare testify to that. But even if one considered Euripides as merely the fourth greatest tragic poet of all time, it would be utterly absurd to suppose that this was grounds for censure.

We will resist the temptation to consider his plays, one by one, conceding weaknesses but showing again and again how, "even though Euripides manages his plays badly in other respects, he is obviously the most tragic of the poets."[23]

VI

E. R. Dodds argued in an early article, long before he succeeded to Gilbert Murray's chair at Oxford, that Euripides, though, of course, a "rationalist" in the sense that he was anti-clerical, was more importantly an "irrationalist."[24] By this Dodds meant two things. His first point, to which most of "Euripides the Irrationalist" is devoted, is grist to my mill. Euripides steadfastly opposed the three claims "that reason (what the Greeks called rational discourse, *logos*) is the sole and sufficient instrument of truth"; "that the structure of Reality must be in itself in some sense rational"; and "that moral, like intellectual, error can arise only from a failure to use the reason we possess; and that when it does arise it must, like intellectual error, be curable by an intellectual process."[25]

Dodds shows this in some detail, calling attention, for example, to Medea's words "in vv. 1078 ff. 'I recognise,' she says, 'what evil I am about to do, but my *thymos* (my passion) is stronger than my counsels: *thymos* is the cause of Man's worst crimes.' Her reason can judge her action, which she frankly describes as a 'foul murder,' (1383) but it cannot influence it: the springs of action are in the *thymos*, beyond the reach of reason."[26]

Dodds's second point, on the other hand, seems dated. He *applauds* what he has spelled out in the above three claims and calls rationalism. "The philosophy thus summed up in its most generalised traits was the decisive contribution of the Greeks to human thought."[27] "Socrates affirmed the supremacy of reason in the

---

[23] Gilbert Murray says very neatly: "There is not one play of Euripides in which a critic cannot find serious flaws or offenses; though it is true, perhaps, that the worse the critic, the more he will find" (*The Literature of Ancient Greece*, p. 273). Murray and Wilamowitz did *not* rank Euripides below his predecessors.

[24] "Euripides the Irrationalist," *Classical Review*, 43 (1929), 97–104.

[25] Ibid., p. 97.

[26] Ibid., p. 98.

[27] Ibid. p. 97.

governance of the universe and in the life of man; in both these spheres Euripides denied it. . . . Some of the passages about the relation between knowledge and conduct do at any rate look like a conscious reaction against the opinion of Socrates, or of other persons who thought like Socrates."[28]

It is surely uncertain whether Socrates really affirmed that reason governed the universe, and Dodds himself goes on to admit that "some of the characteristic features of this [Euripidean] outlook appear already in the *Alcestis*, produced in 438 B.C.; and it is very doubtful if Socrates had emerged as an independent thinker at so early a date."[29] But in that case Dodds might be almost as wrong as Nietzsche, who thought that Euripides got his ideas from Socrates. The truth of the matter might be that Socrates, of whom ancient tradition relates that he attended only the plays of Euripides, was stimulated by this poet—to develop countertheses.[30] This hypothesis goes well with what Socrates says in the *Apology* about the poets: "upon the strength of their poetry they believed themselves to be the wisest of men in other things in which they were not wise."[31] And Plato's attitude toward the tragic poets supports my reconstruction far better than either Nietzsche's or Dodds's.

Philosophers have rarely had any great influence on poets, and that a young philosopher should have decisively influenced a mature poet in whose *oeuvre* we can find no break at all is so improbable that we can safely discount it. The philosophers who did influence important poets did it posthumously; for example, Aquinas, Kant, and Nietzsche. That a mature poet whose work obviously has strong philosophical relevance should influence younger philosophers, even some of his contemporaries, is much more likely; Goethe's strong influence on Schel-

---

[28] Ibid., p. 103.

[29] Ibid.

[30] I find corroboration for this surmise in Bruno Snell, "Das früheste Zeugnis über Sokrates," *Philologus*, 97 (1948), 125–34. He argues that *Medea* 1077 ff. may have led Socrates to formulate his counterthesis, and that *Hippolytus* 380 ff. may be Euripides' reply to Socrates. That Plato's polemic against the view of the multitude (*Protagoras* 352) represents his reply to the *Hippolytus* passage has long been noted, as Snell himself emphasizes (p. 129, note); e.g., by Wilamowitz at the end of a long footnote that documents the ways in which Plato was stimulated by Euripides (*Einleitung*, pp. 24 f.).

In the 2nd rev. ed. of *Die griechische Tragödie*, II (Göttingen: Vandenhoeck & Ruprecht, 1954), pp. 112 f., Max Pohlenz accepts Snell's demonstration that Phaedra's words in *Hippolytus* constitute a direct polemic against Socrates, but not his claim that *Medea*, 1378–80 [sic!], led Socrates to formulate his counterthesis. Pohlenz's brief note bears the signs of haste (he also refers Snell's article to the wrong year) and is unconvincing. See also Snell's *Scenes from Greek Drama* (Berkeley: University of California Press, 1964), chapter 3.

The first to adduce *Hippolytus* 374 against Nietzsche's claim that Euripides shared Socrates' outlook was Wilamowitz in *Zukunftsphilologie! Eine Erwiderung auf Friedrich Nietzsches "Geburt der Tragödie"* (Berlin: Gebrüder Borntraeger, 1872), p. 28. Rohde's defense of Nietzsche on this point lacks all force (*Afterphilologie. Zur Beleuchtung des von dem Dr. phil. Ulrich von Wilamowitz-Möllendorff herausgegebenen Pamphlets: "Zukunftsphilologie!"* [Leipzig: E. W. Fritzsch, 1872], pp. 39 f.).

[31] Plato's *Apology* 22.

ling, Hegel, and Schopenhauer provides a striking example. Even so, Euripides' influence on Socrates remains only probable; but his decisive influence on Plato appears indisputable.

We have noted earlier that Aeschylus stands halfway between Homer and Plato, and Euripides halfway between Aeschylus and Plato. The dialogue between Electra and her mother and other such scenes in Euripides are not great poetry or theatre but point toward a new genre: the Platonic dialogue. To try writing better tragedies than Aeschylus, Sophocles, and Euripides was not an inviting prospect, and Plato, who had tried, destroyed these early efforts when he met Socrates. To try writing better philosophic dialogues than Euripides, wedding the poet's talent to the legacy of Socrates, was the challenge Plato tried to meet.

Dodds's conclusion is utterly unfair to Euripides:

> The disease of which Greek culture eventually died is known by many names. To some it appears as a virulent form of scepticism; to others, as a virulent form of mysticism. Professor Murray has called it the Failure of Nerve.
>
> My own name for it is systematic irrationalism. . . . To my mind, the case of Euripides proves that an acute attack of it was already threatening the Greek world in the fifth century. . . . He shows all the characteristic symptoms: the peculiar blend of a destructive scepticism with a no less destructive mysticism; the assertion that emotion, not reason, determines human conduct; despair of the state, resulting in quietism; despair of rational theology, resulting in a craving for a religion of the orgiastic type. For the time being the attack was averted—in part by the development of the Socratic-Platonic philosophy. . . . Greek rationalism died slowly. . . .[32]

Nietzsche thought that rationalism put an end to the great age of Greece, and found rationalism in Socrates, Plato—and Euripides. Dodds blames irrationalism and considers Socrates and Plato the culmination of the Greek genius—but Euripides is again on the losing side. As Goethe remarked long ago, the classical philologists—and when Nietzsche wrote *The Birth of Tragedy*, he was one—are hard on Euripides.

Suppose we ask for a moment, not of what Greek culture "died"—a rather questionable and misleading metaphor, when you come to think of it—but rather whether the three claims that comprise "rationalism" happen to be true. If, as I think, none of them is, Euripides was wiser than the rationalistic philosophers. What philosophers nowadays would consider reason "sufficient" for the discovery of all truth, particularly when reason is expressly juxtaposed with sense-perception?[33] And who would hold that all moral errors are curable by a purely "intellectual process"? And why speak of "despair of rational theology"? If rational theology is not sound, why not give our poet credit for renouncing it?

---

[32] Dodds, p. 102 f.
[33] Ibid., p. 93.

Since my outlook is close to that with which Euripides is charged by Dodds, I might be considered partisan; and this is not the place for detailed arguments against the kind of rationalism Dodds extols. But we should at least note that a double standard is implicit in this criticism of Euripides: like Hegel and Nietzsche, he is fair game, while Sophocles is not. Surely, Sophocles was not a rationalist in Dodds's sense; he did not believe the three crucial claims, nor did he credit rational theology. But it would never do to use language so negatively charged when speaking about Sophocles.

Dodds's later book on *The Greeks and the Irrational* is not only far more judicious than his early article but an outstanding contribution to our understanding of Greek culture. His early article on Euripides, of which he made some use in the chapter on "Rationalism and Reaction in the Classical Age," is no more representative of Dodds at his best than is *The Birth of Tragedy* of Nietzsche in his prime. And Dodds's edition, with introduction and commentary, of *The Bacchae* is a masterpiece. But it should be plain that we do Euripides a monstrous injustice if we associate him with "the Failure of Nerve." Without any optimistic faith that he could stem the tide of superstition that, seven years after the poet's death, claimed Socrates as one of its victims—and during Euripides' lifetime, it had driven into exile, probably Aeschylus and, without a doubt, Anaxagoras and Protagoras—Euripides fought his public his life long, and died in voluntary exile.

That Sophocles always remained a popular favorite, even at such a time, might raise questions about *him*. But he led his own chorus in mourning for Euripides when the news of his death reached Athens; and in our reading of *Oedipus Tyrannus*—and, of course, of *The Women of Trachis*—we find how far he was both from popular superstition and from "rationalism."

★   ★   ★

In sum, in his first book Nietzsche was wrong about the birth of tragedy, about Aeschylus and Euripides, and about the death of tragedy. Yet the remarks about Hamlet in section 17, much of section 15, and the "Self-Criticsim" added as a preface in 1886, are magnificent; and nobody has ever found a better characterization of Nietzsche than the image of the "artistic Socrates" in section 14. All in all, however, neither *The Birth of Tragedy* nor his other early books can brook comparison with Nietzsche's later works, beginning with *The Gay Science. The Birth of Tragedy* is widely overrated, but the later Nietzsche is inexhaustible.

About the Authors

Max L. Baeumer—Professor of German and Permanent Member, Institute for Research in the Humanities, University of Wisconsin. Author of: *Das Dionysische in den Werken Wilhelm Heinses* (1964); *Heinse Studien* (1966); editor and co-author of: *Toposforschung* (1973); *W. Heinse: Ardinghello* (1975); and author of articles and reviews in his field. Professor Baeumer is currently writing a book on the subject: "Das dionysische Phänomen in der antiken und deutschen Literatur."

Eugen Biser—Professor of Christian Thought and the Philosophy of Religion, University of Munich. Among Professor Biser's writings may be mentioned: *"Gott ist tot": Nietzsches Destruktion des christlichen Bewußtseins* (1962); *Theologische Sprachtheorie und Hermeneutik* (1970); *Theologie und Atheismus* (1972); *Glaubensverständnis: Grundriß einer hermeneutischen Fundamentaltheologie* (1975).

Mark Boulby—Professor of German, University of British Columbia. Author of: *Gerhart Hauptmann: Die Weber* (1962); *Hermann Hesse: His Mind and Art* (1967); *Uwe Johnson* (1974); and numerous journal articles, including studies of Nietzsche and Stefan George.

Ralph S. Fraser—Professor and Chairman of the Department of German, Wake Forest University. Author of articles and translations in his field, he is co-author of *Reimarus: Fragments* (1970), and editor of Uwe Johnson, *Karsch und andere Prosa* (1972).

Sander L. Gilman—Associate Professor and Chairman of the Department of German Literature, Cornell University. Author of a study of Klabund and of liturgical parody in Western letters; editor of the works of Johannes Agricola von Eisleben and F. M. von Klinger. Professor Gilman's articles include studies of Nietzsche.

Peter Heller—Professor of German and Comparative Literature, State University of New York at Buffalo. Author of: *Dialectics and Nihilism* (1966); *"Von den ersten und letzten Dingen": Studien und Kommentar zu einer Aphorismenreihe von Friedrich Nietzsche* (1972), as well as articles on modern literature and aesthetics.

Robert M. Helm—Professor of Philosophy, Wake Forest University. Author of *The Gloomy Dean: The Thought of W. R. Inge* (1962); contributor to the *Catholic Encyclopedia* and other reference works in his field.

Marcus B. Hester—Associate Professor of Philosophy, Wake Forest University. Author of *The Meaning of Poetic Metaphor* (1967) and articles in the field of aesthetics.

Walter S. Kaufmann—Professor of Philosophy, Princeton University. His many books include: *Nietzsche: Philosopher, Psychologist, Antichrist* (1950, 4th edition, enlarged, 1974); *The Portable Nietzsche* (1954, translation of four complete works); *Basic Writings of Nietzsche* (1968, five more works, with commentary); *The Will to Power* (1967) and *The Gay Science* (1974), both with commentary. His most recent books are *Tragedy and Philosophy* (1968) and *Without Guilt and Justice* (1973). Professor Kaufmann has also translated Goethe's *Faust* (1961).

Hugh Lloyd-Jones—Regius Professor of Greek, Christ Church, Oxford University. Among his publications are: an edition of Menander's *Dyscolus* (1960); a translation of Aeschylus' trilogy, *The Oresteia* (1970); *The Justice of Zeus* (1971); and *Females of the Species: Semonides of Amorgos on Women* (1975). Professor Lloyd-Jones is also the author of numerous articles in his field.

James C. O'Flaherty—Professor of German, Wake Forest University, Author of: *Unity and Language: A Study in the Philosophy of Hamann* (1952, rpt. 1966); *Hamann's Socratic Memorabilia: A Translation and Commentary* (1967); (editor), *The Hamann News-Letter* (1953–55, 1961–63); (co-author) *Raabe's Else von der Tanne* (1972); articles on German literature and culture, including studies of Nietzsche.

Helmut Rehder—Ashbel Smith Professor of German, University of Texas. Author of: *J. N. Meinhard und seine Übersetzungen* (1953); (co-author), *Goethe's Faust* (1950, 1955); *Deutsch: Verstehen und Sprechen* (1962) and other texts; (editor) *Literary Symbolism: A Symposium* (1965); numerous journal articles, including studies of Nietzsche.

Karl Schlechta—Professor Emeritus and Director of the Institute for Philosophy, *Technische Hochschule*, Darmstadt. Editor of Nietzsche's *Werke in drei Bänden* (1966); among his numerous publications on Nietzsche are: *Nietzsches großer Mittag* (1954); *Der Fall Nietzsche* (1958); (with Herbert W. Reichert) *International Nietzsche Bibliography* (1960, 1968); *Nietzsche-Chronik* (1975); among his writings on Goethe: *Goethe in seinem Verhältnis zu Aristoteles* (1938); Goethe's *Wilhelm Meister* (1953).

Kurt Weinberg—Professor of French, German, and Comparative Literature, University of Rochester. Author of: *Henri Heine, romantique défroqué, héraut du symbolisme français* (1953); *Kafkas Dichtungen: Die Travestien des Mythos* (1963); *On Gide's Prométhée: Private Myth and Public Mystification* (1972); *The Mind's Body: The Figure of Faust in Valéry and Goethe* (in press); and numerous articles on German and French writers.

Hedwig Wingler—*Dozentin* at the *Technische Hochschule*, Darmstadt, Dr. Wingler lectures on the philosophy of language, the philosophy of science, and aesthetics. Author of articles and a frequent radio lecturer in her field, she is currently writing a book on the Pre-Socratics.

Index

For other volumes in the "Studies" see page ii and following pages.

Send orders to: (U.S. and Canada)
The University of North Carolina Press, P.O. Box 2288
Chapel Hill, N.C. 27514
(All other countries) Feffer and Simons, Inc., 31 Union Square, New York, N.Y. 10003

UNIVERSITY OF NORTH CAROLINA
STUDIES IN THE GERMANIC LANGUAGES
AND LITERATURES

1. Herbert W. Reichert. THE BASIC CONCEPTS IN THE PHILOSOPHY OF GOTTFRIED KELLER. 1949. Reprint.
2. Olga Marx and Ernst Morwitz. THE WORKS OF STEFAN GEORGE. Rendered into English. 1949. Reprint. (See volume 78.)
3. Paul H. Curts. HEROD AND MARIAMNE. A Tragedy in Five Acts by Friedrich Hebbel. Translated into English Verse. 1950. Reprint.
4. Frederic E. Coenen. FRANZ GRILLPARZER'S PORTRAITURE OF MEN. 1951. Reprint.
5. Edwin H. Zeydel and B. Q. Morgan. THE PARZIVAL OF WOLFRAM VON ESCHENBACH. Translated into English Verse, with Introductions, Notes, and Connecting Summaries. 1951, 1956, 1960. Reprint.
6. James C. O'Flaherty. UNITY AND LANGUAGE: A STUDY IN THE PHILOSOPHY OF JOHANN GEORG HAMANN. 1952. Reprint.
7. Sten G. Flygt. FRIEDRICH HEBBEL'S CONCEPTION OF MOVEMENT IN THE ABSOLUTE AND IN HISTORY. 1952. Reprint.
8. Richard Kuehnemund. ARMINIUS OR THE RISE OF A NATIONAL SYMBOL. (From Hutten to Grabbe.) 1953. Reprint.
9. Lawrence S. Thompson. WILHELM WAIBLINGER IN ITALY. 1953. Reprint.
10. Frederick Hiebel. NOVALIS, GERMAN POET—EUROPEAN THINKER—CHRISTIAN MYSTIC. 2nd rev. ed. 1959. Reprint.
11. Walter Silz. REALISM AND REALITY: STUDIES IN THE GERMAN NOVELLE OF POETIC REALISM. 4th Printing. 1965. Pp. xiv, 168. Cloth $6.00.
12. Percy Matenko. LUDWIG TIECK AND AMERICA. 1954. Reprint.
13. Wilhelm Dilthey.. THE ESSENCE OF PHILOSOPHY. Rendered into English by Stephen A. Emery and William T. Emery. 1954, 1961. Reprint.
14. Edwin H. Zeydel and B. Q. Morgan. GREGORIUS. A Medieval Oedipus Legend by Hartmann von Aue. Translated in Rhyming Couplets with Introduction and Notes. 1955. Reprint.
15. Alfred G. Steer, Jr. GOETHE'S SOCIAL PHILOSOPHY AS REVEALED IN *CAMPAGNE IN FRANKREICH* AND *BELAGERUNG VON MAINZ*. With three full-page illustrations. 1955. Reprint.
16. Edwin H. Zeydel. GOETHE THE LYRIST. 100 Poems in New Translations facing the Original Texts. With a Biographical Introduction and an Appendix on Musical Settings. 2nd rev. ed., 1965. Reprint.
17. Hermann J. Weigand. THREE CHAPTERS ON COURTLY LOVE IN ARTHURIAN FRANCE AND GERMANY. 1956. Reprint.
18. George Fenwick Jones. WITTENWILER'S "RING" AND THE ANONYMOUS SCOTS POEM "COLKELBIE SOW." Two Comic-Didactic Works from the Fifteenth Century. Translated into English. With five illustrations. 1956. Reprint.
19. George C. Schoolfield. THE FIGURE OF THE MUSICIAN IN GERMAN LITERATURE. 1956. Reprint.
20. Edwin H. Zeydel. POEMS OF GOETHE. A Sequel to GOETHE THE LYRIST. New Translations facing the Originals. With an Introduction and a List of Musical Settings. 1957. Reprint.
21. Joseph Mileck. HERMANN HESSE AND HIS CRITICS. The Criticism and Bibliography of Half a Century. 1958. Reprint.
22. Ernest N. Kirrmann. DEATH AND THE PLOWMAN or THE BOHEMIAN PLOWMAN. A Disputatious and Consolatory Dialogue about Death from the Year 1400. Translated from the Modern German Version of Alois Bernt. 1958. Reprint.
23. Edwin H. Zeydel. RUODLIEB, THE EARLIEST COURTLY NOVEL (after 1050). Introduction, Text, Translation, Commentary, and Textual Notes. With seven illustrations. 1959, 1963. Reprint.
24. John T. Krumpelmann. THE MAIDEN OF ORLEANS. A Romantic Tragedy in Five Acts by Friedrich Schiller. Translated into English in the Verse Forms of the Original German. 1959. Reprint. (See volume 37.)
25. George Fenwick Jones. HONOR IN GERMAN LITERATURE. 1959. Reprint.
26. MIDDLE AGES—REFORMATION—VOLKSKUNDE: FESTSCHRIFT FOR JOHN G. KUNSTMANN. Twenty Essays. 1959. Reprint.
27. Martin Dyck. NOVALIS AND MATHEMATICS. 1960. Reprint.

For other volumes in the "Studies" see preceding and following pages and p. ii.

Order reprinted books from: AMS PRESS, Inc.,
56 East 13th Street, New York, N.Y. 10003

DATE DUE

2-23-79			